THE GIANTS

Richard Whittingham

THE GIANTS

An Illustrated History

With Photographs by Fred Roe

From the Polo Grounds to Super Bowl XXI

HARPER & ROW, PUBLISHERS, New York

1817 Cambridge, Philadelphia, San Francisco, Washington, London, Mexico City, São Paulo, Singapore, Sydney

Special Thanks

The author, photographer, and publishers wish to offer their grateful appreciation to the New York Giants organization for the generous cooperation and help it provided in the creation of this book.

Special thanks are also extended to the Pro Football Hall of Fame in Canton, Ohio, for the use of its extensive archives and library, especially to curator Joe Horrigan, and to Linda Arenaro of Canon USA for the use of its equipment.

Photo essays by Fred Roe appear as follows: Championships, following page 52; Giants Offense, following page 84; Portraits, following page 116; Giants Defense, following page 148; Time Out, following page 180; and Super Bowl, following page 212. For information about photos in these sections and other photos throughout the text credited to Fred Roe, write to him care of P.O. Box 136, Mt. Arlington, NJ 07856.

Photo on pages ii-iii: New York Giants
Photo on pages iv, vi: Fred Roe

FIRST EDITION

Designer: Sidney Feinberg

Copy editor: Larry Zuckerman

Index by S. W. Cohen and Associates

Library of Congress Cataloging-in-Publication Data

Whittingham, Richard, date
  The Giants: an illustrated history.

  Includes index.
  1. Giants (Football team)—History. I. Title.
GV956.N4W47 1986   796.332'64'097471   86-45162
ISBN 0-06-015648-1

87 88 89 90 91 MPC 10 9 8 7 6 5 4 3 2 1

Contents

Foreword

I was nine years old when my father brought the Giants into the National Football League. It was in the heart of the Roaring Twenties—1925, to be exact—and the league was in just its sixth year of existence.

At that first game in the Polo Grounds against the Frankford Yellow Jackets, I sat in the stands behind the Giants bench with my mother, and in the second half I joined my brother Jack on the sideline, watching the likes of Jim Thorpe, Hinkey Haines, Century Milstead, Jack McBride, Doc Alexander, and Paul Jappe do battle for us. I remember it was a little chilly that day, and my mother, after the game, complained to my father that we had sat in the shade. Why couldn't we go over to the other side of the field and sit in the sun, where we would be nice and warm? she asked. The next game, and from that point on, the Giants sideline in the Polo Grounds was on the sunny side of the field.

It has been a wonderful journey from that day back in 1925, one filled with memories of the good times as well as of the disappointments, the exciting games, the championships, and the many players and coaches and staff who contributed so much over the now more than 60 years of Giants history. And this wonderful book tells the story of the Giants the only way it should be told—fully, with all the ups and downs and all the people and the great moments that were a part of it.

In the beginning, the football team was, to put it mildly, not a financial success. My father was losing a lot of money on it that first year, but we were bailed out when Red Grange came out to the Polo Grounds at the end of the season. My father had wanted him in a Giants uni-

form, but he came as a Chicago Bear instead. Nevertheless, the Galloping Ghost, the most famous football player of his day, drew the fans into the Polo Grounds, more than 70,000 of them, and the franchise was saved. Actually, it was my father and just two assistants who sold those seventy thousand or so tickets out of one small office in the Knickerbocker Building in New York City. Today it would take a staff of twenty people to handle that many tickets.

In those early days, my father's friends all told him it was foolish to try to make a go of it in pro football. I remember Governor Al Smith in our house one day after we lost rather badly to the Green Bay Packers saying, "Pro football will never amount to anything. Why don't you give it up?" My father looked at my brother Jack and me and said, "The boys would run me right out of the house if I did."

We managed to make it through the early years of the NFL and the Depression. Money, needless to say, was very tight in those days. But my father felt sports businesses might prosper somewhat in those economically depressed times because they offered the best entertainment around for the money. And he was right.

It was, of course, a much different kind of game back then. I recall the days when we did not have hash marks. If a player was tackled one yard from the sideline, that is exactly where the ball was put in play. Teams had special plays for that. I remember a tailback from Georgetown, Tony Plansky, a great athlete who drop-kicked for us around 1928. He once drop-kicked a 40-yarder to win a game for us. He normally kicked with his right foot, but he was way over on the left side of the field, so he kicked it with his left foot.

Steve Owen was such an integral part of the Giants in those early days. He came as a player in 1926, took over the head coaching job in 1931, and stayed through 1953. Steve was a true innovator. He developed his version of the two-platoon system in 1937, when the game was restricted to one-platoon football. We had a young team and a very deep bench, so he would just change ten players at the end of the first quarter, then take them out at the start of the second half, and put them back in at the start of the fourth quarter. The only player to stay on the field the full sixty minutes was Mel Hein, because he was just so good on both offense and defense and could handle the full sixty minutes easily.

Benny Friedman was another standout, the game's only great passer of that era. He made a great contribution to pro football off the field as well as on it by going around to high school assemblies during the week and giving tickets away to help promote the game.

There were other great ones, too, including a pair of Hall of Fame ends, Red Badgro and Ray Flaherty, and Harry Newman, another great tailback. Ken Strong, whom we should have gotten in 1929 but finally signed in 1933, was one of the finest all-around players ever to play the game. This book tells how Ken got away to the Staten Island Stapletons when we thought we had him for sure. But after we signed him, he played for us all the way until 1947, and he was forty-one years old that year, although we used him only as a kicker in the later years. He also was a cinch for the Hall of Fame.

Another great was Tuffy Leemans, who made it into the Hall just recently. I recruited him myself, going down to George Washington University for my father and convincing Leemans of the value of a career with the Giants.

The game of pro football changed considerably after the war. The offenses became more sophisticated, there was a lot more passing, and the players were getting bigger and faster all the time.

We had some of our most noteworthy and memorable teams in the 1950s and early 60s. Jim Lee Howell, our head coach for much of that time, had the best pair of assistants ever under one roof: Vince Lombardi handling the offense and Tom Landry the defense. With Charley Conerly and Y. A. Tittle quarterbacking, backs like Frank Gifford and Alex Webster, and pass catchers of the caliber of Kyle Rote and Del Shofner, we provided a lot of exciting offense. And the defense! Well, it was simply one of the best ever: Andy Robustelli, Sam Huff, Rosey Grier, Em Tunnell, Dick Modzelewski, Jim Katcavage, Dick Lynch, and Jimmy Patton, among them.

The game was fun in those earlier days, the men who played it very memorable. Nothing, however, has been more exciting and gratifying than to have watched the Giants of 1986 march through the season and the playoffs, to have sat proudly at the Rose Bowl out in Pasadena and watched the Giants' splendid display of football in the Super Bowl. Our team earned the glory that day, and our many loyal fans deserved the thrill and triumph of it.

It was the Giants first Super Bowl . . . the first of many, we hope.

—WELLINGTON MARA

THE GIANTS

Super Bowl Season

The 1986 football season began for the Giants in midsummer, under a bright, warm sun at their training camp at Pace University in Pleasantville, New York, and ended on January 25, 1987, under a similarly sunny sky some 2,800 miles away, in Pasadena, California. There, the midsummer night's dream of the team and the fans alike—of ultimate conquest in the world of professional football—became an eloquent and gratifying reality.

What turned out to be a joyous journey did not begin that way, however. The Giants had reached the NFC conference championship the year before, but there they had been soundly shut out, 17–0, by the Chicago Bears. Now, in 1986, the championship Bears were still intact, and a lot of pundits were talking about a dynasty. And in the NFC East the Giants had brutal and talented competition awaiting them in the form of the Washington Redskins and the Dallas Cowboys, whose aspirations for a divisional title were as high as their own.

Coach Bill Parcells, in his fourth year at the helm, had had a number of reservations. "In training camp I thought for a while we didn't have a chance. There were a lot of problems early on."

What he was talking about were some very major concerns. Pro Bowl running back Joe Morris was practicing only part-time because of a contract dispute, and there was talk of his perhaps sitting out the season. Lawrence Taylor had had treatment for chemical abuse, which no one was talking about, and there was some wonder if the problem might have an adverse effect on his future performance. Jim Burt was suffering from back problems that threatened his season. Running back George Adams

had a chipped pelvis and would spend the year on the injured-reserve list. "And most of our high draft choices," Parcells pointed out, "reported late and didn't have a clue to what we were doing."

Others, however, were not quite so skeptical. An especially prescient Anson Mount, in *Playboy*'s pro football preview, predicted not only that the Giants would go to the Super Bowl but that they would win it all at that spectacle by defeating the Denver Broncos. "This will be the year of the Giants," he wrote. "There are no obvious weaknesses anywhere. Quarterback Phil Simms has matured, the offensive line may be the best in the league and the running game, with Joe Morris and George Adams, will be spectacular. Best of all is that the Giants are a stable franchise, with no internal bickering or jealousies."

Paul Zimmerman, writing for *Sports Illustrated,* offered an identical prognostication: the Giants to defeat the Broncos in Super Bowl XXI. "A good blocking line, a big booming fullback, Maurice Carthon, knocking people over for Morris . . . it's a good formula," he observed, "and it gets even better when the defense comes out and absolutely stuffs people."

A loss in their first preseason game to the Atlanta Falcons, 31–24, was not a happy harbinger. Nor was the defeat at the hands of the Dallas Cowboys, 31–28, to begin the regular season. It all came together after Dallas, however. Seventeen wins against only one other loss. The most regular-season victories—14—in club history. And triumph.

The odyssey of 1986 brought back to Giants fans

memories of other championship-caliber years, in the distant past but ringing with their own particular carillons of glory. Ken Strong running for a couple of touchdowns against the Bears in 1934. Tuffy Leemans grinding out yardage against the Packers in 1938, and Mel Hein knocking the hell out of the immortal Don Hutson in the same title game. Charlie Conerly rifling a touchdown pass to Kyle Rote and another to Frank Gifford while destroying the Bears in 1956. A valiant band of defenders named Huff, Robustelli, Grier, Modzelewski, and Katcavage battling a blitzkreig of Bears in 1963, and a frustrated Y. A. Tittle leaving the field after his last desperate pass was intercepted at game's end.

Added to those memories now are a frenetic Phil McConkey racing out into the Rose Bowl, Phil Simms' perfect passes, Joe Morris's yardage-gulping runs, Mark Bavaro catching pass after pass, Lawrence Taylor's violent quarterback sacks, a swarming mass of blue Giants defenders, Harry Carson dousing Coach Parcells with Gatorade, and—after it was over—a jubilant Jim Burt hoisting his son on his shoulders in a moving display of triumph.

It was a magnificent climax to what had begun more than six decades earlier when the soft-helmeted members of Tim Mara's newfound franchise trotted out for the first time onto the field at New York's Polo Grounds.

Joe Morris made it happen in 1986: 1,516 yards, the most ever gained rushing by a New York Giant. (Fred Roe)

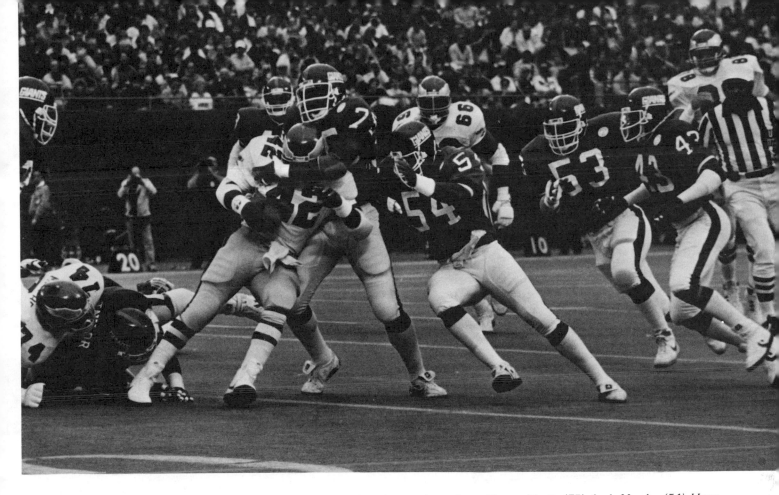

The defense: ever-hungry, always punishing, continually relentless. Among them, above, George Martin (75), Andy Headen (54), Harry Carson (53), Kenny Hill (48); below, Lawrence Taylor (56), Carl Banks (58), Gary Reasons (55), Jim Burt (64), Perry Williams (23). (Fred Roe)

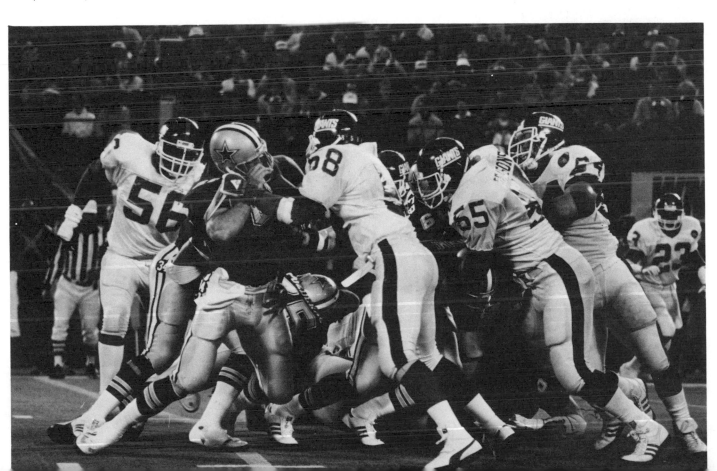

The owners: Wellington Mara and Tim Mara. (New York Giants)

Championship Giants

		Championship Game	Coach
1927	11–1–1	———	Earl Potteiger
1934	8–5–0	30–13, vs. Chicago Bears	Steve Owen
1938	8–2–1	23–17, vs. Green Bay Packers	Steve Owen
1956	8–3–1	47–7, vs. Chicago Bears	Jim Lee Howell
1986	14–2–0	39–20, vs. Denver Broncos	Bill Parcells

Runner-up Giants

1929	13–1–1	———	LeRoy Andrews
1930	13–4–0	———	LeRoy Andrews
1933	11–3–0	21–23, vs. Chicago Bears	Steve Owen
1935	9–3–0	7–26, vs. Detroit Lions	Steve Owen
1939	9–1–1	0–27, vs. Green Bay Packers	Steve Owen
1941	8–3–0	9–37, vs. Chicago Bears	Steve Owen
1944	8–1–1	7–14, vs. Green Bay Packers	Steve Owen
1946	7–3–1	14–24, vs. Chicago Bears	Steve Owen
1958	9–3–0	17–23, vs. Baltimore Colts	Jim Lee Howell
1959	10–2–0	16–31, vs. Baltimore Colts	Jim Lee Howell
1961	10–3–1	0–37, vs. Green Bay Packers	Allie Sherman
1962	12–2–0	7–16, vs. Green Bay Packers	Allie Sherman
1963	11–3–0	10–14, vs. Chicago Bears	Allie Sherman

The braintrust: Phil Simms on the field, Bill Parcells from the sideline. (Fred Roe)

A new tradition: Harry Carson, Gatorade, and a drenched Coach Bill Parcells. (Fred Roe)

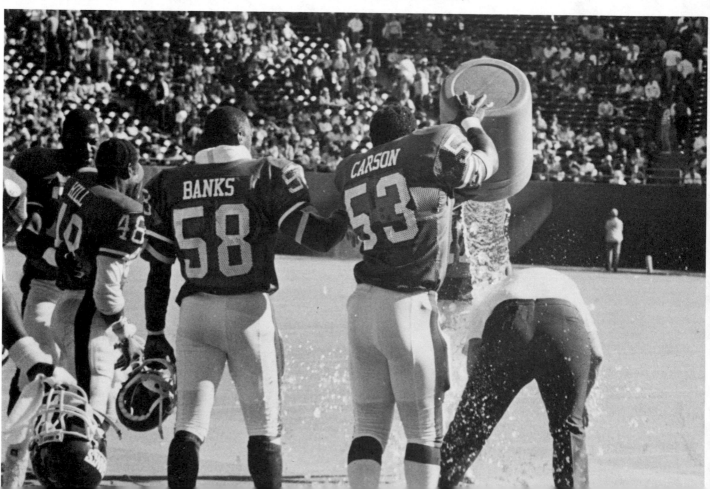

The NFL's Most Valuable Player of 1986, linebacker Lawrence Taylor (56). Besides tackling Washington Redskins runners, he led the league in quarterback sacks with 20½. (Fred Roe)

And the symbol of ultimate triumph in the NFL. (Pro Football Hall of Fame)

2
"I'm Gonna Try to Put Pro Football Over in New York Today"

It was Sunday morning in New York, a clear, sunny October day in 1925. Mass was just letting out at Our Lady of Esperanza Roman Catholic Church, up on 156th Street between Broadway and Riverside Drive. Among the congregation milling about on the sidewalk was a tall, handsome Irishman named Timothy J. Mara, standing there with his wife and one of his two sons, nine-year-old Wellington, and talking with a friend. The boy listened idly to the conversation but looked up suddenly and curiously when he heard his father say to the man, "I'm gonna try to put pro football over in New York today."

And indeed he was. That afternoon the newly enfranchised New York Giants of the National Football League were to take on the Frankford Yellow Jackets at the Polo Grounds in their very first home game. Tim Mara, a thirty-eight-year-old bookmaker (a legal occupation in those days), was to unveil the team he owned and launch what was to become a football institution in New York, and Wellington and his older brother Jack would be there on the sidelines to begin a lifelong association with the club.

Tim Mara was successful in business and a colorful promoter who could claim among his closer friends Governor Al Smith of New York and at that time the soon-to-be mayor Jimmy Walker. Another associate of Mara's was Billy Gibson, who managed boxer Gene Tunney, among other interests. As the story goes, Mara wanted to invest in Tunney, but on the day of the meeting to discuss that particular deal, Gibson was sidetracked by another potential investment. Harry March, a retired army doctor from Ohio who wanted to see an NFL franchise opened in New York, and Joe Carr, the league commissioner, were trying

to entice Gibson into putting up the money to found a team. Gibson, who had been burned before in an attempt to bring pro football to the city, was apprehensive. Into the midst of this discussion appeared Mara, which prompted Gibson to suggest that perhaps the franchise would be better off in the bookmaker's hands. Mara asked, "How much will the franchise cost?" Some say the price tag was $500; others, $2,500, and no one really knows for certain.

Tim Mara knew it was a risky venture, but that kind of thing had never fazed him before. So he took it, and the football Giants became a reality in New York City.

Dr. Harry March, with the title of club secretary, quickly assumed the duties of putting the team together. Tim Mara came up with the approximately $25,000 necessary to provide players, a coach, a stadium lease, equipment, transportation, and other sundry business expenses.

First to be hired was Bob Folwell as head coach. Folwell had been a college coach for a number of years, most recently at Navy. Together March and Folwell set about building a team.

Mara knew that for the venture to succeed in New York, the team had to be a good one, and the players had to be at least fairly well known. So he and March decided to try to sign the biggest football name around, Jim Thorpe, who the year before had played for the Rock Island (Illinois) Independents. He would not be difficult to sign, Mara told March, because there was a kind of mutual disenchantment between the new coach at Rock Island and the then football-elderly and reputed imbiber Thorpe. March got in touch with Thorpe and asked him to come to New York and talk over the possibility of playing for

Tim Mara, a New York bookmaker and renowned man about Manhattan, bought an NFL franchise for his hometown for, some say, $500; others claim $2,500. Whatever the figure, he launched the Giants in 1925, saw them through the tough times, and passed the team ownership on to the able hands of his two sons, Jack and Wellington. He was honored in 1963 as one of seventeen charter members of the Pro Football Hall of Fame. (Pro Football Hall of Fame)

the new franchise. Thorpe was delighted at the prospect of coming to New York, and in Tim Mara's office in Manhattan he quickly came to terms with the club.

The only problem was that Thorpe was now thirty-seven and not in very good shape, but Mara wanted him for his presence on the team, not necessarily for his performance. He was signed to a unique contract in pro football history: Thorpe was to be paid $200 "per half game" because it was clear he would not be able to go a full sixty minutes.

At the same time, the Giants lined up some first-rate talent that was both young and in good condition. Century Milstead had been a consensus All-American tackle at Yale in 1923. Five-foot-ten-inch, 165-pound tailback Henry "Hinkey" Haines from Penn State and fullback Jack McBride of Syracuse were considered to be two of the best backs coming from the college ranks. Joe Alexander, who was also a physician and called "Doc" by his fellow players, had been an All-American guard at Syracuse in 1918 and 1919, then played several years in the pros with the Rochester Jeffersons, signed on to play center for the Giants.

Life in the six-year-old NFL in 1925 was obviously quite different from what it is today. An average player earned somewhere between $50 and $150 a game, the bigger-name stars perhaps as much as $400 a game. They all worked at regular jobs during the week, and therefore practices had to be scheduled after ordinary working hours. The top price for a ticket at the Polo Grounds that year was $2.75, the cheapest seat in the stadium a mere half-dollar. The NFL itself claimed twenty franchises in 1925, with teams from such towns as Pottsville, Pennsylvania; Canton, Ohio; Hammond, Indiana; and Duluth, Minnesota. And one team, the Milwaukee Badgers, was fined $500 for using four high school players in a game against the Chicago Bears.

The brand-new New York Giants made their debut in early October at their only preseason game, a match staged in New Britain, Connecticut, with a team known as Ducky Pond's All Stars, which was not a member of the NFL. (Pond had been a standout on Yale teams of 1922–24, but never played in the NFL. He would, however, return to his alma mater as head coach from 1934 through 1940.) To get the franchise off on the proverbial right foot, the Giants demolished Ducky Pond's All-Stars that afternoon, 26–0.

The regular-season schedule called for the Giants to play two road games and then host nine straight games at the Polo Grounds. The first was against the Providence Steam Roller up in Rhode Island, another newcomer to the NFL that year, and the Giants flopped in their regular-season football debut, losing 14–0. Six days later the Giants appeared in Philadelphia to take on the Frankford

Yellow Jackets, a team led on the field and coached by Guy Chamberlain, one of the greatest of the early players. Frankford won that one, 5–3, the winning margin coming from a safety.

That game was held on a Saturday, and after it both teams entrained for New York to meet again the next day at the Polo Grounds.

Tim Mara brought his wife and two sons to the stadium that afternoon, joining about 25,000 other fans for the home opener. Jack Mara, who was seventeen at the time, got to sit on the sidelines; Wellington, eight years younger, sat with his mother in the stands but managed to talk his way into a seat on the bench just before the second half got under way.

Perhaps Tim Mara hadn't prayed hard enough that morning in church, or maybe the Giants were a little nervous on their formal introduction to New York; whatever the reason, they lost, 14–0, and now had a record of 0–3. Jim Thorpe, slowed by age and an injured knee, was ineffective. He did not play a full half but still collected his $200. It was his last game as a New York Giant. He was released by Mara, whereupon he returned to Rock Island to finish out the season with the Independents, who decided they still wanted him despite his condition.

After that, the Giants pulled together, especially the defense, and treated New Yorkers to four straight shut-outs: 19–0 over the Cleveland Bulldogs, 7–0 over the Buffalo Bisons, 19–0 over the Columbus Tigers, and 13–0 over the Rochester Jeffersons. Three more wins over the Providence Steam Roller, Kansas City Cowboys, and the Dayton Triangles brought their record to 7–3–0.

But as successful as the Giants now were on the field, they were not at the gate, at least in terms of those who

The First Captain

Bob Nash, born in Ireland and raised in New Jersey, has the distinction of being the first captain of the New York Giants. He was 34 years old in 1925, a sometime end and sometime tackle who had played with the famous black athlete and singer Paul Robeson in his college days, and then gone on to play with pro teams in Massilon and Akron, Ohio, and Buffalo, New York, before joining the newly founded Giants.

Nash also has claim to being the source of the first NFL player transaction when the Akron Pros sold him for $300 (or $500 depending on who tells the story) to the Buffalo All-Americans. He played with the Giants that charter year and then retired from the game, but was brought back as an honored guest, at the age of 83, to the opening of Giants Stadium in the New Jersey Meadowlands in 1976.

actually paid to get into the Polo Grounds. The home opener had been a big draw, but more than half of the 25,000 spectators had been admitted free of charge. By the time the Chicago Bears came out to New York in early December, the Giants were deep in debt—probably about $40,000—and Tim Mara's friends and colleagues, almost to a man, were urging him to forget altogether what they felt was the ill-fated business of professional football. Wellington Mara remembered one evening at the Mara home around this time when Governor Al Smith, a frequent visitor, said to Tim Mara, "Pro football will never amount to anything. Why don't you give it up?" Mara paused for a moment, looked at his two sons, and said, "The boys would run me right out of the house if I did."

Financial resurrection was at hand, however. The Chicago Bears were on the way to New York with their most recent acquisition, Red Grange, who had played his last college game the Saturday before Thanksgiving and his first pro game on Thanksgiving Day. The East Coast had

Starting Lineup, Opening Day, October 18, 1925	
LE	Bob Nash
LT	Century Milstead
LG	Art Carney
C	Doc Alexander
RG	Joe Williams
RT	Al Bednar
RE	Lynn Bomar
QB	Dutch Hendrian
LH	Jim Thorpe
RH	Heinie Benkert
FB	Jack McBride
Coach	Bob Folwell

Dr. Harry March, a retired Army doctor and erstwhile advocate of "postgraduate football," as he called the pro game in the 1920s, was instrumental in convincing Tim Mara of the efficacy of bringing the sport to New York City. After Mara bought the franchise, March was appointed secretary and contributed much to the development of the team and the organization, eventually succeeding to the club presidency. (Pro Football Hall of Fame)

been deprived of watching the fabulous back zigzag his way through three years of the best of college defenses. Tim Mara was now giving them their chance to experience the phenomenon.

The Galloping Ghost, as Grange had been dubbed by famed sportswriter Grantland Rice, was still technically a senior in college, but he was as well-known a sports figure in 1925 as Babe Ruth, Jack Dempsey, Bobby Jones, and Bill Tilden. At Illinois, where he had won All-American honors three years in a row, he became the most dazzling runner the game of football had yet seen. His finest day had been against Fielding Yost's top-ranked Michigan team in 1924 when he scored four touchdowns in the first twelve minutes of the game (a 95-yard kickoff return and runs of 67, 55, and 44 yards). He ran for another touchdown later in the game and passed for still another as he led his team to an upset 39–14 victory over the Wolverines.

The game was scheduled for December 6, a propitious time because it was the week after the Army-Navy game at the Polo Grounds, always a major attraction, and thousands of extra seats were still in place from that spectacle. Mara, with the help of two employees, manned the ticket office in the Knickerbocker Building. And New York responded. By game time more than 70,000 tickets had been sold and more than 100 press credentials issued. In the press box were such sports-writing luminaries of the day as Damon Runyon, Grantland Rice, Paul Gallico, and Westbrook Pegler.

Damon Runyon later observed, "Seventy thousand men, women, and children were in the stands, blocking the aisles and runways. Twenty thousand more were perched on Coogan's Bluff and the roofs of apartment houses overlooking the baseball home of McGraw's club,

Before the 1925 regular season got under way up in Providence, Rhode Island, this was the projected starting lineup, pictured here at the Polo Grounds. Top row, left to right: the backfield—wingback Dutch Hendrian, tailback Hinkey Haines, halfback Jim Thorpe, fullback Jack McBride. Bottom row, left to right: the line—end Lynn Bomar, tackle Century Milstead, tackle Ed McGinley, center Doc Alexander, guard Joe Williams, guard Art Carney, end Paul Jappe. There were some changes by the time the team debuted in New York City, and the fabled Thorpe only made it through three games with the Giants. (New York Giants)

content with just an occasional glimpse of the whirling mass of players on the field far below and wondering which was Red Grange." Actually *more* than 70,000 squeezed and squashed their way into the 65,000-seat-capacity Polo Grounds that afternoon, at the time by far the largest crowd ever to attend a professional football game.

All eyes were on Grange once the game started, including those of the Giants' defense who were keying on him. This was unfortunate because it enabled the Bears' diminutive quarterback, Joey Sternaman, to pull off what had become his favorite play: a fake handoff to Grange going around one end and then a Sternaman bootleg around the other. By the end of the first quarter, Little Joey, as he was known, had scored two touchdowns, and the Bears had a 12–0 lead.

The Giants came back in the second quarter with a concerted drive, the touchdown coming on a 3-yard plunge by fullback Phil White. The score remained 12–7 well into the fourth quarter, when the Giants decided to take a very risky gamble. With third down and 8 yards to go for a first down and deep in their own territory, the Giants lined up in punt formation. But it was a fake, and the Giants' kicker heaved a pass to Jack McBride racing along the sideline, only to have Red Grange step in front of him, pick it off, and then do what everyone had come

to see him do. He raced with it 35 yards through pursuing Giants to add another touchdown for the Bears.

That was the extent of the scoring that historic afternoon in New York: the final score was the Bears 19, the Giants 7. When the tally from the gate was figured, the word was that Grange's share alone was $30,000 (see

---

Profitable Day

Paul Vidmer, writing for the New York Times, *had this boxed introduction to his article reporting the debut of the Chicago Bears and Red Grange at the Polo Grounds, December 6, 1925:*

How Grange Earned $30,000

- Played all of one quarter and parts of two others
- Gained 53 yards on eleven plays from scrimmage
- Ran back two kicks for total of 12 yards
- Threw three forward passes, two of which were completed for total gain of 32 yards
- Received one forward pass for gain of 23 yards
- Intercepted one forward pass and ran 35 yards for a touchdown

---

sidebar). For the Giants, not only was Tim Mara's $40,000 deficit wiped out, but at season's end he showed a profit of about $18,000.

The Giants played the Bears one more time that year, a week later at Cubs Park in Chicago, a game tacked on to the schedule because of the Grange/Bears tour. During that seven-day span, the Bears and Red Grange had played exhibition games in Washington, D.C., Providence, Pittsburgh, and Detroit. In fact when they took the field against the Giants that day in Chicago the Bears had played seven games in eleven days. It was not surprising that the bedraggled and battered Bears fell victim to the New Yorkers, 9–0, that frigid December day. A touchdown from Phil White and a field goal booted by Jack McBride was all that was needed, and the Giants' first season was over with a respectable record of 8–4–0 and a standing of fourth place in the twenty-team National Football League.

Red Grange, with his accompanying flood of publicity and fan-following, had done for the Giants, and profes-

Henry "Hinkey" Haines, a five-foot-ten, 165-pound tailback from Penn State, proved to be one of the best rookies the Giants acquired during their maiden season and was a mainstay in the backfield through the 1928 season. (Pro Football Hall of Fame)

sional football in general for that matter, just what Tim Mara thought he would. Mara's only regret was that the redhead was not doing it as a Giant.

Going to Get Grange

In the second half of the season, Tim Mara was all too aware that he was doling out much more money than the Giants were bringing in. He felt he had to do something to get paying customers into the Polo Grounds, and he had an idea.

Mara told Harry March that he was going out to Illinois to sign up the most dazzling star ever to hit college football, Harold "Red" Grange. The great breakaway back, who could lure 60,000 to 70,000 fans into college stadiums to see him run with a football, was about to play his last college game. Mara's plan was to sign him and get him in a Giants uniform to play against the Chicago Bears at the Polo Grounds. It would save the franchise, Mara told March, and then he promptly reserved a drawing room on the 20th Century Limited to Chicago. From there he would go to Champaign to meet with Grange.

Wellington Mara remembers that everyone was very excited about the prospect, and after a few days, the family received a telegram:

Partially successful STOP Returning on
train tomorrow STOP Will explain STOP
                                    Tim Mara

"We couldn't figure out what 'partially successful' meant," Wellington Mara later explained. They found out on his father's return. "He'll be playing in the Giants-Bears game here," the elder Mara told them. "Only he'll be playing for the Bears."

George Halas and Dutch Sternaman, co-owners of the Chicago Bears, had been dealing with Grange's manager, C. C. Pyle, earlier and had struck an incredible deal to get Grange. Pyle would arrange two postseason tours of the United States, seventeen games in all, and it would take the Bears from New York to Florida to California, with Grange and Pyle splitting profits fifty-fifty with the Bears. It was a deal that would bring Grange and Pyle approximately $250,000 in gate receipts alone, and one that was impossible for Mara to compete with. Still, Tim Mara had been "partially successful" in getting Red Grange to play at the Polo Grounds in 1925.

Red Grange, on the bench next to Chicago Bears and future Hall of Fame center George Trafton, awaits his turn as a pro. Right: Out of uniform, resplendent in the style of the 1920s, the redhead poses with his agent, entrepreneur extraordinaire C. C. "Cash and Carry" Pyle. Sought desperately by Tim Mara, Grange made it to New York as a Chicago Bear instead of as a Giant, but saved the franchise by attracting more than 70,000 to the Polo Grounds to see him gallop. (Pro Football Hall of Fame)

Memorabilia from the game that saved the New York franchise: the Giants versus the Chicago Bears and Red Grange. (New York Giants)

Official Program 1925

"77"   "77"

Chicago Bears vs. New York Giants
SUNDAY, DEC. 13th 2:15 P. M.
CUBS PARK
Price **10** Cents

Red Grange was still the feature when the Giants came out to Chicago seeking revenge for the 19–7 defeat they had suffered at the hands of the Galloping Ghost and his teammates the week before at the Polo Grounds. And they got it, with a 9–0 victory, to end their first season in the NFL.

Where it all began: the Polo Grounds, on the banks of the Harlem River, just beneath Coogan's Bluff. The first Giants home game was played there in early autumn 1925, but the New Yorkers stumbled in their debut and fell to the Frankford Yellow Jackets, 14–0. Jim Thorpe made a fleeting appearance that opening day, Red Grange came there later in the year in a Bears uniform and helped to fill the stadium and save the franchise, while Tim Mara and his sons, Jack and Wellington, were steady dwellers on the sidelines. During the thirty-one years that the Giants claimed the Polo Grounds as their home field, they won three national championships and nine division titles. The last game that the Giants played there was near the end of the 1955 season, a 35–35 tie with the Cleveland Browns. (New York Giants)

3

Hanging In There

The appearance of Red Grange in a football uniform in New York City, so delightfully redemptive for the Giants in 1925, took on a totally different aspect in 1926. Instead of drawing masses into the Polo Grounds to nourish Tim Mara's pleasure and bank account, the spectral Grange would be across the Harlem River enticing potential paying customers of the Giants into Yankee Stadium to watch him perform in a brand-new uniform of the New York Yankees' football franchise.

C. C. Pyle, Red Grange's agent and the organizer of the Bears-Grange barnstorming tour the year before, and the co-owners of the Chicago Bears were unable to come to terms on a contract for the 1926 season. Pyle's demand of a third of the ownership of the ballclub was quite a bit more than George Halas and Dutch Sternaman were willing to part with even for Grange's magisterial presence. So "Cash and Carry" Pyle, as the entrepreneur was known, went to NFL president Joe Carr and formally requested a franchise of his own in New York City, where he had secured a deal to play in Yankee Stadium.

The idea of a competing franchise not a lot more than a Hail Mary pass away from the Polo Grounds, one showcasing the nation's best-known football player, obviously had little appeal to Tim Mara. Knowing how difficult it was to get people to pay their way into the Polo Grounds on a Sunday afternoon *without* competition, Mara, along with Harry March, went to the now-annual NFL owners meeting determined to block Pyle's incursion into New York. Pyle went too. But the Giants' owner pleaded his case as convincingly as Clarence Darrow might have, with the result that the other owners sided with him and voted against granting Pyle a franchise.

Undeterred, Pyle said fine; he would take Grange and launch another league to compete with the entire NFL, and the New York City franchise would be his, would feature Grange, and would play in Yankee Stadium. And wizard of a promoter that he was, Pyle did indeed organize the first American Football League with franchises in nine cities and an impressive array of players who were lured out of the NFL.

Not only were the Yankees and Grange going to play over in the Bronx, the AFL set up franchises in Brooklyn and Newark as well, and the NFL sanctioned still another team, the Brooklyn Lions, who would play at Ebbets Field. The Giants also lost their best lineman, Century Milstead, and coach Bob Folwell to the new league.

The Giants passed Folwell's head coaching duties to Doc Alexander and acquired a five-foot-ten-inch, 225-pound tackle named Steve Owen, who the year before had played for the Kansas City Cowboys and the Cleveland Bulldogs, launching a Giants career as player, then coach, that would last through the 1953 season. They also added two fine rookie backs, Jack Hagerty of Georgetown and Walt Koppisch from Columbia.

With Hinkey Haines and Jack McBride still leading the attack, the Giants breezed through their first two games against a pair of pushovers, the Hartford Blues and the Providence Steam Roller. But then the Giants took the train to Chicago to face the powerful Bears, now without Grange but led by the best tailback in the game, triple-threat Paddy Driscoll. The ensuing 7–0 loss in the Windy City was the Giants' first of the season and was followed

N. Y. FOOTBALL GIANTS
(National Football League)
VS.
PHILADELPHIA QUAKERS
(American Football League)

Captain JACK McBRIDE
Fullback
New York Football Giants

Sunday
ember 12, 1926

Polo Grounds
New York

Fullback Jack McBride, the Giants' second captain and program coverboy in 1926. An alumnus of Syracuse, he was a premier running back for New York during the first five years of the club's existence. After a three-year sojourn with the Brooklyn Dodgers, he returned to round out his career with the Giants from 1932 through 1934. (Pro Football Hall of Fame)

ignominiously by back-to-back shutouts, each 6–0, at the hands of the Frankford Yellow Jackets, who were destined to win the NFL title that year. After that, however, Doc Alexander's boys pulled together and salvaged a respectable season. They won five of their last six games, ending up with a record of 8–4–1, good enough for seventh place in the now twenty-two–team NFL. Jack McBride was the league's fifth-most profuse scorer (48 points), scoring 5 touchdowns and kicking a field goal and 15 extra points.

With the regular season over, Mara challenged Pyle and his AFL Yankees to an "intracity championship game." Pyle at first agreed but later backed out. So Mara invited the AFL-champion Philadelphia Quakers, the team that had pirated Folwell and Milstead before the season, to come to the Polo Grounds and face his Giants. They agreed. On December 12 the two teams lined up before 5,000 chilled fans on a snow-covered field that, before the afternoon was over, would be churned into a marbled veneer of snow, mud, and slop.

The Quakers were confident; some even boasted in the newspapers before the game of the trifling concern they had for the seventh-place Giants of the NFL. Perhaps they should have concerned themselves more.

The game was pure defense in the slush of the first half, but Jack McBride managed a field goal to give the Giants a 3–0 lead at intermission. Then all hell broke loose. McBride burst in for a score early in the third period, and on their next possession Hagerty skidded in with another. In the final period, McBride picked off a Quaker pass and ran it back for a touchdown; a little later, Tillie Voss snatched away another and carried it in for 6 more points. Besides all that, Jack Hagerty had raced 65 yards for a touchdown, but it was called back because of a penalty; and another penalty nullified a 52-yard TD run by McBride. The Giants' defense allowed the Quakers only one first down the entire game, and when it was over the seventh-place NFL Giants had outscored the AFL-champion Quakers, 31–0. Babe Parnell, a tackle who played the full sixty minutes for the Giants, said of it much later, "Everyone on the Giants wanted to win that one. The

---

Sunday Pro Football Games Here Are Defended by Court

"I attend the games myself, and I fail to see any basis for such charges."

With this statement Magistrate James Barrett in Washington Heights Court dismissed charges that players of the New York and Cleveland professional football clubs violated Sabbath "blue laws" in playing on Sunday at the Polo Grounds. Summonses were handed to the captains and to Dr. Harry March, sponsor of the local club, following a game at the Polo Grounds on November 1, but when the case came before him Magistrate Barrett on lack of evidence that the game disturbed the peace as was charged, dismissed the complaint.

A Loss That Saved the Franchise, December 6, 1925

New York Giants		Chicago Bears
Paul Jappe	LE	Duke Hanny
Century Milstead	LT	Ed Healey
Art Carney	LG	Hunk Anderson
Doc Alexander	C	George Trafton
Joe Williams	RG	Jim McMillen
Babe Parnell	RT	Don Murry
Lynn Bomar	RE	George Halas
Mike Palm	QB	Joey Sternaman
Hinkey Haines	LH	Red Grange
Heinie Benkert	RH	Laurie Walquist
Jack McBride	FB	Dutch Sternaman

Giants	0	7	0	0 —	7
Bears	12	0	0	7 —	19

Touchdowns—*Giants:* White; *Bears:* J. Sternaman (2), Grange.
PATs—*Giants:* McBride; *Bears:* J. Sternaman.

Quakers thought the Giants were pushovers, but we kicked the bleep out of them." And so ended the Giants' 1926 football season.

The bad news for Tim Mara was that his organization had lost $40,000. Better news perhaps was that Pyle's Yankees dropped $100,000, and the AFL collapsed.

The Yankees and Pyle, however, did not go away. The NFL granted them a franchise for the 1927 season, although they would have to play all but four of their sixteen games on the road. But they would prove to be no competition on the field, despite having Red Grange and Eddie Tryon in their backfield, Iron Mike Michalske in the line, and a pair of Hall of Fame–bound ends in Ray Flaherty and Red Badgro—the reason being simply that the Giants were the best team in the league that year, with a defense so niggardly that they gave up only 20 points in thirteen games. When the Giants did meet up with Pyle's Yankees, they shut them out, 14–0, at the Polo Grounds and 13–0 at Yankee Stadium on successive Sundays in December.

The NFL was down from twenty-two teams to twelve by 1927. At season's start, the class of the league appeared to be the Chicago Bears with Paddy Driscoll and Joey Sternaman, the Green Bay Packers with Curly Lambeau and Red Dunn, the Cleveland Bulldogs behind rookie tailback Benny Friedman, and the Providence Steam Roller with Wildcat Wilson and Jimmy Conzelman. And, of course, the Giants.

Harry March had wanted to beef up the Giants' defense, and so he recruited a six-foot-two-inch, 235-pound All-American tackle, Cal Hubbard, from Centenary College in Shreveport, Louisiana. In addition, March talked Century Milstead into redonning a Giants uniform. Along with Steve Owen, Al Nesser, Hec Garvey, Mickey Murtagh, and Chuck Corgan, the Giants had a virtually impregnable front wall. Wingback Mule Wilson was acquired to join Hinkey Haines and Jack McBride in the backfield, as was thirty-four-year-old Indian Joe Guyon. And Messrs. Mara and March decided to replace coach Doc Alexander, whose medical practice was taking too much of his time, with Earl Potteiger.

The Giants knocked off the Providence Steam Roller up in Rhode Island, 8–0, to open the season. But over at Cleveland, the Bulldogs held New York scoreless; fortunately, the awesome defense of the Giants also prevented Benny Friedman and his cohorts from putting a point on the scoreboard. Two weeks later, however, after an easy win over the Pottsville Maroons, they were not so lucky. Hosting Cleveland at their home opener in the Polo Grounds, the Giants again failed to score, but Friedman got the Bulldogs a touchdown that gusty October afternoon, and New York suffered its first loss of the season.

But after that the Giants' running game came to life, most excitingly on the legs of Hinkey Haines, Jack McBride, and Jack Hagerty, and their defense allowed only two touchdowns in their next nine games. With nine straight victories, they easily took the NFL crown. Only the Chicago Bears, late in the season, gave them a first-class fight. Still harboring hopes for the title, George Halas brought his Bears to the Polo Grounds with a

Never Sneak Up on an Indian

From Richard Whittingham, The Chicago Bears, *Rand McNally, 1979:*

In 1927 an aging Joe Guyon (34) was in the backfield for the Giants. As he faded back for a pass, George Halas, the Chicago Bears' right defensive end, burst through. Guyon's back was to Halas, a perfect set-up for a blind-side hit, maybe a fumble, but if nothing else a reminder that the game of football was a rough one. At the last second, however, Guyon unloaded the pass and wheeled around to greet the charging Halas with his knee. It broke several of Halas' ribs. Guyon shook his head at the grimacing Chicago Bear on the ground. "Come on, Halas," he said. "You should know better than to try to sneak up on an Indian." And making Halas even more miserable, the referee called him for clipping and marched off 15 yards against the Bears.

Steve Owen, as both player and coach, was a Giants institution for twenty-eight years. He arrived from the Kansas City Cowboys in 1926 as a five-foot-ten, 225-pound tackle, played through 1933, and served as coach from 1931 through 1953. Notorious as a brutal tackler when he was a player and famed for his "umbrella defense" as a coach, he was enshrined in the Pro Football Hall of Fame in 1966. (Pro Football Hall of Fame)

record of 6–2–2, not an insurmountable stride behind the 8–1–1 Giants with several games still to play in the season.

The field was muddy from an early morning rain that November day, the sky overcast (and with dropping temperatures was threatening snow), part of the reason a crowd of only about 10,000 fans showed up. The Bears marched from the outset and ended up in a fourth-down, goal-to-go situation from the Giants' 1-yard line. But when a Bears back hit the line he ran smack into Giants guard Al Nesser, who dropped him just short of the goal.

The game remained a battle of the defenses through the first half. Several more times during the period the Bears pounded their way deep into New York territory, but each time the Giants' defense rose up and stopped them. In the third quarter, it was a different story, however. Now it was the Giants' turn to threaten, moving to the Bears' 2 in the third quarter. Jack McBride cut off tackle and fell into the end zone with the game's first score. Later in the period, the Giants again moved the ball, this time to the 1, from where McBride again bulled it in. The Bears, trailing 13–0 in the fourth quarter, came back and posted a touchdown of their own on a pass from Laurie Walquist to Joey Sternaman. The remaining ten minutes were brutal and bloody, especially at the line of

Benny Friedman

"He was the best quarterback I ever played against," Red Grange said of Benny Friedman. "There was no one his equal in throwing a football in those days." Indeed, and the Giants wanted him so badly they bought the entire franchise of the faltering Detroit Wolverines in 1929 to get him.

Only five foot eight inches and weighing about 170 pounds, he came from Cleveland, Ohio, but played his college ball at Michigan under the legendary Fielding "Hurry Up" Yost. He led the league in passing (19 touchdown passes) his first year with the Giants and again the following year (14), throwing to such able receivers as Ray Flaherty and Len Sedbrook.

But passing wasn't all that Friedman could do. Paul Gallico wrote in Liberty *magazine back in the 1930s, "The things that the perfect football player must do are kick, pass, run the ends, plunge the line, block, tackle, weave his way through broken fields, drop and place kick, interfere, diagnose plays, spot enemy weaknesses, direct an offense, and not get hurt. I have been describing Friedman's repertoire to you."*

New York's first NFL championship team, which won eleven games. The season's record was marred only by one loss and a tie to the Cleveland Bulldogs. Top row, left to right: Joe Alexander, Pete Henry, Riley Biggs, Al Nesser, Dick Stahlman, Steve Owen, Cal Hubbard, Charley Corgan, George Murtagh, Arthur Harms, Paul Jappe. Bottom row, left to right: Phil White, Doug Wycoff, Jack Hagerty, Talma Imlay, Hinkie Haines, Earl Potteiger (coach), Jack McBride, Joe Guyon, Faye Mule Wilson, Cliff Marker. (New York Giants)

scrimmage. At the gun, defense had prevailed, and the score remained the Giants 13, Bears 7.

A few years later, Steve Owen recalled:

> That was the roughest, toughest game I ever played. I played sixty minutes at tackle opposite Jim McMillen, who later became a world wrestling champion. When the gun went off, both of us just sat on the ground in the middle of the field. He smiled in a tired way, reached over to me, and we shook hands. We didn't say a word. We couldn't. It was fully five minutes before we got up to go to the dressing room.

When the season closed, the Giants were 11–1–1, comfortably ahead of the Green Bay Packers (7–2–1) and the Bears (9–3–2). It was their first NFL championship, which made Tim Mara and Harry March quite happy, although they were still a ways from putting some profits in their pockets.

If there had been a Most Valuable Player Award in the NFL, it would have to have gone to Jack McBride. He led the league in scoring with 57 points, in touchdowns rushing (6), in extra points kicked (15), kicked 2 field goals, and threw 6 touchdown passes, the latter exceeded only by Benny Friedman of Cleveland, who was universally acknowledged as the best passer in the game. Hinkey Haines, along with Ray Flaherty of the New York Yankees, caught the most TD passes (4). And no one doubted

The Way It Was

Home opener in 1926 against the Frankford Yellow Jackets. From Barry Gottehrer, The Giants of New York, *G. P. Putnam's Sons, 1963:*

> Everyone was ready for the big afternoon. [Tim] Mara had hired baseball comics Nick Altrock and Al Schacht to entertain, 4,000 Frankford rooters were in town with their own band and cheerleaders, and a crowd of more than 35,000 was expected. Then, the rains came. The game was delayed almost an hour to wait for Mayor Jimmy Walker to arrive and officially kick out the first ball, then started without him. He finally did make his appearance, late in the second quarter, minutes after Frankford had scored on a 46-yard pass, stayed until halftime, marched around the field with Tim Mara, waved to the 15,000 fans, and quickly left the ballpark. He didn't miss a thing.

The game ended at 6–0, the Giants' third straight defeat.

that the Giants had far and away the best defense in the league. It had been a year to remember, but that would be the only solace for them during the long, depressing season of 1928 that they were about to face.

Tim Mara was talking about a repeat championship before the 1928 season ever got under way. After all, he had virtually the same team back and what looked like a very promising new back in rookie Bruce Caldwell from Yale. Hinkey Haines had decided to retire at age twenty-nine, but Mara and March were in the process of talking him back into uniform.

The schedule called for five road games to start the season, then four at home. Pottsville was easy (12–0), Green Bay a bit tougher (6–0), but the team had a decidedly lackluster appearance on both playing fields. Harry March told Tim Mara they would never beat the Chicago Bears or the Detroit Wolverines, their next two opponents, unless they shaped up. He was only too right. The Bears mauled them, 13–0; then the Wolverines chewed

Cal Hubbard, the only player to be enshrined in both the Pro Football Hall of Fame and major-league baseball's Hall of Fame (as an umpire), came to the Giants in 1927 and played tackle for them for two years before going to the Green Bay Packers in one of the Giants' more lamentable trades. The six-foot-two, 260-pounder proved to be one of the greatest linemen of his time, and in 1936, at age 35, he returned to New York to play out the last year of his career. He was elected a charter member of the Pro Football Hall of Fame in 1963. (Pro Football Hall of Fame)

Friedman Remembers . . .

From Pro Football's Rag Days, *Bonanza Books, 1969):*

I think one of the highlights along the charity trail was when we played the Notre Dame alumni for Mayor Jimmy Walker's unemployment fund in the depths of the depression. . . .

There were a couple of funny things that came out of it. Just before the game Rockne walked into our dressing room with a cane—he wasn't well at the time. I was getting my ankles taped . . . I looked up at him—he was one of my idols—and said, "Hi, coach," and he said, "Hello, Benny."

[He asked how I was.] I said, "Fine."

He said, "That's too bad."

I asked, "What can I do for you?"

He started giving me a story about some of these old men that he had, and he told me that one of these guys had taken a big step off a Pullman and got a charleyhorse. He said, "I think we ought to have free substitution."

I said, "Okay, coach, anything else?"

He said, "Yes, I think we ought to cut the quarters down to ten minutes—from fifteen."

I said, "Oh, Lord, we can't do that. There are 45,000 people out there who have paid five bucks apiece to see this game. I'll tell you what we'll do—we'll cut it down to twelve minutes and a half and if it gets bad we'll cut it down some more in the second half." I then said, "Anything else?"

He said, "Yes, for Pete's sake, take it easy."

them up, 28–0, behind the passing and running of Benny Friedman, whom Detroit had acquired from Cleveland.

The players were disgruntled, mostly because the Giants were a no-frills team in 1928. After losing money two years in a row, Tim Mara had appropriately tightened the proverbial purse strings (witness: the team stayed at the YMCA in Chicago). And the word came down from Tim and Harry March that if the players didn't start playing respectable football, they might find themselves even more disgruntled looking for other jobs.

It worked somewhat. The Giants squeaked by their in-town rivals, the Yankees, by a field goal, then held a fine Frankford team to a scoreless tie (the Yellow Jackets would finish second at the end of the year with a record of 11–3–2). Another win over Pottsville, and they were ready to face Detroit again, this time in the friendly sweep of the Polo Grounds. At least they were ready through the first three quarters. Taking a 19–7 lead into the final period, the Giants felt they were vindicating themselves. Benny Friedman had other ideas, however, and led his Wolverines down the field twice, capping each drive with a touchdown pass. Friedman's only problem was that he failed to kick either conversion (a mistake he would make

End Ray Flaherty came from the New York Yankees to the Giants in 1928 and starred for them on offense and defense for six seasons thereafter. After his playing days ended, he went on to become head coach of the Redskins in Boston and then Washington, and, after the war, of the New York Yankees in the All-America Football Conference (AAFC). He was inducted into the Pro Football Hall of Fame in 1976. (Pro Football Hall of Fame)

only 7 times out of 26 attempts that year), and the Giants escaped with a 19–19 tie.

After that, it was disastrous. The Giants lost their last five games in a row, two of them in fact to their hated neighbors, the Yankees. The Giants tumbled from the NFL throne down to sixth place, with a record of 4–7–2, having averaged only 6 points a game. And the organization lost somewhere in the vicinity of $40,000. The mood was a little gloomy in the front office.

Not surprisingly, coach Earl Potteiger was the first to get the message. He would not be back the following year. Then practically everybody on the team followed him out the door at the request of the management. The only returnees of any note were tackle Steve Owen and backs Jack Hagerty and Mule Wilson (and only Owen would start on the 1929 Giants).

In all, eighteen Giants departed as Mara and March carried out one of the most massive slate-cleanings in football history. Tim Mara knew what he wanted for the Giants, or perhaps more precisely *whom* he wanted:

Benny Friedman, the tailback he had watched pick apart his Giants the year before. To obtain his exclusive services, Mara had to buy the entire Detroit team, part-owner/coach Roy Andrews included. It was neither difficult nor expensive because the Detroit franchise was in deep financial trouble and about to go out of business. In essence, all Mara had to do was to sign up Andrews and then negotiate with the Detroit players that he wanted. An-

Playing in the late 1920s and early 1930s at the end opposite Ray Flaherty was Morris "Red" Badgro. Winning a post on three of the first four All-Pro teams (1931, 1933–34), he was, in the words of Red Grange, who often played against him, "one of the best half-dozen ends I ever saw." Badgro played with the Giants from 1928 through 1935, taking a year off in 1929 to play baseball for the St. Louis Browns in the American League. Like Flaherty, he too was elected to the Pro Football Hall of Fame, although the redhead had to wait until 1981 for the honor. (Pro Football Hall of Fame)

drews was installed as head coach of the Giants, and the best of the Detroit players were retained. To keep superstar Friedman happy, Mara dug deep and signed him for $10,000 for the season, by far the most ever paid to a pro player up to that time, excluding, of course, the Red Grange deal with the Chicago Bears in 1925.

Among the other standouts that the Giants acquired from Detroit were tackle Bill Owen (Steve's brother), wingback Len Sedbrook, a fine blocking back by the name of Tiny Feather, and center Joe Westoupal. They also added end Ray Flaherty from the now-defunct New York Yankees.

It was a new show at the Polo Grounds, and it paid off, at least on the field. Only two teams were in contention for the NFL crown during that season, the Giants and the Green Bay Packers. Like the Giants, the Packers had made some key acquisitions—one that would especially come back to haunt the Giants many times over the next five years, and that was monolithic Cal Hubbard. Tim Mara would rue many times having let the Hall of Fame–bound tackle get away from New York. Two other future Hall of Famers picked up by the Pack were halfback Johnny "Blood" McNally and guard Iron Mike Michalske.

The Giants were a little shaky coming out of the starting blocks that season, however. They were held to a scoreless tie by the Orange Tornadoes of New Jersey, a newcomer to the NFL. But that would be the last mishap during the next two months. Behind Friedman's pinpoint passing and the fine running of fullback Tony Plansky, a second-year man who had been injured for most of the preceding season, and an absolutely stalwart defense, the Giants beat and battered their next eight opponents by the collective score of 204–29. Among those triumphs was a 34–0 drubbing of the once-proud Chicago Bears, who, after the Yankees' demise, once again showcased Red Grange.

During the same period of time, the Packers also went undefeated in their nine games, having allowed their beleaguered opponents a paltry total of 16 points.

The clash of the two unbeatens took place at the Polo Grounds on November 24. Curly Lambeau told his team that if they were to beat the Giants, they had to stop Friedman's passing. All week before the game the Green Bay defense worked on rushing the passer. They had probably the biggest and strongest line in the league, but Lambeau said they also had to be fast enough to put great pressure on Friedman.

The Packer defense did its job that day. Friedman was totally thwarted in the first half, and when he tried the running game the Pack shut it down as well. The Giants' defense was no slouch either. They held the Packers during the first half until they lost the ball on a fumble deep in their own territory, which Green Bay took advantage of and got the half's only touchdown. In the third quarter,

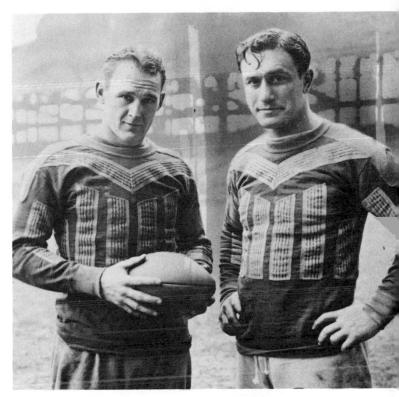

The pro game's first great passer, Benny Friedman (right) poses here with rookie Cliff Montgomery when both were with the Brooklyn Dodgers. Friedman came to the Giants in 1929, and during his three seasons with the club he was the highest paid player in the NFL ($10,000 per year). His 19 touchdown passes in 1929—a time when other passers might throw 5 or 6 at best in a season—remained the NFL standard until Cecil Isbell of the Packers broke it in the much more pass-oriented season of 1942. (Pro Football Hall of Fame)

Friedman finally escaped the Packer pressure and hit Tony Plansky for a touchdown, but missed the extra point, and New York trailed 7–6. Later in the half, however, Green Bay faked a punt, and the pass to Johnny Blood brought them well into Giants territory. A sustained march followed, the icing applied when fullback Bo Molenda charged in for the score. Johnny Blood added another touchdown before time ran out, and the Packers had the win, 20–6.

It was the Giants' only loss all season, which ended with an impressive record of 13–1–1. But Green Bay remained on top with a final record of 12–0–1. (Schedules were not uniform in those days, so some teams ended up playing more games than other teams.) However, Benny Friedman had proved to be the imposing force that Mara and March believed he would. His 19 touchdown passes were more than three times the 6 thrown by runners-up Red Dunn of Green Bay and Ernie Nevers of the Chicago

Cardinals. And Friedman's 20 of 32 extra points were well above the next kicker in that column, Red Dunn, who booted 11 of 22. The top three receivers, at least in terms of touchdowns that year, were all Giants: end Ray Flaherty with 8 and backs Len Sedbrook and Hap Moran with 6 and 5, respectively. Only Ernie Nevers scored more points than the 66 registered by Sedbrook and Tony Plansky's 62.

It was a most pleasant reversal, Tim Mara noted. And not only that, people were finally coming out to watch his team play ball. More than 25,000 had shown up to watch the fateful game with the Packers, and when the season's final figures were toted up Mara's Giants had earned about $8,500, the first black ink on the register since Red Grange came out with the Bears to top off the 1925 football season.

4

"What, and Leave Me Here All Alone?"

The bad news for Tim Mara and the Giants' staff in 1930, besides the Great Depression, seemed to come from all directions. It began with losing Ken Strong, the All-American triple threat from New York University, whose services Mara and March wanted so desperately to keep on Manhattan Island, to the Staten Island Stapletons. It was a blow of major proportions. Watching the refurbished Chicago Bears sign rookie fullback Bronko Nagurski was discomforting, to say the least. Noting that the Green Bay Packers, with the addition of an unheralded but quickly impressive all-around back named Arnie Herber, appeared even stronger than they had in winning the NFL crown the year previous was not overly encouraging. To top it off, Benny Friedman took an additional job coaching at Yale and was noticeably fatigued by the daily round-trip commute from Brooklyn to New Haven, Connecticut, and back to Brooklyn, which he was forced to make before each Giants' practice session.

Outside the world of professional football, Tim Mara had suffered substantial losses in the stock market crash of 1929 and was embroiled in a multithousand-dollar lawsuit in which he was suing world heavyweight champion Gene Tunney and his manager Billy Gibson, whom Mara had formerly been associated with, for money that was due him, he claimed, but that had not been paid. With the overriding fear that the financial setbacks of that dismal time and the litigation in which he was involved might possibly result in the loss of the franchise, Mara turned over total ownership in the ballclub to his sons Jack, twenty-two, and Wellington, fourteen, certainly the youngest owners in the history of professional football (they

were titular owners then, not taking part in management, but later the team would become the life work of both).

Although the Giants hadn't signed Ken Strong, they did make some fine acquisitions that year. End Red Badgro, who had played for the New York football Yankees for two years and then taken a year off to play major-league baseball for the St. Louis Browns, was lured to the Giants. And through press coverage of college games and word of mouth they learned about and also hired a strong running back named Dale Burnett from Kansas State Teachers College and a spunky guard by the name of Butch Gibson from a school called Grove City College in Pennsylvania. The Giants were certainly considered in the running for the NFL title in 1930.

After two easy wins, however, the Giants traveled out to central Wisconsin to take on the Packers and found they were mortal, losing 14–7. If anything, it brought the team closer together because the New Yorkers sailed through their next eight straight games without another defeat, on the way shutting out the Chicago Bears, 12–0, despite the Bears' running combo of Grange and Nagurski, twice clobbering the Chicago Cardinals and Ernie Nevers, and annihilating the hapless Frankford Yellow Jackets by a score of 53–0. An especially pleasing victory during that streak involved thwarting Ken Strong and his Staten Island Stapletons. Because Messrs. Mara and March were under the misapprehension that Strong had snubbed them and their generous salary offer of $10,000 a year (see sidebar), they very much wanted the triple threat to see what he was missing by not playing for the Giants. The game brought out one of the better crowds

27

seeking revenge for their earlier loss. They were 4–4–1 at the time and virtually out of the race for the title. The Giants were a predictable favorite at this point in the season. But there were several factors, other than Red Grange and Bronko Nagurski, that would contribute to the New Yorkers' second defeat of the regular season. After just edging the Chicago Cardinals, 13–7, by scoring two touchdowns late in the fourth quarter the previous Sunday, the Giants stopped off in Cincinnati, Ohio, on their way back from the Windy City to play an Armistice Day exhibition game against a local pro team known as the Ironton Tanks. But the Tanks proved not to be the pushover the Giants surmised. They were a determined team coached by Greasy Neale and guided on the field by tailback Glenn Presnell, both of whom would soon make their names very well known in the NFL. Neale, who also played seven years of baseball with the Cincinnati Reds (he was their leading hitter in the 1919 fixed World Series against the Chicago "Black Sox"), would coach the Philadelphia Eagles throughout the 1940s and earn his way into the Pro Football Hall of Fame. Presnell would make his mark as an outstanding runner and passer with the Portsmouth Spartans and the Detroit Lions.

The Giants scored first on a pass from Hap Moran to Mule Wilson, but Presnell brought the Tanks right back

Chris "Red" Cagle, an All-American from Army who joined the Giants in 1930, puts a move on a would-be tackler during a Giants scrimmage. The fleet redheaded halfback, at five-foot-ten and 170 pounds, was a breakaway runner but also a respected blocker and tackler. He left the Giants after the 1932 season to launch the Brooklyn Dodgers with fellow Giant departee Shipwreck Kelly. (New York Giants)

of the season to the Polo Grounds, about 18,000, but it almost didn't turn out as the Giants' brass had anticipated. After an overly zealous Giants defense knocked Strong unconscious early in the third quarter, the Stapleton star cleared the fog from his head, came back onto the field, grabbed a short pass, and raced 60 yards for a touchdown. He then booted the extra point to put Staten Island ahead, 7–6. The lead held until late in the fourth quarter. Then Benny Friedman, who was having an uncommonly poor day, moved the Giants to the Staten Island 35-yard line, and on fourth down with just two minutes to go, kicked a field goal to give New York a 9–7 win. By November 10, the Giants boasted a handsome record of 10–1, but the Green Bay Packers remained ahead of them with a mark of 8–0.

The Chicago Bears then came to the Polo Grounds,

On Losing Ken Strong

Wellington Mara was only a youngster when Ken Strong entered the NFL, but he remembers the loss well.

Ken Strong had been a great back at New York University in the years when my brother Jack was going to Fordham. That made him a hated rival, of course, but we still thought he was the greatest. We wanted him for the Giants very badly. My father had this employee who was instructed to make every effort to sign Ken Strong. But he failed, and we were very upset when Ken signed with the Staten Island Stapletons, who were a key rival of ours. He then came over and beat us a couple of times.

When the Staten Island team disbanded, Strong came to us. My father said, "Well, Ken, you are three years too late. I never understood why you went over there for less money than we offered you."

Ken said, "What do you mean?"

"We offered you ten thousand dollars a year."

"No, you didn't. You offered me five thousand dollars."

Apparently our employee was going to pocket the five thousand dollars' difference, or else he thought he was going to save the club some money and make some points for himself. I don't know which; all I know is that's how we lost Ken Strong.

Tim Mara presents his good friend and New York's mayor Jimmy Walker with a check for $115,153—the proceeds of the postseason exhibition game played between the Giants and Knute Rockne's Notre Dame All-Stars. The benefit to aid the New York Unemployment Fund during the Depression-racked time was the brainchild of Mara, and more than 55,000 watched the Giants drub the former Fighting Irish, 22–0, at the Polo Grounds. (Pro Football Hall of Fame)

with a 40-yard touchdown pass to Tex Mitchell, and the score at the half was 6–6. After the kickoff to start the second half the Giants marched the length of the field, and Len Sedbrook carried it in from the 1, but the try for an extra point was fumbled away. From that point on, the Tanks totally shut down the New York offense. And in the final minutes of the game, Presnell stunned the Giants by running and passing his Ironton team to a last-second touchdown, the garland a 28-yard toss to Jack Alford, who stepped into the end zone with only seconds remain-

ing. The successful extra point gave Ironton a 13–12 triumph and sent a surprised and morose Giants team back to New York to face the Bears five days later.

With the Giants running head to head into the final stretch for the NFL crown and such superstars as Grange and Nagurski performing for the Bears, it would have seemed the rush for tickets to the game at the Polo Grounds would be substantial. But the rains came Sunday morning and continued into the afternoon, and only about 4,000 stalwarts showed up to watch the two teams

One for the City

The postseason exhibition game of 1930 was played to benefit the unemployed of New York City.

New York Giants		Notre Dame All-Stars
Red Badgro	LE	Chuck Collins
Bill Owen	LT	Joe Bach
Les Caywood	LG	Hunk Anderson
Mickey Murtagh	C	Adam Walsh
Rudy Comstock	RG	Noble Kizer
Len Grant	RT	Rip Miller
Glenn Campbell	RE	Ed Hunsinger
Benny Friedman	QB	Harry Stuhldreyer
Len Sedbrook	LH	Don Miller
Ossie Wiberg	RH	Jim Crowley
Tiny Feather	FB	Elmer Layden
Benny Friedman	Coach	Knute Rockne

New York Giants	2	13	7	0 —	22
Notre Dame All-Stars	0	0	0	0 —	0

Touchdowns—*Giants:* Friedman (2), Campbell. PATs—
Giants: Friedman, Moran.
Safety: Stuhldreyer.

---

wallow in several inches of mud.

It was a game the Giants truly needed because arriving the next week would be undefeated Green Bay. Friedman tried to pass his team to victory, but his receivers slipped and slid all over the rain-soaked, windswept field, and he had little control over the slippery ball. Pass after pass fell incomplete (he completed only three all afternoon). At the same time the Bears' vaunted running attack was also stalled in the mire. The two teams merely exchanged possession of the ball through the first three scoreless quarters. But in the fourth quarter Red Grange found his footing and zigzagged his way 30 yards to the Giants' 15. Reserve running back Joe Lintzenich then carried it to the 6, and Nagurski blasted through for a touchdown on the next play. With time running out, Friedman now passed in desperation and the Bears picked one off. With only seconds left, Nagurski took a pitchout and stormed around right end, shaking off Giants tacklers for 20 yards before sloshing into the end zone. The final score was 12–0. The only solace was the news announced in the dressing room that Green Bay had also fallen that day in its encounter with the Chicago Cardinals.

The sports pages heralded the game between the Giants and the Packers as the one that would decide the

1930 national championship. To aid their cause the Giants lured Army's three-time consensus All-American back, Chris "Red" Cagle, up to New York from his coaching job at Mississippi A & M. The breakaway back was signed for $7,500, it was reported, one of the highest salaries in the league.

Cagle made hardly any difference in his professional debut, however. He was injured in the first quarter and contributed very little when he returned in the second half. But, as it turned out, the Giants didn't really need him that cold November afternoon. With about 45,000 fans shivering in the Polo Grounds, the Giants put the first score on the board in the second quarter on a 22-yard pass from Friedman to Red Badgro. Friedman booted the conversion for a 7–0 lead. In the third quarter, with the Giants deep in their own territory, Hap Moran surprised every-

Dale Burnett came to the Giants in 1930 from Kansas State Teachers College and earned a starting assignment in the backfield the following year. He proved to be a fine runner and pass catcher during his ten-year career with the Giants. (Pro Football Hall of Fame)

one in the stadium, especially the Packers, by faking a punt and then racing around end 84 yards before he was dragged down at the Green Bay 1-yard line. Moments later Friedman carried it in for the touchdown.

Green Bay came back in the last period, Verne Lewellen scoring from the 5 after a concerted drive. The Pack threatened again in the closing minutes of the game, moving down to the Giants' 5-yard line. Three plunges got them to the 1, and, on fourth down, substitute fullback Hurdis McCrary bolted through for the score, but offsides was called on both teams, and the touchdown was nullified. McCrary tried again on the next play, but the Giants' line stopped him short of the goal. The game ended with the Giants on top, 13–6, and in first place with a record of 11–2, three wins better than Green Bay's 8–2 (the Giants had played three weeknight games during the season).

It was the acme of their season as it turned out because the next week the Giants fell to the Stapletons, the winning touchdown contributed by none other than Ken Strong, and the following Sunday they were beaten by the

Brooklyn Dodgers, a newcomer to the NFL that year. It was enough to cost Roy Andrews his head coaching job and the Giants the NFL crown. They ran second (13–4–0) to Green Bay (10–3–1). Benny Friedman had had a spectacular year, justifying his hefty salary in Tim Mara's eyes. The versatile tailback, as expected, threw the most touchdown passes that year (14), and he was second in total points scored (55), just two short of former Giant Jack McBride of the Brooklyn Dodgers. In addition, he was second in touchdowns rushing, his 7 only one fewer than Verne Lewellen's total for Green Bay.

There was, however, a most colorful epilogue to the 1930 season. Tim Mara had approached his friend Mayor Jimmy Walker and told him he would like to do something to help the many unemployed in his Depression-racked hometown. He suggested his Giants play a charity game against a Knute Rockne–coached team of former Notre Dame greats, including the fabled Four Horsemen. Charles Stoneham, owner of the baseball Giants and the Polo Grounds, would provide the stadium free of rent, and all income from the contest would be turned over to

An action shot from the early 1930s shows the great Ernie Nevers downed with the ball at the Polo Grounds, surrounded mostly by Chicago Cardinals teammates. (Pro Football Hall of Fame)

On the Bench

In 1931, there weren't a lot of restrictions as to who might sit on the bench along with the team and coaches. Paul Gallico, one of the best sportswriters of the time before he turned his authorial talents to fiction, remembers one incident in an article for Liberty *magazine that year, which also gives an insight into the talents of Benny Friedman.*

Late this fall I sat on the sidelines at the Polo Grounds in New York with Leroy Andrews, coach of the New York Giants, Tim Mara's professional football team. They were playing the Providence Steam Roller pretty even. The score was 0–0. Benny Friedman was on the field as captain and quarter back of the New Yorkers.

Suddenly Andrews dug a huge elbow into my side. "Look at that half back!" he cried, pointing to the defensive right half back of the Providence team. I couldn't see anything wrong with him. He looked reasonably alert, and I said so.

"Alert, hell! He's two yards out of position. It's the spot for a pass and a touchdown. Watch Benny now! I wonder . . ."

The ball was snapped while he was still talking and a blue-shirted Giant streaked through the left side of the line and in a second was out and beyond the Providence man. Even then the defender failed to catch the scent of danger, because Friedman, who was drifting lazily slantwise to the side line, was looking down the other side of the field, where decoys were spreading out fanwise. Not until he had pulled his arm back did Friedman suddenly whirl and spiral the ball down to the lone runner. The defensive half back who had been standing those bare, and to the layman imperceptible, two yards out of position, never had a chance. The receiver was beyond him, he turned, raising his right shoulder, and the ball was at his finger tips—touchdown!

the mayor to be used to help New York's unemployed.

Despite a bitingly cold day, the contest attracted a crowd of more than 55,000, including Mayor Walker and former New York governor and presidential candidate Al Smith. Knute Rockne knew his former collegians were undersized, less experienced, and fashioned into a team in just one week. In the locker room before the game he told them, "Boys, these Giants are big and heavy, but slow. Go out there and score two or three touchdowns on passes right off, and then defend." Then thoughtfully he added, "And don't get hurt."

Out of their league, so to speak, the All-Stars went out there and got throttled, the final score being 22–0. The day's action was probably best summed up in a story Notre Dame guard Noble Kizer often told later. At the line of scrimmage during the second quarter, Kizer whispered to center Adam Walsh, "I think they're going to pass. I'm going to pull out and take the inside back." Walsh looked

over at him wide-eyed, and said, "What, and leave me here all alone?"

On the plus side, Tim Mara was able to hand Mayor Walker a check for the New York Unemployment Fund totaling $115,153, the entire gate receipts. The $15,000 worth of expenses that had been promised to Rockne and his players was paid out of Tim Mara's personal bank account.

The 1931 season was not a memorable one, at least the way the Giants played. After being a solid contender the year before, they suffered through a 7–6–1 season, land-

A Providential Postmaster in Providence

Mel Hein tells the fateful story of how he became a New York Giant in 1931:

I went from Washington State to the New York Giants but I almost went with another team. I had a contract offer from the Providence Steam Roller out of New England. I hadn't received anything from the Giants, although I'd heard they were planning to make me an offer. Well, Jimmy Conzelman was the Steam Roller coach, and he was pushing me, so I signed with Providence for $125 a game.

After I signed the contract, I went down to Spokane for a basketball game, another sport I played at Washington State. We were playing Gonzaga, and Ray Flaherty, the Giants' captain, coached them in the off-season. He came down to the dressing room after the game and asked me if I'd received a contract yet from the Giants.

"No, I haven't," I said. "But if one's on the way, it's too late now. I signed one with Providence and mailed it back to them yesterday."

"Oh, no," Ray said. "How much are they paying you?"

I told him and he said, "The Giant contract is a better offer, $150 a game. I know that's the figure, and I know the contract's on its way to you. Damn." A little later he came back to me and said, "Why don't you go down to the postmaster when you get home and see if he won't send a telegram to the postmaster in Providence to see if he would intercept the letter?"

The next morning I did, but the postmaster said he wouldn't do it. He said that I could try myself, but he truly doubted I'd get the letter back. So I sent the telegram myself and, sure enough, the postmaster in Providence sent the letter with the signed contract back. In the meantime, the Giants' contract for $150 a game had arrived. I signed with the Giants and tore up the other contract. I think at that time $150 a game was probably the highest pay of any lineman in the league. It was pretty good money, even though it wouldn't sound that way now in the 1980s, but you could buy a loaf of bread for a nickel and get a full meal for thirty-five cents in the Automat back then. And you had no income tax!

ing in fifth place in the then ten-team NFL. But there were some significant events that would have very positive effects on the Giants' future.

Among them were the appointment of Steve Owen as head coach and the signing of a tall, rangy center from Washington State by the name of Mel Hein. At the start of the season the Giants lost Benny Friedman, who decided to make his coaching job at Yale full-time, but after the Giants lost three of their first four games, Tim Mara took on the assignment of talking Friedman into coming back. By November 1, he succeeded. The return of Friedman helped at the gate and, at least for the first two games, on the field. With a renewed passing attack, the Giants knocked off the undefeated Portsmouth Spartans (8–0 going into the game) and then the Frankford Yellow Jackets. But success was short-lived. Over the next three weeks, New York was manhandled successively by the Bears, Packers, and Stapletons. The Giants won their last two games of the year, beating Brooklyn and surprising the Chicago Bears, but it proved to be the first of two disappointing seasons. Still, two Giants were selected to the first All-Pro team, end Red Badgro and guard Butch Gibson.

Team Poet Laureate

On the occasion of "Tim Mara Day" at the Polo Grounds in November 1932, Westbrook Pegler, in his syndicated column "Speaking Out," observed a new Giant in the fold:

They have hired cheerleaders from time to time and yesterday a poet laureate bobbed up in the literature of the official program (price, 15 cents) with a new alma mater song dedicated to Tim Mara, entitled "My Song." . . .

The new alma mater song, struck from the lyre of Poet Thomas J. McCarthy, runs about a hundred lines, which is somewhat longer than the formula for such works, but then it probably was written on space, and it was demonstrated years ago in the newspaper business that the space system made for length.

A few lines will serve to tell you about the new song:

Each fall my joy is without bounds,
On Sundays at the Polo Grounds.
For when our football Giants play,
Just try to keep this guy away.

It is a little better than most college songs, but, then, the college poets are amateurs, like the college players, and cannot be expected to write as well as the pros.

The Giants of 1931, the first team coached by Steve Owen. They expected to be a title contender, but could only muster a fifth-place, 7–6–1 season. Top row, left to right: Steve Owen, Johnnie Kitzmiller, Len Sedbrook, Hap Moran, Dale Burnett, Tim Mara, Dr. Harry March, Doug Wycoff, Ted Bucklin, Chris Cagle, Benny Friedman. Bottom row, left to right: Sam Stein, Ray Flaherty, Len Grant, Bill Owen, Lester Caywood, Mel Hein, George Murtaugh, Butch Gibson, Laurie Walquist, Corwan Artman, George Munday, Glen Campbell, Red Badgro. (New York Giants)

Benny Friedman left the Giants for good before the start of the 1932 season. He had asked for a piece of the ballclub as well as his salary, but Tim Mara told him the organization was going to remain a family operation. Friedman signed with the Brooklyn Dodgers, and the Giants went in search of a tailback, one who could pass the ball well. With Friedman in Ebbets Field, the Dodgers no longer needed Jack McBride and released him, so the Giants hired their former tailback to join Red Cagle, Dale Burnett, and Bo Molenda (acquired from Green Bay that year) in the backfield. New York still had two of the classiest ends in the league, Ray Flaherty and Red Badgro, and the finest center in the game, Mel Hein. They also took on a swift and cagey running back from the University of Kentucky, John Simms "Shipwreck" Kelly (see sidebar). But they hardly played as a team, and in their first six games could come up with only one win, a 20–12 rout of Benny Friedman and his Dodgers. It got a little better after that, with three wins and a tie in their last four games, the highlight being a 6–0 upset of the defending NFL-champion Green Bay Packers.

When the season ended, the Giants had a record of 4–6–2 and resided in sixth place, finishing ahead of only the Providence Steam Roller and the Staten Island Stapletons. End Ray Flaherty was the only Giant to earn All-Pro honors. But times were about to change in the Giants' camp.

Shipwreck, as in Kelly

John Kieran, writing for the New York Times, *described the coming to the Giants in 1932 of Shipwreck Kelly, who would become one of the more colorful figures in pro football as well as New York's café society over the next four or five years:*

It was in the summer that a big, lanky, redheaded chap came into Tim Mara's office on Twenty-third Street.

"Ah'm Shipwreck Kelly," explained the visitor.

"What?" said Mr. Mara. "The fellow who sits on flagpoles?" (One of the more famous characters of the stunt-filled Roaring Twenties was a flagpole sitter who had dubbed himself Shipwreck Kelly.)

"No, suh," said the visitor. "Ah play football. Played foh Kaintucky."

Barry Gottehrer later elaborated on the story.

Mara, who had been given a list of the top college prospects by his sixteen-year-old son Wellington, suddenly realized who his visitor was. "Welcome," said the Giants' owner, smiling and offering a chair. "I've heard of you, my boy. Here, look at this." Opening his drawer, Mara pulled out a folder crammed with clippings detailing the exploits of Shipwreck Kelly of Kaintucky.

"I've seen them all," said Kelly, "and I'd lak to play football

this fall with yah Giants. Ah hear it's a right smart team, suh."

Mara and the Giants needed Kelly but not at his price—a percentage of the gate similar to the deal Red Grange had back in 1925. "I'd love to have you, but I can't afford you," said Mara. "Well, the news about the depression will get back to the hills of Kentucky sooner or later, and you might as well be the one to carry the word."

The Giants had not heard the last of Shipwreck Kelly. . . . Totally unannounced, the drawling redheaded halfback reported to the Giants' training camp at Magnetic Springs, Ohio.

"Glad to have you," said [coach Steve] Owen, "but really we weren't expecting you."

"That's why I came," drawled Kelly. "I do the most ahstonishing things. Nevah know why myself. Now, Coach, there's nothing to do but give me the ball and let me get going."

Shipwreck got the chance to prove himself early in the 1932 season and proved to be an exciting, elusive runner as well as a fine punter. He quickly became the focus of the fans at the Polo Grounds. But:

For the Portsmouth game, Kelly's picture was on the cover of the program. . . . Only one thing was missing—Kelly himself. When he didn't show up by game time, the band started playing "Has Anybody Here Seen Kelly?" but Shipwreck obviously had better things to do for the afternoon. . . .

"What happened to Kelly?" a writer asked Owen after the game.

"Maybe he's sitting on a flagpole," quipped one of the Giants.

"As far as I'm concerned, he can sit on a tack," said Owen. "He's suspended." And colorful John Simms "Shipwreck" Kelly, who never fully explained his mysterious absence, never played another game as a Giant.

Shipwreck Kelly did explain his absence to the author in an interview in 1983: "I played about six or seven games with the Giants that year, but then I quit because the doctor told me I wasn't in shape for it. I had a small touch of rheumatic fever, and I didn't feel very good, and they weren't paying me very much money anyway. I had some money myself, and so I went back to Kentucky."

THE NEW YORK NATIONAL LEAGUE FOOTBALL CO., INC.

DR. HARRY A. MARCH
PRESIDENT
235 WEST 103D STREET
DAY AND NIGHT PHONE
ACADEMY 2-7241

PRESENTS
THE GIANTS

JOHN V. MARA
VICE PRESIDENT
AND TREASURER

JOHN J. MARA
SECRETARY

STEVE OWEN
COACH

"Post Graduate" Football amid "The Sidewalks of New York"

March 25, 1931

Shipwreck Kelly, one of the more colorful characters both on and off the field in New York, poses with a ball he could run with, catch, and kick with equal talent. His field performances were notedly erratic, but his exploits in New York cafe society were legendary. Kelly remained with the Giants for only one season (1932), then went over to Brooklyn with Chris Cagle to own and lead the Dodgers. (Pro Football Hall of Fame)

Mel Hein, whom the Giants were almost too late in signing, was named the NFL's All-Pro center an unprecedented and un-equaled eight consecutive times (1933–40). A Giant of legend-ary proportions, he holds club service records of fifteen seasons (1931–45) and most consecutive games played (172). His Giant jersey number, 7, has been retired. Hein was a charter enshrinee in the Pro Football Hall of Fame in 1963. (Pro Football Hall of Fame)

5

Three Championship Seasons

The year 1933 was an important one in the NFL. A variety of rules changes "modernized" the game and opened up the art of offense considerably. The ball itself, which had gradually been slimming down over the past decade and a half, received a further paring that year, bringing it to the shape it is today, which made it much easier to pass but which at the same time signaled the demise of the dropkick.

Among the rules changes was a provision allowing a back to pass from anywhere behind the line of scrimmage (previously the passer had to be at least 5 yards back of the scrimmage line). The goalposts were moved from the end lines up to the goal lines, a big help for field-goal kickers and designed to boost the scoring. Hash marks were introduced for the first time, and after any play that ended within 5 yards of a sideline, the ball was placed on the hash mark line, which was set 10 yards in from the sideline.

George Preston Marshall, owner of the then–Boston Redskins in their second year in the league, lobbied for dividing the ten-team NFL into two divisions and the holding of a championship game between the two division leaders at the end of the regular season. It was accepted unanimously.

The Giants were placed in the Eastern Division along with the Redskins, Brooklyn Dodgers, and two new franchises, the Philadelphia Eagles, owned by Bert Bell and Lud Wray, and the Pittsburgh Pirates, headed by Art Rooney.

With the passing game revitalized now in the NFL and Benny Friedman lost forever to the Giants, Tim Mara was

determined to add someone to pilot an aerial attack. The person he saw in that role was a five-foot-eight-inch, 175-pound All-American quarterback from Michigan named Harry Newman, whom Wellington Mara aptly described later as a "perfect clone of Friedman." But Newman had decided not to come out to the East Coast cheaply. He bargained with Mara and March and finally worked out a deal in which he was guaranteed a percentage of the Giants' gate receipts, one that would prove quite lucrative for him and cause more than a little consternation in the New York front office during the course of the next two years.

Another prize was unearthed when the Staten Island Stapletons went out of business, leaving triple-threat back Ken Strong unemployed. This time Mara did not dispatch an emissary to talk with Strong; he did it himself and signed the great back the same day. The Giants now had the best backfield in the Eastern Division, rivaled in the entire NFL by only the Chicago Bears with Nagurski and Grange.

Steve Owen felt confident that, with Newman's passing, Strong's running and kicking, and a defense that he was especially proud of, the Giants had a good shot at being the Eastern Division representative in the NFL's first championship game. After the first four games of the regular season, however, his confidence was severely eroded. Losses to the Portsmouth Spartans and the Boston Redskins gave them only a .500 record, with some of their toughest games still to be played, including two with the Chicago Bears, who had handily won their first four games.

The First NFL Championship Game, 1933

New York Giants		Chicago Bears
Red Badgro	LE	Bill Hewitt
Len Grant	LT	Link Lyman
Butch Gibson	LG	Zuck Carlson
Mel Hein	C	Ookie Miller
Potsy Jones	RG	Joe Kopcha
Bill Owen	RT	George Musso
Ray Flaherty	RE	Bill Karr
Harry Newman	QB	Carl Brumbaugh
Ken Strong	LH	Keith Molesworth
Dale Burnett	RH	Gene Ronzani
Bo Molenda	FB	Bronko Nagurski

Giants	0	7	7	7 — 21
Bears	3	3	10	7 — 23

Touchdowns—*Giants:* Badgro, Krause, Strong; *Bears:* Karr (2). Field goals—*Bears:* Manders (3). PATs—*Giants:* Strong (3); *Bears:* Brumbaugh, Manders.

Those first four contests were all on the road. Owen pleaded and berated his players to make a good showing at their hometown debut; he wanted the Giants' fans convinced that the team was as good as he felt they were. He obviously got through to them; the Giants systematically destroyed the Philadelphia Eagles before 18,000 fans at the Polo Grounds by the score of 56–0, then the highest score in the club's history and a standard that would remain until 1972. Newman got the scoring going in the first period with a touchdown pass to Hap Moran, then threw him another for the point after touchdown. Throughout the game, he marched the Giants up and down the field and made everyone forget the passing wizardry of Benny Friedman. When the home opener finally came to an end, fullback Bo Molenda had rushed for two touchdowns, Ken Strong another, and Kink Richards another, and Stu Clancy had raced 46 yards for still another. Jack McBride came off the bench and tossed two touchdown passes in the fourth quarter to Richards and to Dale Burnett.

The following week more than 30,000 fans filed into the Polo Grounds to watch the Giants take on the Brooklyn Dodgers. It was a reunion of sorts, the Dodgers' backfield featuring former Giants running backs Red Cagle and Shipwreck Kelly, who were co-owners of the franchise, and, of course, tailback Benny Friedman. Newman set the tone on the third play of the game. Dropping back to pass, he couldn't find a receiver, so he legged it himself

25 yards for a touchdown. Later in the half he hit end Glenn Campbell with an 18-yard TD strike. On the first play of the second half Kink Richards zigzagged his way 70 yards for a third New York touchdown. The Dodgers got one, but that was it for the day, 21–7, and the Giants were on their way to their first divisional title.

The game also contained one of the unique plays in pro football. With the score 7–0, Ken Strong sent a punt spiraling deep down the field. Shipwreck Kelly trotted back under it and, as the two teams thundered down the field toward him, calmly caught the ball and instead of running with it simply punted it straight back up the field. It was also noted in the next day's sports pages that "Kelly and [Ray] Flaherty, hard workers both, played without headgears . . . Shipwreck had more hair to protect him though."

The Giants lost only one other game in 1933, a 14–10 squeaker to the Bears out in Chicago. When the Chicagoans came out to the Polo Grounds, Steve Owen's proud defense held them scoreless, and Ken Strong's lone field goal provided the margin of victory. The Giants' record of 11–3–0 was far ahead of second-place Brooklyn (5–4–1). In the Western Division, the Bears hadn't surprised anyone by taking the title with a record of 10–2–1. And so the stage was set for the NFL's first championship battle.

The scene was Wrigley Field in Chicago, December 17, a cold, overcast day with a mist that from time to time would turn to a drizzle. The baseball park that the Chicago Cubs played in had a capacity of about 40,000, and some 26,000 seats were occupied for the premier NFL championship match.

The Giants had prepared well. They were not only fired up, but they came with a pocketful of tricks as well. The most memorable was a play devised by Harry Newman and later described by Mel Hein as the "center-with-ball-

All Don't Come from the Draft

Steve Owen got this letter, postmarked Garden Grove, Iowa, in early summer of 1933:

I think I could be a pretty good back. . . . Weight 190 . . . Simpson College last three years. . . . Led Iowa Conference in scoring two years. . . . I'll pay my own expenses east for a tryout. . . . Name is Elvin Richards.

Owen wrote back tersely: "Come on along."
Elvin "Kink" Richards not only made the team but was a mainstay in the Giants' backfield from 1933 through 1939.

PRICE **10** CENTS

NEW YORK FOOTBALL GIANTS
vs.
PORTSMOUTH SPARTANS

KEN STRONG (Giant Back)

POLO GROUNDS   **NOVEMBER 5, 1933**

The Giants finally got Ken Strong into a uniform in 1933 after a recruiting snafu had let him get away to the Staten Island Stapletons four years earlier. A great running back and kicker, he was a key force in the divisional champion Giants of 1933, 1934, and 1935. He came back to the Giants as a kicking specialist in 1937 and again from 1944 through 1947, then retired with a host of club scoring and kicking records. Strong was inducted into the Pro Football Hall of Fame in 1967. (Pro Football Hall of Fame)

The Power of Prayer

In 1933, Ken Strong kicked a field goal to defeat the Chicago Bears, 3–0, in a game at the Polo Grounds that eventually enabled the Giants to meet the Bears for the NFL title that year. On his first attempt, however, New York was offside, and the ball was moved back. Strong kicked again, and again it was good.

Steve Owen fumed on the sideline, not because of the offside penalty but because he had observed his brother Bill, a tackle, on both kicks. Bill had made no attempt to pulverize the Bear across the line from him, guard Joe Kopcha. "Why didn't you destroy that Kopcha," he shouted at Bill at the sideline after the second kick. "He just knelt there at the line of scrimmage, and you didn't do anything."

"I couldn't," Bill said, shaking his head in dismay. "On each kick Kopcha raised his eyes toward the heavens and said 'Please, God, don't let him make it.' Gosh, Steve, I couldn't belt a guy when he was praying."

hidden-under-shirt-keeper-play." Center Hein explained the play as follows: "We put all the linemen on my right except the left end. Then he shifted back a yard, making me end man on the line, while the wingback moved up on the line on the right. Harry Newman came right up under me, like a T-formation quarterback. I handed the ball to him between my legs, and he immediately put it right back in my hands—the shortest forward pass on record." Hein quickly stuffed the ball under his shirt and began strolling downfield while the Bears' defense was rushing after Newman, who was fading back as if to pass. About 30 yards downfield Bears safety Keith Molesworth saw Hein begin to run and tackled him, thereby preventing a touchdown.

The Bears were the first to get on the scoreboard, on a 16-yard field goal from Automatic Jack Manders. He followed that with a 40-yarder. The Giants' offense did not get going until well into the second quarter, which was when Kink Richards slashed through the Bears' defense for 30 yards, and then Newman hit Red Badgro with a 29-yard TD pass. Ken Strong's extra point gave New York a 7–6 lead at the half. The field was muddy by now and the air raw and damp, hardly a setting for what lay ahead, one of the most exciting halfs ever to be played in an NFL title game.

On the opening series of the second half, the Bears marched down to the Giants' 13, where Manders booted another field goal to return the lead to Chicago. The Giants came right back, Newman throwing five consecutive completions that ate up 61 yards before Max Krause lugged it in from the 1-yard line. Then it was the Bears' turn. At their own 25 with long third-down yardage, reserve halfback George Corbett rolled out and tossed one to Carl Brumbaugh, who shook loose for 67 yards, leaving the ball on the Giants' 8-yard line. The Giants keyed on Bronko Nagurski, expecting him to hammer into the line. He did take the handoff but suddenly reared back and hoisted a floater into the hands of end Bill Karr in the end zone. Manders's extra point put the Bears back on top, 16–14.

In the fourth quarter now, Newman continued his deadly passing game: four straight completions this time, to bring the ball to the Bears' 8. Then with a little razzle-dazzle, albeit unplanned, the Giants regained the lead. Ken Strong described it later:

Newman handed off to me on a reverse to the left, but the line was jammed up. I turned and saw Newman standing there [back at about the 15-yard line], so I threw him the ball. He was quite surprised. He took off to the right, but then he got bottled up. By now I had crossed into the end zone, and the Bears had forgotten me. Newman saw me wildly waving my hands and threw me the ball. I caught it and fell into the first-base dugout.

He clambered out of the dugout and kicked the extra point to put the Giants ahead, 21–16.

With time running out, the Bears were now forced to eschew their powerful running game and go to the pass. Molesworth arched one to Brumbaugh, and suddenly the Bears were on the Giants' 33 yard line. Nagurski got the ball on the next play, started around the end, and then rifled a short pass to end Bill Hewitt over the middle. Hewitt headed for the sideline with two Giants defenders in pursuit, and just as one of them was about to pounce on him he flipped a lateral to Bill Karr, who was streaking behind him. Karr carried the ball in for the final touchdown of the game.

The Bears won it, 23–21, but they almost didn't. With just a few seconds remaining, the Giants had the ball and Newman spotted Red Badgro downfield. He hit him with his twelfth completion of the afternoon. Only Red Grange stood between Badgro and the Bear goal line. Trailing behind Badgro was Dale Burnett, waiting to take the lateral when Grange tackled Badgro. But Grange was not only one of the most talented defensive backs in the game, he was also one of the shrewdest, and so instead of tackling Badgro low he hit him high in a bear hug, pinning the ball between them. They both went down in a heap—the lateral thwarted—prompting Tim Mara to say after the game: "Red Grange saved the game for Chicago . . . that quick thinking prevented a score on the last play."

Harry Newman, an All-American from Michigan, was coaxed into joining the Giants in 1933 to replace tailback Benny Friedman. Newman could pass and run with the best and proved to be, in the words of Wellington Mara, "a clone of Friedman." In his rookie year, Newman led the entire NFL in the three major areas of passing stats, with 53 completions for 973 yards and 9 touchdowns. He guided the Giants to a divisional championship that year and an NFL title the following season. Newman left the Giants and the NFL for the new AFL in 1936, when he and his former club could not agree on salary terms. (New York Giants)

Each of the Giants went back to New York richer by $142.22, their individual shares of the title game gate; the Bears collected $210.34 apiece.

When the statistics were in for 1933, Harry Newman led the NFL in pass completions (53), passing yardage (973), and touchdown passes (9). Kink Richards had the best rushing average in the league (6.2 yards per carry), and Ken Strong kicked the most extra points (14) and the most field goals (5). Newman, Red Badgro, and Mel Hein won All-Pro recognition.

The Giants earned the opportunity to avenge themselves against the Bears in 1934 in what turned out to be one of the strangest and most storied NFL championship games in history. But it was not nearly as easy getting to the title game, the first ever held at the Polo Grounds, as everyone in the organization thought before the season got under way.

Tim Mara had gone over to the Bronx to snare two Fordham grads who would start fine Giants careers that year. They were tailback Ed Danowski and guard/center Johnny Dell Isola. The team was favored to take the Eastern Division title, with only the Boston Redskins being considered to have a chance at unseating them.

The Giants, however, got off to a dismal start, posting only 6 points in losses to Detroit and Green Bay in the first two games of the season. Coach Steve Owen railed at them all week before they traveled to Pittsburgh to take

---

Runyon Predicts

The first night football game to be played at the Polo Grounds pitted the College All-Stars against the New York Giants in the 1936 preseason, a benefit for the New York Herald Tribune *Fresh Air Fund, and Damon Runyon devoted several of his "Both Barrels" syndicated columns to it:*

It's our private opinion, and don't let it get around any more than you can help as it might affect the odds, that the College All-Stars will knock the spots off the New York Giants. . . .

It is to be held at night on a light-flooded field, which in itself is a tremendous novelty in New York and may be the beginning of regular night football and baseball, too, here.

They are presenting against the professionals a team of college stars that will include some of the most famous players in the United States, under the coaching of Bernie Bierman, who is accounted one of the smartest football generals alive.

Neighbor Caswell Adams reports from Evanston, Ill., where the College All-Stars are training, the presence of fellows like Wayne Millner and Bill Shakespeare of Notre Dame, Phil Flanagan of Holy Cross, Amerino Sarno of Fordham, and Dick Crayne, Sheldon Beise, Riley Smith and numerous others whose names and exploits threaded the football news last Fall.

Jay Berwanger, of Chicago, halfback selection on everybody's All-American is there. So is Joe Maniaci, Dick Pfefferle and Dale Rennebohm. . . . We think the collegians are a fair bet to beat the Giants.

The Giants won, 12–2.

on the team then known as the Pirates, whose only real claim to distinction that year was speedster Johnny Blood, whom Art Rooney had acquired from the Packers. Fortunately for the Giants, Blood was sidelined that week with an injury.

The thus-far disappointing Giants barely got by Pittsburgh, 14–12, but the turn had been made. New York beat down its next four opponents, looking better each game. Then it was out to Chicago to face the unruly Bears, who were undefeated in five games. It was not yet time for revenge, however. The Giants were blown out of Wrigley Field, 27–7.

The next chance came two weeks later at the Polo Grounds, and it was much more respectable for the Giants. A Giants-loyal crowd of about 55,000 warmed Tim Mara's heart, as did a Ken Strong touchdown in the second quarter. New York added 2 points with a safety when the defense smothered Bears halfback George Corbett in the end zone on the kickoff to open the second half, enabling the Giants to take a 9–0 lead into the fourth quarter.

It did not come without cost, however. Harry Newman was sacked at one point and had to be helped off the field. He tried to come back a bit later but ended up limping off again. The next day X rays showed that he suffered two

The "Sneakers" Championship, 1934

New York Giants						Chicago Bears
Ike Frankian		LE				Bill Hewitt
Bill Morgan		LT				Link Lyman
Butch Gibson		LG				Zuck Carlson
Mel Hein		C				Eddie Kawal
Potsy Jones		RG				Bert Pearson
Tex Irvin		RT				George Musso
Ray Flaherty		RE				Bill Karr
Ed Danowski		QB				Carl Brumbaugh
Dale Burnett		LH				Gene Ronzani
Ken Strong		RH				Keith Molesworth
Bo Molenda		FB				Bronko Nagurski
Giants	3	0	0	27	—	30
Bears	0	10	3	0	—	13

Touchdowns—*Giants:* Strong (2), Frankian, Danowski; *Bears:* Nagurski. Field goals—*Giants:* Strong; *Bears:* Manders (2). PATs—*Giants:* Strong (2), Molenda; *Bears:* Manders.

The Giants visited the Hollywood set of a motion picture starring Jimmy Cagney (front center) in the mid-1930s on one of their exhibition tours to California. The cast, including actor/comedian Joe E. Brown (directly behind Cagney), posed with the Giants in front of a movie-lot set of a prison. Identifiable Giants include Jack Mara and Tom Jones at the far left. (New York Giants)

broken bones in his back, and he was out for the remainder of the season. Ed Danowski took over the duties at tailback that afternoon against the Bears and for the rest of the year.

It was still not time for the Giants to reap their revenge—so the Fates and a few Bears decreed. In the fourth quarter, with Bronko Nagurski both carrying the ball and on other plays leading the blocking for the swift Beattie Feathers, the Bears marched down the field and scored. Jack Manders's extra point put them within two points of the Giants.

The Giants had the ball with less than two minutes to play, but disaster struck when Max Krause fumbled on his own 33-yard line and the Bears recovered. Chicago powered to the 16, where, with only a few seconds left, Manders booted a game-winning field goal.

The Giants won two of their last three games, posting a record of 8–5–0, good enough to earn the divisional crown, comfortably ahead of the runner-up Boston Redskins, who were 6–6–0.

No one had come close to the 10–2–1 Bears in the NFL West, and so the stage was set for the Giants' third confrontation that year with their everlasting nemesis from Chicago. The site for the NFL's second championship game was the Polo Grounds, and the day, December 9, was bitterly cold (nine degrees above zero at game time). The field was frozen hard and coated with a treacherous veneer of ice.

The conditions prompted end Ray Flaherty to come up with a brainchild that would be forever remembered in the annals of pro football. "Why don't we wear sneakers?" he suggested to coach Steve Owen before the game. "When I was playing for Gonzaga we did that once on a frozen field, borrowed them from our basketball team, and we went out and beat a team a lot better than us." Owen wisely took him up on the idea (see sidebar) and dispatched the now quasi-immortal Abe Cohen to procure some.

The paid attendance was officially only 35,059, but according to the *New York Times* there were about 46,000 fans shivering in the stadium at kickoff time. The Giants posted the only score in the first period when Ken Strong booted a 38-yard field goal. Both teams were sliding all over the field as Abe Cohen was still trying to round up sneakers.

The power of the larger Bears proved to be the factor in the second quarter. They were able to push the Giants down the slippery field, with Nagurski the prime mover on a long drive that did not end until he bucked in for a touchdown. Later in the period, the scenario was replayed, and the Bears marched all the way to the Giants' 10-yard line. The drive stalled there, but Jack Manders came on to boot the field goal. The score at the half was

---

**Eating on the Road, 1930's Style
New York Football Giants**

DINNER
One Dollar and Fifty Cents

Puree of Tomato Soup, Croutons   Consomme

Broiled Tenderloin Steak, Fresh Mushroom Sauce
Chateau Potatoes   New Stringless Beans

Assorted Bread

Lettuce and Beet Salad, French Dressing,
Chopped Eggs

Mince Pie, *Hot or Cold*
Ice Cream   Chilled Grapefruit

Tea   Coffee   Milk

December 1, 1935

PENNSYLVANIA RAILROAD

---

the Bears 10, the Giants 3, and, with another Manders field goal in the third period, Chicago was clearly in command.

But then just before the fourth quarter began Abe Cohen showed up with the sneakers. The gymshoe-clad Giants took hold and suddenly were running around and away from the slipping and sliding Bears. Ken Strong ran a punt back 25 yards. Danowski took to the air, and his receivers had little trouble getting free from the Bears' defenders. Four straight completions to Flaherty, Burnett, Strong, and Ike Frankian, and the Giants had their first touchdown of the game. On the next possession, Ken Strong broke loose on a 42-yard touchdown jaunt, and New York had the lead. The Giants took the ball away from the Bears on an interception a minute or so later and marched down the field, with Strong adding another 6-pointer. The Giants snared still another interception from the stunned and stumbling Bears, and moments later Danowski carried the ball into the end zone. The 27-point fourth quarter gave the Giants a 30–13 victory over the Bears in what would be known forever after as the "sneakers" championship.

Harry Newman, who was still troubled with his back injury from the previous season, was making too much

Sneakers Stats

Giants-Bears Statistics

	First Half		Second Half		Full Game	
	Giants	Bears	Giants	Bears	Giants	Bears
Number of rushes	15	24	21	20	36	44
Ground gained rushing	29	67	128	27	157	94
First downs rushing	2	3	5	4	7	7
Number of passes	5	6	7	9	12	15
Passes completed	3	3	4	3	7	6
Ground gained passes	29	39	86	35	115	74
First downs passes	2	1	3	2	5	3
Number of punts	4	4	2	5	6	9
*Average distance of punts	40	38	35	32	38	35
Runback of punts and kickoffs	34	65	46	100	80	165
Fumbles	2	2	0	0	2	2
Ball lost fumbles	2	0	0	0	2	0
Penalties	0	3	0	1	0	4
Ground lost penalties	0	15	0	15	0	30

*Punts averaged from line of scrimmage
The Giants intercepted three passes, the Bears two.

money because of the structure of his contract, the Giants' front office felt. Comfortable in the fact that Ed Danowski had proven himself a most able passer, Tim Mara decided the deal had to be changed, but it did not sit well with the talented tailback. As Newman later explained it:

In 1935, I had a contract dispute with the Maras. And I decided to hold out. In that last game that I'd played in, in 1934, the one against the Bears, we filled the Polo Grounds. Because I was on a percentage, they had to pay me a lot of dough. As a result they wouldn't give me the same kind of contract for the next year. . . . I held out but it didn't do me a lot of good. The season started, and I kept myself sort of busy scouting for coach Kipke back at the University of Michigan.

Newman did come back later in the season, but his playing time was limited. Also leaving in 1935 was guard Butch Gibson. And the Giants' two All-Pro ends, Flaherty and Badgro, thirty-one and thirty-two, respectively, were thinking seriously now about their own postfootball ca-

Sneakers, Abe Cohen, and a Championship

Hero of the New York Giants' first triumph in an NFL title game, the "sneakers" championship of 1934, was five-foot-two-inch, 140-pound Abe Cohen. Wellington Mara tells of how Cohen achieved his immortality:

At the Polo Grounds on Sunday morning, the field was completely frozen. We had a little fellow on the payroll named Abe Cohen, a sort of jack-of-all-trades. Abe was a tailor by profession, and he also worked for Chick Meehan, who was a famous coach at Manhattan College and was quite a showman in his own way. Meehan was the first coach to put what we call satin pants on a football team. He had done that first at NYU in the days of Ken Strong. Abe was his tailor and made the pants for the players so that they would fit properly. Steve Owen asked Abe to go up to Manhattan College, to which he had access—he had a key to their equipment room and the gym—and borrow the sneakers from the lockers of the basketball players and bring them over to the Polo Grounds for our players.

Abe got in a taxi and went to Manhattan. I think he had to break into the lockers. At any rate he got back around half-time of the game with nine or ten pairs of sneakers.

Some of the players didn't want to put them on, but those who did had so much success that eventually most of our players put them on. Ken Strong, who kicked off for us, placekicked with the sneakers on, and he lost a toenail on his big toe. In the second half we began moving the ball. One of the Bears' players went over to the sideline and told George Halas that we were wearing sneakers. "Step on their toes," Halas shouted to his players.

The following week after the championship game—in those days you had barnstorming trips after the season was over—the Bears were playing an exhibition game in Philadelphia, and Steve Owen and I went down to see the game. We went into the Bears' dressing room, I guess to crow a little bit, and the first thing we saw was about twenty-four pairs of sneakers on top of the lockers. Halas said to us, "I'll never get caught like that again."

And as for Abe Cohen, Lewis Burton summed it up best in the December 10, 1934, edition of the New York American: *"To the heroes of antiquity, to the Greek who raced across the Marathon plain, and to Paul Revere, add now the name of Abe Cohen."*

reers. The most promising newcomer was a raucous and outspoken end from West Virginia, Tod Goodwin, who not only won a starting job but became Danowski's favorite receiver.

The Giants started the season by demolishing the Pittsburgh Pirates, 42–7, before 24,000 spectators, at the time the largest crowd ever to witness a game in Pittsburgh.

Abe Cohen Wasn't the Only Hero

From Pro Football Inquirer, *December 1976:*

When the water buckets froze during the "sneakers" game, trainer Gus Mauch thought of something else to give the Giants' players during time outs.

"It was sometime during the fourth quarter," says Mauch. "I asked Jack Mara [team president] if he had a bottle of whiskey. I only wanted it for medicinal purposes . . . something to warm 'em up out there. During the next time out I poured some whiskey in each of the paper cups and took them out on a tray. On the next play, Ken Strong ran a reverse and took it all the way for a touchdown.

"During the next time out, I did the same thing and we scored again," says Mauch. "By that time the bottle was empty. So Jack Mara went to some of his friends sitting in the field boxes right behind our bench. Judge Phelan, the boxing commissioner and Jack's father-in-law, was there. So was Mayor [Jimmy] Walker and Jim Farley, the postmaster general."

Mauch says Mara returned with another bottle and the trainer made another visit to the players. "This time they told me, 'We've got this thing won now; we don't want to get drunk.' They chased me off the field."

Johnny Dell Isola, initially a center on offense, was switched by Steve Owen to a guard because of Mel Hein's monopoly on the position, and played linebacker on defense. He joined forces with the Giants in 1934, after a fine college career at Fordham, and became an important figure in the Giants' offensive and defensive alignments for seven seasons. Johnny Dell Isola made All-Pro in 1939, and came back to the Giants as an assistant coach from 1957 through 1959. (Pro Football Hall of Fame)

The famous lateral that did in the Giants during the last minute of the 1933 NFL championship game. Helmetless, Bill Hewitt of the Bears, after catching a pass and about to be tackled by Giants defender Ken Strong, wheels and pitches the ball back to Bill Karr (22), who would then carry it for a touchdown to give the Chicagoans a come-from-behind 23–21 victory. (Pro Football Hall of Fame)

The NFL East was acknowledged as the weaker division, much weaker in fact, with the Giants considered to be the only forceful team in it. The Western Division, with only four teams now that Cincinnati had dropped out of the league, was the class of the NFL. And that proved to be true. The Giants lost only three games all season, and those were to Green Bay, the Chicago Bears, and the Chicago Cardinals, all from the NFL West. When the season was finished, the Giants (9–3–0) were the only team in the East with a record better than .500, the other teams posting a collective mark of 13–31–2, while in the West all four teams had winning seasons.

The best in the West, it turned out in 1936, was the Detroit Lions (7–3–2), edging out the Green Bay Packers (8–4–0) for the divisional title. The Lions were anchored around triple-threat tailback Dutch Clark, who led the league in scoring that year with 55 points. They also had in the backfield another of the game's most versatile backs, Glenn Presnell, and one of the most powerful of fullbacks, Ace Gutowsky.

The Giants' strength was passing. Ed Danowski led the league in three categories: completions (57), passing yardage (795), and TD passes (11). Tod Goodwin caught the most passes in the NFL (26), and in receiving yardage was only a single yard behind Boston Redskin end Charley Malone, who gained 433. Mel Hein was named the All-Pro center for the third year in a row, and Danowski and tackle Bill Morgan earned similar honors that year.

So for the third time in three years of NFL championship games, New York was the Eastern Division representative. It had rained off and on for four days before the game, and the field at the University of Detroit had taken on characteristics of the Florida Everglades. The rain was gone by game day; it had not really stopped but had simply turned into snow. Only about 15,000 stalwarts turned out for it, but the highly partisan Detroit fans were rewarded almost instantly. The Lions took the opening kickoff and marched 61 yards in six plays, culminated when Ace Gutowsky bulled in for the touchdown. A little later in the quarter, Dutch Clark raced 40 yards for another Detroit tally. The Giants showed a little life in the third period when Ken Strong scored on a 42-yard pass play from Ed Danowski. But that and Strong's extra point proved to be New York's only points of that wintry afternoon. The Lions added a pair of touchdowns in the final quarter to give them a 26–7 victory.

And it was now time for the Giants to take a two-year leave of absence from the NFL title game.

The Giants tried desperately to earn the title of spoilers when they entertained the undefeated Bears late in the 1934 season at the Polo Grounds, but this field goal in the last minute by Jack Manders squelched the 9–7 New York lead and gave the Chicagoans a 10–9 triumph. The Bears went on to a 13–0 season, but the Giants got their revenge in this same stadium in the title tilt. The two Giant defenders are tackle Bill Owen (36) and end Red Badgro (17). (Pro Football Hall of Fame)

A Cold and Lonely Championship

New York Giants		Detroit Lions
Ike Frankian	LE	Ed Klewicki
Bill Morgan	LT	Jack Johnson
Potsy Jones	LG	Regis Monahan
Mel Hein	C	Clare Randolph
Bill Owen	RG	Ox Emerson
Len Grant	RT	George Christensen
Tod Goodwin	RE	John Schneller
Ed Danowski	QB	Glenn Presnell
Ken Strong	HB	Frank Christensen
Kink Richards	HB	Ernie Caddel
Red Corzine	FB	Ace Gutowsky

Giants	0	0	7	0 —	7
Lions	13	0	0	13 —	26

Touchdowns—*Giants:* Strong; *Lions:* Gutowsky, Clark, Caddell, Parker. PATs—*Giants:* Strong; *Lions:* Presnell, Clark.

The Giants eventually stopped Bronko Nagurski during the bitterly cold contest for the NFL title in 1934. Some evidence of it is shown here as Mel Hein (left) and Ray Flaherty wrestle him to the ground. Stopping Nagurski and donning sneakers for the second half enabled the Giants to turn a 10–3 deficit at the intermission into a 30–13 victory and the NFL title. (Pro Football Hall of Fame)

One of the most formidable things the Giants had to contend with in the 1934 NFL title game besides the ice-coated field was the game's most powerful runner; six-foot-two, 235-pound Bronko Nagurski of the Bears, here about to take a pitchout from Carl Brumbaugh and test the mettle of the New York defense. The bruising fullback scored the game's first touchdown, which gave Chicago a lead they would not relinquish until Abe Cohen arrived at halftime with a dozen pairs of sneakers which transformed a bunch of slip-sliders into sure-footed Giants. (Pro Football Hall of Fame)

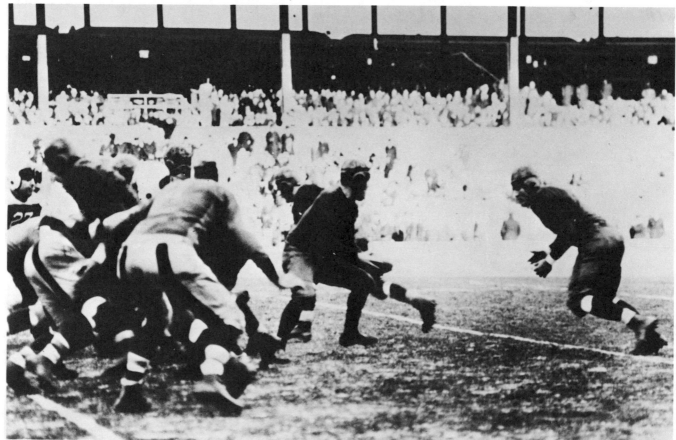

Price 10 cents

N. Y. GIANTS
·VS·
PITTSBURGH PIRATES

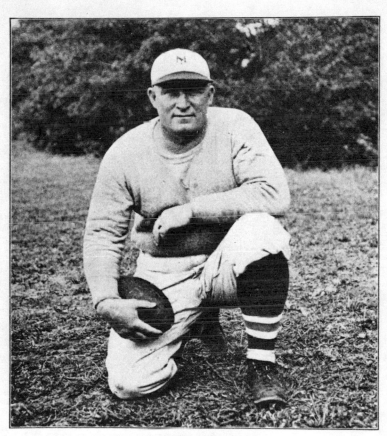

STEVE OWEN
New York Giants Coach

•

POLO GROUNDS
Sunday, December 8, 1935

While this program was being hawked at the Polo Grounds, the Giants easily clinched the NFL East title. Their 13–0 victory over Pittsburgh gave them a 9–3 record for the season and the right to meet the Detroit Lions for the NFL title of 1935, the Giants' third consecutive battle for the championship. (New York Giants)

The NFL champion New York Giants of 1934. Top row, left to right: Charles Porter (trainer), Jack Mara (president), Red Badgro, Bill Morgan, Dale Burnett, John Dell Isola, Stuart Clancy, Ed Danowski, Harry Newman, Gus Mauch (trainer). Middle row, left to right: Kink Richards, Hank Reese, Len Grant, Bill Owen, Tom Jones, Mel Hein, Harrison Stafford, Willis Smith. Front row, left to right: Steve Owen (coach), Ike Frankian, Butch Gibson, Ray Flaherty, Cecil Irvin, Bo Molenda, Max Krause, Ken Strong, Bob Bellinger. (New York Giants)

6

More NFL Championship Games Than Any Other Team

The first NFL draft was held in 1936, and the Giants' first pick in it was Art Lewis, a tackle from Ohio University, who, as it turned out, would have only a one-year football career in New York. But the year before, a youthful Wellington Mara, then nineteen and a student at Fordham University, had gone down to the nation's capital and recruited running back Alphonse "Tuffy" Leemans of George Washington University, an acquisition who would prove to be more valuable than any first-round draft pick over the next fifteen years.

Although he was only a junior in college, Wellington Mara had already immersed himself in what was to become his career—an integral and guiding force in the New York Giants' management. His special forte was finding talent. He kept files on hundreds of college players, scouring newspapers and magazines for information on them, writing letters to college coaches, friends, and Giants alumni for firsthand information about them. Leemans was one he thought had special potential even though he was playing for a small and unheralded college football team.

Wellington suggested to his father the efficacy of his going down and talking Leemans into a career in professional football. "Go ahead," Tim Mara told his son.

"I sent him a telegram setting up a meeting and signed my father's name to it," Wellington explained later. "It was to be in front of the gymnasium at George Washington. When I got there, he thought I was a kid who wanted his autograph. He looked at me, strangely suspicious, and said he was meeting Tim Mara, the owner of the New York Giants. But I was able to eventually convince him

that I was in fact a legitimate emissary, and he did listen to me. And, of course, we got him for the Giants."

The Giants lost three familiar names to the new American Football League: Ken Strong, Harry Newman, and Red Badgro. And Ray Flaherty resigned to take on the head coaching duties for George Preston Marshall of the Boston Redskins. Still, the Giants were favored to garner another divisional crown. Their vulnerability became apparent, however, early in the season with losses in their first two games to the hapless Philadelphia Eagles (which would turn out to be the Eagles' only win in twelve games that year) and the Pittsburgh Pirates.

Chiefly behind the running of Tuffy Leemans, who was fast proving to be one of the league's most effective rushers, Steve Owen's New Yorkers rebounded, winning four games and tying another. But then the Chicago Bears throttled them, 25–7, at the Polo Grounds. The next week it was the Lions in Detroit who battered them, 38–0. Then the Green Bay Packers came to Gotham and whipped the Giants, 26–14. A win over the Brooklyn Dodgers gave them a record of 5–5–1 going into the last game of the season, but as disappointing as the year had been, it could all be rectified at the Polo Grounds on December 6. That afternoon they were scheduled to face the Boston Redskins, who had a record of 6–5–0. The Pittsburgh Pirates had already finished their season with a record of 6–6–0. So a Giants win would put them on top by dint of a 6–5–1 record.

But on a mud-soaked field with rain falling intermittently throughout the game, the Giants could not get going. Their offense was overwhelmed, principally by

A family and a friend—the brain trust of the Giants circa the late 1930s. From right to left: Wellington Mara (secretary), Tim Mara (founder), Jack Mara (president), Steve Owen (coach). (New York Giants)

Redskin All-Pro tackle Turk Edwards, who was seemingly in on every tackle, recovered fumbles, and blocked kicks. Cliff Battles stunned the well-dampened 17,000 fans at the Polo Grounds by weaving his way 74 yards to return a New York punt for a touchdown. That, and another TD by fullback Don Irwin, were enough to give Boston a 14–0 shutout and the divisional title.

New York's record of 5–6–1 marked only the third time in the franchise's twelve-year history that it fell below .500. On an individual level, however, rookie Tuffy Leemans led the entire NFL in rushing with 830 yards and was named All-Pro. The only other Giant All-Pro was center Mel Hein.

The Maras, unhappy at the sudden decline of their team, vowed some changes. And so when the Giants took the field in 1937, there were seventeen rookies on the twenty-five-man roster. That wasn't all that was new. The uniforms were fresh from the tailor, now with blue jerseys and silver pants. The offense was revamped, too; Steve Owen sent his team out with a backfield alignment he devised called the A formation.

The Giants' first-round draft pick in 1937 was consensus All-American tackle Ed Widseth of Minnesota. Two rookie backs, wingback Ward Cuff from Marquette and fullback/halfback Hank Soar of Providence, would spend a lot of time in the backfield that year with Danowski and Leemans. Jim Poole, out of Mississippi, replaced the retired Tod Goodwin at end, and Jim Lee Howell from

Arkansas was slated for a good deal of work at the other end.

But for all the newness, the Giants still had to settle for the role of runner-up. And in almost a repeat from the year before, they gave the title to the Redskins, who were now situated in Washington. In the last game of the season. The Giants were 6–2–2 when they hosted the Redskins on December 5 at the Polo Grounds. The Redskins were 7–3–0. The winner would claim the NFL East title.

The Redskins, deftly guided by rookie tailback Slinging Sammy Baugh, had defeated the Giants in the first game of the regular season, 13–3, but going into the finale were listed as a slight underdog by the oddsmakers. George Preston Marshall, flamboyant owner of the Washington franchise, shrugged it off and said of his Redskins, "The Indians have come to reclaim Manhattan Island." And to support his contention he brought along a fifty-five piece marching band dressed in Indian costumes as well as 10,000 fans who came by train and chartered buses and led them in a march up Broadway the day of the game.

The hype worked, at least in the second half. With the Giants a touchdown behind midway through the third quarter, the Redskins suddenly went on the rampage and, behind the passing of Baugh and the running of Cliff Battles, raked off four unanswered touchdowns, turning a 21–14 contest into a 49–14 massacre.

Ed Danowski had passed for 814 yards that year, second to sensational rookie Sammy Baugh, who became only the second passer to throw for more than 1,000 yards (1,127). And Mel Hein was named All-Pro center for the fifth consecutive time. The youthful team showed a lot of promise, Tim Mara thought as he closed the books on the 1937 Giants; so did the game of professional football in New York, with the Giants attracting more than 260,000 spectators to their seven home games and their ledger solidly in the black.

Ed Danowski did not have far to move when he went from Fordham, where he was a standout tailback, to the Polo Grounds and the Giants in 1934. The following year he took over as starting tailback, replacing Harry Newman, who was holding out for more money, and kept the job until he retired after the 1939 season (he resumed the position for the 1941 season before going into the military). (Pro Football Hall of Fame)

News Brief

New York, August 2—The New York Football Giants today became the first major league professional gridiron club to purchase a minor league team.

John V. Mara, president of the Giants, announced that the New York eleven had purchased the franchise of the Stapleton team in the American Association and would operate in that circuit as the Jersey City Giants playing home games in the new Roosevelt Stadium in Jersey City.

The new team will be coached by Bill Owen, brother of Steve Owen, present New York Giants tutor. Bill is a former tackle on the Giants and makes his home in Kinsley, Kansas.

Perhaps "It seems I've heard this song before" should have been the refrain played by George Preston Marshall's marching band that again paraded up Broadway before the last game of the 1938 season. In the balance at the Polo Grounds for the third consecutive year was the Eastern Divisional crown. The young Giants sported a record of 7–2–1, and the Redskins were a shade behind at 6–2–2.

Foresight!

Arthur J. Daley wrote of this friendly encounter between NFL owners in 1938 in the New York Times:

The Giants were playing the Redskins in Washington early this season before the largest crowd ever to see a professional football game in the capital. The youthful Jack Mara, president of the New Yorkers, strolled out on the field before the battle with George Preston Marshall, grand high mogul and panjandrum of the Redskins.

With an innocence that was belied by the twinkle in his eyes, Jack turned to the Magnificent Marshall and asked, "Tell me, George, where are you going to put the extra seats for the play-off game?"

George Preston took a running broad jump into the trap for a new Olympic record. "See those seats out in center field?" answered the Magnificent One with a grandiloquent wave of his hand. "We'll build extra stands in back of them and then we'll put more seats in right field and"—

"Or maybe, George," interrupted Jack, "you'll come up to the Polo Grounds to see the Giants in the play-off."

As it turned out, the Giants did host the championship game that year, and George Preston Marshall did attend it, watching benignly as New York defeated the Green Bay Packers, 23–17.

The New Yorkers' only two losses had come in the second and third games of the regular season, 14–10 to Philadelphia and 13–10 to the Pittsburgh Pirates. After that the Giants soared, even topping the Redskins midway through the season.

The Redskins and their huge tribe of fans arrived and marched in Manhattan with the same exuberance they had the year previous. But the song they had heard before ended on a distinctly different note in 1938. The tone was set in the first quarter when Hank Soar burst through the Redskins' line and raced 42 yards for the Giants' first touchdown of the day. Thirty unanswered points after that, the Giants had a 36–0 triumph, the NFL East title, and a sweet taste of revenge for the 49–14 drubbing they had received the year before.

Again Ed Danowski had proved to be one of the game's most dangerous passers. His 70 completions were the most in the league in 1938, and his 848 yards gained passing trailed only Ace Parker of the Brooklyn Dodgers and Sammy Baugh of the Redskins. Ward Cuff kicked the most field goals (5) and extra points (18) in the NFL. And big Ed Widseth joined seemingly permanent resident Mel Hein on the list of All-Pros.

The Green Bay Packers had won the NFL West behind the passing combination of Cecil Isbell to Don Hutson and the powerful running of Clarke Hinkle, and were a slight favorite to beat the Giants. The largest crowd to attend an NFL championship game up to that time, 48,120, filled the Polo Grounds to watch a contest that was both suspenseful and savage. Arthur J. Daley described it this way in the *New York Times:*

The Giants and the Packers delved into the realm of fiction for a storybook football game at the Polo Grounds yesterday. . . . Perhaps there have been better football games since Rutgers and Princeton started the autumnal madness sixty-nine years ago, but no one in that huge crowd would admit it. This was a struggle of such magnificent stature that words seem such feeble tools for describing it. . . . What a frenzied battle this was! The tackling was fierce and the blocking positively vicious. . . . Tempers were so frayed and tattered that stray punches were tossed around all afternoon. This was the gridiron sport at its primitive best.

The Giants got on the scoreboard first. A Clarke Hinkle punt was blocked in the first quarter by Jim Lee Howell,

Mixing Metaphors

After the Giants whipped the favored Green Bay Packers, 23–17, for the NFL title of 1938, Arthur "Bugs" Baer, writing for the International News Service, had trouble containing himself:

It was a game of vibrating behemoths against fermenting goliaths. Every man on the field was six feet tall, three feet wide and a yard thick. There was every kind of official on the turf except the one they needed most. And that was a knock-down timekeeper.

When the two lines rushed at each other it was like a freight train kissing the depot. You could hear the crash from the rockbound shores of Maine to far prettier places. The score, 23 to 17, sounds like the little-potato-hard-to-peel had met the lumberyard skullbusters who decided to mash them instead.

It was a backwoods vendetta in the high rent district. . . . With the winners getting about $135 extra per man, it was this extra bit of muscular bribery that made the lads go to town like a wolf in famine.

The result the boys were as earnest as a sneak thief in a lock and key store. And as tough as veal breaded in marble dust.

They went at each other like dogs meeting in a sausage machine. And mixed like the stuff they put in a Martini.

It was a throwback to the apes. Twenty-two muggs got an assist on the play and the apes get credit for the put-out. . . .

It was mostly a barroom fight outdoors. Close to 50,000 innocent bystanders looked upon the resumption of gang warfare in America. It was terrific.

CHAMPIONSHIPS

Frank Gifford (16) follows blocker Al Barry (68) against Gino Marchetti and Big Daddy Lipscomb of the Colts in the 1958 championship game.

The beginning of a historic play in the 1958 game: Charlie Conerly (42), leaping high in the air, passed to Kyle Rote, who carried to the Baltimore 25-yard line, where he fumbled. Alex Webster then recovered the fumble and carried the ball to the Baltimore 1—a total gain of 86 yards.

Johnny Unitas (19), the great Baltimore quarterback (above), unleashing a pass to his favorite receiver, Raymond Berry (82, below), in the 1958 championship game. Giants defensive players include Harland Svare (84), Andy Robustelli (81), Dick Modzelewski (77), and Jim Katcavage (75).

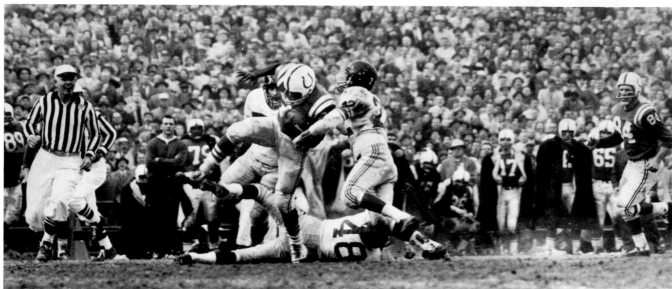

Bill Stitts (48), Dick Lynch (22), and Sam Huff (70) try to stop, and then finally bring down, Baltimore's Lenny Moore in the 1959 championship game.

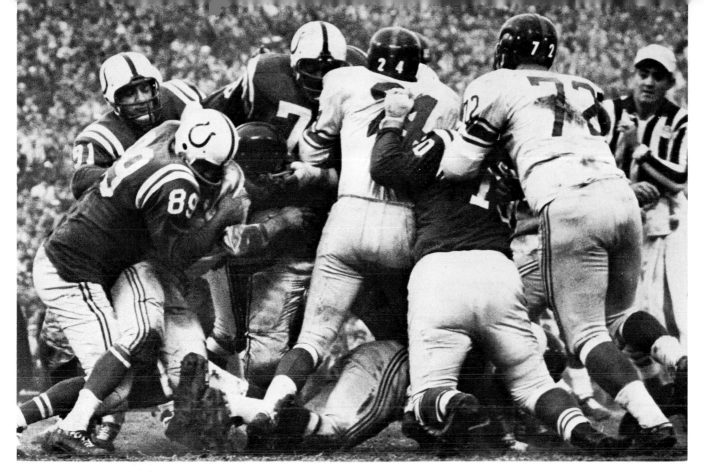

A mass of Colts and Giants converge on Frank Gifford in the 1959 game. Left to right: Ordell Brasse (81), Gino Marchetti (89), Big Daddy Lipscomb (with his hand on Gifford's face mask), Phil King (24), Art Donovan (holding King's shirt), and Frank Youso (72).

Charlie Conerly (42) running for his life from Art Donovan (70) and Gino Marchetti (89) of the Colts in the 1959 game. Giants include Frank Youso (72), Jack Stroud (66), and Mel Triplett (33).

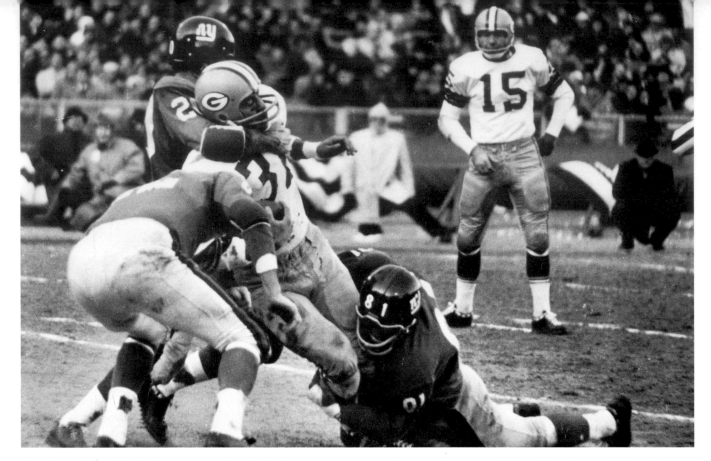

Bart Starr (15) of the Packers watches Jim Taylor being brought down by Andy Robustelli (81) and Jim Patton (20) in the 1962 championship game.

Y. A. Tittle (14) unleashes a pass in the 1963 game. Bookie Bolin (63) tries to block Doug Atkins (81). No. 33 is the Bears's Larry Morris.

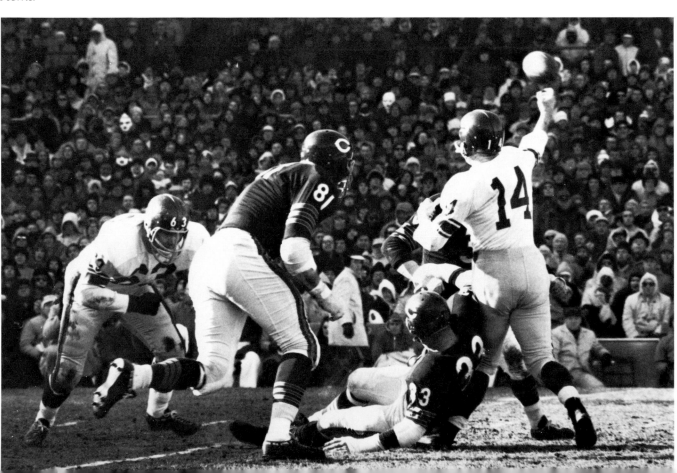

While the Giants huddle, the Packers wait in the cold and wind-swept dust of Yankee Stadium in the 1962 championship game. The Packer defenders are Hank Gremminger (46), Willie Davis (87), Hog Hanner (79), Ray Nitschke (66), and Henry Jordan (74).

Bears quarterback Bill Wade scores the decisive touchdown in the 1963 game. Other Bears are Ronnie Bull (29), Ted Karras (67), and Mike Pyle (50)

Phil King (with the "24" barely visible on his helmet) drives just short of the goal line in the 1963 championship game, won by the Bears. Blockers shown are Darrell Dess (62), Greg Larson (53), and Rosey Brown (79); the Chicago defender on the ground is Fred Williams (75).

N. Y. GIANTS
·vs·
DETROIT LIONS

POLO GROUNDS

Sunday, November 1, 1936

KINK RICHARDS
Star Giant Back

Sunday, November 8, 1936, Kickoff 2:15 P.M.
AT POLO GROUNDS
NEW YORK GIANTS vs. CHICAGO BEARS

His name was Elvin Richards, but he was better known around the Polo Grounds as "Kink" once he came out of obscurity (Simpson College in Iowa) in 1933 and worked his way into a backfield with such luminaries as Ken Strong, Harry Newman, and Dale Burnett. Richards became the second Giant to rush for more than 100 yards in a game, a feat he accomplished against the Brooklyn Dodgers in 1933 only a week after Harry Newman set the century standard. He led the club in rushing in 1935, with 449 yards, and stayed around through the 1939 season. (Pro Football Hall of Fame)

and the Giants took over on the Green Bay 7-yard line. Three plays failed to score, and then Ward Cuff booted a field goal. On the next series of downs, Cecil Isbell dropped back to punt for the Packers, and this time Jim Poole knifed in to block it, giving the Giants the ball on the Green Bay 27-yard line. And this turnover resulted in a touchdown a few plays later when Tuffy Leemans lugged the ball into the end zone.

In the second quarter, it was the Giants' turn to make a mistake. Tiny Engebretsen, a six-foot-one-inch, 240-pound guard for the Pack, intercepted a Giants pass, and moments later Arnie Herber dropped back and rifled a 40-yard bomb to Carl Mulleneaux for a touchdown. The Giants redeemed themselves, however, with a concerted march down the field, highlighted by runs by rookie halfback Len Barnum and culminating in a 20-yard touchdown pass from Ed Danowski to Hap Barnard. And still the first-half scoring was not over, although time was running out. Isbell hit end Wayland Becker with a short pass, and he scampered 66 yards before Hank Soar could catch him and drag him to the turf at the New York 17-yard line. Then Clarke Hinkle hit the Giants' line five times in a row, finally smashing in for 6 Packer points. The

Fullback Hank Soar was one of the seventeen rookies to join the Giants in 1937, and he wound up as a starter. In fact, he gained the most yards rushing for the team that year, 442. Soar would prove to be a dependable runner and blocker throughout his nine-year Giants career. After football, he went on to become a famous major-league baseball umpire. (New York Giants)

Tuffy Leemans, shown here carrying the ball against the Green Bay Packers, came to the Giants in 1936 after a teenage Wellington Mara went down to George Washington University and recruited him the year before. To prove Mara's sagacity, Leemans as a rookie led the entire NFL in rushing with 830 yards. Moving out to block for him here are Leland Shaffer (20) and Dale Burnett (18). (Pro Football Hall of Fame)

score at the half was the Giants 16, the Packers 14.

During that period of play, Don Hutson, Green Bay's great pass receiver, had to leave the game with an injured knee; Mel Hein, kicked in the cheekbone, suffered a concussion; Johnny Dell Isola was taken from the field on a stretcher straight to St. Elizabeth's Hospital, where he was treated for a spinal concussion that was feared to be but fortunately was not a fractured vertebra.

Then came the second half. The Packers were on the move from the opening kickoff, a 63-yard drive all the way to the Giants' 5-yard line. That is as far as they went, so Tiny Engebretsen stood back and kicked a 15-yard field goal to give Green Bay its first lead of the day, 17–16. But the Giants were far from foundering, and they came right back with a march of 62 yards, the highlight of which was a picture-perfect pass from Danowski to Hank Soar at the

6, where he shook off a tackler and stormed into the end zone.

Green Bay fought back magnificently in the fourth quarter, dominating the action. The Pack reached the New York 38 on one drive and the 17 on another. But the first was stalled, and the second resulted in a fumble. After that the Packers moved again, and Arnie Herber connected on a pass to end Milt Gantenbein at the Giants' 40-yard line; but the Packers' flanker back had edged up to the line of scrimmage, which made Gantenbein an ineligible receiver. The ball was turned over to the Giants at the point of the foul—the rule of the day—which was the Green Bay 43-yard line. The Packers still put together two more drives during the fourth quarter, both into Giants territory, but both were stopped. There were no points scored in the fourth quarter, but many observers said it was one of the most exciting, hard-fought periods in the history of NFL championship games. Both teams were brutally beaten as they left the field that December

---

Champs a Second Time, 1938

New York Giants		Green Bay Packers
Jim Poole	LE	Wayland Becker
Ed Widseth	LT	Champ Seibold
Johnny Dell Isola	LG	Russ Leftow
Mel Hein	C	Lee Mulleneaux
Orville Tuttle	RG	Buckets Goldenberg
Ox Parry	RT	Bill Lee
Jim Lee Howell	RE	Milt Gantenbein
Ed Danowski	QB	Herman Schneidman
Hank Soar	LH	Cecil Isbell
Ward Cuff	RH	Joe Laws
Leland Shaffer	FB	Clarke Hinkle

Giants	9	7	7	0 — 23
Packers	0	14	3	0 — 17

Touchdowns—*Giants:* Leemans, Barnard, Soar; *Packers:* Mulleneaux, Hinkle. Field goals—*Giants:* Cuff; *Packers:* Engebretsen.
PATs—*Giants:* Cuff (2), *Packers:* Engebretsen (2).

One Title Tilt Better Forgotten, 1939

New York Giants		Green Bay Packers
Jim Poole	LE	Don Hutson
Frank Cope	LT	Baby Ray
Johnny Dell Isola	LG	Russ Letlow
Mel Hein	C	Earl Svendsen
Orville Tuttle	RG	Buckets Goldenberg
John Mellus	RT	Bill Lee
Jim Lee Howell	RE	Milt Gantenbein
Ed Danowski	QB	Larry Craig
Kink Richards	LH	Cecil Isbell
Ward Cuff	RH	Joe Laws
Nello Falaschi	FB	Clarke Hinkle

Giants	0	0	0	0 — 0
Packers	7	0	10	10 — 27

Touchdowns—*Packers:* Gantenbein, Laws, Jankowski. Field goals—*Packers:* Engebretsen, Smith. PATs—*Packers:* Engebretsen (2), Smith.

---

afternoon, and every player on the field knew that he had truly been in a savage football game. The final score stood at 23–17, giving the Giants victory and the right to be known as the first team to win two NFL championship games.

The season was not over for the Giants when they dragged their bruised and bloodied bodies from the Polo Grounds after the NFL championship melee. Ahead was the league's first "Pro Bowl" game, a contest to be staged across the country at Wrigley Field in Los Angeles. On January 15, 1939, the Giants took on a select cast of pro all-stars, which included such future Hall of Famers as Sammy Baugh, Clarke Hinkle, Joe Stydahar, and Bruiser Kinard. But the Giants displayed for the California audience their championship form, coming back from a 10–3 deficit in the fourth quarter with a 22-yard touchdown pass from Ed Danowski to Chuck Gelatka and a Ward Cuff field goal to win, 13–10.

Their next encounter that year was another all-star game, this one against the College All-Stars, a tradition begun by sports columnist Arch Ward and the *Chicago*

Owen's Favorite

Arthur Daley wrote in the New York Times *of Steve Owen's response when he was asked who of his old ballplayers he missed the most:*

"That's easy," he drawled. "Hank Soar. I rode him unmercifully every season, but I guess he was my favorite. He had such a blazing team spirit, such a will to win and such good humor at all times that I hate to see him gone."

Hank was strictly a money player, at his best when the chips were down and the going at its very toughest. Never will any Giant forget that terrific battle with the Redskins a few seasons back when Slingin' Sammy Baugh was trying desperately to pitch to victory in the closing minutes.

Soar, playing safety, kept glancing back at the clock. "Don't look at the clock," roared Stout Steve from the sidelines, "watch the ball."

Hank's classic answer was delivered with an annoyed wave of his hand. "Don't bother us, Steve," he shouted back, "we're busy out here."

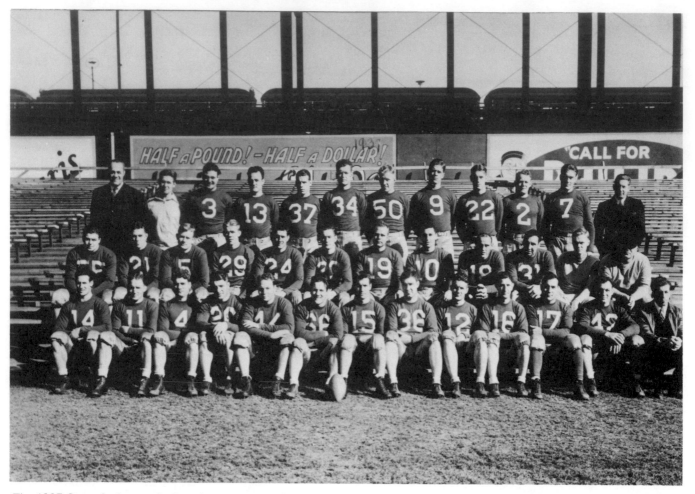

The 1937 Giants had a new look, with seventeen rookies on the twenty-five-player roster, yet they just missed winning the NFL East title in the last game of the season. Top row, left to right: Charles Porter (trainer), Bo Molenda (assistant coach), Len Grant, Kink Richards, Ray Hanken, Bunny Galazin, Ed Widseth, John Haden, Ed Danowski, John Dell Isola, Mel Hein, Gus Mauch (trainer). Middle row, left to right: Jerry Dennerlein, Jim Lee Howell, Kayo Lunday, Chuck Gelatka, Will Walls, Jim Poole, Ewell Phillips, Mickey Kobrosky, Dale Burnett, Larry Johnson, Wellington Mara (secretary), Steve Owen (coach). Front row, left to right: Ward Cuff, Tony Sarausky, Tuffy Leemans, Leland Shaffer, Ox Parry, Tarzan White, Hank Soar, Pete Coal, Jim Neill, Tillie Manton, Les Corzine, Orville Tuttle, Joe Carroll. (New York Giants)

Tribune in 1934. The idea was to pit the NFL champs from the year before against the best players coming out of college that year in a game at Soldier Field in Chicago before the start of the pros' regular exhibition season.

This was the Giants' first appearance in the spectacle, which annually drew 75,000 to 80,000 fans into cavernous Soldier Field. Since its inception the pro champs had won only once, the All-Stars twice, and they had played to one tie. The collegians had won the two previous encounters, embarrassing the Packers and the Redskins respectively, and the pros were eager to regain their self-esteem. Among the more notable college All-Stars that year were Heisman Trophy winner Davey O'Brien of Texas Christian, Marshall Goldberg from Pittsburgh, Bob MacLeod of Dartmouth, and Bowden Wyatt from

Tennessee. It was a less than thrilling game, but the pros could once again look demeaningly upon their younger challengers as the result of a 9–0 victory by New York. The points came on two field goals by Ken Strong, back in a Giants uniform for the first time since 1935 after his three-year adventure in other pro football leagues, and another from the toe of Ward Cuff.

Ken Strong was thirty-three years old now, and his contributions would be pretty well restricted to the kicking game. The Giants' backfield was spoken for, so to speak, with division title veterans like Danowski, Leemans, Soar, Barnum, and Cuff. And their defense, keyed by Widseth, Hein, and Dell Isola, was overwhelming. In fact, the Giants gave up an average of only 6 ½ points in their first six games of the 1939 season.

Rice on Owen

Dean of sportswriters Grantland Rice used his poetic pen to describe Steve Owen in the mid-1940s:

"Stout Steve" is the name you've got—the moniker that
    you've earned—
Stout in body and stout in heart, wherever the tide has
    turned,
One of the best who has come along in this morbid vale
    of tears,
A massive fellow who rides the storm in the march of
    the passing years.
Never a boast and never a brag and never an alibi,
But the breed we label in any sport as a typical four-
    square guy,
A mighty hunk of the human mold, blown from the
    rugged West,
Whatever the odds from the off-side gods—a fellow
    who gives his best.

Sixth Trip to the Championship Game, 1941

New York Giants		Chicago Bears
Jim Poole	LE	Dick Plasman
John Mellus	LT	Ed Kolman
Kayo Lunday	LG	Danny Fortmann
Mel Hein	C	Bulldog Turner
Len Younce	RG	Ray Bray
Bill Edwards	RT	Lee Artoe
Jim Lee Howell	RE	John Siegal
Nello Falaschi	QB	Sid Luckman
George Franck	LH	Ray Nolting
Ward Cuff	RH	Hugh Gallarneau
Tuffy Leemans	FB	Norm Standlee

Giants	6	0	3	0 —	9
Bears	3	6	14	14 —	37

Touchdowns—*Giants:* Franck; *Bears:* Standlee (2), McAfee, Kavanaugh. Field goals—*Giants:* Cuff; *Bears:* Snyder (3).
PATs—*Bears:* Snyder, Maniaci, Artoe, McLean.

As it had been since 1936, the NFL East was a fierce battle between New York and the Redskins, one that would again go down to the very last game of the season. The Giants had lost only to the Lions, an upset out in Detroit, and had played Washington to a 0–0 tie while defeating eight other opponents. The Redskins had an identical record of 8–1–1, having lost only to the Green Bay Packers.

And so, as New York sports columnist Bill Corum observed, "At the head of a 150-piece brass band and 12,000 fans, George Preston Marshall slipped unobtrusively into New York today," for what had become the traditional December NFL East title decider.

It was rainy that day, but to prove conclusively that professional football had come into its own in New York City more than 62,500 filled the Polo Grounds to see who would earn the right to represent the NFL East in that year's championship game. On a messy field, the game was a plodding one, with defense the overriding factor. The Giants proved the stronger through the first three

Big Ed Widseth was a vintage addition to the Giants' front line in 1937. A consensus All-America tackle from Minnesota, he earned All-Pro honors his sophomore year in the NFL and played four years with the Giants. (Pro Football Hall of Fame)

quarters of play, holding the Redskins scoreless and maintaining a 9–0 lead on two field goals by Ward Cuff and another from Ken Strong. That lead was diminished in the final quarter, however, when tailback Frank Filchock threw to end Bob Masterson for a Redskins touchdown. The conversion brought them within two points of New York. Then, with less than a minute remaining, the Redskins, on the Giants' 10-yard line, lined up for a field goal. Bo Russell booted the ball, and the Washington players watching it began leaping in jubilation at what presumably was the game-winning, title-clinching 3 points. But they

Ed Danowski (left) and trainer Gus Mauch, two very familiar faces around the Giants' locker room during the late 1930s, share a little canned libation during Danowski's last year (1941) as a Giant. Danowski led the team in passing every year from 1935 through 1939 and was named as an All-Pro twice (1935 and 1938). (Pro Football Hall of Fame)

Ward Cuff was another rookie find in 1937—a multitalented halfback from Marquette, in the days when the Milwaukee school fielded a football team. Cuff quickly earned a steady job in the Giants' backfield and led the team in scoring every year from 1937 through 1942. He could run with the ball, catch passes, and kick field goals and extra points; he was also a fine defensive back during his nine-year Giants career. (Pro Football Hall of Fame)

were stopped in their proverbial tracks by referee Bill Halloran, who was signaling that the attempt was not good. There was a lot of screaming and yelling from the Redskins' players and their coach, Ray Flaherty, who raged after Halloran, and there was a small riot among players and spectators on the field after time expired, but the ruling held, and the Giants were the winner by the score of 9–7. The call was controversial and never proven correct or incorrect by later photos, the angles of some showing the kick to be good, and others showing it to be not good. Later Steve Owen said, "I thought the call was right, but I didn't have the best angle to judge it." Ray Flaherty said, "If that guy [Halloran] has got a conscience,

The way the Redskins came to town, circa 1938. This was the band and the followers of the Washington Redskins, whom George Preston Marshall, the flamboyant team owner, led "unobtrusively into New York" (in the words of New York sports columnist Bill Corum) to support their team against the Giants. It did not do them a lot of good, however, as the Giants lambasted the Redskins, 36–0, to secure the NFL East title that year. (Pro Football Hall of Fame)

he'll never have another good night's sleep as long as he lives!"

The Green Bay Packers had narrowly edged out the Chicago Bears in the NFL West and were to serve as host for the title tilt, not in their hometown, however, but instead at the State Fair Park in Milwaukee, which could accommodate a larger crowd. The 9–2–0 Pack still sported the backfield of Isbell, Herber, and Hinkle, the dazzling pass catching of Don Hutson, a fine defense, and the able coaching of Curly Lambeau.

It was a typically cold, windy December day in Wisconsin, but that hardly hampered the Packers. They were hot for revenge for the defeat the Giants had handed them in the championship match the year before. And the Giants were as cold as the frozen turf of State Fair Park. Green Bay scored midway through the first quarter on a pass from Arnie Herber to Milt Gantenbein. The Giants had several opportunities to score, but two field-goal attempts by Ward Cuff and another by Len Barnum were all unsuccessful. The Pack had a 7–0 lead at the halftime intermission. From that point on, the game was Green Bay's alone. Scoring 10 points each in the remaining two quarters and picking off pass after Giants pass (the Packers intercepted six passes that afternoon), Green Bay humbled the Giants by the most decisive score up to that time in NFL championship play, 27–0. The $455.37 each

Tuffy Leemans bursts through the Green Bay line in the 1938 championship game for a few valuable yards for the Giants. Leemans scored New York's first touchdown of the day, a 6-yard run in the first quarter. Those six points contributed to the winning margin of the Giants' 23–17 title triumph that afternoon at the Polo Grounds. (Pro Football Hall of Fame)

Giant took back to New York as shares of the gate was little consolation (each Packer received $708.97).

Still, it had been a fine season, bringing the team's second straight divisional crown and the claim to the NFL's most niggardly defense by having allowed opponents only 85 points in 11 games. The Giants also set an NFL record of 14 successful field goals: Ward Cuff kicked 7, the most in the league, Ken Strong had 4, and Len Barnum 3. And they landed four players on the All-Pro listing: center Mel Hein (his seventh straight year), halfback Tuffy Leemans, end Jim Poole, and guard Johnny Dell Isola.

The New York Giants should have probably been overjoyed at not having had to go to the NFL championship game of 1940; that was the one in which the Chicago Bears—Sid Luckman, George McAfee, Bill Osmanski, Ken Kavanaugh, Joe Stydahar, Bulldog Turner, Danny Fortmann, Jack Manders & Co.—annihilated the Washington Redskins, 73–0, and undoubtedly shortened George Preston Marshall's life by a decade or two.

Ed Danowski had retired before the start of the 1940 season, and replacing him was Ed Miller, who had come from the University of New Mexico and had been drafted by the Giants the year before. And there was a lot of hope for two rookie backs, Grenny Landsdell from USC and Kay Eakin of Arkansas. But the spark that had fired the two previous divisional champs was not there, illustrated graphically in an opening-day tie with the Pittsburgh Pirates, who had had a record of 1–9–1 the year before and would be 2–7–2 at the end of the 1940 season. The Giants followed that performance by a 21–7 beating at the hands of the Redskins.

Midway through the season and just before having to face the Chicago Bears, Tuffy Leemans was lost for the rest of the year with a back injury. A pounding by the Bears, 37–21, and a loss to the Brooklyn Dodgers, 14–6, gave the Giants four losses at the end of the season against six wins and a tie, good enough only for third place. Mel Hein was the only Giant to win All-Pro honors, accomplishing that for the tenth year in a row.

With a world war looming and a disappointing season to start the decade, the 1940s did not seem all that promising for the Mara family business.

The Giants, however, managed to put together a quite respectable team in 1941. Ed Danowski was lured out of retirement, Tuffy Leemans's back had healed, and Mel Hein had been talked out of a contemplated retirement. There was an especially promising crop of rookies, most notably for the backfield: George Franck from Minnesota, Frank Reagan of Pennsylvania, Len Eshmont from Fordham, and Andy Marefos of St. Mary's. The New Yorkers virtually sailed through their first five games, only the Redskins coming within a touchdown of them as they collectively outscored their opponents, 122–27. But the Brooklyn Dodgers, coached by Jock Sutherland and guided on the field by All-Pro tailback Ace Parker, dealt them their first loss of the season over at Ebbets Field. Then, after an upset by the cellar-dwelling Chicago Cardinals of the NFL West, the Giants got back on track.

By the last game of the season, the Giants had clinched the NFL East title with a record of 8–2. It mattered little that they lost that Sunday, December 7, at the Polo Grounds to the Dodgers, 21–7. It mattered much more, of course, that while they were playing that game Pearl Harbor was under attack by the Japanese, and for the United States World War II had formally started.

The title game two weeks later attracted little interest in a nation otherwise preoccupied. Only 13,341 spectators showed up at Wrigley Field in Chicago, the smallest crowd ever in the history of NFL championship games. The Bears, the pride of George Halas with a regular-

Green Bay fullback Clarke Hinkle meets a stubborn Giants defense in the second quarter of the 1938 title game and is brought down a yard from the goal line. On the next play, however, Hinkle bulled it in for a Packer touchdown, but the Wisconsonians still ended up on the short end of the score that December day. No. 17 on Green Bay is tailback Cecil Isbell. (Pro Football Hall of Fame)

season record of 10–1–0, who had outscored their regular-season and playoff opponents (they had to defeat the 10–1–0 Packers for the divisional crown) 429–161, were a legitimate favorite. But by the end of the first quarter, they trailed the Giants, 6–3, the result of a 31-yard touchdown pass play from Tuffy Leemans to George Franck.

The Bears' hibernation came to an end in the second half, however, with four touchdowns and almost complete domination. The final score was 37–9, and the Bears became the first team in NFL history to win back-to-back championships.

The Giants could find solace in the fact that they had rebounded respectably to win their sixth divisional title and held the honor now of having played in more NFL championship games than any other team in the league.

7
World War II

The National Football League continued to operate during World War II, but many of the best players were in Europe and Asia fighting for their country. In all, 638 NFL players saw military duty during the war, and 21 of them were killed in action. Fifty-two New York Giants were in military service during the 1942–45 period, and two did not return. A scant six weeks after playing in the 1944 championship game for the Giants, tackle and now lieutenant Al Blozis, a starter from 1942 through 1944, was killed on his first combat mission in the Vosges Mountains of France on January 31, 1945. A little more than two months later, Lieutenant Jack Lummus, an end on the 1941 Giants team, was killed while leading an attack during the battle of Iwo Jima.

The 1942 Giants lost a lot of familiar names to the military: Ed Danowski, Jim Poole, Nello Falaschi, Len Eshmont, Frank Reagan, John Mellus, Kayo Lunday, and Orville Tuttle among them. Merle Hapes, a running back from Mississippi, was New York's first-round draft choice and not only worked his way into the starting lineup but proved to be the club's leading rusher that year. At six foot six inches and 250 pounds, Al Blozis from Georgetown became an immediate and imposing figure in the Giants' front line. Tuffy Leemans took on the duty of signal calling and the role of chief passer at quarterback in the decimated Giants backfield. The team was a mere splinter of the divisional champions from the year before. "I took one look at the squad, and I felt like crying," Leemans said. "It hurt to see the Giants I loved having as miserable a group as we had there."

The season was a lackluster one, including a 5–5–1

record and third place in the NFL East. Hapes was the leading ground gainer with 363 yards, but his average carry was only 3.8 yards. Leemans passed for 555 yards, the team standard in a year when Cecil Isbell gained 2,021 yards passing for the Green Bay Packers, and four others threw for more than 1,000 yards (Sammy Baugh of the Redskins, 1,524; Tommy Thompson of the Eagles, 1,410; Bud Schwenk of the Chicago Cardinals, 1,360; and Sid Luckman of the Bears, 1,023). Only guard Bill Edwards made All-Pro.

The Giants' roller coaster began its climb upward in 1943. The league was hanging in there by several threads, with many players gone, many empty seats on Sunday afternoons in the ballparks, and those taking the field often old or second-rate. The NFL was down to nine teams after the financially plagued Pittsburgh Steelers and Philadelphia Eagles combined forces to form a team called the Steagles, which managed to beat the Giants in the opening game of the regular season, 28–14.

In New York, rookie Bill Paschal from Georgia Tech was a nice addition to the backfield, Steve Owen admitted. And Al Blozis was playing All-Pro caliber at tackle although there were no All-Pro selections officially made during the war years. But everything else was much the same. Tuffy Leemans, now thirty and in the last year of his playing career, was still at quarterback. Mel Hein, after twelve years with the Giants, retired to take a teaching and coaching job in upstate New York, but Steve Owen talked him into coming back to the city on weekends to play (see sidebar). Because of the age of many of the starters and an otherwise dearth of talent, the Giants of 1943 appeared to most as not much better than mediocre.

By the time the Chicago Bears came to town in mid-November, the Giants were 2–2–1 and were about to be shocked by the worst defeat in their then nineteen-year history. Sid Luckman, the Bears' outstanding T-formation quarterback, was a native of Brooklyn and had played his college football on Manhattan Island for Lou Little at Columbia. On November 14, he reappeared in New York before one of the largest crowds ever to watch a football game at the Polo Grounds, 56,591, and put on an aerial exhibition unlike any the Giants' fans had suffered before. Luckman passed for seven touchdowns to set an NFL record and gained 453 yards passing, breaking the previous mark set by Cecil Isbell of the Packers by a full 120 yards. The final score was 56–7.

The humiliation served a purpose, however. After that, Steve Owen turned his team around, and it won the remaining four regular-season games, including back-to-back triumphs over the Washington Redskins, with whom, as a result, the Giants were tied for the divisional title. The playoff match was set for December 19 at the Polo Grounds, and after their two convincing victories on preceding Sundays, the Giants were the favorite. But for

one reason or another the Giants' pass defense reverted to its earlier ineptness. Sammy Baugh came out slinging: three touchdown tosses and 199 yards gained on 16 passes. Besides that, Baugh intercepted two New York passes, running one of them back 44 yards to set up another touchdown, and got off a 67-yard quick kick at another point in the mismatch. The final score was 28–0, and the Giants' 1943 season was over.

Bill Paschal led the league in rushing that year with 572 yards, an average gain of 3.9 yards per carry. His 10 touchdowns rushing were the most in that category, and the 72 points he scored was second only to Don Hutson's 117. Ward Cuff averaged 6.5 yards on each of his 80 carries that year, another NFL high.

With Tuffy Leemans truly retired in 1944, the Giants talked former Green Bay Packer tailback Arnie Herber, now thirty-four, out of retirement and into a Giants jersey. They even coaxed thirty-eight-year-old Ken Strong back into a football uniform, something he had not donned

Sunday Center

Mel Hein retired after the 1942 season to take the head coaching job and to teach physical education at Union College in Schenectady, New York. But because of the war, the school decided to disband its team for 1944. When Steve Owen heard of that decision, he phoned Hein and talked him into coming down to New York City to join the Giants on weekends. So the thirty-five-year-old Hein taught classes all week, got on a train for Manhattan on Friday nights, worked out with the team on Saturdays, resumed his slots at center and linebacker on Sundays, and then commuted back to Schenectady on Sunday nights. One sportswriter dubbed him the "Sunday Center."

"It wasn't easy," Hein remembered. "That first game! I went into it without any physical contact before it that year. We were up in Boston, and our center, who had worked out with the team in the preseason, was supposed to start until I'd gotten myself into decent shape. But he got hurt in the last preseason game against the Bears. So I had to play the full sixty minutes, and I think it was the hottest day Boston ever had. What a toll it took. I could hardly get on the train to get to Schenectady that night. It took about three weeks to get rid of all that soreness. Still, the next week I had to go sixty minutes again."

Tackle Al Blozis from Georgetown made an immediate impression on the wartime Giants, arriving in 1942 and quickly earning a starting berth. If All-Pro selections had been made during the war years, he would have been on two or three of them. Blozis played in the 1944 championship game which the Giants lost to the Packers, 14–7, then was sent almost immediately overseas, where as a lieutenant in the army he was killed in action in France a brief six weeks later. (Pro Football Hall of Fame)

since the 1939 season. Thirty-five-year-old Mel Hein was still commuting between Schenectady and New York City on weekends.

But if the Giants were antiquated, so were the other four teams in the NFL East. The only competition of note came from the Philadelphia Eagles, with their impressive rookie halfback Steve Van Buren, and the Washington Redskins, who were paced by Sammy Baugh and Frank Filchock. But as it turned out, the Giants' defense prevailed.

The New Yorkers gave up only two touchdowns and a field goal in winning their first three games. The brunt of the offense was the running of Bill Paschal, having another noteworthy year, and Ward Cuff. The only loss came in the fourth game of the season when the Eagles came up from Philadelphia and eked out a one-touchdown victory despite Paschal's rushing for 139 yards. The only stain on the rest of the season was a 21–21 tie with the Eagles down in the alleged City of Brotherly Love.

When the season was over, the 8–1–1 Giants had five shutouts to their credit, including a 24–0 drubbing of the NFL West–champion Green Bay Packers. Collectively New York outscored its opponents, 206–75. Paschal carried the ball more often (196 times), gained more yards rushing (737), and scored more touchdowns rushing (9) than any other back in the league. Ken Strong's elderly foot booted the most field goals in the NFL (6) and connected on 23 of 24 extra points; and Howie Livingston, a rookie back from Fullerton Junior College, led the league with nine interceptions. The Giants were back on top.

In the division to the west, the champion Packers had lost only one other game besides the one to the Giants, another shutout, this one at the hands of the Bears, and

Wartime Humor

This story has been told by many and is probably close to being to true. Steve Owen was riding down to New York from Camp Devens, Massachusetts, with one of his more prized possessions, former safety, now Private, Hank Soar, who had been given a leave of absence to play in a Giants football game.

The ever-football-conscious Owen leaned over and asked Soar, "How's your pass defense these days?"

"Wonderful, Steve," was the answer from the ebullient Soar. He reached into his pocket and took from his wallet a piece of official-looking paper. "Here it is. No MP can stop me. A pass signed by Colonel Winfield Shrum himself. Good for three days, too!"

Wartime Logic

Bob Considine, in military uniform but still writing for the New York Herald Tribune, had this observation about the first sudden-death playoff game in NFL history, which involved the Giants and the Redskins in 1943.

The Giants are favored today for such trite reasons as the fact that they've beaten the Redskins these past two Sundays, that they're in much better shape from a manpower standpoint, that the Reds are still jittery over their gambling charges, that three key men will not be able to play for Dutch Bergman's team, and that the Giant players are much hungrier for the league playoff dough than are the Redskin players.

The Redskins, therefore, should win. That's the only conclusion that can be safely drawn from a study of the recent eruptions of form in the pro league. The Redskins were embarrassing favorites to win against the Giants two Sundays ago, and lost 14–10. The following week they got the Giants in their own bailiwick, were in better shape, and were obviously ready to administer a terrible revenge. So the Giants won 31–7.

It follows naturally that the Redskins will win today. We have been checking an unauthoritative report that Sammy Baugh has a broken leg and two tennis elbows. That would be the clincher. . . . So, if Sammy's ailing very grievously this afternoon, and the outlook of the Redskins is as dark as a cow's belly, please let me have two dollars' worth of their chances at whatever odds the generous Giants rooters want to give. If these dire things befit Baugh and the Reds, the Washington team will be a cinch—as things go these days.

As prognosticator Considine reasoned, the Redskins did prove the paradox and won, 28–0.

had an 8–2–0 record. Their source of success was the passing of Irv Comp, his 1,159 yards gained being the most in the NFL, and the pass catching of Don Hutson, who led the league in receptions (58), yards gained receiving (866), and touchdown catches (9).

The Giants had the homefield advantage, hosting the Pack on the same ground where they had humbled them by 24 points a few weeks earlier. They were a favorite among sportswriters and oddsmakers alike, although only a slight one, and they had to feel confident going into this rematch. But Curly Lambeau still felt the smarting of the earlier loss, and he did everything to ignite his Packers before the game.

Neither team, however, could get going in the first quarter, but Green Bay got the spark in the following period. On one drive, highlighted by a 20-yard run by Joe Laws and another for 27 yards by Ted Fritsch, the Packers got

Slated as the starting eleven for the 1943 Giants. Many would soon be gone, exchanging football uniforms for those of the military. Top row, left to right: the backfield—Ward Cuff, John Chickerneo, Merle Hapes, Tuffy Leemans. Bottom row, left to right: the line —Will Walls, Al Blozis, Chuck Avedisian, Mel Hein, Ed Lechner, Frank Cope, O'Neal Adams. (New York Giants)

to the 1-yard line. The Giants' respected defense repulsed them on three power plays, but on fourth down Fritsch bucked in for the score. Later in the quarter, the Pack moved again, this time on passes from Irv Comp. First he hit Don Hutson, which got the ball well into New York territory. On the next play, he used the triple-teamed Hutson as a decoy, sending him down one side of the field and then tossing to Ted Fritsch in the flat on the other side. Fritsch ran it 27 yards into the end zone. Along with two extra points from Hutson, the Packers had a 14–0 lead at intermission.

The Giants moved in the second half and scored when Ward Cuff carried it in from the 1-yard line on the first play of the fourth quarter. Late in the game, they marched again, only to see it come to nothing when defensive back Paul Duhart picked off an Arnie Herber pass at the Green Bay 20-yard line. The game ended with the score 14–7. After seven trips to the NFL title game, the Giants had been disappointed now five times.

The good news in 1945 was that the war ended; the bad news, at least for the New York Giants, was that they posted their worst record since Tim Mara brought the team to life back in 1925. After an impressive win over the Pittsburgh Steelers in the regular-season opener, 34–6, it was all downhill. Bill Paschal only played the last half of the season after coming home from military service; and Mel Hein at thirty-six, Ken Strong at thirty-nine, Arnie Herber at thirty-five, and Ward Cuff at thirty-two had clearly seen better times on the football field. When the season mercifully ended the Giants had a record of 3–6–1, the fewest wins in their twenty-one-year history, ahead of only the 2–8–0 Pittsburgh Steelers in the standings. With the 1945 season over, Mel Hein, after fifteen years a Giant (a team service record that still stands), retired for good; so did Arnie Herber, who had spent eleven years as a Green Bay Packer and two as a New York Giant—both headed for the Pro Football Hall of Fame, which was still to be instituted.

For the Giants, the year 1946 was to be very different from the one that preceded it—in a variety of ways. First, they would have some competition at the box office. Across the Harlem River, Dan Topping's football Yankees were scheduled to play in Yankee Stadium in the new All-America Football Conference (AAFC), which materialized that year to challenge the NFL's monopoly on professional football. Second, the Giants would for the first time play a regular-season game against a team from California, now that the Cleveland Rams had relocated in Los Angeles. It was different, too, in the fact that the Giants were once again a winning team destined to end up on top of their division, a rather striking turnaround from their worst season ever. And lastly, they would be the focus of the first scandal to hit professional football.

The most important addition to the Giants of '46 was quarterback Frank Filchock, who was acquired from the Washington Redskins. Filchock was not only a fine runner but would also reinstitute the Giants' passing attack, which had been sorely lacking since Ed Danowski had run down about six years earlier. Two other key figures were rookie tackles Dewitt "Tex" Coulter, who was a six-foot-four-inch, 225-pound All-American from Army, and six-foot-two-inch, 225-pound Jim White, who hailed from Notre Dame.

The Giants were 2–0 when they went to Washington to face Frank Filchock's old pals in Redskins uniforms. He especially wanted the win after so many years of existing in the shadow of Sammy Baugh. But it was not to be; Washington dealt the Giants their first loss of the year, 24–14.

At home afterward, New York pulled off two impressive wins against expert passing teams, the Chicago Cardinals, with their hurler Paul Christman, and the Chicago Bears, with Sid Luckman. A loss in Philadelphia to the Eagles was avenged the following week at the Polo Grounds when the Giants annihilated the Philadelphians, 45–17, their most explosive performance of the year. The Giants also lost to the Los Angeles Rams, who had come

Radar, Selling Tickets, Etc.

Bill Corum loved to tell stories of Tim Mara in his column for the New York Journal-American. *From one:*

Squire Tim Mara, of Spring Lake, N.J., told the tale in Toots Shor's restaurant the other evening. The Squire had come up from his Jersey estate to while away an evening with the sports crowd.

Then he told us how his son, Lieut. Wellington Mara, of the Navy, had dictated the signing of [Tuffy] Leemans as a backfield coach and possible spot player. "Lieut. Well," by the way is a Radar expert and Steve Owen can scarcely wait for the war to be over, so he can find out if Radar will help him pick up the signals of the Redskins and Bears.

From another:

This will give you an idea of how much loose money there is around. Along with most everybody else, Tim Mara, who owns the N.Y. Giants professional football team, is finding it hard to get help these days.

So last week before the Giants and Bear game, when his ticket seller was out of the office, Tim took over the window himself.

He hadn't been there long when a young man came along who wanted twenty-five box seats.

"The only box seats left are in the lower stands back of the goal posts," Mara told him.

"I'll take 'em," said the young man.

Tim counted out the tickets and the buyer proffered a hundred-dollar bill. Tim made the change and was taken aback when the young fellow shoved a ten-dollar bill back through the window, saying: "Stick this in your kick."

"Oh, no," said Mara, returning the bill.

"You mean, you don't want ten dollars?" said the ticket buyer.

"Not as a tip," replied Tim. "You see, I happen to be the owner of the Giants."

"Are you Tim Mara?" asked the young fellow.

"That's right," replied Tim.

"Well, keep the ten anyhow," said the surprised buyer. "It's worth that to meet you."

An Unwelcome Surprise, 1944

New York Giants					Green Bay Packers
O'Neal Adams		LE			Don Hutson
Frank Cope		LT			Baby Ray
Len Younce		LG			Bill Kuusisto
Mel Hein		C			Charley Brock
Jim Sivell		RG			Buckets Goldenberg
Vic Carroll		RT			Paul Berezney
Frank Liebel		RE			Harry Jacunski
Len Calligaro		QB			Larry Craig
Arnie Herber		LH			Irv Comp
Ward Cuff		RH			Joe Laws
Howie Livingston		FB			Ted Fritsch

Giants	0	0	0	7 —	7
Packers	0	14	0	0 —	14

Touchdowns—*Giants:* Cuff; *Packers:* Fritsch (2).
PATs—*Giants:* Strong; *Packers:* Hutson (2).

New York Football Giants Service Roster

Adams, O'Neale	E	Army	1944
*Avedisian, Chas.†	G	Marines	1942
Barrett, Emmett†	C	Army	1942
*Blozis, Al ★	T	Army	1944
*Brown, Dave	HB	Navy	1943
*Buffington, Harry	QB	A.A.C.	1942
Cantor, Leo	HB	A.A.C.	1942
Chickerneo, John	QB	A.A.C.	1942
*Cole, Pete	T	Army	1940
Cuff, Ward†	HB	A.A.C.	1943
Damiani, Frank	T	Army	1944
*Danowski, Ed	QB	Navy	1941
*DeFilippo, Louis	C	Navy	1941
*Dennery, Vincent	E	Navy	1941
Eakin, Kay[1]	HB	Army	1941
*Eshmont, Len	HB	Navy	1941
*Falaschi, Nello	QB	N.A.C.	1941
*Franck, George	HB	N.A.C.	1941
*Gelatka, Chas.[2]	E	A.A.C.	1940
*Gladchuck, Chet	T	Navy	1941
Hapes, Merle	HB	A.A.C.	1942
*Hiemstra, Edward	G	Army	1942
*Horne, Richard	E	A.A.C.	1941
*Howell, Jim Lee	E	Marines	1942
*Keahey, Eulis	T	Marines	1942
*Kline, Harry[3]	E	Navy	1942
*Lansdell, Granville	HB	A.A.C.	1940
Lascari, John	E	Army	1942
*Lechner, Edgar	G	Navy	1942
Liebel, Frank†	E	Army	1942
*Lieberum, Don	HB	Navy	1942
*Lunday, Ken	C	A.A.C.	1941
*McClain, Clint	FB	Navy	1941
*Lummus, Jack ★ ★	E	Marines	1941
Marefos, Andy	FB	Army	1942
Mellus, John	T	Army	1941
*Miller, Eddie	QB	Army	1940
*Neilsen, Walter	FB	Army	1940
*Oldershaw, Doug	G	A.A.C.	1941
*Owen, Al	HB	Navy	1942
Paschal, Wm.[4]	FB	Army	1944
*Pedersen, Win	T	Army	1941
Petrilas, Wm.	HB	Navy	1944
*Poole, Jim	E	Navy	1941
Principe, Dom	FB	Navy	1942
*Pugh, Marion[5]	HB	Army	1941
*Reagan, Frank	HB	Marines	1941
Seick, Earl	G	Navy	1943
Soar, Hank	HB	Army	1942
*Sohn, Ben[6]	G	Marines	1941
Stenn, Paul	T	Army	1942
Trocolor, Robert†	HB	Marines	1943
*Vosberg, Don	E	Navy	1941
*Yeager, Howard[7]	HB	A.A.C.	1941
Younce, Len	G	Army	1944
*Mara, Wellington	Co-owner	Navy	1941
*Palm, Mike	Ass't Coach	N.A.C.	1941

*Commissioned officer.
1. Awarded Bronze Star (Normandy).
2. Awarded Air Medal, Distinguished Flying Cross, and two Presidential citations (Darwin and Papoon areas).
3. Awarded Purple Heart and honorable discharge.
4. Medical discharge from Army Air Corps. Drafted into Army out of Maritime Service.
5. Purple Heart with Oak Leaf cluster (ETO).
6. Purple Heart (South Pacific).
7. Awarded Soldier's Medal for Heroism.
†Medical discharge.
★ Killed in France on January 31, 1945.
★ ★ Killed on Iwo Jima.

to the East Coast to introduce Bob Waterfield and Tommy Harmon, their two prize backs.

But when the regular season was over, the Giants were firmly entrenched at the top of the NFL East with a record of 7–3–1. Filchock had passed for 1,252 yards, the first Giants passer ever to toss for more than 1,000 yards, and his 87 completions and 12 touchdown passes set two other Giants standards. Filchock also led the club in rushing with 371 yards. It was enough to earn him All-Pro honors. Jim White also made All-Pro in his freshman year.

So, for the eighth time since the NFL began holding championship games in 1933, the Giants had earned their way to the classic, and for the fourth time they would be facing the Chicago Bears, whom they had beaten once and lost to twice. The Bears, behind NFL passing leader Sid Luckman (1,826 yards, 17 touchdowns), had easily taken the NFL West with a record of 8–2–1 (one of their only losses administered by the Giants at the Polo Grounds, 14–0, the only game that year in which the Bears did not score at least 21 points).

On Saturday, December 14, the day before the championship game, Giants owner Tim Mara and coach Steve Owen learned that two of their mainstays, Frank Filchock and fullback Merle Hapes, were under investigation for bribe offers in a scheme to get them to throw the championship game (see sidebar). Bert Bell, in his rookie year as NFL commissioner, was informed of the facts of the case, at least what was known of them at the time—that Hapes had been offered a bribe by gambler Alvin Paris, had not taken it, but had not informed his coach or team officials of the offer, and that Filchock had associated with

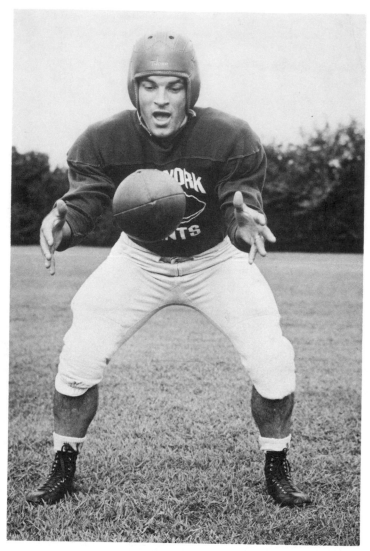

Merle Hapes, pictured here just after returning from military service in 1946, had been the club's leading ground gainer in 1942 before going off to war, rushing for 362 yards and leading the team in both punt and kickoff returns. Hapes was suspended indefinitely by Commissioner Bert Bell before the 1946 championship game between the Giants and Chicago Bears for not reporting a bribe which was offered to him and teammate Frank Filchock. (New York Giants)

Paris but claimed that he had not been offered a bribe. Bell decided to suspend Hapes, but Filchock was allowed to play in the championship game.

The Bears did not look anything like the team that had been embarrassed at the Polo Grounds two months earlier after, as one New York scribe called it, the "tainted title tilt" got under way. Luckman hit All-Pro end Ken Kavanaugh with a 21-yard touchdown pass in the first quarter; then Dante Magnani snatched a Giant pass and raced 19 yards for another touchdown in the same period.

But the Giants were far from out of it. Filchock, playing his heart out because of the scandal that hung over him that day, came back with a 38-yard bomb to end Frank Liebel; then, in the third quarter, he lobbed another to Steve Filipowicz in the end zone. With forty-year-old Ken Strong's two extra points, the Giants had a tie at 14 points going into the final period.

In the fourth quarter, however, Sid Luckman came up with a little razzle-dazzle that proved to be the Giants' undoing. He described it this way:

> We had a play called "Bingo keep it" where I ran with the ball. It worked like this. We had George McAfee at halfback, and he was such a tremendous threat as a runner, a breakaway back, that they always had to watch out for him. So in the fourth quarter of that championship game I took a timeout and asked Coach Halas if I could call the "Bingo" play. He said okay. When I got the snap, I faked to McAfee, who went around the left end with the defense in hot pursuit. Everyone was chasing McAfee, so I just danced around right end with the ball and then along the sidelines for a touchdown.

It was a 19-yard run, during which Luckman shook off a Giant tackler, and it proved to be the decisive play of the game.

The final score was the Bears 24, the Giants 14. From the wallets of the 58,346 fans who had passed through the turnstiles at the Polo Grounds that day, the gross gate of $282,955.25 was the most up to that time for an NFL title game. Each Giants player went home with $1,295.57, while each of the victorious Bears pocketed $1,975.82.

Frank Filchock had played hard and well, had even suffered a broken nose early in the game, and assured everyone that the gamblers had had no influence on his performance. After the game, however, he, too, was suspended from professional football by Commissioner Bell when it became known that he had also been offered a bribe by Alvin Paris and had lied about it before the game.

The 1946 title was the eighth that the Giants had participated in, but it was to be their last trip to the NFL championship for a decade.

It was a devastating drop for the divisional champion Giants of 1946 to the cellar of the NFL East in 1947, the first time in the franchise's history that the team hit bottom. Filchock and Hapes were, of course, gone, and the Giants were virtually without a quarterback in the beginning of the season.

After tying the Boston Yanks, 7–7, in the season opener, New York lost seven straight games. Four games through the dreadful season the desperate Giants traded their most consistent running back, Bill Paschal, to the Boston Yanks for their quarterback, Paul Governali. A graduate of Columbia, Pitching Paul was in his second

Scandalous Doings

Steve Owen tells the story (in his book My Kind of Football, *David McKay Company, 1952):*

I know of only one time anything in the game made me mad and sick and worried. That was the time in 1946, just before we were to meet the Bears in the Polo Grounds for the world championship, that two of our boys, Frank Filchock and Merle Hapes, were accused of having to do with gamblers.

That thing broke Saturday afternoon, the day before the big game. The Maras and I were called to the mayor's [William O'Dwyer's] residence in Gracie Square, and then went to police headquarters, where we dug into the thing to get at the truth.

One Alvin Paris, who later was sentenced to prison, was charged with having offered a bribe to Hapes to influence the outcome of the game with the Bears. Filchock knew of this offer but did not report it. Worst of all, both boys had associated with this Paris and his crowd—you know, bright lights and smart entertainment.

The police had Paris as well as the two boys in for questioning, and you might say Paris was in no hurry to cooperate. I said to Commissioner Arthur W. Wallander: "If you will let me take this so-and-so into the inspector's room for a few minutes, while you look the other way, I guarantee I'll get his confession."

Wallander looked at me, with a tight little grin on his face, and answered: "I believe you would, Steve, but you know I can't let you do it that way."

Finally, it was disclosed that neither boy was criminally involved. But there was no doubt that Hapes, although he did not take a bribe, had led Paris on by permitting the fixer to wine and dine him.

Filchock was just plain foolish for not telling what he knew, the minute he knew it.

The police cleared the boys, and that put a decision up to Bert Bell, commissioner of the league. Hapes had gone too far to be permitted to play football, and the commissioner so ruled. In the case of Filchock, he permitted him to play against the Bears, and no one ever saw a boy give a more spirited and courageous performance on the football field. Honestly, it choked you up, knowing how hard he was trying. The Bears defeated us, 24–14, but it was not for lack of effort by Filchock. The boy's nose was broken early in the game, but he kept on fighting through every play with blood and mud coating his face and uniform. In his heart he hoped the past would be forgotten.

But Bell in the end banned Filchock as well as Hapes.

Except for the Fourth Quarter, 1946

New York Giants		Chicago Bears
Jim Poole	LE	Ken Kavanaugh
Tex Coulter	LT	Fred Davis
Bob Dobelstein	LG	Rudy Mucha
Chet Gladchuk	C	Bulldog Turner
Len Younce	RG	Ray Bray
Jim White	RT	Mike Jarmoluk
Jim Lee Howell	RE	George Wilson
Steve Filipowicz	QB	Sid Luckman
Dave Brown	LH	Dante Magnani
Howie Livingston	RH	Hugh Gallarneau
Ken Strong	FB	Bill Osmanski

Giants	7	0	7	0 —	14
Bears	14	0	0	10 —	24

Touchdowns—*Giants:* Liebel, Filipowicz; *Bears:* Kavanaugh, Magnani, Luckman. Field goals—*Bears:* Maznicki.

PATs—*Giants:* Strong (2); *Bears:* Maznicki (3).

---

passing for 1,461 yards and throwing a total of 14 touchdowns. He managed to get the Giants a pair of wins late in the season, one of which was over the Chicago Cardinals and their "dream backfield" of Paul Christman, Charlie Trippi, Elmer Angsman, and Pat Harder, the team that would win the NFL championship that year. But that was certainly the only bright spot of 1947. The Giants' final record, the worst up to that time in the team's history, was 2–8–2.

As good a passer as Paul Governali was, he lost his job in 1948 to a lanky, raw-boned All-American from Mississippi who was destined to become a fixture in the New York Giants' backfield, Charlie Conerly. From his rookie year through eleven additional seasons as a starting quarterback and two others as backup, Conerly would virtually rewrite the club's passing records.

Conerly was not the Giants' first-round draft pick that year; he was in fact acquired from the Washington Redskins, who already had Sammy Baugh and Harry Gilmer to handle their passing game. The Giants' top pick in the 1948 draft was Tony "Skippy" Minisi, a halfback from Pennsylvania. They also drafted All-American end Bill Swiacki from Columbia, who would prove to be the team's most productive pass receiver his rookie year.

There was also a notable milestone in 1948; the Giants signed the first black in club history. The young man simply walked into the Giants' office one day and asked

---

year in the NFL and had already proven himself an accomplished passer. And he showed off those credentials from the start in New York. In the eight games he played for the Giants in 1947, Governali set two club records by

Charlie Conerly

Charlie Conerly was a lanky rookie when he lined up as tailback in the Giants' A formation on a blustery December afternoon in 1948 at the Polo Grounds and gazed across the line of scrimmage at the menacing Pittsburgh Steelers. When the afternoon was over, he had thrown an NFL-record 36 completions out of 53 attempts.

Conerly, born in Clarksdale, Mississippi, and a consensus All-American back at Ole Miss in 1947, had been drafted by the Washington Redskins in 1945, but when he became eligible for the pros in 1948, they traded him to the Giants after obtaining Alabama tailback Harry Gilmer. Fourteen years later, at age forty with the distinction of being the oldest player in the NFL, Conerly finally took off his Giants uniform for the last time. In all Giants history only Mel Hein has played longer for the team.

No Giants passer has completed more passes than Conerly's 1,418 nor gained more yardage hurling the ball than his 19,488. He represented the Giants in three Pro Bowls (1951, 1952, 1957) and was named the NFL's Most Valuable Player in 1959. When he retired after the 1961 season, only Sammy Baugh, Bobby Layne, and Norm Van Brocklin had thrown more touchdown passes than Conerly's 166. (N.Y. Giants)

for a tryout. He had played for the University of Toledo for one year, he told Wellington Mara, but he broke his neck. Then he had gone into the Coast Guard, and when he came out of that had played some ball at Iowa. He got his tryout, made the team, and Emlen Tunnell began a pro football career that would land him eventually in the Hall of Fame, recognized as one of the greatest defensive backs ever to play the game.

It was a year of rebuilding, according to stout Steve Owen. But it soon became clear that one element was not taking to the reconstruction process: defense. In the second, third, and fourth games of the season, the Giants gave up 41 points to the Redskins, 45 to the Eagles, and 63 to the Chicago Cardinals. The 63–35 loss to the Cardinals set an NFL record for the most points scored in a game up to that time, 98, eclipsing the 87 scored the year before when the Philadelphia Eagles beat the Washington Redskins 45–42. The 63 points was the most scored against the Giants since the team was born.

On offense, however, the rebuilding was going nicely. Charlie Conerly was proving to be a masterful passer and an inspiring team leader. Against the Pittsburgh Steelers, he set an NFL record of 36 completions, a league stan-

dard that would remain until George Blanda completed 37 for the Houston Oilers in 1964.

Because of their porous defense, the Giants could only manage to win four of their twelve games in 1948. But Conerly had passed for 2,175 yards on 162 completions and thrown 22 touchdown passes, all team records. The 10 touchdown catches made by Bill Swiacki tied the team record set by Frank Liebel in 1945, and the 550 yards he gained on pass receptions was the second most in club history at the time.

The Giants needed some help in their running game, Steve Owen was well aware, and, needless to say, a complete overhaul on defense. Things would be better the next year, he assured the Maras; rebuilding takes some time. He was right.

The Giants were back to .500 ball in 1949, a record of 6–6, the result of a rampaging offense and a slightly improved defense. They had added a fine defensive tackle in rookie Al DeRogatis from Duke, a good offensive guard in Bill Austin from Oregon State, and an expert placekicker who had defected from the AAFC, Ben Agajanian.

It was the year that Steve Owen decided to do away with his A formation and switch to the T. Conerly, he felt,

The Conerly Controversy

Red Smith, writing for the New York Herald Tribune *in 1948, reported the intracity squabble for the rights to Charlie Conerly, who had just finished an illustrious career at Mississippi and was ready to become a pro. It seems both the New York Giants and the Brooklyn (football) Dodgers of the All-American Football Conference wanted his quarterbacking services.*

Branch Rickey [the Brooklyn owner], the most dangerous switch orator since Demosthenes, got carried away by his own eloquence yesterday. The effects threaten to be as far-reaching as his rich barytone voice. . . .

[He informed] members of the Brooklyn Gridiron Club that he had offered $110,000 to a rookie football player named Charlie Conerly of the University of Mississippi. Then he hauled off and swung a transpontine haymaker at the football Giants, who expect to hire Conerly. . . .

It was, the Reverend went on, the best offer Conerly received, but the kid had to turn it down because he was already committed to the National League Giants, interborough rivals of Rickey's All-America Conference Dodgers. So here, the orator thundered, was a case of a boy in a "free American sport" being unfree to accept the best offer for his services. Going oracular, the Reverend predicted the Giants would always have a "morale problem" with Conerly because he would remember that he had not been allowed to make a better deal. "It seems un-American to me," declaimed the Reverend, "and you can take that for what it's worth—in New York or Mississippi." . . .

"Maybe," said [Tim] Mara, who had just finished reading about Rickey signing Ralph Branca to pitch for $14,000 [for the baseball Dodgers], "the kid figures he'll have greater security with the Giants than with an organization that puts such a price on a 21-game winner.

"Maybe he's looked over the All-America Conference and realized that we've been in business here twenty-four years, whereas Brooklyn has had three–four owners. . . . I do not know where this guy gets off talking about morale problems and stuff, considering the business he's in. . . . A hundred and ten thousand dollars," he mused. "That would be out of our reach. I thought United Cigar Company coupons were out of print these days."

Conerly, of course, signed with the Giants and stayed around for fourteen seasons—his first contract was reportedly for $62,500 over five seasons and a $10,000 signing bonus.

Sid Luckman, famed Chicago Bears T-formation quarterback, drops back to toss one against the Giants in November 1943. It was during this game at the Polo Grounds that Luckman, much to the chagrin of the Giants, set two NFL records—throwing 7 touchdown passes and gaining 433 passing yards—in a 56–7 rout. No. 32 on the Giants is tackle Al Blozis; the Bears' No. 35 is tackle Bill Steinkemper. (Pro Football Hall of Fame)

would be a most effective T-formation quarterback. To aid in the transition, Owen hired Allie Sherman, an acknowledged T scholar, to work with Conerly.

At season's end, Conerly had completed 152 passes for 2,138 yards, including 17 TD tosses. Bill Swiacki had set two team records by gaining 652 yards on 47 receptions. But the biggest surprise was Gene "Choo-Choo" Roberts, a halfback in his second year with the Giants, who led the entire NFL in scoring with 102 points on 17 touchdowns. The 634 yards he gained rushing was the third most then in Giants history, trailing only Tuffy Leemans (830 in 1936) and Bill Paschal (737 in 1944).

The several years of renovation were now over. Both the NFL and the New York Giants would have a new look for the 1950s.

Bill Paschal, like Tuffy Leemans, was a halfback out of George Washington University. Paschal came to the Giants in 1942 and set a passel of club records in 1943, scoring 72 points on 12 touchdowns (10 rushing). During the war years, he was the team's most productive rusher and scorer. His Giants career ended during the 1947 season, when he was traded to the Boston Yanks. (Pro Football Hall of Fame)

Don Hutson, the most immortal pass catcher of his time, hauls one in here for the Packers in the 1944 NFL championship game against the Giants. He did not catch a touchdown pass that afternoon, but he did kick two extra points in Green Bay's 14–7 victory. No. 24 of the Giants, here in frustrated pursuit, is Howie Livingston. (Pro Football Hall of Fame)

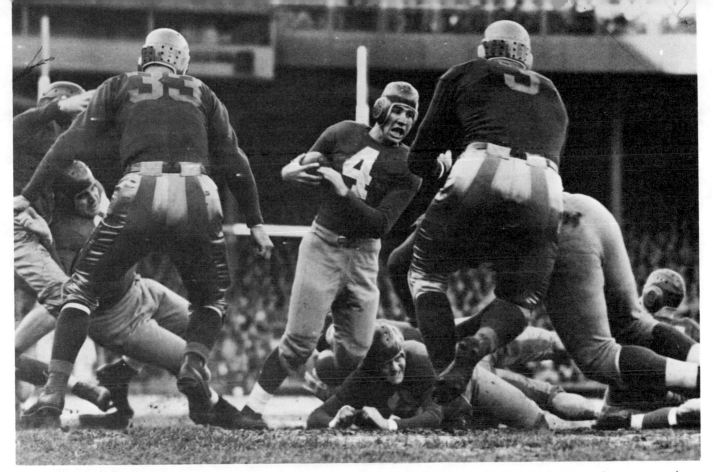

Tuffy Leemans, shown here doing what he did so well in the late 1930s and early '40s: breaking through a hole to rack up some yardage for the Giants. When he retired after the 1943 season, he had the distinction of then being the Giants' all-time leading rusher (3,132 yards). Today, he ranks seventh in that category. Leemans was inducted into the Pro Football Hall of Fame in 1978. (Pro Football Hall of Fame).

Frank Filchock came to the Giants in 1946 to take over tailbacking duties after serving as Sammy Baugh's understudy with the Redskins. He did well enough that year for New York to win All-Pro honors, but was an unfortunate subject involved in the offer of bribes to throw that year's championship game. (Pro Football Hall of Fame)

Howie Livingston goes up high in this sequence to intercept a Chicago Bears pass intended for end Ken Kavanaugh in the battle for the 1946 NFL crown. It helped for the moment, but in the end the Giants fell to the Bears, 24–14. No. 15, in the last panel, is Hank Soar of the Giants. (Pro Football Hall of Fame)

Frank Filchock (40) is corraled here by Bears linebacker Bulldog Turner in the 1946 NFL title game. Filchock, a figure in the bribe offer before the game, was allowed to play because it was believed that a bribe had not been offered directly to him, only that he knew an offer had been made to Merle Hapes. He played well that day, going through most of the game with a broken nose, but after it he was suspended indefinitely, like Hapes, when it came to light that he had in fact been offered a bribe. (Pro Football Hall of Fame)

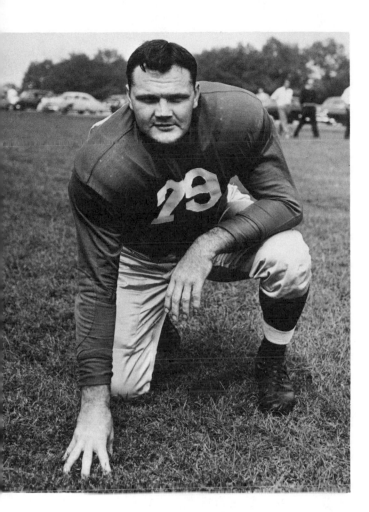

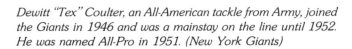

Dewitt "Tex" Coulter, an All-American tackle from Army, joined the Giants in 1946 and was a mainstay on the line until 1952. He was named All-Pro in 1951. (New York Giants)

Emlen Tunnell walked into the Giants' offices one day, before the start of the 1948 season, and asked Wellington Mara for a tryout. No black had ever worn a Giants uniform before, but Tunnell got his tryout, made the team, became a four-time All-Pro, set a variety of NFL records as a defensive back, and earned his way into the Pro Football Hall of Fame as one of the greatest safeties of all time. His records of 1,282 yards gained on interceptions and 258 punt returns are still NFL standards; and his 79 career interceptions are exceeded only by the 81 registered later by Paul Krause of the Redskins and Vikings. Tunnell ended his eleven-year Giants career after the 1958 season. (New York Giants)

Bill Swiacki, remembered for his diving, acrobatic catch for Columbia that enabled them to upset Army in 1947, came to the Giants in 1948 and played three seasons. Swiacki led the team in pass receptions all three years and set two team records in 1949, when he caught 47 passes for 652 yards. (Pro Football Hall of Fame)

Beginning of a New Era

The All-America Football Conference, founded by *Chicago Tribune* sports editor Arch Ward in 1946, had run its course in competing with the NFL after the 1949 football season. But the AAFC bequeathed three teams to the NFL—the Cleveland Browns, San Francisco 49ers, and Baltimore Colts—all of whom would make distinctive marks in the expanded league. The divisions were realigned and renamed, becoming the American Conference and the National Conference instead of the Eastern and Western divisions.

The New York Giants were assigned to the American, along with the NFL's reigning champion Philadelphia Eagles, Pittsburgh Steelers, Washington Redskins, Chicago Cardinals, and Cleveland Browns. They were no longer sharing the Polo Grounds with the New York Bulldogs, now known as the New York Yanks, who had moved their act over to Yankee Stadium.

Due to the demise of the AAFC, the cream of its talent was infused into the NFL. The Giants were especially rewarded, acquiring such AAFC veterans as tackle Arnie Weinmeister, guard John Mastrangelo, and defensive backs Tom Landry, Otto Schnellbacher, and Harmon Rowe. In the college player draft they selected Auburn quarterback Travis Tidwell and later added fullback Eddie Price from Tulane and end Bob McChesney of Hardin-Simmons.

The NFL was rife with offensive football talent in 1950. In the American Conference, the Eagles had Steve Van Buren, Tommy Thompson, and Pete Pihos; the Steelers, Joe Geri and Lynn Chandnois; the Cardinals, Charlie Trippi, Pat Harder, Elmer Angsman, and Bob Shaw; the Redskins, Sammy Baugh, Bullet Bill Dudley, and Charley "Choo Choo" Justice; and the Cleveland Browns had Otto Graham, Marion Motley, Dub Jones, Mac Speedie, and Dante Lavelli.

Over in the National Conference, the Los Angeles Rams had Bob Waterfield, Norm Van Brocklin, Glenn Davis, Dick Hoerner, Tom Fears, and Elroy "Crazylegs" Hirsch; the Bears, Sid Luckman, Johnny Lujack, Ken Kavanaugh, and Jim Keane; the New York Yanks, George Ratterman, Buddy Young, George Taliaferro, and Zollie Toth; the Lions, Bobby Layne, Doak Walker, Bob Hoernschmeyer, Cloyce Box, and Leon Hart; the Packers, Tobin Rote and Billy Grimes; the 49ers, Frankie Albert, Joe Perry, and Emil Sitko; and the Colts, Y. A. Tittle and Chet Mutryn.

The forte of the Giants in 1950, however, was defense, and therefore most of the preseason pundits suggested they were doomed to a dull and mediocre season, much like that of 1949. But it was a revolutionary defense that Steve Owen devised, called the "umbrella" (see sidebar), which immediately proved to be highly successful, especially against a passing offense.

The Giants opened on the road in 1950 with a win over Pittsburgh, 18–7. Then it was on to Cleveland, where the mighty Browns lay in wait. Paul Brown's magnificent eleven had won the AAFC title in each of the four seasons of the team's existence, compiling a record of 51–4–3 in the process. To open their maiden season in the National Football League, the Browns destroyed the Philadelphia Eagles, the team that had won the NFL championship the year before, 35–10.

Cleveland was heavily favored the day they faced the Giants, but Owen's umbrella was opened up for the first time, and the Browns were both mystified and frustrated. Pass after pass from Otto Graham was batted away or intercepted. The invincible Browns were to their uncharacteristic chagrin totally vanquished, held scoreless for the first time in the team's history. Rookie Eddie Price, who had earned the starting berth at fullback, scored to give the Giants a 6–0 victory.

The Redskins were the next victim, 21–17, and the Giants sat at the top of the American Conference with a record of 3–0; a reign short-lived, however, when Pittsburgh surprised them the following week. When the Browns came to the Polo Grounds, they had a record of 4–1, and the Giants were 3–1 (the Browns had opened their season a week earlier). Again the Browns were the favorite among oddsmakers, most choosing to ignore the Giants' earlier triumph. And it looked as though they were correct, at least at the half, with Cleveland holding a 13–3 lead by dint of two Lou "The Toe" Groza field goals and a Giants turnover on their own 1-yard line that was converted to a Browns touchdown. But New York came back, the umbrella once again shutting down the Browns. And while the Giants' defense held Cleveland scoreless in the second half, their offense came alive. A touchdown in the third quarter brought them within three of the Browns; and another touchdown in the fourth quarter gave the Giants a 17–13 win and undisputed claim to the top tier of the conference.

Again it was short-lived. The Chicago Cardinals dished

Newsletter Notes, 1952

Em Tunnell has fully recovered from the dislocated shoulder he suffered in the Pro Bowl game in California last January. Em can't wait to rejoin Otto Schnellbacher on the back line. While he's waiting, Tunnell works as a beer salesman in his hometown of Garrett Hill, Pa. . . . Kyle Rote is a building contractor in Corpus Christi, Tex., in the off-season. . . . Bob Wilkinson, brand new dad of a daughter, has graduated from stunt stuff to a featured part in Hollywood. . . . Lots of news on Giants in service: Sonny Grandelius is a second looey at Fort Slocum in New Rochelle, N.Y. . . . Jack Stroud is at Fort Jackson, S.C. . . . Both Stroud and Grandelius are scheduled for Far Eastern service. . . . Ray Wietecha is with the Marines at Quantico. . . . Bud Sherrod starred with the Carswell Air Base national service champions. . . . Bill Milner is expected to be mustered out of the Marines by Fall. . . . Milner coached and played with the Camp LeJeune team, which lost the Cigar Bowl game, 20–0, to Brooke Army Medical Center. . . .

them a loss at Comiskey Park in Chicago the following week, and again they were forced to share the lead with the Browns. And that's the way it remained for the rest of the season. Neither the Giants nor the Browns suffered another loss. Among the impressive Giant wins were a 51–21 drubbing of the Cardinals at the Polo Grounds, a 55–20 devastation of the Colts down in Baltimore (at the time the second highest number of points a Giants team had compiled in a single game, only a point less than the

Fullback Eddie Price came to the Giants in 1950 from Tulane and averaged 5.6 yards a carry as a rookie, gaining 703 yards rushing (then the third-highest total in club history). The following year he led the entire NFL with 971 yards. Twice an All-Pro, Price stayed through the 1956 season and ranks sixth in rushing in club annals with 3,292 yards. (Pro Football Hall of Fame)

56 run up against the Eagles in 1933), and a 51–7 shel-lacking of the New York Yanks. No one was remarking on the Giants' alleged lack of offense any longer.

At season's end the Giants and Browns each had rec-ords of 10–2 and would decide the title in a playoff game at Municipal Stadium in Cleveland.

December 17 was brutally cold, an ice-winded seven-teen degrees at game time. There were slightly more than 33,700 fans on hand to see if the New Yorkers could once again shut down the otherwise offensively volatile Browns. Cleveland edged ahead in the first quarter when a drive was stopped at the 4-yard line and Lou Groza drilled one through the uprights for a 3–0 advantage.

That lead, in a totally defense-dominated game, lasted into the fourth quarter. And then the Giants had a won-derful chance to go ahead. Having driven to the Browns' 36, the Giants surprised the Clevelanders when Choo Choo Roberts took a reverse and scampered around end all the way to the Browns' 4-yard line. Two running plays advanced the ball only to the 3, where, on third down, Charlie Conerly rifled one to Bob McChesney in the end zone. But a red flag lay on the field, and the signal was that New York had been offside. Several plays and several penalties later, the Giants found themselves on fourth down at the Cleveland 13. Randy Clay came on to kick the game-tying field goal.

As the fourth quarter wore on, the Browns ground away at the Giants, and finally, with only fifty-eight sec-onds left in the game the truest toe in professional foot-ball, Lou Groza, kicked a 28-yard field goal. Not too many seconds later, Charlie Conerly, looking for a receiver from his own end zone, was tackled by Cleveland All-Pro Bill Willis for an additional but unneeded two points. The final score was 8–3, and the Browns won the right to represent the American Conference in the NFL championship of 1950.

It had been a fine year for the Giants, however; they were back above .500 for the first time since 1946. They had shown Cleveland—and the entire NFL, for that mat-ter—how effective Steve Owen's umbrella defense was in the hands of the game's finest secondary: defensive half-backs Tom Landry and Harmon Rowe and safeties Emlen Tunnell and Otto Schnellbacher.

Eddie Price rushed for 703 yards with an impressive 5.6-yard average per carry, and Choo Choo Roberts picked up another 483 yards on the ground. Arnie Weinmeister was the only Giants All-Pro in the last year before the listings would honor offense and defense sepa-rately.

Just as the New York Giants and the Washington Red-skins clashed for divisional titles in the late 1930s, the same scenario was taking shape in the fifties between the Giants and the Cleveland Browns; at least it would be

played that way through the first three years of the dec-ade. In 1951, there would be virtually no other competi-tion in the conference except for those two teams.

The Giants began the year on a note of good fortune. In those days, the very first pick in the college draft was a "bonus" pick; each team drew a slip of paper from a hat, one of which was designated the bonus, and the lucky winner got the pick of that year's crop regardless of where the team had ended up in the preceding year's standings. In 1951, as Wellington Mara remembers, "My brother Jack or I ordinarily drew from the hat, but that year I said something like, 'Let's see if we can change our luck if Steve does the picking.' So he reached in, and he sure in fact drew the bonus, and we promptly drafted Kyle Rote." An All-American tailback and Heisman Trophy runner-up, Kyle Rote of Southern Methodist had been a most capa-ble successor to Doak Walker's role as a triple threat at SMU and was touted as the best pro prospect that year, coveted by every team in the league. The acquisition of Rote was especially welcome in Giantdom in that starting halfback Choo Choo Roberts had abandoned the team for the new Canadian Football League.

But the Giants' luck reversed itself in the preseason. First, Rote injured his knee and therefore saw only limited service during the regular season. Then Charlie Conerly

Kyle Rote

Notre Dame's coach Frank Leahy in 1950 called him the "most underrated back in football." A year later Steve Owen said, "He receives, runs, and kicks with power, polish, and determination."

Kyle Rote, coming from San Antonio and the heir at Southern Methodist to Doak Walker's tailback spot as well as All-American status, came to the New York Giants in 1951 as their first-round draft pick and stayed around for eleven seasons. Beleaguered by a knee injury his first year and shortly afterward overshadowed in the backfield by Frank Gifford, Rote was converted to a flanker in the mid-1950s by Jim Lee Howell.

As a prolific receiver of passes thrown by Charlie Con-erly and later Y. A. Tittle, Rote played in four NFL cham-pionship games (1956, 1958, 1959, and 1961), and went to the Pro Bowl four times (1954–57). He stands eighth in all-time scoring for the Giants, having toted up 312 points on 52 touchdowns (48 of them on pass receptions, a team record). Only Joe Morrison, Frank Gifford, and Bob Tucker have caught more passes for the Giants than Rote, who pulled in 300 for a total of 4,797 yards.

aggravated a shoulder injury to his throwing arm, which would hamper his passing considerably throughout the year.

The Giants were surprised in the first game of the regular season and held to a 13–13 tie by the Pittsburgh Steelers. It was not all doom and gloom, however, when word came in that the Browns had been soundly defeated out in California by the revitalized San Francisco 49ers. But any elation there was soon ended because the Browns did not lose another game the entire season. Among their eleven consecutive victories were two over the Giants, the first a 14–13 squeaker in Cleveland and the next a more decisive 10–0 shutout at the Polo Grounds. As it turned out, those were the only two losses New York suffered that year, but they were enough to sentence them to second place once again. "If we could only have beat the goldarn Browns," Steve Owen said later, "we would have been champs of everything that year [1951]. We could have beat the Rams [the NC champ], and anybody else except those Browns."

Still, it had been a most respectable season. Eddie Price led the league in rushing and set a Giants record with 971 yards gained on the ground, 141 more than Tuffy Leemans toted up back in 1936. Price's 271 carries set an NFL single-season mark, eclipsing the 263 jaunts that Steve Van Buren had for the Eagles in 1949 when he set the NFL rushing record of 1,146 yards.

Emlen Tunnell was the top punt returner in the NFL with a total of 489 yards on 34 returns, his total yardage a club record that still stands today. And Otto Schnellbacher's 11 interceptions were the most in the NFL and also a new Giants standard.

When the All-Pro selections were made, the Giants landed two players on the offensive unit, fullback Eddie Price and tackle Tex Coulter; and five on the defensive squad, tackles Arnie Weinmeister and Al DeRogatis, guard Jon Baker, and defensive backs Emlen Tunnell and Otto Schnellbacher.

In 1952, with Kyle Rote's leg better and the addition of first-round draft choice Frank Gifford, an outstanding halfback from Southern Cal, the Giants proved they could in fact beat the Browns. First, they handed them a 17–9 shellacking in Cleveland and took over first place with a record of 3–0. But when they slipped by them, 37–34, in the last game of the season it did not really matter because, going into the game the 6–5 Giants had already been mathematically eliminated by the 8–3 Browns.

It was a frustrating season after such a fine start. Losses to the Chicago Cardinals and the Philadelphia Eagles after knocking off the Browns brought the Giants back to earth with a thud. But the most bone-crushing defeat was yet to come. The sorry site was Pittsburgh, and the Steel-

Today one seldom sees Tom Landry hatless, but back in 1950, the year he came to the Giants from the New York Yankees of the AAFC, he posed that way. An outstanding defensive back through 1955, he ranks sixth in all-time interceptions with 31, three of which he returned for touchdowns. Landry was an All-Pro in 1954, served as a player/assistant coach in 1954 through 1955, and was the Giants' full-time assistant coach for defense from 1956 through 1959 before moving to Dallas to take over the head coaching duties of the newly enfranchised Cowboys. (Pro Football Hall of Fame)

ers, a team that had won only three of nine games that year, were the perpetrators. The Giants were annihilated that afternoon, 63–7, the most points at that time ever given up by a New York Giants team. In that game, Charlie Conerly left the game with a rewounded shoulder. Then his replacement, rookie Fred Benners from SMU, was knocked out of the game. Steve Owen sent Tom

The Umbrella Defense

Steve Owen invented the defense that came to be known as the "umbrella," and he described its versatility:

The nickname refers to the four backs, who roughly assume the shape of an open umbrella, with the two halfbacks shallow and wide and two safety men deep and tight. Then, when we have a 6-1-4 formation, there is the backer-up to suggest the handle of a bumbershoot.

In general, it is the role of the umbrella to act as a sort of flexible basket and adjust itself to contain any attacking situation, by moving in one side or dropping back on the other, but always as a unit, and never without interdependence.

To give another idea of variations on a basic formation, we use the umbrella most often in a 5-2-4 and work eight changes off it.

1. We can red-dog the backers-up through the line, with the ends holding to protect the outside.

2. We can send in an end from one side and a backer-up from the other, with the backer-up on the end side sliding off to cover, and the end on the backer-up side dropping a few yards to protect the vacated area.

3. We can send all seven linemen and backers-up charging in.

4. With a man-in-motion, we can wheel the umbrella to pull three men onto the strong side. We do that depending on the quality of the opposition.

5. We may play zone defense in the backfield, with backers-up dropping straight back watching out for hook passes.

6. We may play man-for-man in the backfield, with the backers-up covering the fullback and one flat. To give that a minor change-of-pace variation we sometimes slide an end out to cover the flat, in lieu of the backer-up.

7. We may go into a 5-1-5, with a combination of some men man-for-man and others in zone defense.

8. We may go into a 6-1-4, to shift rapidly into a 4-3-4, with a combination of man-for-man and zone, if a pass develops after the snap.

Landry in to quarterback the ballclub, a position he had not played since his days at Texas in the mid-1940s. The Giants' record of 7-5 left them in a tie with the Philadelphia Eagles for second place in the American Conference, once again short of the Cleveland Browns.

There were not a lot of highlights from the 1952 season. Eddie Price rushed for 748 yards, second only to Dan Towler of the Rams, who picked up 894. Emlen Tunnell actually gained more yardage running on special teams and on defense than any offensive runner in the league. Between punt and kickoff returns and interception runbacks, Tunnell gained a total of 924 yards for the Giants. Three New Yorkers made All-Pro: fullback Eddie Price,

defensive tackle Arnie Weinmeister, and defensive back Emlen Tunnell.

If 1952 was disappointing, 1953 could only be described as disastrous, despite the appearance of a number of new and promising faces in the starting lineup. Three rookies moved into the offensive line: tackle Roosevelt "Rosey" Brown from Morgan State, guard Jack Stroud of Tennessee, and center Ray Wietecha from Northwestern. In the backfield, another rookie, halfback Sonny Grandelius, would see quite a bit of action after Eddie Price and Kyle Rote were forced to sit out much of the season with injuries. Arnie Galiffa, an All-American at Army in 1949, was back in football as a Giant and was scheduled to be Charlie Conerly's backup. And Steve Owen decided to use Frank Gifford on offense as well as defense (as a rookie Gifford was used almost exclusively as a defensive back).

In a reversal of the season before, the Giants lost their first three games of 1953, solid defeats at the hands of the Rams, Steelers, and Redskins. With Cleveland winning its first three games easily, it became apparent that the Giants were not going to race the Browns to the title that year.

As it turned out, the Giants won only three games in 1953, two wins over the hapless Chicago Cardinals, the only team in what was now called the Eastern Conference to have a record (1–10–1) worse than the Giants that year, and an upset over the Philadelphia Eagles. Their record of 3–9 was the most dismal since recording a 2–8–2 season in 1947. The most embarrassing afternoon came in the next-to-last game of the year when the Giants went out to Cleveland and were lambasted, 62–10, the second-worst beating in their twenty-nine-year history.

Arnie Weinmeister was the only Giant to make All-Pro. He would be gone the following year, however, defecting to the Canadian Football League. And another one-time New York tackle would also depart, one who had spent the past twenty-three years patrolling the Giants' sidelines and guiding their on-field actions: Steve Owen.

Don Smith, former publicity director of the Giants, wrote of perhaps the most difficult decision the Mara family had to make in the first thirty years of the team's existence.

As much as the Maras, Jack, Wellington, and the late T. J., hated to admit it, they had to agree that the gridiron parade had passed by their old warhorse. Never before had the Giants fired a coach. . . . During Owen's long and successful tenure, it was unthinkable that he would be the first to be replaced. Stout Steve was so close to T. J. Mara that neither had ever considered a signed contract necessary. Steve and the elder Mara . . . simply shook hands before each season. . . .

Arnie Weinmeister takes on two white-shirted Giants blockers in a practice session during the early 1950s. An All-Pro tackle in each of his four years with the Giants (1950–53), Weinmeister was considered as fast as most of the backs in the NFL despite his 250-plus–pound bulk. (Pro Football Hall of Fame)

The day after the humiliating defeat by Cleveland, Owen was summoned to the Giant office. All three Maras were there when big Steve heaved into a wicker chair and asked, "What's up?"

It was an awkward moment in the lives of all four men.

Jack Mara acted as spokesman. He told Steve of the decision to hire a new, younger coach. He also expressed a genuine hope that Steve would remain with the Giants as head of college personnel.

Steve Owen did stay around the Giants' front office in 1954, but attended to few duties and then left to go back into coaching, first as a line coach at Baylor down in Waco, Texas, and later as a defensive coach with the Philadelphia Eagles. The man selected to replace him was a surprise to just about everybody, especially Jim Lee Howell himself. But Howell, who had been serving as the Giants' end coach, was the Maras' choice to guide the team.

Among the first things Howell accomplished was a most masterful selection of a staff. He hired one of Earl Blaik's assistant coaches at Army, Vince Lombardi, to handle the offense, and appointed Tom Landry to direct the defense as a player-coach.

Charlie Conerly, who had been battered and bruised for six long seasons as a pro, especially during the last few years when New York's offensive line was less than protective, announced he was retiring from the game. Howell, who had always had great faith in Conerly's abilities as a T-formation quarterback, promptly went after him. As he later explained:

> I tracked him down and found him somewhere in Missouri or Iowa. He was putting out fertilizer on his farm, wearing those high rubber farm boots. When I asked him about coming back, he told me he didn't want to be hurt anymore. I told him I'd get him a line that would protect him, that would be the first order of business, and Charlie said okay, he'd come back.

The next step was to rebuild the stale roster, Howell felt, and when the regular season opened there were quite a few newcomers in Giants uniforms. From the college draft, Howell plucked two quarterbacks to back up Charlie Conerly and his troublesome shoulder, Bobby Clatterbuck from Houston and Don Heinrich of Washington; and he also selected a fine defensive back, Dick Nolan from Maryland, and solid running back Bobby Epps of Pittsburgh.

Howell also went to the trading table and acquired linebacker Bill Svoboda from the Chicago Cardinals. Then he signed a former All-American end at both Army

Automatic Ben

They called Ben Agajanian "Automatic Ben," and they also called him "The Toeless Wonder," the reasons being that he was one of the finest placekickers in the game and that he had only one toe on his kicking foot. He managed to kick 147 field goals in his nine-year NFL career, which ranks him fourth on the all-time list, only Lou Groza (300), George Blanda (201), and Pat Summerall (152) having booted more field goals.

How it all came about was described by Gerald Es-kenazi in his book There Were Giants in Those Days:

He went to the University of New Mexico on a scholarship. But the scholarship did not pay his way. He was poor. He washed pots and pans, refusing to ask his parents for money. The dishwashing job sapped his strength, and he found himself too weak to work out with the club. So he quit for a softer job in a soda-bottling plant.

One day he took the freight elevator, which was loaded with barrels of syrup. He did not realize that his right foot protruded a few inches over the edge of the elevator floor. Four toes were sheared off when they hit a well extending out. Before the surgeon operated, he told him, "Don't worry, Aggie, I'll square off your stumps and you'll kick better than ever."

The surgeon was right.

The Best of the First Twenty-Five Years

In 1950, Steve Owen, who had been at the helm of the Giants for two decades, was asked to select the greatest Giants by position. His choices:

		Years as a Giant
E	Jim Poole	1937–41, 1946
E	Ray Flaherty	1928–35
E	Red Badgro	1927–35
T	Al Blozis	1942–44
T	Ed Widseth	1937–40
T	Cal Hubbard	1927–29, 1936
G	Len Younce	1941–48
G	Johnny Dell Isola	1934–40
G	Butch Gibson	1930–34
C	Mel Hein	1931–45
C	George Murtaugh	1926–32
C	Joe Alexander	1925–27
QB	Ed Danowski	1934–41
QB	Bennie Friedman	1929–31
QB	Jack Hagerty	1926–30
HB	Tuffy Leemans	1936–43
HB	Kink Richards	1933–39
HB	Ward Cuff	1937–45
HB	Hinkey Haines	1925–28
FB	Ken Strong	1933–35, 1939, 1944–47
FB	Jack McBride	1925–28, 1932–33
FB	Phil White	1925–27

and Mississippi, Barney Poole, from the Baltimore Colts, and another highly regarded end, Bob Schnelker, from the Philadelphia Eagles. In addition, Howell signed up two returning servicemen, end Ken MacAfee and linebacker Cliff Livingston.

It was a new look, and it was a better one. The Howell-led Giants won four of their first five games in 1954. The snarling and the boos at the Polo Grounds disappeared, and more people began to take seats in the stadium on Giant-game Sundays. But the Giants were once again having trouble with Paul Brown's dynasty from Cleveland. They fell to them twice in 1954, as the invincible Browns marched to their fifth consecutive conference title.

The Giants won seven of their twelve games that year, a much-improved record over 1953. And there was a lot

Kyle Rote, an All-American tailback from Southern Methodist University, signs his first pro contract with the Giants in 1951 under the delighted eyes of Wellington Mara. It signaled the beginning of an illustrious Giants career which would last through the 1961 season. (New York Giants)

to be optimistic about. Frank Gifford was proving to be a valuable and versatile back on offense, posting an average gain of 5.6 yards on each rush that year before being injured. Kyle Rote had become a capable receiver, complementing the passing game from his slot at halfback. Charlie Conerly was throwing well, and now that his line was blocking effectively for him he seemed happy to have resumed his career. Both ends Bob Schnelker and Ken MacAfee proved to be most able receivers. Only defensive back and defensive coordinator Tom Landry made All-Pro from the Giants that year, but everyone agreed things were looking up.

In 1954, NFL Commissioner Bert Bell had stood before a special press conference and announced, "The war is on." The conflict of figurative arms he was referring to was with Canada, the Canadian Football League to be precise, which had been raiding the National Football League for talent. It reached untenable proportions, Bell felt, when Giant Arnie Weinmeister, the finest tackle in the league, and Redskins quarterback Eddie LeBaron had been lured north of the border.

There were no prospects for peace or even a truce as the 1955 football season approached. Bell and some of the NFL owners had made concerted efforts to bring the Canadian forays to an end but had gotten nowhere. It had reached a point where the owners directed that all college players selected in the NFL draft that year were to be immediately and personally contacted in an effort to persuade them to stay and play in America.

The Giants were especially hard hit when three key linemen—Bill Albright, Ray Collins, and Billy Shipp—decided on Canada. The Maras had had it. "We've got to do something about it," Wellington Mara said. "We have to teach *them* a lesson, and I think I know how to do it. Let's go after the best they have. Let's turn the tide on them." And he did. The CFL's leading rusher and MVP in 1954 had been powerful halfback Alex Webster of the Montreal Alouettes. Webster had been a star running back at North Carolina State but had been cut from the Washington Redskins by Curly Lambeau before the 1953 season. In his last year of coaching in the NFL, Lambeau told Webster, "You're just not good enough to make it in the pros, son."

After an exceptional two years at Montreal, Webster was the most prized possession in the Canadian league. So Mara went after him and got him for the Giants, and although it was not, in the war between the leagues, the fall of Berlin, to the Canadian league it was akin to the D-day landing.

The Giants' first-round draft pick in 1955 was a halfback from Notre Dame, Joe Heap, who would carry the ball for them eight times during the regular season, gain

Andy Robustelli

Andy Robustelli, a native of Stamford, Connecticut, went to tiny Arnold College in Milford in his home state, hardly a breeding ground for future NFLers. But he made the pros; made it in fact all the way to the Pro Football Hall of Fame.

Don Smith, of that illustrious organization, wrote:

> Andy Robustelli almost didn't make it to the Pro Football Hall of Fame for the really excellent reason that he almost didn't play pro football.
>
> Andy was drafted in the 19th round by the Los Angeles Rams in 1951 and the only "bonus" he received was his air transportation to the California training camp of the Rams. Even if he stuck with the club, his starting salary was set at $4,250!
>
> For long hours, Robustelli and his wife Jean weighed the possibility of a pro football career against a high school teaching job which "would offer more security." Even some of his closest friends advised him to take the job. . . .
>
> Once he made the decision to report to the Rams—camp opened on his second wedding anniversary—Robustelli immediately had reason to doubt the wisdom of his choice. He had been considered an outstanding offensive end in college but with the Rams, he would have to compete with a host of talented veterans, including future Hall of Famers Tom Fears and Elroy "Crazylegs" Hirsch.
>
> How could a raw rookie from a small college beat out those guys?
>
> The answer, of course, was that he couldn't and Rams coach Joe Stydahar immediately informed him of this.
>
> "If you make it AT ALL," he instructed Robustelli, "it will be as a defensive end and that is where we are going to give you your shot."

Robustelli was honored as an All-Pro defensive end seven times in his fourteen-year NFL career, five of them as a New York Giant, and was inducted into the Pro Football Hall of Fame in 1971.

29 yards, and then depart the pro game for good. But they fared much better with some of their later picks that year. There was Roosevelt "Rosey" Grier, a six-foot-five-inch defensive tackle from Penn State, who was somewhere between 260 and 280 pounds when he arrived at his first training camp, depending on who is telling the story. Then there was fullback Mel Triplett from Toledo and defensive back Jim Patton, who had played for Mississippi. In a trade with the Los Angeles Rams, Mara picked up linebacker Harland Svare. They were handsome additions to a roster that still boasted names like Gifford, Rote, Schnelker, MacAfee, Brown, Tunnell, and Landry.

GIANTS OFFENSE

Y. A. Tittle (14) passes to Joe Morrison (40) in a game against the Cleveland Browns. Players to the left are Darrell Dess (62), Phil King (24), and Frank Parker (78).

Two immovable objects: Rosey Brown (79), the Giants' great blocker, and Paul Wiggin, Cleveland's great defensive tackle, in a standoff at Yankee Stadium.

Frank Gifford (16) heads for the goal line past Bob Pellegrini (53) of the Redskins.

Rob Carpenter (26) vaulting the line against the Rams.

Kyle Rote (44) eludes Philadelphia's Tom Brookshier.

The late Doug Kotar (44) fights his way for extra yardage against the Cowboys. No. 53 is Bob Breunig.

Zeke Mowatt (84) pulls down a pass in the Dallas end zone, as Butch Woolfolk (25), and two defenders watch.

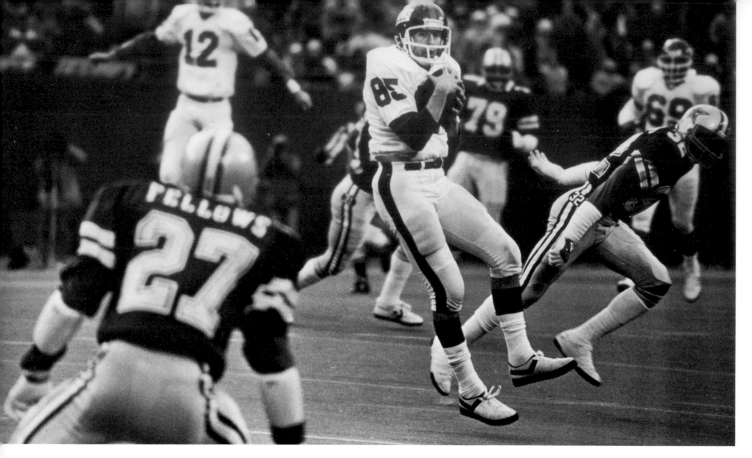

John Mistler (85) clutches a pass from Scott Brunner (12), as Ron Fellows of the Cowboys moves in.

Joe Morris (20) bursts through a large gap in the Pittsburgh line as defensive back Dwayne Woodruff (49) tries to close it.

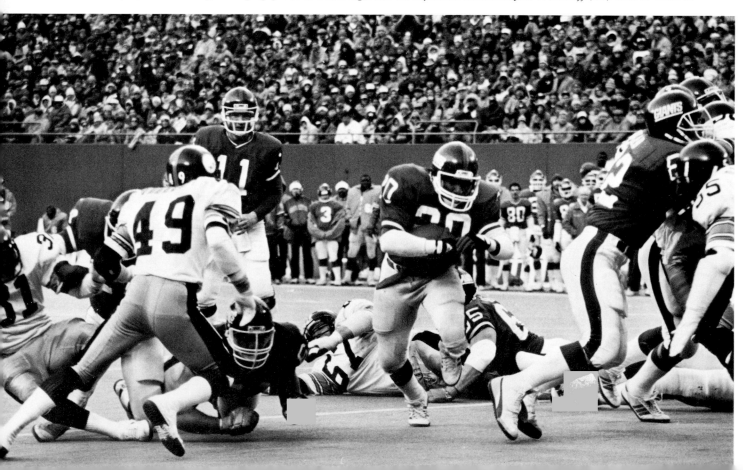

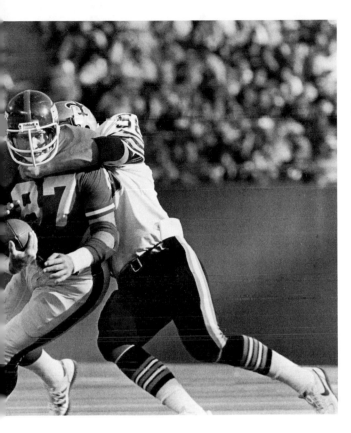

Tight end Gary Shirk (87) carries a New Orleans Saint on his back. Note the defender's right hand reaching in to strip the ball.

Ron Johnson, the first Giant to gain 1,000 yards rushing in a season.

Wide receiver Earnest Gray (83), one step behind Green Bay defender Estus Hood (38), pulls in a pass, sprints for the end zone, and raises the ball in triumph.

There was a lot of hope for the Giants of 1955 in the front office. The team seemed to be truly taking shape. Jack Mara was quoted in the *New York Times:* "We are a strong team, capable of meeting and defeating any team in the league." The fans and the sportswriters were a little more skeptical, however, and that became evident both at the box office and in the space devoted to Giants football on the New York sports pages. In 1954, the Giants had drawn a little more than 190,400 fans into the Polo Grounds, far below the more than 326,000 that the Los Angeles Rams and the Detroit Lions had attracted to their stadiums, or the 269,000-plus credited to the San Francisco 49ers and the 243,000-plus to the Chicago Bears. In 1955, the Giants would drop to a figure of 183,847 in home attendance, one of the few teams in the NFL to lose at the box office that year.

Part of that problem was attributable to the Giants' awful start in 1955. Despite a seemingly stellar cast taking the field, they lost decisively in the opening three games to the Philadelphia Eagles, Chicago Cardinals, and Pittsburgh Steelers, all second-rate teams in their conference. Those three games had been on the road, so when the Giants arrived at the Polo Grounds for their home opener against the Cardinals, they were the only team in the NFL Eastern Conference without a win to its credit.

The foremost power in the conference that year was the Cleveland Browns. Otto Graham was still around, although he had threatened to retire before the season, backed up at quarterback by George Ratterman. And so were Dante Lavelli, Lou Groza, Frank Gatski, Abe Gibron, and Len Ford, as well as such relatively eminent newcomers as Curley Morrison, Ed Modzelewski, and Chuck Noll, among others. The Washington Redskins were another force with which to contend since Eddie LeBaron had decided to come back from Canada, and they also had former Heisman Trophy winner Vic Janowicz to carry the ball and kick field goals and extra points for them.

The Giants went into their first encounter with the Redskins with the undistinguished record of one win and four losses, but proceeded to destroy the favored Redskins, 35–7. The next week, however, they fell to the Browns, a team that, at this point in the season, with a record of 6–1, had virtually wrapped up the conference title, at least as far as the Giants were concerned.

There were five more games remaining in the 1955 season, and that was when the Giants offered the harbinger of what was to come. They stomped all over the Baltimore Colts and the Philadelphia Eagles, the defense allowing each team only a single touchdown. Then Cleveland came to the Polo Grounds for a game that would prove to be historic. It was to be the last Giants game played in the Polo Grounds, the team's home since its inception back in 1925. (The Maras had decided to move

The first-round draft pick of 1952 for the Giants was a providential one: halfback Frank Gifford from Southern Cal. He starred for the Giants for twelve years (missing 1961 because of a concussion suffered in the last game of the 1960 season), earning All-Pro honors four times and making eight trips to the Pro Bowl. The Giff is the second leading all-time scorer for the Giants (484 points: 78 TDs, 2 FGs, 10 PATs), the second-leading pass receiver (with 367 catches), and the third-leading rusher (with 3,609 yards). He was inducted into the Pro Football Hall of Fame in 1977. (New York Giants)

to the more spacious Yankee Stadium after the 1955 season.)

And the game with the conference-leading Browns was a fitting cap to all the pro football excitement that had occurred on the grass beneath Coogan's Bluff during the thirty-one years the Giants held court there. Going into the fourth quarter, the score was tied at 21 apiece. The Browns marched in the final period and iced the drive with a touchdown when Ed "Big Mo" Modzelewski bucked in from the 1-yard line. But the Giants came right back with a drive of their own and climaxed it when Charlie Conerly rifled one to Kyle Rote in the end zone. The 28–28 tie did not last long in that volatile quarter. A few minutes later the Giants had the ball again, but this time Conerly's pass ended up in the hands of Cleveland linebacker Chuck Noll, who returned it for a touchdown.

An undaunted Conerly came right back, passing the Giants down the field until he culminated the drive with a touchdown pass to Frank Gifford. The score stood at 35–35. Thirty-three-year-old Otto Graham, playing out his last season as a pro, was not to be outdone, however. He moved the ball steadily against a desperately clawing New York defense as time wore down to the final seconds. Graham got the Browns just inside the New York 15-yard line, with fourth down and only a few seconds on the clock. In came Lou, the ever-faithful toe, Groza, by this time universally recognized as the finest placekicker in history of the game. The holder lined up just back of the 20-yard line, a straight line from him directly through the goalposts. But in a flash after Groza's immortal toe sunk into the ball Giants linebacker Pat Knight got high enough to slap the ball away, and the final score remained 35–35.

The Giants left the Polo Grounds for the last time that afternoon, went out and won their last two games, beating a favored Redskins team and the Detroit Lions to round out a 6–5–1 season. What was most pleasant about it was that the team had gotten its act together in midseason and had turned into not just a winning club but also a dominating force in the conference.

It was the beginning of a new Giants era. They would do justice to the house that Babe Ruth built over in the Bronx. Like the Yankees that ruled the baseball world so often, the football Giants would begin an eight-year epic of outstanding football in which they would lay claim to their conference title six times and become a fixture in NFL championship games.

Kyle Rote, with a look of grim determination, takes off around end in this 1953 game. Rote was the team's leading pass receiver that year, but the Giants had a dismal 3–9 record and ended up in fifth place in the NFL East. No. 31 is Giants fullback Eddie Price. (New York Giants)

Steve Owen accepts a silver token of the Giants' esteem for his sterling career as coach of the Giants on the occasion of his retirement from the job after the 1953 season. Looking on are the Giant owners: (from left to right) Wellington, Tim, and Jack. (New York Giants)

Defensive back Dick Nolan, from Maryland's national championship team of 1953, joined the Giants in 1954 and stayed through the 1957 season. Nolan played in the defensive backfield with Tom Landry and later served as an assistant to Landry in Dallas before moving on to head coaching jobs with the San Francisco 49ers and the New Orleans Saints. (New York Giants)

Two Giants youths, Frank Gifford (left) and quarterback Don Heinrich (right), visit with then Vice President Richard Nixon at West Point, where all three were attending President Eisenhower's Youth Fitness Conference. (New York Giants)

Ray Poole, posed here, was only one of three members of the famous football-playing Poole family of Mississippi who at one time or another donned a Giants uniform. An end, Ray played for New York from 1947 to 1952. His brother Barney, also an end, was an All-American at both Army and Mississippi and played for the Giants in 1954. The oldest brother, Jim, still another end, played with the Giants from 1937 through 1941. (New York Giants)

Bill Svoboda became a Giant in 1954, acquired in a trade with the Chicago Cardinals. He held a linebacking slot until retiring from the game after the 1958 season. (New York Giants)

Dick Alban (42) of the Redskins picks off a pass from Charlie Conerly intended for Frank Gifford (16) in this 1954 game. The Giants destroyed Washington, however, in both their encounters that year: 51–21 in the nation's capital and 24–7 at the Polo Grounds. No. 89 on the Redskins is defensive end Joe Tereshinski. (New York Giants)

Roosevelt "Rosey" Grier, after three years as the cornerstone of the Penn State line, joined the Giants in 1955. One of the most imposing defensive tackles of his time, Grier played seven years with the Giants, missing the 1957 season for military service, before going to Los Angeles to join the Rams' famous "Fearsome Foursome." (New York Giants)

Frank Gifford finds plenty of running room in this 1955 game against the Eagles—the next to last game that the Giants played in the Polo Grounds. They beat Philadelphia that day, 31–7. The other Giants are guard Jack Stroud (66) and quarterback Charlie Conerly (42); the Eagles are tackle Lum Snyder (73) and linebacker Bob Hudson (being blocked by Stroud). (New York Giants)

Giants defensive end Walt Yowarsky has the leg of Pittsburgh halfback Lynn Chandnois and is not about to let go of it in this 1955 game at the Polo Grounds. New York lost that day, 19–17, one of five losses against six wins and a tie during that third-place season. No. 61 of the Giants is defensive lineman Ray Beck. (New York Giants)

Mel Triplett, one of seventeen children of a Mississippi share-cropper, honed his running skills at the University of Toledo before being drafted by the Giants in 1955. The powerful full-back played for the Giants through the 1960 season before moving to the Minnesota Vikings. Triplett is the tenth leading rusher in Giants history, toting up 2,289 yards. (New York Giants)

Harland Svare was traded to New York by the Rams in 1955 and was a key linebacker through the 1960 season, playing in three NFL title games. Svare served as an assistant coach with the Giants after retiring as a player and later went on to head coaching jobs with the Los Angeles Rams and the San Diego Chargers. (New York Giants)

One of the smallest players drafted by the Giants in 1955 was six-foot, 180-pound defensive back Jimmy Patton from Mississippi, who would turn out to be one of the biggest contributors to the Giants' awesome defense over the next decade. Patton made All-Pro five times, and his 52 interceptions are exceeded in New York history only by Emlen Tunnell's 74. (New York Giants)

Alex Webster was recruited from the Canadian Football League by Wellington Mara and made his New York debut in 1955. For the next ten years he would prove to be one of the Giants' all-time greatest running backs. No one in team history has rushed for more yardage than the 4,638 he gained, and only Joe Morris has more rushing touchdowns than his 39. The 336 points Webster scored on 56 touchdowns ranks him as the fifth-highest New York scorer. Webster came back as head coach of the Giants from 1969 through 1973, compiling a 29–40–1 record. (Pro Football Hall of Fame)

9

The Famine's Over

The last sporting event New Yorkers were treated to at Yankee Stadium before the Giants made their debut in that illustrious edifice was the fifth game of the 1956 World Series, the one in which Yankee hurler Don Larsen pitched the only perfect game in Series history. When this fact was mentioned by one of the coaching staff to the players during a session devoted to extolling their new home, one player allegedly remarked to head coach Jim Lee Howell, "And you want us to top that?" When Howell did not respond, the player added, "Do we get more than one game to do it?"

Jack and Wellington Mara as well as coach Howell were expecting good things from their ballclub that year. They had gone out and rounded up a number of new faces, in what would prove to be one of the most lucrative bounties of acquisition in the club's history. The first-round draft choice, fullback Henry Moore, notwithstanding—he would spend only a year on the Giants' bench before being dealt to the Colts—New York drafted Sam Huff, a twenty-one-year-old linebacker from the coal-mining region of West Virginia who had made several All-American teams playing for the state university there. They also drafted a defensive end from Dayton, whose name was menacing but as yet not well known in the national football community; Jim Katcavage. They also drafted punter, placekicker, and occasional halfback Don Chandler from Florida.

In trades, New York first acquired defensive end Andy Robustelli from the Rams. Next was Dick "Little Mo" Modzelewski from the Steelers, who told coach Howell on his arrival, "Last year, you know, Brown [Paul, coach of

the Cleveland Browns] made a trade for my brother [Ed] and won the championship. This year it's your turn." And to augment the defensive backfield Ed Hughes was acquired, also from Los Angeles. Infusing this flush of savagery and talent into a defense that already boasted such stalwarts as Rosey Grier, Harland Svare, Bill Svoboda, Emlen Tunnell, Dick Nolan, and Jim Patton, New York now had the foundation of what was to become one of the most legendary fortifications in pro football history.

This was combined with an offense that featured Frank Gifford, Charlie Conerly, Alex Webster, and Mel Triplett in the backfield, along with receivers like Kyle Rote and Ken MacAfee, and a line to protect them peopled by the likes of Rosey Brown, Jack Stroud, Dick Yelvington, and Ray Wietecha. There was reason in New York City to be optimistic.

The Giants were scheduled to play their first three games on the road in order to accommodate the New York Yankees, the almost perennial hosts of the World Series. The Browns and the Redskins had been the powerhouses of the NFL East the year before. Cleveland in fact was the reigning NFL champ. But Paul Brown had lost Otto Graham to retirement, and many of his other old-line veterans had slowed noticeably. And Washington had lost Vic Janowicz, who had been severely injured in an automobile accident during training camp.

The Giants opened the season in San Francisco. The 49ers had had a miserable season the year before and were now under the tutelage of their former quarterback Frankie Albert. They had Y. A. Tittle at quarterback and such running backs as Hugh McElhenny, Joe Perry, and

John Henry Johnson, but their defense left much to be desired. And the Giants took advantage of it, racking up 38 points while allowing the San Franciscans just 21.

The next game brought them to Chicago to face the Cardinals, who had surprised the title-bearing Browns in their opener. Behind the running of Ollie Matson and the passing of Lamar McHan, the Cardinals proved they were a force to contend with that year by beating the Giants, 35–27. On to Cleveland and the faltering Browns, where the doom of the "electronic quarterbacks" was sealed (see sidebar); there New York sent the longtime ruler of the NFL East reeling, a fall that would continue throughout the season and result in the team's first finish below .500. The score was 21–9, and as the Giants returned to New York to introduce themselves in their new Bronx home there was a lot of ink in the local papers about the heartening prospects of this new New York Giants team.

The Steelers, who had finished last in the NFL East the year before, were in a state of reconstruction, or so their public relations staff stated. Quarterbacked by Ted Marchibroda, they had upset the Redskins in their home opener but then lost the next two. They were to serve as the bow on which the Giants would break the bottle of champagne to christen Yankee Stadium.

By October 21, the Yankees had abandoned the stadium after trimming the Brooklyn Dodgers in the World Series, and such illustrious baseballers as Mickey Mantle,

The Famine's Over, 1956

New York Giants		Chicago Bears
Kyle Rote	LE	Harlon Hill
Rosey Brown	LT	Bill Wightkin
Bill Austin	LG	Herman Clark
Ray Wietecha	C	Larry Strickland
Jack Stroud	RG	Stan Jones
Dick Yelvington	RT	Kline Gilbert
Ken MacAfee	RE	Bill McColl
Don Heinrich	QB	George Blanda
Frank Gifford	LH	Bob Watkins
Alex Webster	RH	John Hoffman
Mel Triplett	FB	Rick Casares

Giants	13	21	6	7 —	47
Bears	0	7	0	0 —	7

Touchdowns—*Giants:* Triplett, Webster (2), Moore, Rote, Gifford; *Bears:* Casares. Field goals—*Giants:* Agajanian (2).

PATs—*Giants:* Agajanian (5); *Bears:* Blanda.

Razzle-Dazzle, 1956 Style

From a Giants program of the time:

The Giants must be the hardest team in the National League to scout. Every week, Coach Jim Lee Howell and his staff come up with some fancy new offensive wrinkle. The "Belly 26 Reverse Pass" from Gifford to MacAfee that scored the first touchdown against Washington last Sunday was a real gem. It involved faked handoffs by Don Heinrich to Mel Triplett, plunging into the line, and then to Alex Webster, slicing toward his left tackle. Don then delivered the ball to Gifford, who had started to his left from left halfback, then wheeled back to the right. Led by Jack Stroud, who executed a reverse pull from right guard, Gifford headed out around right end. With an option to run or pass, he passed when he saw that MacAfee had a lead on Washington's left corner man, who had been drawn in by the faked runs to the other side, and threw a 35-yard strike to Ken in the end zone.

Yogi Berra, Billy Martin, Hank Bauer, Gil McDougald, Enos Slaughter, Whitey Ford, and Don Larsen had emptied their lockers so the Giants could fill them with pads and cleats and helmets. The Giants took the field that afternoon before 48,108 expectant fans. And they got what they came to see, a New York rout. With Conerly passing well, Gifford doing everything right, and the defense simply overwhelming the Steelers, the Giants walked off with a 38–10 victory to inaugurate nearly a decade of exceptional football in New York.

The Eagles and the Steelers again fell to the Giants before the obviously rejuvenated Chicago Cardinals came to Yankee Stadium. The Giants were 5–1, and so were the Cardinals, both well ahead of the rest of the division. Even this early in the season, it was clearly a two-team race for the divisional crown.

Coach Jim Lee Howell and his two assistants, Vince Lombardi and Tom Landry, knew that to win they had to stop the Cards' running game, principally that of the division's leading ground gainer, Ollie Matson, but also the power rushes of fullback Johnny Olszewski. The coaches felt that if the Giants could control the run, the Chicagoans' preferred mode of attack, the game was theirs. Middle linebacker Sam Huff was given the chore of keying on Matson, and, after a series of brutal hits he made it clear to the Cardinal running back that he was in for a painful day. And for the Giants it was the defense that carried the day. Matson was held to a mere 43 yards rushing, and the team to 10 points. Meanwhile the Giants' offense put 23 points on the board and gained sole pos-

NEW YORK GIANTS
1956 WORLD'S CHAMPIONS

1956 NEW YORK FOOTBALL GIANTS

First row: Ray Wietecha, Jim Patton, Herb Rich, Gene Filipski, Mel Triplett, Kyle Rote, Coach Jim Lee Howell, Bill Svoboda, Dick Modzelewski, Walt Yowarsky, Sam Huff, Gerald Huth, Dick Yelvington, Wellington Mara, Pete Previte.

Second row: John Johnson, John Dziegiel, Dick Nolan, Jack Stroud, Frank Gifford, Charley Conerly, Don Heinrich, Ray Beck, Ed Hughes, Roosevelt Brown Jr., Henry Moore, Harland Svare, Ed Kolman, Ken Kavanaugh, Pete Sheehy.

Third row: Em Tunnell, Bob Clatterbuck, Jim Katcavage, Andy Robustelli, Cliff Livingston, Alex Webster, Ken MacAfee, Roosevelt Grier, Bob Schnelker, Bill Austin, Don Chandler, Sid Moret, Tom Landry, Vince Lombardi.

session of first place in the NFL East. After the game, Huff, a rookie in only his third game as a starter, was asked by a New York sportswriter about the savagery with which he went after All-Pro Matson. "I learned right off," he said, "there's no room for nice guys in pro football. When I go out there on the field, I'm mad at everyone. The hell with them all. Tell them to look out for old Sam Huff. He's mean today."

The game had been an important one, and the Giants had prevailed in such a way that a letdown the following week was not improbable. But one like that which occurred in Washington was totally unexpected. The Redskins had gotten off to a miserable start, losing their first three games in a row, but they were on a roll when New York came down, counting three wins in a row. And they added a fourth with devastating force, by crushing the Giants 33–7.

It was a game the Giants had wanted particularly to win because the next week the Chicago Bears were coming to Yankee Stadium, bringing with them a record of 7–1. They were tied for first place in the NFL West and naturally not anxious to jeopardize their race to the title with a loss to New York. Their offense was the best in the entire NFL that year, concentrated around the powerful running of fullback Rick Casares and the passes of Ed Brown to Harlon Hill and Bill McColl. The defense showcased future Hall of Famers Doug Atkins and Bill George.

But the Monsters of the Midway, as they were called around Chicago, hardly seemed the stuff of their press clippings, at least through the first three quarters of the game that day at Yankee Stadium. The Giants took a 17–3 lead into the final period, confident their defense would maintain the game for them. But it did not, and the two touchdowns the Bears scored before time ran out gave them a tie at the final whistle.

A rebound win over Washington was more than satisfying after the way the Giants had been treated down in the nation's capital two weeks earlier. Next up was Cleveland, with an unprecedented lowly record of 4–6. The Giants, playing at home, were a solid favorite. The team's chief scout, Jack Lavelle, a corpulent character about town, who, if he had not been real, could well have been a creation from the pen of Damon Runyon or Paul Gallico, was wary, however, after having watched the Browns defeat the Eagles the week before. Lavelle wrote in an article for the game program:

> I have warned Jim Lee Howell to tell the boys to be ready to fight for their lives today. Those Browns will come to town with the sincere meanness that you develop when somebody takes something you own. They held the Eastern Conference

title for so long that they figured it belonged to them permanently. I promise that they will not look upon the Giants with friendly eyes.

Portly Jack Lavelle was absolutely correct. The bloodthirsty Browns came and left with a 24–7 shellacking of the Giants. But, as it turned out, it didn't matter. Out in Chicago, the Cardinals fell to their crosstown rivals, the Bears, leaving them with a record of 6–5. The resurgent Washington Redskins had also lost that weekend to the Steelers, reducing their record to 6–5 as well. The Giants, standing at 7–3–1, had clinched the division title. The victory the following week over Philadelphia was superfluous, but it did give them their best record since 1951.

Not since 1950 had a Giants team earned its way to the NFL championship game. And not only were they there in 1956, but the oddsmakers gave them a slight edge over the Chicago Bears, whose record of 9–2–1 was just a smidgen better than the 9–3 Detroit Lions in the NFL West.

The afternoon of December 30 was bitterly cold in New York, as it had been all the previous week, and the field was a marble slab. The Giants were prepared for it, having obtained basketball shoes the day before (see sidebar). That was apparent to the 56,836 bundled-up fans in Yankee Stadium from the opening kickoff. Gene Filipski took it for the Giants and streaked 53 yards with it. Three plays later the Giants were at the Bears' 17-yard line. Mel Triplett hit the middle of the Bears' line, shook off a tackle or two, and plowed straight through to the end zone. On the Bears' possession, Rick Casares fumbled the ball, and New York recovered, capitalizing on it with a Ben Agajanian field goal, the first of two from him that period.

In the second quarter, the Giants increased their lead to 20–0 when Alex Webster plunged in from the 3-yard line. The Bears then got on the scoreboard when Casares found a hole and bulled his way 9 yards for a touchdown. But the Giants were in total control. One writer aptly put it, remembering the famous "sneakers" game of 1934, "As some racehorses take to mud the Giants in title contention apparently took to ice." Two more New York touchdowns were scored before the half, and the Giants went to the locker room with a 34–7 lead.

The game was really over before the third quarter started. But the Giants kept going. Charlie Conerly, who had come off the bench in the second quarter, hit Kyle Rote for a touchdown and then found Frank Gifford for the Giants' sixth touchdown of the day. The final score: Giants 47, Bears 7.

It was the Giants' first NFL championship since 1938 when they had drubbed the Green Bay Packers in the old Polo Grounds. In 1956, each victorious Giants player received $3,779.19 for his effort; back in 1938, the take

Howell's Best

Ten years after Steve Owen picked his all-time Giants team of the first quarter-century (1925–50), coach Jim Lee Howell was asked to list his all-time Giants postwar team (1946–60). The best were, according to Howell:

Offense

Ends	Kyle Rote	(1951–61)
	Bill Swiacki	(1948–50)
Tackles	Rosey Brown	(1953–65)
	Tex Coulter	(1946–52)
Guards	Jack Stroud	(1953–64)
	Len Younce	(1941–48)
Center	Ray Wietecha	(1953–62)
	(also) John Rapacz	(1950–54)
Quarterback	Charlie Conerly	(1948–61)
Halfbacks	Frank Gifford	(1952–60, 1962–64)
	Alex Webster	(1955–64)
Fullback	Eddie Price	(1950–55)

Defense

Ends	Andy Robustelli	(1956–64)
	Ray Poole	(1947–52)
Tackles	Arnie Weinmeister	(1950–53)
	Al DeRogatis	(1949–52)
Linebackers	John Cannady	(1947–54)
	Bill Svoboda	(1954–58)
	Sam Huff	(1956–63)
Halfbacks	Otto Schnellbacher	(1950–51)
	Tom Landry	(1950–55)
Safeties	Emlen Tunnell	(1948–58)
	Jim Patton	(1955–58)

had only been $504.45.

With the Yankees winning the World Series and the Giants winning the NFL championship, it had been a most worthy year in Yankee Stadium. No one on the Giants made individual history in the vein of Don Larsen, but the statistics were noteworthy. Frank Gifford was the fifth most productive rusher in the league with 819 yards, and his 5.2-yard-per-carry average was outstanding; the Giff was the third top receiver in the NFL with 51 catches for 603 yards. He scored 9 touchdowns and passed for 2 others, and was an easy choice for All-Pro.

Charlie Conerly threw for 1,143 yards, including 10 touchdowns, and was ranked number three among all quarterbacks in the NFL that year. Sam Huff was named Rookie of the Year. Besides Gifford, others achieving All-Pro honors included Emlen Tunnell, Andy Robustelli, Rosey Brown, and Rosey Grier.

It would not have been surprising if Jack and Wellington Mara had closed the books on the year humming "This could be the start of something grand."

It turned out to be less than grand in 1957, however, but it was still an exciting season, at least until the last three games. There were essentially no new faces, the Giants having given up their first-round draft choice in an earlier trade, but there was a conspicuous absence. All-Pro tackle Rosey Grier had departed for the army and would spend the season at Fort Dix, New Jersey, instead of Yankee Stadium.

For the most part, preseason picks had the Giants repeating as the NFL champ. Most felt the runner-up Cardi-

nals of the year before had played over their heads, and that would prove to be true. The Browns were certainly going to be helped by their first-round draft choice, a muscular six-foot-two-inch, 228-pound, twenty-one-year-old running back named Jim Brown, although no one then realized just how much a factor he would become in the NFL.

The Giants were wary of him, however. Tom Landry went on record on various occasions, touting the danger Brown presented to any team he ran against, including the vaunted defense of the Giants. He even designed a special defense to thwart him, basically having Sam Huff key on Brown on practically every play.

With Jim Brown, Paul Brown's Browns quickly proved they were a restored champion. The Giants met them on opening day in 1957 in Cleveland, and the battle went right down to the last minute of the ballgame. Landry's special defense worked against the Browns, although Jim Brown gained 87 yards rushing and averaged over 4 yards per carry, holding them to a mere 3 points until the

Roosevelt "Rosie" Brown blocks Cleveland's Paul Wiggins (84) as Frank Gifford slips through with the ball. Brown played at Morgan State before joining the Giants in 1953. The ultimate blocking tackle, he paved the way for New York runners and protected Giants passers through the 1965 season, earning All-Pro recognition eight times. He was inducted into the Pro Football Hall of Fame in 1975. (Fred Roe)

Thanks for a Late Plane

One of the most often-told tales among Giants nostalgics concerns a pair of twenty-one-year-old disheartened rookies in 1956, linebacker Sam Huff and kicker Don Chandler, whose professional careers almost ended before they ever began.

Huff, a third-round draft choice, and Chandler, a fifth-rounder, were not happy with the way things were going at the Giants' training camp up at St. Michael's College in Winooski, Vermont. Huff had played tackle at West Virginia, but, at six foot one inch and 230 pounds, he was considered too small for that position in the pros. The rumor that a few of the coaches thought he was too slow for any other position got back to him, and he was, in his words, "disheartened, miserable, and homesick." Chandler was suffering from an injured shoulder and not doing well in camp, and therefore was often the butt of Jim Lee Howell's "bellering," as the players called the coach's remonstrations.

One day after workouts, the two decided it was hopeless and that they might as well go home. Line coach Ed Kolman heard about the situation and cornered Huff. "You'll never forgive yourself if you leave now," he told him. "You'll feel like a quitter."

Huff shook his head. "It's not working out. I'm just wasting my time here."

"I've seen some great ones," Kolman said. "And I think if you stick it out you could be one of them in a few years. You've got talent, and I mean it. Don't throw it away by leaving."

The vote of confidence was enough to persuade Huff to stay, but when the linebacker tried to talk Chandler out of departing he couldn't. So he agreed to drive his friend to the airport in Burlington, Vermont. What happened there is described by Don Smith, former publicity chief of the Giants, in a book he wrote in 1960.

There they were informed that Chandler's flight would be late. It might be an hour or more before he could leave. The players drifted into the hot waiting room and plopped down on a bench. As the minutes ticked by, Huff began to wonder if he'd made the right decision; whether or not he should get his bags and join Chandler as they had originally planned. Despite Kolman's comforting words, Sam was losing his confidence again.

Just then a station wagon roared up to the terminal and out bolted [Vince] Lombardi. He dashed through the waiting room and pursued Chandler almost to the revved-up plane, which had just taxied up to the passenger gate.

"Hold on," Lombardi shouted in a voice that was disturbingly familiar to all Giant rookies. "You may not make this ballclub, Chandler, but you're sure as hell not quitting on me

now. And neither are you, Huff, in case you've got any ideas about running out." With that, he packed the the rookies into the station wagon and delivered them back to camp.

"If that plane had been on time," Huff recalls, "Chandler would have been on it. And maybe I would have gone with him."

Electronic Quarterbacks

There was an innovation in pro football at the start of the 1956 season, referred to in the press as "electronic quarterbacks." The electronics referred to were devices that allowed a coach on the sidelines to communicate by radio directly to his quarterback on the field, who had a receiver in his helmet.

In the offices of the National Football League, especially the one belonging to Commissioner Bert Bell, the practice was "absurd, disruptive to the game, and takes away the human element." Still, many teams were using the devices as the season got under way, but not the Giants, at least in the way the other teams were.

When the Giants traveled to Cleveland for the third game of the season, they brought some transistors of their own along. But not for Jim Lee Howell to talk from the sideline to Charlie Conerly on the field. Instead they were set to the wavelength that Cleveland coach Paul Brown was transmitting over to his quarterback, George Ratterman. Rookie end Bob Topp sat on the bench with earphones, picking up the plays Brown was sending to his quarterback. Topp quickly relayed them to defensive coach Tom Landry, who, in turn, shouted them to his defense on the field.

It only lasted for several plays, however, and then Ratterman disconnected the receiver because he could no longer hear Brown over the roar of the crowd.

Commissioner Bell, a few days later, decided radio communications and electronic spying on the field was just too much and outlawed the whole thing. "It was a good thing," Giant end and chief spy Bob Topp said later. "If the trend continued, the number-one draft choice of the Giants next year would probably have been the valedictorian of MIT."

last twenty seconds of the game. Unfortunately the Giants could post no more than three themselves, and with just a third of a minute left to play the sure-footed Lou Groza came on to kick a 47-yard game-winning field goal.

The Giants rebounded with three straight wins over the Eagles, Redskins, and Steelers, but then were stunned by a fired-up Washington team in a 31–14 embarrassment. It was forgotten over the next four weeks, however, as the Giants rolled to four consecutive victories, giving them a record of 7–2 for the season. It was only good for second place in the NFL East because a revived Browns powerhouse had carried Cleveland to a 7–1–1 record.

Then, for some still unexplainable reason, the football field fell out from under the Giants, and they lost their last three games to San Francisco, Pittsburgh, and finally Cleveland. In the Browns game, however, the Giants gave them a mighty fight despite the fact they were already out of any chance for the title. They lost, 34–24, but they left a distinct impression on Paul Brown that the Giants were

the team to worry about in the upcoming season. "We beat them twice last year," he said before the start of the 1958 season, "but we were in two brutal battles. They're the team that will give us the most trouble."

New York ended up with a record of 7–5 in 1957. Frank Gifford, Andy Robustelli, and Rosey Brown were named All-Pro. Charlie Conerly had a good year, passing for 1,712 yards and 11 touchdowns, good enough to rank him number four among all NFL quarterbacks. Gifford had led the Giants in rushing (528 yards, 3.9-yard average) and in receiving (41 catches for 588 yards). And Don Chandler led the entire NFL with a punting average of 44.6 yards, which also set a Giants record.

Although the season was a bit of a disappointment, one would shortly be able to look on the bright side and deem it nothing more than an intermission between NFL championship games. The Giants were about to treat New Yorkers to a marvelous six years of football in which they would prevail in their division five times.

Sneakers Game II

If the Super Bowl warrants Roman numerals, so should the two classic "sneakers" games played between the Giants and the Chicago Bears. In 1934, little Abe Cohen was the hero of the hour; in 1956 it was somewhat of a joint effort.

Wellington Mara remembered the 1934 classic that was saved by his team's wearing basketball shoes in the second half. And when he saw how frozen the field was the week before the 1956 title game, he talked with coach Jim Lee Howell about the situation and the shoes that might just make a difference.

Howell tested the turf. He sent back Gene Filipski out to run around wearing basketball shoes and defensive back Ed Hughes with cleated shoes. Hughes slid about on the frozen field, but Filipski ran smoothly. So Mara and Howell spoke with defensive end Andy Robustelli, who, on the side, had a sporting goods store, and asked him to put through a rush order for rubber-soled basketball shoes. As Robustelli recalls, "It was for four dozen pairs, sizes nine to thirteen."

The order came through in time, and the ever-responsible defensive end carted them to Yankee Stadium for the Giants. It helped once again. Perhaps even more in 1956: the Giants won, 47–7, and in 1934 they had only won by a score of 30–13.

One of the game's all-time great defensive ends, Andy Robustelli came out of Arnold College, a school not overly well known for its football teams, and served a five year apprenticeship with the Rams before donning a Giants jersey in 1956. He was named All-Pro five times as a Giant (and twice previously with Los Angeles). He was inducted into the Pro Football Hall of Fame in 1971. (Fred Roe)

Frank Gifford (16) was at the acme of his career in 1956, shown here carrying the ball along the road to an NFL championship. Gifford led the team in scoring (65 points), rushing (819 yards), and receiving (51 catches for 603 yards), and predictably was named All-Pro. The other Giants here are Gene Filipski (40), Jack Spinks (62), and Mel Triplett (33). (Fred Roe)

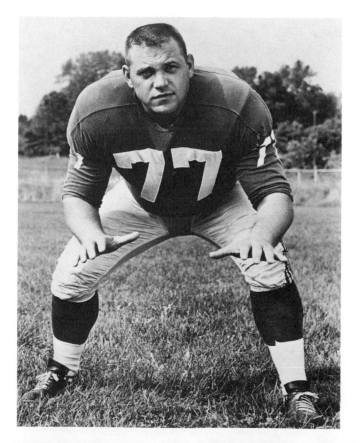

Dick "Little Mo" Modzelewski was traded to the Giants by the Steelers in 1956 and took his place in a line that featured such stalwarts as Andy Robustelli, Rosey Grier, and Jim Katcavage. Modzelewski stayed with New York through the 1963 season, then went over to the Cleveland Browns. "Little Mo" was anything but little—he weighed about 260 pounds during most of his Giants career. (New York Giants)

Don Chandler almost left the Giants before he was able to kick a single football, but the disillusioned kicker was brought back into the fold by assistant coach Vince Lombardi during summer camp in 1956. Chandler placekicked and punted for the Giants until 1965, when he was traded to the Green Bay Packers and was reunited with Lombardi. He still holds the Giants' record for the most PATs in a season (52), and the "Babe," as he was called by some, has the standard for punting average during a career (43.8 yards) and in a single season (46.6 in 1959). (New York Giants)

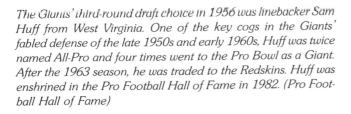

The Giants' third-round draft choice in 1956 was linebacker Sam Huff from West Virginia. One of the key cogs in the Giants' fabled defense of the late 1950s and early 1960s, Huff was twice named All-Pro and four times went to the Pro Bowl as a Giant. After the 1963 season, he was traded to the Redskins. Huff was enshrined in the Pro Football Hall of Fame in 1982. (Pro Football Hall of Fame)

The Giants and the Cleveland Browns have had some real roustabouts over the years. One who always contributed a certain amount of discomfort was Jim Brown (32), shown here awaiting a flat pass from Frank Ryan (13). The Giants defenders are Dick Modzelewski (77), Andy Robustelli (81), Rosey Grier (76), and Jim Katcavage, who is applying a bit of muscle to quarterback Ryan's upper torso. (New York Giants)

10

Sudden-Death Overtime

The year 1958 seemed filled with suspense and excitement on all fronts. The army launched the nation's first satellite into orbit around the earth, Explorer I, to initiate the space age. President Eisenhower sent the U.S. Marines into Lebanon, the first real military action since the Korean War ended. The New York Yankees, trailing the Milwaukee Braves in the World Series three games to one, pulled off a miraculous comeback, thanks to the hitting of Moose Skowron and Gil McDougald and the pitching of Bob Turley, and won the world championship of baseball, four games to three. And not to be outdone, the Giants treated New York football fans to one of the most heart-pounding, edge-of-the-seat seasons in the history of pro football.

The football year for the Giants would not go down merely to the last game of the regular season, although it was an absolutely crucial one for them, but to a winner-take-all conference playoff game, and the first sudden-death overtime championship game in NFL history.

It was the last year that Vince Lombardi and Tom Landry would be working together as an assistant coach tandem for Jim Lee Howell. The next year Lombardi would leave to take the head coaching job in Green Bay, and the year after that Landry would depart for the same position with the Dallas Cowboys. It was also the year that the Giants, with noticeable jubilation, welcomed Rosey Grier back from the army—and one in which they aided their cause substantially with a few key acquisitions. From the Chicago Cardinals, they got defensive back Lindon Crow and placekicker Pat Summerall, both of whom would make significant contributions in 1958. Al Barry, a fast,

strong offensive guard, was picked up from Green Bay, and defensive back Carl Karilivacz was obtained to back up the four regular secondary defenders. From the draft, most notable was Phil King, a hard-running six-foot-four-inch, 225 pound back from Vanderbilt, offensive tackle Frank Youso from Minnesota, and offensive guard Bob Mischak of Army.

The preseason was hardly a harbinger of what was to come, however. They lost five of six exhibition games, and Howell, Landry, and Lombardi were scrambling to figure out what was going wrong with a team so filled with proven talent.

The season opener with the Chicago Cardinals was set in Buffalo because the Yankees still occupied Yankee Stadium and the White Sox were playing at the Cardinals' home, Comiskey Park in Chicago. The Giants were a heavy favorite despite their awful exhibition season; the Cardinals had only won three games the year before and had occupied the NFL East cellar. Their defense was considered among the more porous in pro football, and it lived up to that demeaning reputation when the Giants met them in the 1958 season opener: the final score New York 37, Chicago 7.

Despite that blowout, the Giants were far from the team they would be later in the season. They proved that they were still struggling the following week when they fell to the Philadelphia Eagles, 27–24 (one of the only two games the Eagles would win that year). They managed a one-touchdown win over a weak Washington Redskins team, but then were shocked in their home opener at Yankee Stadium by the Chicago Cardinals, 23–6 (also one of only two games the Cardinals would win in 1958). To add to the woe, Frank Gifford was in the hospital after it with a leg injury. A lot of soul-searching was going on as the Giants took their 2–2 record into the game with the Pittsburgh Steelers, especially when the standings showed that the Cleveland Browns stood at 4–0, having scored no fewer than 27 points in any of the four games.

The Giants dispatched the Steelers with relative ease, and then went back to prepare for a major confrontation against the 5–0 Browns at Cleveland. Jimmy Brown was already on his way to a record-breaking season rushing— he would demolish Steve Van Buren's nine-year-old total-yardage mark of 1,146 yards by gaining 1,527 and set another NFL standard with 17 touchdowns rushing.

Charlie Conerly, who had been benched the week before, was back at quarterback to face the Browns. Sam Huff again had the assignment of stopping the mercurial and monstrous Brown. A record crowd in Cleveland filled Municipal Stadium, 78,404, to watch their allegedly title-bound team squelch the New Yorkers. Only it did not turn out that way. With Charlie Conerly having one of his finest

---

Notes and Quotes from the NFL East Playoff, 1958

Mel Triplett, explaining the events that led to his ejection after a fight in the second period: "No. 86 [Paul Wiggin] kicked me, and Don Colo grabbed the bar on my mask. That's when we started to go at it. It was just one of those things. But the officials ought to know it takes two to make a fight."

Paul Brown, after being informed that this was the first time the Browns had been shut out in 114 consecutive NFL games: "If you're going to lose, you might as well be shut out. Now maybe we can start another streak" [114 games earlier, in 1950, it was the Giants who shut them out, 6–0, in Cleveland].

Jim Lee Howell on his defense: "I have never seen a game where two equal teams were playing, where one defense overpowered the other team so completely. Landry and the defense deserves the credit. Andy Robustelli is a real money player, and Dick Modzelewski played his heart out. Katcavage and Huff are newcomers, they don't know the meaning of defeat."

And, from the New York World Telegram: *"Giant fans were so confident of victory that many of them left in the third quarter to go outside and stand in line for tickets to the championship game next week."*

---

days in some time, the Giants rallied all their forces and subdued the favored Browns, 21–17. Mel Triplett even outrushed Brown, 116 yards to 113.

If the Giants had their proverbial hands full with the Browns, the following week promised an armload. Coming to Yankee Stadium were the Baltimore Colts, 6–0 in the NFL West and just coming off a 56–0 humiliation of the Green Bay Packers. The "Hosses," as they liked to be called in the late '50s, were coached by Weeb Ewbank and had risen steadily since he arrived in 1954. In five years, he had put together a team that was laden with famous football names: Johnny Unitas, Alan Ameche, Lennie Moore, Ray Berry, Jim Parker, Gino Marchetti, Art Donovan, Big Daddy Lipscomb, and Jim Mutscheller, among them.

The biggest crowd ever to watch a Giants game in New York City (with the exception of the Red Grange/Chicago Bears encounter in 1925, whose attendance was estimated at more than 72,000) showed up at Yankee Stadium, a turnstile total of 71,163 (a record that would endure until the Giants moved to the Meadowlands in the late 1970s). And again the Giants were ready, helped incidentally by the sidelining of Unitas, who had suffered some cracked ribs in the game the week before. The game was a seesaw battle, but the Giants were able to pull it out in the last quarter. With about two minutes left to play and the score tied at 21, Pat Summerall came on for New York and booted a 28-yard field goal to give them the victory.

Cleveland lost that same day, a surprise at the hands of the otherwise unimpressive Detroit Lions, and so the Giants had earned their way to a tie for the conference with a record now of 4–2. The Giants lost one more game before going into the last game of the 1958 season, a 31–10 sting by the Pittsburgh Steelers; but the Browns (9–2) did not lose another game and led the Giants (8–3) by a game.

That last game of the year pitted the two against each other, and a Giants win would bring the NFL East title race to a dead heat and necessitate a playoff game to determine the champ. The Giants had the homefield advantage, if there was any such thing in the snow and ice that blanketed Yankee Stadium that bitter December afternoon. Wellington Mara took a look at the conditions and felt that the extremely inclement weather might turn the game one way or another on just a break or two. "Everyone is going to be stalled in this," Vince Lombardi said before the game, and altered his offense accordingly.

No one, however, told Cleveland's Jim Brown that. On the first play of the Browns' first possession, he took a handoff from Milt Plum, slid out of the grasp of Sam Huff, and raced 65 yards for a touchdown.

It was the only score of the first period. The Giants got

Gifford's Visitor

While Frank Gifford was having his injured knee attended to in a New York hospital in 1958, he awoke at about 5:30 one morning to find a large, trembling young man at the foot of his bed. The immobilized Gifford watched as the man shook the bed and ranted, "What's the matter with your Giants? What's the matter with all of you, Gifford?"

The man walked over to the venetian blinds and ran his hand up and down them to make noise. "What you need is someone like me, a killer. I was in Korea."

Gifford grabbed the water pitcher beside his bed. "If he was going to come at me I was going to gong him," Gifford said later. The man didn't, but he also did not leave. He just stood there, running his hand along the blinds.

Gifford finally said to him, "If you really think you can help the team, get your ass down to Yankee Stadium. Tell them what you can do." The man sort of nodded and left, much to Gifford's relief.

However, the man did take the Giff's advice and went to Yankee Stadium. He managed to get into the locker room, where most of the players by that time were suiting up for practice, and began screaming at 260-pound Dick Modzelewski first and then at some others. According to sportswriter Barry Gottherer, the man then began drop kicking footballs around the room, castigating the team before several policemen arrived to take him away.

As he was leaving, Gottherer quoted him as shouting back, "All right, so you don't appreciate me. I'll go down to Baltimore and help Johnny Unitas out."

Mel Triplett (33) bulls his way through Philadelphia's line in the second game of the 1958 season. The Giants lost during that day in the city of brotherly love, 27–24, but it was only one of three losses that year, and New York ended up on top of the NFL East. No. 55 on the Giants is center Ray Wietecha. The two Eagles whom Triplett is dragging along are Eddie Bell (left) and Marion Campbell (right); No. 72 is Jess Richardson. (New York Giants)

a field goal from Pat Summerall in the second quarter, but Lou Groza matched it for the Browns and sent them to the locker room at the half with a 10–3 lead. Neither team scored in the third period, nor in the first four minutes of the final quarter. The game had turned into a plodding battle on a slippery, windswept field, not much more than an exercise in exchanging punts. But then the Giants got a break. Milt Plum fumbled on his own 25-yard line, and Andy Robustelli fell on it.

The Giants took immediate advantage of it. On certainly the most exciting play since Brown broke loose in the first quarter, Frank Gifford took a pitchout from Charlie Conerly and started around right end, but suddenly he pulled up and threw diagonally across the field to Kyle Rote, who was racing down the opposite sideline. Rote grabbed it and broke a tackle, finally being slung into the snow at the 6-yard line. Gifford took a handoff on the next play, but was knocked for a yard loss. On the next

Sudden Death, 1958

New York Giants		Baltimore Colts
Kyle Rote	LE	Ray Berry
Rosey Brown	LT	Jim Parker
Al Barry	LG	Art Spinney
Ray Wietecha	C	Buzz Nutter
Bob Mischak	RG	Alex Sandusky
Frank Youso	RT	George Preas
Bob Schnelker	RE	Jim Mutscheller
Don Heinrich	QB	Johnny Unitas
Frank Gifford	LH	L. G. Dupre
Alex Webster	RH	Lenny Moore
Mel Triplett	FB	Alan Ameche

Giants	3	0	7	7	0 — 17
Colts	0	14	0	3	6 — 23

Touchdowns—*Giants:* Triplett, Gifford; *Colts:* Ameche (2), Berry. Field goals—*Giants:* Summerall; *Colts:* Myhra.

PATs—*Giants:* Summerall (2); *Colts:* Myhra (2).

play, it was again a pitchout to Gifford, who pumped a fake to Rote this time and then rifled the ball to Bob Schnelker, who had button-hooked just inside the end zone. Summerall's extra point tied the game at 10.

The Giants' defense responded as well, not giving up a single first down the remainder of the game. The Giants staged a 45-yard march to the Browns' 25, but there Summerall missed the field goal with about five minutes remaining. A few minutes later, after a shanked punt, the Giants got the ball at what was estimated as the Cleveland 43- or 44-yard line—no one could tell for sure because the field was totally covered with snow. Three passes from Conerly fell incomplete, and it was now fourth down with just over two minutes remaining and the snow falling in a profusion that would have stirred Bing Crosby to song if he had been there. A punt, and the game would surely end in a tie, and a tie would do the Giants no good. They could try for a first down, but that was 10 yards away, and the chance of it being made quite remote. The only thing perhaps more remote was a field goal, somewhere around a 50-yarder through the swirling snow. Jim Lee Howell, to almost everyone's dismay, yelled to Pat Summerall to go in and boot it. Perhaps it was the shock of being told to do it under the conditions that fueled the adrenaline release, but, whatever it was, it spurred Summerall to kick the longest field goal in his Giants career, officially logged as a 49-yarder (see sidebar). The Giants won it in the snow, 13–10.

The two teams had a week to rest, recover, and prepare for a repeat meeting. The coin toss to determine who would host the playoff game was won by the Giants, and therefore they would convene again at Yankee Stadium. The snow had stopped in New York, but the biting cold was still there, and the field was frozen.

This time Jim Brown did not start the game with a flourish. In fact, the Giants' stoked-up defense shut him down completely the entire day, not to mention the rest of the Cleveland attack. It was the Giants who burned the Browns in the first quarter of this game. The play was unorthodox, to say the least, but it worked. New York had gotten to the Cleveland 19-yard line, and Vince Lombardi sent in a special play. Charlie Conerly took the snap and handed off to Alex Webster, who then on a double reverse gave the ball to Frank Gifford. The Giff made his way past the line of scrimmage, then at the 8-yard line as he was about to be tackled lateraled to thirty-seven-year-old Charlie Conerly, who ran it in for the score. "The double reverse didn't surprise me," Paul Brown said after the game. "But the lateral to Conerly? That couldn't have been planned. What the hell was he doing there?" Conerly was elated with the touchdown. "I don't know when I scored last. But it was great for an old guy like me to run it in." He also explained that it was not a fluke, either;

Summerall's Moment in the Snow

Many unpredictable things have happened on a professional football field, but not many were less likely than Pat Summerall's miraculous 49-yard field goal in a dizzying snowstorm in 1958 to defeat the Cleveland Browns and clinch a tie for the NFL East crown. Gerald Eskenazi described the astonishing deed in his book There Were Giants in Those Days.

"I couldn't believe Jim Lee was asking me to do that," says Summerall. "That was the longest attempt I'd ever made for the Giants. It was on a bad field, and it was so unrealistic. Most of the fellows on the bench couldn't believe it either."

Meanwhile, Wellington Mara was up in the press box in the upper stand . . . [and said,] "That Summerall kick was the most vivid play I remember. I was sitting next to Ken Kavanaugh and Walt Yowarsky and we all said, 'He can't kick it that far. What are we doing?' "

It is credited as a 50-yard [actually 49 yards] attempt but, according to Summerall, "No one knows how far it had to go. You couldn't see the yard markers. The snow had obliterated them. But it was more than 50 yards, I'll tell you that. . . .

"I knew as soon as I touched it that it was going to be far enough. My only thought was that sometimes you hit a ball too close to the center and it behaves like a knuckleball, breaking from side to side. It was weaving out. But when it got to the 10, I could see it was breaking back to the inside."

In the locker room after the game, Tim Mara was as happy as his sons Jack and Wellington, coach Jim Lee Howell, and Summerall, all rolled into one. "What a kick," he said. "What a kicker. But what the hell, that's what I pay him for, and I'm glad to see he earned his money today."

Records Broken in the 1958 Championship Game

Those worth noting:

Most yards passing	Johnny Unitas	349
Most passes caught	Raymond Berry	12
Most yardage receiving	Raymond Berry	178
Most championships participated in	Giants	10
Most first downs	Colts	27
Most first downs passing	Colts	17

What a kick! (New York Giants)

"The lateral was an option, Vinnie [Lombardi] came up with the play just for this game."

That was all the Giants needed that day, although Pat Summerall added a field goal in the second quarter. The final was 10–0, and the stats from the game tell the story of the invincibility of the New York defense that December afternoon.

	Giants	Browns
Total yards gained	317	86
Yards gained rushing	211	24
Yards gained passing	106	62
Total first downs	17	7
First downs rushing	12	2
First downs passing	5	5

As Paul Brown put it after the game, "We were soundly defeated by a team that was in an inspired state of mind, that's all." And so the Giants, with five All-Pros (Rosey Brown, Ray Wietecha, Andy Robustelli, Sam Huff, and Jim Patton), were headed to the NFL championship game, what would be the club's tenth appearance since the league began playing the classic back in 1933, more than any other team at that time in the NFL.

The squad the Giants were facing, to no one's great surprise, was the awesome Baltimore Colts, who had won their division with a record of 9–3. The Giants had beaten them during the regular season, but at the same time they were well aware of how explosive the Colts' offense was —their average of 31.8 points a game and total of 381 points scored was the best in the entire NFL; in fact Baltimore led in almost all categories of offense that year. In addition, the Colts' defense was acknowledged as one of the league's strongest and most consistent.

There was more than the usual hype for this title game, perhaps because television was boosting professional football up to a level of national interest that the game had never experienced before. Perhaps too because the Giants now had a large and devoted following who were thoroughly excited about the team that had come from behind to snatch the conference crown on a seemingly impossible field goal by Pat Summerall one week and a defense as sweeping and impenetrable as the Great Wall of China the following Sunday.

Baltimore was equally enraptured with its team, its first ever to go for the NFL title. As a matter of fact, the last time a Baltimore team won a major professional sports crown had been back in 1896 when Ned Hanlon's old Orioles were baseball's tops, and that was five years before they started playing the World Series. Now, sixty-two years later, "Coltaphrenia" was what the sportswriters called the sports madness sweeping Baltimore, and it had been so intense during the regular season that one writer referred to Baltimore's Memorial Stadium as an "outdoor insane asylum." Now 15,000 of those fans had come by train, bus, and automobile to New York, to become a frenzied and vocal part of the more than 64,000 fans assembled to watch the Colts take on the Giants at Yankee Stadium.

It was expected to be a close game, a classic confrontation of Baltimore's great offense and New York's magnificent defense, and it was as close as any game could possibly be.

Fateful Fourth Quarter, 1959

New York Giants		Baltimore Colts
Kyle Rote	LE	Ray Berry
Rosey Brown	LT	Jim Parker
Darrell Dess	LG	Art Spinney
Ray Wietecha	C	Buzz Nutter
Jack Stroud	RG	Alex Sandusky
Frank Youso	RT	George Preas
Bob Schnelker	RE	Jim Mutscheller
Charlie Conerly	QB	Johnny Unitas
Frank Gifford	LH	Mike Somner
Alex Webster	RH	Lenny Moore
Mel Triplett	FB	Alan Ameche

Giants	3	3	3	7 —	16
Colts	7	0	0	24 —	31

Touchdowns—*Giants:* Schnelker; *Colts:* Moore, Unitas, Richardson, Sample. Field goals—*Giants:* Summerall (3); *Colts:* Myhra.
PATs—*Giants:* Summerall; *Colts:* Myhra (4).

On Second Thought . . .

Jimmy Cannon, one of the finest sportswriters of his time, proved his fallibility the week before the 1959 title game between the Giants and the Colts when he laid a prediction on the line in his column in the New York Daily News.

The Giants are what all college football squads struggle to be but seldom achieve. That's why I think they will win the championship of the National League by beating the Colts in Baltimore this Sunday. They are the perfection of the team ideal.

In all the seasons I have been reporting games at which men work for a living, I've never covered an athletic group that was closer. They belong together, each and every one, as if they were the brothers of an immense family connected by something more dramatic than a pay roll. . . .

The defensive unit has been honored by the game's scholars as the best ever to function for wages. . . . I think the Giants will win because the Giants' defensive guys will be able to get to Unitas.

Defense prevailed in the first quarter, the Giants systematically holding off the Colts' balanced rushing/passing attack. Pat Summerall drove a 36-yarder through the uprights for the only score of the period, but the Giants' lead was a brief one.

Offense took charge in the second quarter as the Colts started a drive that ended on the Giants' 2-yard line, where Alan "The Horse" Ameche bulldozed in to give the Colts the lead. Later in the same period, Baltimore began another march, this one from its own 14-yard line. At the Giants' 15-yard line, twenty-five-year-old Johnny Unitas dropped back and found Raymond Berry for another touchdown, and the Colts had a 14–3 lead at the half.

Again in the third quarter the Giants' renowned defense bent to the pressure of the Unitas-led attack. The Colts surged all the way to the New York 3-yard line, but there the Giants' defense lived up to its reputation. Three plays failed to gain a yard, and when, on fourth down, Ameche tried to bruise his way through to the end zone, as he had earlier, linebacker Cliff Livingston met him and dropped him at the 5-yard line. The Giants took over, suddenly revitalized by the goal-line stand, and after a pair of running plays Charlie Conerly threw long to Kyle Rote, who grabbed it at the Colts' 40 and ran it as far as their 25 where, as he was being dragged down, he fumbled the ball. It bounced crazily, but Alex Webster managed to scoop it up and race for the goal line. He made it only to the 1-yard line, but moments later Mel Triplett carried it

Alex Webster gains a few yards for the Giants in 1958 despite the efforts of the Cleveland defense. The Giants met the Browns three times that year—twice in the regular season and once in the divisional playoff—and defeated them all three times. The other Giants are tackle Frank Youso (72) and center Ray Wietecha (55). The Browns' defenders are Frank Costello (50), Henry Jordan (72), Bob Gain (79), and Walt Michaels (34). (Pro Football Hall of Fame)

in for the score, and the Giants were right back in the ballgame, trailing by only four points.

The momentum had changed, no doubt about it, and Conerly took advantage of it. At the start of the fourth quarter, he hit Bob Schnelker for 17 yards and on the following play for 46 more. With the Giants at the Baltimore 15, Conerly changed targets and fired a sideline pass to Frank Gifford at the 5, who shook off two tacklers and scored. Summerall's extra point gave New York a 17–14 lead.

There were a little more than two minutes remaining in the game when the Giants were faced with a third-and-four situation. With Baltimore looking for a pass, Conerly pitched to Gifford on a sweep to the right. Big Gino Marchetti was outside for the Colts, so Gifford slashed in off tackle. Marchetti grabbed him and brought him to the ground, but not until after it appeared he had made the

Before he became a spokesman for Tru-Value, as well as one of pro football's most popular broadcasters, Pat Summerall spent his time putting his toe to the football. Summerall played for the Detroit Lions and the Chicago Cardinals before coming to the Giants in 1958, and stayed with New York through the 1961 season. He is the seventh-leading scorer in Giants' history, his 313 points coming on 59 field goals and 136 extra points. (New York Giants)

This momentary ballet features Frank Gifford with one of the foremost blockers in Giants history, tackle Rosie Brown (79). Together they were instrumental in bringing New York six divisional titles between 1956 and 1963. (New York Giants)

The coaching staff, 1959. From left to right: Johnny Dell Isola, Tom Landry, Ken Kavanaugh, Jim Lee Howell (head coach), Walt Yowarsky, and Allie Sherman. (New York Giants)

first down. As they went down, however, Big Daddy Lipscomb, all 290 pounds of him, fell across Marchetti's leg and broke it. Amid the screams of pain and the scramble by everyone to get off Marchetti, the referee neglected to mark the ball. When the chaos subsided, the ball was finally placed down, but it was about a foot and a half behind where it should have been marked, according to most observers and all Giants. "I know I made that first down," Gifford said later. "The referee was so concerned about Marchetti that he forgot where he picked up the ball. I saw him pick it up at his front foot, but he put it down where his back foot was." The ensuing measurement showed the Giants six inches shy of a first down.

At their own 43-yard line, Howell had no desire to take a chance at that late moment in the game and sent Don Chandler in to punt. It was a fine kick, and Baltimore was back at its own 14-yard line with two minutes to go. After two incompletions, it appeared the game was securely in the hands of the Giants. But then the ice-cold engineer Johnny Unitas went to work. It took seven plays in just about a minute and a half for the crew cut quarterback to move the Colts all the way to the Giants' 13-yard line. Highlights of the journey were three completed passes to Raymond Berry for a total of 62 yards, all while he was double-covered. With only seven seconds remaining Steve Myhra came on to boot the game-tying field goal.

And so, for the first time in NFL history, the title had to be decided in a sudden-death overtime period. The Giants won the toss and obviously chose to receive. They were stymied, however, and forced to punt. Unitas and his "Hosses" got the ball at their own 20-yard line. This time Unitas carefully interwove runs with his passes and moved the ball steadily down the field. The most significant play was a 23-yard run by Alan Ameche that brought Baltimore to the Giants' 20 and within field-goal range. But the surging Colts did not need a field goal. They continued the march all the way to the 2, then Unitas gave the ball to Ameche, who simply stepped through a gaping hole between tackle and end on the right side of the line, opened by perfectly executed blocks by tackle George Preas and end Jim Mutscheller.

The most exciting NFL championship up to that time in history came to a close with the Giants on the short end of a 23–17 score. As the lead line in the *New York Times* the next day pointed out, "Time and fortune finally ran out on professional football's Cinderella team, the New York Giants." It was a heartbreaker indeed for the Giants, but there was still an abundance of pride. Jim Lee Howell said in the locker room after the game, "I'm very proud of my men. This team went a long way this season. Our kids were always straining against teams which should have been better than they were. We were only twenty seconds and a few inches away from winning it all today."

Dick Lynch (22), after a college career at Notre Dame and a year with the Redskins, became a Giant in 1959. Shown here facing off with Washington end Fred Dugan, Lynch was an important member of New York's defensive backfield in the early 1960s and earned All-Pro recognition in 1963. He had 35 career interceptions and returned four of them for touchdowns. (Fred Roe)

And mountainous Dick Modzelewski added, "We did pretty good for a team that was so low after we lost five exhibition games. You can't come any closer to winning the championship than we did. We outfought Baltimore, but they outplayed us." And so ended suspenseful and exciting 1958.

The year 1959 began on a sad note in the Giants' organization when founder Tim Mara died on February 16. The elder Mara had been a major force in the development of professional football and would be a charter member of the Pro Football Hall of Fame when it was created in 1963. Through the hardest of times he kept the NFL franchise in New York, his mission to provide the people of New York with a good professional football team and leave a bequest to his two sons that he knew they wanted so much. In the thirty-four years he was the titular head of the Giants, they won three NFL championships and took eight divisional titles.

Vince Lombardi left to launch his dynasty at Green Bay, taking over a Packer team that had finished last in the NFL West the year before with a record of 1–10–1. Allie Sherman, who had organized the T formation for the Giants some years earlier, was hired to handle the offense

A somewhat aged Norm Van Brocklin lets one fly for the Philadelphia Eagles in 1959, the next to last year of his career. The Eagles handed the Giants one of their only two losses that year, an embarrassing 49–21 defeat in Philadelphia. No. 70 on the Giants is linebacker Sam Huff. (Fred Roe)

in Lombardi's stead.

With Charlie Conerly somewhere around thirty-eight or thirty-nine—no one really knew for sure just how old the drawling quarterback was in those days—the Giants drafted a promising quarterback from Utah in the first round, Lee Grosscup. And suddenly what the Giants ended up with was a plethora of quarterbacks because they still had Don Heinrich; they traded for George Shaw, who had been Unitas's backup at Baltimore the year before; and gilded halfback Frank Gifford announced his intention of trying out for the position at training camp.

Gifford said that he had always wanted to play that position in the pros—he had played it in high school and at USC for a time—and had mentioned the desire to his roommate and good friend Charlie Conerly. The elderly Conerly did not mind; instead he seemed almost bemused by the idea. Coach Jim Lee Howell said, "Why not?"

By the end of the preseason, however, Grosscup was relegated to the taxi squad, and Gifford was back at halfback, where he had already set so many club records: scoring, rushing, receiving; his talent and versatility at that position was unequaled in Giants annals.

The most important reaping from the draft that year was halfback Joe Morrison, although his contributions would not come until a few years down the line. By way of trade, the Giants picked up cornerbacks Dick Lynch from the Redskins and Dick Nolan, reacquired from the Cardinals. And offensive guard Darrell Dess came over from the Steelers to a starting berth on the Giants.

The Los Angeles Rams, New York's opponent in the 1959 opener, were not a good team that year, one that would only win two games all season, but they were ready for the Giants and almost pulled off a major upset. No one in New York was worried about the Giants' defense. As Vince Lombardi had said when he was leaving for Green Bay, "Any team that hopes to get by in this conference somehow has to figure how to get past New York's defense. It may be the best in the history of the game." The offense was the worry. Could Charlie Conerly, who despite his advanced age had won the starting slot at quarterback over all the 1959 competition, play championship-caliber ball? Could the Giants score when they had to? Would Conerly be able to bring them back, say, like a Unitas, when he had to? Those questions were, or at

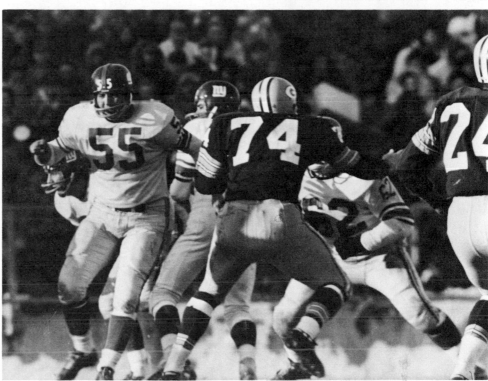

A little action with Green Bay. Ray Wietecha (55) moves out for the Giants as Henry Jordan (74) moves in for Green Bay, while Charlie Conerly (his head between the two) drops back to pass. (Fred Roe)

least should have been, put to rest after the Rams game out in Los Angeles.

Conerly came out passing, and the Giants built a 17–0 lead, but surprisingly the defense went stale in the second half, and the Rams scored three touchdowns to take a 21–17 lead. Without a lot of time remaining, Conerly passed the Giants 74 yards downfield, where Pat Summerall came on to boot a field goal and narrow the margin to a single point. The defense returned the ball to the Giants' offense, and Conerly started again. This time he was faced with a fourth-down-and-11 situation. Too late in the game to punt, Conerly felt, and Jim Lee Howell agreed. So old Charlie dropped back in the pocket, faked a pass to Gifford, then sailed one to Bob Schnelker for the first down. He then moved the Giants to the Los Angeles 18, where Summerall came on again and kicked the game-winning field goal. At game's end, Conerly had completed 21 of 31 passes for 321 yards, and Summerall was three for three from the field-goal tee.

Giants fans did not know it at the time, but they had seen a forecast of the upcoming season in microcosm that afternoon in Los Angeles. It was going to be a memorable year of Conerly's passes and Summerall's kicks, and, of course, a defense that was, as Conerly once put it, "as reliable as an old hound dog."

But the old hound dog must have dozed off the next week when the Giants traveled to Philadelphia because there they were annihilated by the Eagles, 49–21. Not since the Cleveland Browns ran up 62 points against them in 1953 had a team scored so many points against the Giants' defense.

Cleveland, with Jimmy Brown, Bobby Mitchell, Milt Plum, and Billy Howton, was the real concern for the Giants in 1959. But Sam Huff and his brawling gang had found the way to handle them. Three times they had beaten them the year before; in 1959 they would do it twice. The first was a simple 10–6 victory, the second a 48–7 humiliation in the next-to-last game of the season.

The latter trouncing stood a chance of not getting into the record books, however. As Tex Maule reported in *Sports Illustrated:*

> New York fans poured out of the stands about two minutes before the game ended and made a determined effort to tear down the goal posts while the two teams were going through the motions of finishing the game. Police were powerless to stop them, then the public-address announcer informed the unruly that unless they cleared the field, the game could be declared forfeit to the Browns. In the face of so grievous a contingency, the mob reluctantly squeezed itself behind the side and end lines and the game was played out.

After the game, Cleveland coach Paul Brown, perpetrator of many similar devastations himself over the previous ten years, said, "I wouldn't have asked for a forfeit even

End Bob Schnelker (85) is ready to gather in a Charlie Conerly pass here in the 1959 NFL championship game. The Baltimore defenders are Johnny Sample (47) and Andy Nelson (80). Schnelker caught a touchdown pass late in the fourth quarter, but it was too little too late, and Baltimore triumphed, 31–16. Sample intercepted two Conerly passes that day and Nelson another on a less than memorable afternoon. (New York Giants)

if the last two minutes hadn't been played. We didn't even belong on the same field with them today."

In between those two games with rival Cleveland, the Giants won six others and lost but one, 14–9, to Pittsburgh, then capped the season with a win over the Redskins to give them a 10–2 record and easy access to the NFL East title for the second year running.

The Giants' defense had given up an average of 14 points a game in the twelve regular-season contests, but discounting the anomaly that occurred in Philadelphia, New York's defense only allowed 11 points in each of the other eleven games. They in fact led in just about every major defensive category, most notably: fewest points allowed, fewest points per game, fewest first downs allowed, fewest rushing yards allowed, fewest passing yards allowed, and fewest rushing and passing touchdowns.

The worrisome offense offered little to worry about as it turned out, scoring a total of 284 points for an average of almost 24 points a game. Charlie Conerly ended up the top-ranked quarterback in the entire league, completing 113 of 194 passes for 1,706 yards, including 14 touchdowns. The 4 interceptions he threw were the least a Giants passer had thrown since Tuffy Leemans back in 1942, and it still remains the club standard. Pat Summerall kicked the most field goals in the NFL, 20 of 29, and his success ratio of 69 percent was also tops that year; he was also 30 for 30 on extra points. Don Chandler's punting average of 46.6 yards a boot is still the best ever by a Giant, although it was second in the league that year to Detroit's Yale Lary (47.1). Frank Gifford, proving his placement at halfback was truly proper, led the team in rushing once again (540 yards, 5.2-yard average per carry), and in receiving (42 for 768 yards). All-Pro honors went to Frank Gifford, Rosey Brown, Sam Huff, Andy Robustelli, and Jim Patton.

The championship battle of 1959 commanded repeat performances from the Giants and the Colts, who had ended their season with a record of 9–3, only this time Baltimore would host the event.

The Colts sent their ordinarily raucous fans into hysteria early in the first quarter when Johnny Unitas unloaded a pass to Lenny Moore that covered 59 yards and put the first 6 points on the scoreboard. But the frenetics wound down steadily as the Baltimore offense stalled under immense pressure from the Giants' defense. Through the rest of that quarter and the second and third as well, the Colts' ordinarily volatile offense was shut down. Meanwhile, for the Giants, Webster, Triplett, and Gifford ground out yardage, and Conerly connected from time to time, and even though they were unable to get into the end zone they were able to get close enough in each quarter for Pat Summerall to kick a field goal. Going into the fourth quarter the Giants had a 9–7 lead.

The momentum, which the Giants seemed to have had on their side, took a dramatic reverse, however, when late in the third quarter New York, on the Baltimore 27 with a fourth-and-one-foot situation, disdained the field goal and went for it. Alex Webster hit the line but was repulsed. The Colts took over and proceeded to disembowel the Giants from that point forward. Unitas moved his team down the field, the highlight being a 36-yard pass to Lenny Moore. When he got the Colts to the Giants' 4, he faked a pass to Jim Mutscheller and then carried it in unmolested for the touchdown.

The Giants came back passing, but a Conerly toss was intercepted by Andy Nelson and returned to the New York 17. A few plays later, Unitas hit rookie flanker Jerry Richardson for a 12-yard touchdown. Conerly, his day growing worse by the minute, went to the air again, and this time defensive back Johnny Sample picked it off and

To the victors go the spoils. Kyle Rote (left) and Andy Robustelli (right) both had whirlwind careers with the Giants which were part of the period from 1956 through 1963, during which New York took six divisional titles. Rote retired after the 1961 season and Robustelli retired after the 1964 season. (New York Giants)

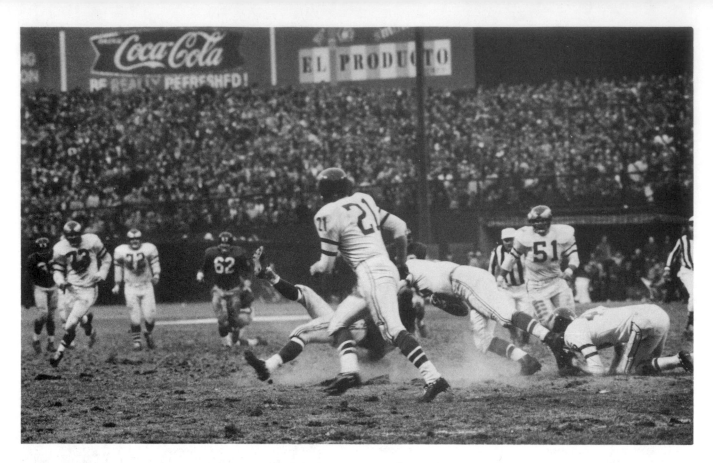

This sequence shows the hit on Frank Gifford by Eagles linebacker Chuck Bednarik that resulted in a serious concussion which ended the Giff's 1960 season and kept him out of action the following year as well. Top: The collision can be seen behind Philadelphia's Jimmy Carr (21). Bottom: The ball skitters away from the kayoed Gifford on the ground as Bednarik (60) watches it. A recovered Gifford made a comeback, but not until 1962. (Fred Roe)

PORTRAITS

Alex Webster.

Giants defensive stalwarts Andy Robustelli, Rosey Grier, Dick Modzelewski, and Jim Katcavage.

Jack Stroud.

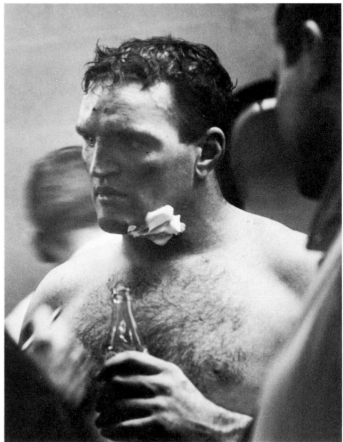

Dick Lynch.

Greg Larson.

Rosey Brown.

Joe Morrison (40) and Don Chandler.

Vince Lombardi, after he moved to Green Bay.

Kyle Rote and Ray Beck.

Harry Carson.

Lawrence Taylor.

Mark Bavaro.

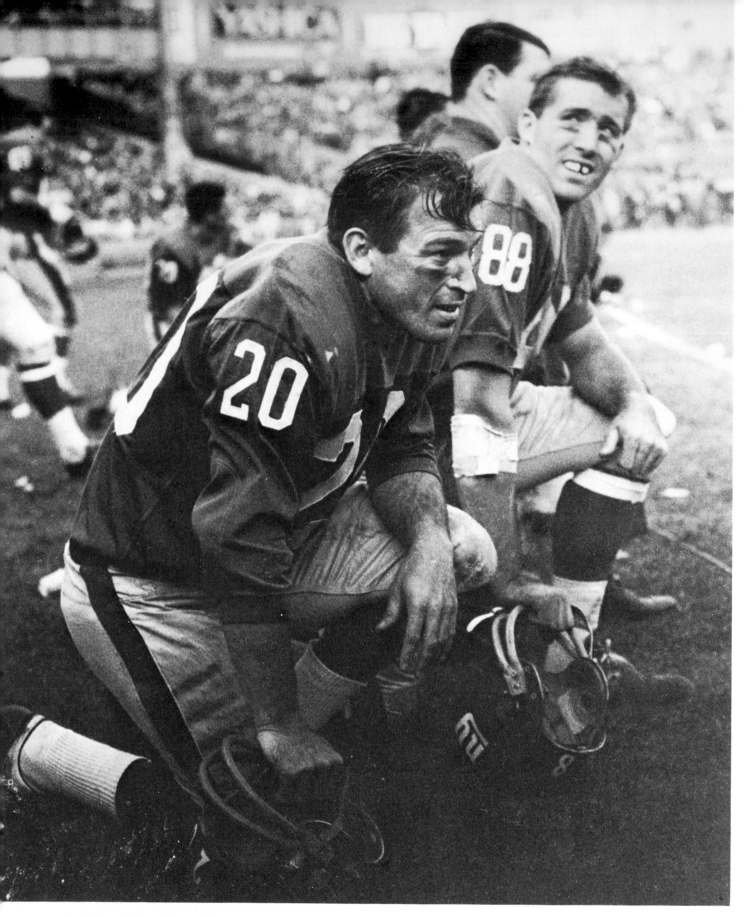

Jim Patton (20) and Aaron Thomas.

ran 42 yards for another Baltimore touchdown. The score stood at 28–9, Colts.

Not too much later, Sample did it to Conerly again, returning this one 24 yards, which set up a Steve Myhra field goal. The Giants managed an inconsequential touchdown in the last minute of the game, but went down soundly to defeat, 31–16.

If only the championship games of the late 1950s had ended earlier, Giants fans must have thought, just seconds in 1958 and a quarter in 1959, if only. . . . But they had not; their nemesis named Unitas and his loyal compatriots had seen to that.

NFL Commissioner Bert Bell had died during the 1959 season, and the job was held on an interim basis by acting commissioner Austin Gunsel. The owners were divided on giving him the job permanently, however, and after four days of meetings were still at an impasse. It was at that point that Giants vice-president Wellington Mara offered a compromise candidate, the thirty-three-year-old general manager of the Los Angeles Rams, Pete Rozelle, and the owners confirmed him.

Rozelle, of course, inherited a league that was expanding—the Dallas Cowboys were entering it in 1960, and the Minnesota Vikings were scheduled to join the following year—and one that was about to face the largest and most serious challenge of its then forty-year history, the well-organized and well-financed American Football League.

On the New York Giants front, it was a year of ailments and injuries. Among those up but mostly down were Frank Gifford, Charlie Conerly, Alex Webster, Jim Katcavage, and various others. Adding to the misfortune was the departure of defensive genius Tom Landry, returning to his home state to guide the fortunes of the maiden Dallas Cowboys.

The Giants got off to a decent start, winning their first three games, but dropped from first place after a tie with the Redskins and a loss to the now St. Louis Cardinals. They struggled through to the eighth game of the season, posting a record of 5–2–1, still definitely in the race. But in that game, Gifford suffered a severe concussion after a savage hit by Philadelphia Eagles' All-Pro Chuck Bednarik. It knocked him out for the season, and the Giants folded after that, winning only one of their four remaining games. Their record of 6–4–2 left them in third place in the NFL East, behind the Eagles and the Browns.

George Shaw had done the majority of quarterbacking for the Giants in 1960, relieving forty-year-old and often injured Charlie Conerly, and his stats were mediocre at best. Perennial All-Pros Rosey Brown, Andy Robustelli, and Jim Patton once again reaped those honors.

The Giants were far from over the hill, however, as the next three seasons would delightfully prove. There would be two important new faces: Allie Sherman on the sideline as head coach, replacing Jim Lee Howell, who chose to retire to the Giants' front office, and a thirty-four-year-old, bald-headed quarterback by the name of Y. A. Tittle. And there would be three thrilling trips to NFL championship games.

The Potentates of the East

11

From 1961 through 1963 the Giants were once again the undisputed masters of the Eastern Conference. Although many of the veterans from the title teams of the late 1950s were on hand for the new era of ascendancy, it was a markedly different offense that was to conduct come-from-behind victories game after game and season after season during a glorious three-year romp in the NFL East.

Although 1960 was the only year during the previous three that the Giants did not end the season at the top of the Eastern Conference, the third-place finish resulted in substantial changes within the Giants' organization. Jim Lee Howell, head coach since 1954, announced his retirement. The Mara brothers appointed him director of personnel and expressed hope that his move to the front office would make room for Green Bay's Vince Lombardi to rejoin the team, this time in the capacity of head coach. But when Lombardi failed to accept the invitation to come back to New York, assistant coach Allie Sherman was promoted to the top slot.

Now working with new Commissioner Pete Rozelle, the NFL owners lengthened the regular-season schedule from twelve games in 1960 to fourteen in 1961. They also welcomed the league's fourteenth franchise, the Minnesota Vikings, an addition planned earlier as part of the same expansion program that had brought the Dallas Cowboys into the league the previous season. And in the first game of the Vikings' first season, rookie quarterback Fran Tarkenton threw four touchdown passes and ran for a fifth in a 37–13 drubbing of the Chicago Bears. People in New York were impressed, and none surmised that "Sir Francis" would one day play for New York.

During the off-season, the Maras and Coach Sherman had valid worries that the floundering Titans of the struggling American Football League, now approaching its second season, might raid the Giants' roster. However, the fears proved unfounded. With no major defections to contend with, Allie Sherman went to work reshaping the club's offense.

Charlie Conerly, at age thirty-nine, had at last seemed to be fading during the 1960 season. In a move that soon proved to be inspired, Sherman traded second-year tackle Lou Cordileone to the San Francisco 49ers in exchange for quarterback Yelberton Abraham Tittle.

"Who else did they get besides me?" Cordileone asked, shocked that a lineman was swapped for a seasoned All-Pro quarterback. But the San Francisco brain trust seemed happy with the trade. They were convinced that Y. A., thirty-five years old then (appearing even older because of his baldness), was no longer fast enough for the scrambling required by their newly installed shotgun offense. It was one of the grandest miscalculations in the history of pro football.

With the quarterback question now settled, at least in Allie Sherman's mind, the new coach turned his attention to another pressing problem. The great Frank Gifford, knocked out by a stinging hit from the future Hall of Famer Chuck Bednarik of the Eagles during the 1960 season, decided not to return for 1961. Sherman hoped to overcome the loss of Gifford by acquiring a pair of fine receivers. The most important of the acquisitions was a lean and lithe six-foot-three-inch, 186-pound end named Del Shofner, a four-year veteran from Los Angeles. During the next three seasons, Shofner and Tittle would help to rewrite the Giants' and the NFL's record books in passing.

Sherman also acquired an offensive end from Washington named Joe Walton, and the rookie crop included linemen Greg Larson and Mickey Walker and halfback Bob Gaiters.

As for the defense, all the great Giants' stars were back: Rosey Brown, Andy Robustelli, Rosey Grier, Sam Huff, Jim Katcavage, and the rest—none had jumped to the AFL. And new to the defensive backfield was Erich Barnes, a three-year veteran acquired from the Bears. Barnes would soon make his mark in the Giants' secondary, but at the start of the season his most distinguishing characteristic was the peculiar way he pronounced his first name: "It's *EE*-rich," he insisted.

Mel Triplett was traded to the Minnesota Vikings, a move that ultimately reinstalled Alex Webster in the Giants' backfield. After a disastrous season in 1960, Webster had worked hard conditioning his legs and felt he was ready to resume an important role in the New York offense.

The unproven head coach had made his preseason moves, but by the end of the first game of the 1961 season, fans at Yankee Stadium sensed disaster. While Y. A. Tittle watched glumly from the sidelines, an aged Charlie Conerly managed only nine completions for a total of 75 yards in a 21–10 loss to the St. Louis Cardinals in the season opener.

During the first half of the next game in Pittsburgh, the Giants' offense was sluggish, to put it delicately. Some New York fans, watching their first televised game of the season, were already screaming for Sherman's head when he pulled Conerly and gave Tittle his chance to run the show.

Del Shofner caught seven passes during that game, as it turned out, including one for a touchdown. Added to Joe Morrison's touchdown reception, the score was knotted at 14, paving the way for Pat Summerall's winning field goal. The come-from-behind victory was about to become a way of life for the New York Giants of the 1960s.

When the Giants played their third game in Washington's new D.C. Stadium, Tittle again replaced Conerly, this time in the first quarter, with New York already down by two touchdowns. His first pass was intercepted, which allowed the Redskins to set up their third touchdown. But then the "Bald Eagle," as Tittle was sometimes called, settled down to engineer another come-from-behind miracle.

With Tittle wresting the starting assignment from Conerly, and with Rote, Webster, Shofner, and Summerall all in fine form, the Giants' offense swung into high gear,

scoring impressive victories over the Cardinals, the Cowboys, and the Rams. Although he lost the starting job, Conerly was a dependable backup. The Giants lost by 17–16 in the second game against Dallas, but they were back in form when they slaughtered Washington, 53–0, the following week. Helping to pile up the points were three touchdown passes from Tittle to Shofner.

The ninth game of 1961, played in Yankee Stadium on November 12 against the Eagles, was a battle for first place in the East. Luck seemed to be with the Giants from the outset. Running for his life from a ferocious Philadelphia blitz, Tittle threw a wounded-duck pass toward Kyle Rote, but before it could reach him an Eagle safety tipped it high in the air toward the Philadelphia goal line. Diving for the ball, another Eagle player batted it back into the air, where Del Shofner grabbed it in midflight and carried it into the end zone. The final score was 38–21, and the victory put the Giants in first place.

Wins over Pittsburgh and Cleveland followed. In the Browns game, New York's tough defense managed to hold star running back Jim Brown to a total of 2 yards rushing in the second half, after having given up 72 yards to him in the first half. But just when it appeared that the conference title was theirs, the Giants fell, 20–17, to the Green Bay Packers. The loss, coupled with a Philadelphia victory, put New York again in a tie with the Eagles. The Eastern Conference championship was on the line in the next-to-last game of the season when the Giants faced the Eagles in Philadelphia.

Surprisingly, it was elderly Charlie Conerly—not Y. A. Tittle—who led the Giants to victory in the most important game of the season. Injured during the second quarter, Tittle watched from the sidelines as Conerly dissected the injury-ridden Philadelphia secondary. Despite Sonny Jurgensen's NFL-leading aerial attack, the Eagles' weak running game and their injured and inexperienced defensive backs could not hold back the Giants' surge. The final score was 28–24, New York; three touchdown passes had been hauled in by Shofner.

Only a tie in the season finale was needed to clinch the Eastern Conference title for the Giants, and New York, as it turned out, indeed could do no more than that in that final game, played against Cleveland. Plagued by fumbles, interceptions, and missed field goals, the Giants managed only a 7–7 tie.

For the third time since 1958, the Giants were within one victory of the NFL championship. But in 1961 so were the Green Bay Packers, champions of the Western Conference and in the earliest years of the Lombardi dynasty that would put the Pack at or near the top of the NFL throughout most of the 1960s. Despite five conference titles in earlier years, Green Bay was hosting only its first championship game on December 31, 1961.

Frozen Out in Green Bay, 1961

Offense

New York Giants		Green Bay Packers
Del Shofner	LE	Max McGee
Roosevelt Brown	LT	Bob Skoronski
Darrell Dess	LG	Fuzzy Thurston
Ray Wietecha	C	Jim Ringo
Jack Stroud	RG	Forrest Gregg
Greg Larson	RT	Norm Masters
Joe Walton	RE	Ron Kramer
Y. A. Tittle	QB	Bart Starr
Joel Wells	LH	Paul Hornung
Kyle Rote	RH	Boyd Dowler
Alex Webster	FB	Jim Taylor

Defense

Jim Katcavage	LE	Willie Davis
Dick Modzelewski	LT	Dave Hanner
Roosevelt Grier	RT	Henry Jordan
Andy Robustelli	RE	Bill Quinlan
Cliff Livingston	LLB	Dan Currie
Sam Huff	MLB	Ray Nitschke
Tom Scott	RLB	Bill Forester
Erich Barnes	LCB	Hank Gremminger
Dick Lynch	RCB	Jesse Whittenton
Joe Morrison	LS	John Symank
Jim Patton	RS	Willie Wood

Packers	0	24	10	3 —	37
Giants	0	0	0	0 —	0

Touchdowns—*Packers:* R. Kramer (2), Hornung, Dowler.
  Field goals—*Packers:* Hornung (3).
PATs—*Packers:* Hornung (3).

As 39,029 fans bundled up in freezing Lambeau Field, they saw their team give a chilly reception to the champions of the East. For a time, it seemed as if New York would take the lead. Kyle Rote, in his eleventh and final season as a player, dropped a sure TD pass in the first quarter, which then ended in a scoreless tie. It appeared he might score again in the second quarter when he broke free in the end zone for an option pass from halfback Bob Gaiters, but Gaiters overthrew him. The Giants were running out of opportunities, and the Packers took advantage of it by scoring three unanswered touchdowns in the second quarter, one on a Paul Hornung rush, followed by two on Bart Starr passes.

In the second half, the Packers' offense and crushing defense continued to dominate. On the other hand, the Giants' running game was ineffectual, and Green Bay defender Jesse Whittenton did a fine job of covering the ordinarily elusive Shofner tightly, allowing him only three receptions the entire game. Green Bay racked up a total of 183 yards rushing to 31 for New York. In the passing game, the Giants fared only slightly better. Tittle and Conerly threw for 119 yards, while Starr accounted for 164 for the Pack. Two second-half Hornung field goals and another touchdown made it a certified rout. The Giants' hopes for a championship were frozen out in Green Bay by the final score of 37–0.

It was a bitter end to an otherwise fine season for the New York Giants. Y. A. Tittle, deemed "too old and too slow" to play in San Francisco, was named league MVP. Allie Sherman was Coach of the Year in his rookie season. Erich Barnes, Rosey Brown, Sam Huff, Jim Katcavage, Jim Patton, Andy Robustelli, Del Shofner, Y. A. Tittle, and Alex Webster were all invited to the Pro Bowl; and All-Pro honors were bestowed on five Giants: Tittle, Shofner, Brown, Patton, and Barnes.

The statistics from 1961 give solid evidence of the

The great Bobby Layne (22) unleashes one here for the Pittsburgh Steelers in an early 1960s game against the Giants. Applying the pressure is Sam Huff (70) and Rosey Grier (76). (Fred Roe)

Out of uniform, the Giants' offensive punch of the early 1960s. From left to right: Joe Walton, Joe Morrison, Frank Gifford, and Del Shofner. (New York Giants)

team's excellence. The defense allowed 3 fewer points than Green Bay's, for a league-leading minimum of 220. The fleet-footed defensive backs gave up the stingiest percentage of pass completions in the NFL (45.6 percent) while the passing duo of Tittle and Conerly was third in total yards gained (3,035). The Giants netted the most first downs (275) and gave up the fewest (212). Del Shofner set a team record of 68 receptions during the season, and the defense led the league with 33 interceptions. One of the greatest pickoffs of the decade was made by newcomer Erich Barnes in a game against Dallas in 1961. Intercepting a Cowboy pass in the end zone, Barnes scampered 102 yards for the touchdown, a new (and still-standing) Giants record.

Although Allie Sherman and the Giants eventually proved them wrong, many sportswriters and oddsmakers saw the NFL East being dominated in 1962 by the Paul Brown–coached Cleveland Browns. Featuring the running attack of star fullback Jim Brown, perennial NFL rushing leader, they appeared to be even stronger when Heisman Trophy winner Ernie Davis, a halfback from

Syracuse, was selected in the college draft. What many thought could be the greatest one-two rushing attack in the history of pro football ended in tragedy before it ever began, when Davis was struck down with leukemia before playing a single NFL game. Jim Brown, as it turned out, was finally unseated as NFL rushing champ, and the Browns managed only a third-place finish in the East.

For the Giants, the pressure to repeat as conference champions fell squarely on the aging shoulders of Y. A. Tittle. Charlie Conerly, who had been so effective as Tittle's backup during the 1961 season, decided to call it quits at the age of forty. The new reserve quarterback was Ralph Guglielmi, a veteran from the Washington Redskins by way of the St. Louis Cardinals. Guglielmi's services were limited, however, because Y. A. Tittle was starting a two-season passing streak that virtually rewrote the record books.

In addition to Conerly, two other Giants stars were gone by the start of the 1962 season. Halfback Kyle Rote, after eleven years of steady service, retired as a player to become backfield coach. Kicker Pat Summerall also retired to pursue his already developing career in television and radio. Don Chandler now handled placekicks as well as punts. Bobby Gaiters was traded to San Francisco for end Aaron Thomas. Cliff Livingston went to Minnesota in exchange for defensive back Dick Pesonen, and Dick Nolan was sent to Dallas for a draft pick.

Draftees making the team were Bookie Bolin, an offensive guard from Mississippi; Jim Collier of Arkansas, another offensive end; a five-foot-ten-inch, 170-pound halfback from Illinois, Johnny Counts; and Bill Winter, a linebacker from St. Olaf. Of the four rookies, only Bolin managed to remain in the NFL longer than three years.

Rejoining the team after sitting out the 1961 season was Frank Gifford. At the start of the season, Sherman decided to use Gifford as a flanker. Although he was no longer a rushing threat, Gifford would haul in enough passes in the 1962 season to give him second place for total yards among Giants receivers, behind Del Shofner. Although they still had the spirited rushing of Alex Webster, the Giants knew that it would take another great passing season from Tittle—and consistent performance from the defense, still largely intact from the previous seasons—to capture the Eastern crown.

The Giants were put to the test in the first game of the 1962 season, held before a capacity crowd in Cleveland. The defense performed relatively well, but New York's vaunted aerial attack stumbled badly. Helped by three interceptions of Tittle passes, the Browns triumphed, 17–7.

The following Sunday, however, Cleveland began its long slide toward a disappointing 7–6–1 record in a close loss to Washington. And with just one minute gone in the Giants' second game, it appeared as if it might be a long season for New York as well; the Eagles' Sonny Jurgensen completed a 75-yard scoring pass to Timmy Brown. But it was the last Philadelphia touchdown of the afternoon. The defense stiffened, and Tittle, Shofner, Gifford, and the rest of the Giants' air force began their blitzkrieg. It lasted the remainder of the season and the next one as well. New York trounced the Eagles that day, 29–13.

The third game of the season pitted against each other two explosive offenses: the Giants' offense versus Bobby Layne's Pittsburgh Steelers. Tittle threw four touchdown passes, hitting all three of his favorite receivers, Shofner, Gifford, and Webster. It was too much even for the high-powered Steeler attack. Layne's final attempt at a game-winning drive ended when Erich Barnes intercepted his pass in the New York end zone. The Giants won, 31–17.

The Giants' home opener did not come until the fifth game of the season, when the Steelers came to New York seeking revenge, and Layne and his cohorts found just that in a bruising 20–17 victory. For New York fans, the defeat was aggravated by an apparently serious injury to Del Shofner's shoulder late in the fourth quarter.

But by the next game, with visiting Detroit, Shofner was back and so were the Giants. Despite the fact that Tittle was forced to sit on the sidelines for much of the first half following a fierce end-zone tackle at the end of a scoring bootleg early in the game, the Giants managed a 17–14 victory. It was the beginning of a nine-game winning streak that would extend through the last game of the regular season.

There was some question as to how seriously Tittle had been injured in the Detroit game, but the fears were put to rest the following Sunday when he tied a long-standing NFL record by throwing seven touchdown passes in an important New York victory over first-place Washington (see sidebar). It was the most astounding performance by a quarterback most New Yorkers had ever seen. The victory placed New York (at 5–2) just one game behind the Redskins, whose record now stood at 4–1–2.

By the time the season was over, Y. A. Tittle had captured the imagination of every armchair quarterback in

Del Shofner literally ran out of his shoe after catching a pass from Y. A. Tittle in this 1961 game against the Eagles. He carried the ball in for a touchdown before retrieving his shoe. New York went on to win, 38–21. The Eagles are Glen Amerson (46) and Jess Richardson (72). (New York Giants)

Tittle's Day

The game was at Yankee Stadium, October 28, 1962, against the Washington Redskins, and it was to be one of the most memorable afternoons ever to thrill the heart of a Giants fan. It was to be Y. A. Tittle's day.

Losing 7–0 in the first quarter, Tittle engineered a touchdown drive in the first half with passes to Del Shofner, Frank Gifford, and finally, the 6-pointer to Joe Morrison. Then, after Erich Barnes intercepted a Norm Snead pass on the next Washington possession, Tittle again went to the air with two passes to Shofner and a short lob to Joe Walton for Y. A.'s second scoring toss of the day. As the two-minute warning approached in the first half, Tittle completed a 53-yard toss to Shofner, and, after two futile running plays, fired a bullet to Joe Morrison in the end zone, and the Giants had a 21–13 lead.

On the first play following the Giants' kickoff to start the second half, Snead launched one to Bobby Mitchell for an 80-yard touchdown, his third of the game as well. On the next New York possession, however, Tittle moved a stride ahead of Snead by throwing his fourth touchdown pass of the afternoon.

The thirty-six-year-old balding New York quarterback was back at it again after the next Washington drive stalled and the Giants took over at their own 49-yard line. Tittle completed three consecutive passes, the last to Joe Walton, who carried it into the end zone for passing touchdown number five.

In the press box, reporters were scrambling through their media guides to see just which records Tittle was approaching. Two loomed as possibilities: Y. A. had completed 11 passes in a row at this point, and the NFL record was 13, set by Minnesota's Fran Tarkenton the previous December; and there was the long-standing NFL mark of 7 touchdown passes in a single game, set by Sid Luckman of the Chicago Bears in 1943 (against the Giants at the Polo Grounds) and tied by Adrian Burk of the Philadelphia Eagles in 1954. Midway through the third quarter, Tittle was two completions shy of both records.

Tittle completed his twelfth consecutive pass, this one to Alex Webster, when the Giants got the ball again, but he lost his bid for the record when his next toss fell incomplete. He made up for it on the succeeding throw, however, a bomb to Frank Gifford that resulted in a 63-yard touchdown. Then, in the fourth quarter, came Tittle's record-tying pass. First, a 50-yard completion to Shofner brought the ball to the Redskins' 15-yard line. A few plays later, the Bald Eagle tossed a 5-yarder to Joe Walton, who, after racing across the goal line, tossed the historic ball high into the air.

When his record-setting day was over, Tittle shared the NFL standard of seven touchdowns in a single game and established a Giants' record of 505 yards gained passing (27 completions in 39 attempts), a mark that still stands today.

Late in the game, fans screamed for Tittle to go for touchdown number eight, but he never did. "It would have been bad taste," Tittle was quoted in the New York Times *the next day. "If you're leading by so much [the final score was 49–34], it just doesn't sit right with me to fill the air with footballs. I'm the quarterback. It would be showing off."*

New York. He threw an NFL-record–shattering total of 33 touchdown passes, eclipsing the mark of 32 held jointly by Johnny Unitas and Sonny Jurgensen. But it was his calm, steady demeanor in the pocket as much as his glittering statistics that awed the Sunday audiences. Week after week he calmly picked out Shofner or Gifford for the bomb, Webster for the quick screen, and he even scrambled like a twenty-five-year-old when he was forced out of the pocket. His completed passes went farther than anyone else's in the NFL that year, averaging exactly 16 yards each.

The Giants' winning ways made them heroes in New York, helped by the fact that they were rapidly becoming the only football show in town. Playing before empty seats in the old Polo Grounds, the rival AFL's New York Titans franchise collapsed. As Tittle and the Giants were passing and receiving their way into the record books, the Titans players' paychecks were bouncing at banks all over the metropolitan area. Fearing a total collapse of the American Football League should the New York team fail to finish the season, AFL Commissioner Joe Foss was forced to run the Titans for the remainder of the year.

The Giants finished out their season with victories over St. Louis, Dallas, Washington, Philadelphia, Chicago, Cleveland, and Dallas once again to post a record of 12–2–0. The 41–31 Giants victory in the season finale featured six Tittle touchdown passes, the last one being his thirty-third of the year. Asked to comment on that record-breaking pass, he said, "I was going to run it in if I could."

Even before the regular season was history, the Giants could afford to joke. They had clinched their fifth Eastern Conference title in seven years with two full games remaining to be played when they edged out the tough Chicago Bears, 26–24, in early December. The remaining games were nothing more than warm-ups for the championship contest, which once again would be with Green Bay.

For New York fans, however, the final two games of the 1962 season were particularly frustrating. Both were played in New York. According to NFL rules in effect since 1954, all games played at home were blacked out from local television coverage. Adding to the fans' frustration was the fact that New York City was in the midst of a disastrous newspaper strike. While the Giants were wrapping up a sensational season, not a single daily newspaper was published in New York to document the achievement.

As they had for the past several seasons, thousands of New York fans flocked to area motels, where enterprising owners had erected tall antennas capable of pulling in a television station in Hartford which broadcast the game. So many fans crowded into some motel complexes that vendors and cheerleaders were attracted to the sites. One large motel presenting the Hartford coverage even brought in a high school marching band to entertain at the half. Some pundits remarked that there were more spectators glued to motel televisions in Westchester County, Connecticut, and eastern Long Island than there were fans in Yankee Stadium.

While the Giants were playing out their season, the Green Bay Packers were also finishing another spectacular year, posting a 13–1–0 record in earning a third consecutive Western Conference title. With offensive standouts Bart Starr, Paul Hornung, and fullback Jim Taylor (who had just taken the NFL rushing crown from Jim Brown), Green Bay headed east fully expecting to face the renowned aerial attack piloted by Y. A. Tittle.

To the Giants' bitter disappointment, however, conditions at game time were far from favorable for the forward pass. The 64,892 fans jammed into Yankee Stadium on December 30 found the temperature at kickoff time was nineteen degrees and falling; a thirty-five-mile-per-hour wind, with gusts in excess of forty, precluded any passing threat that afternoon. Not a single passing point was scored by either team. Instead, a brutal ground game was fought in the trenches. Green Bay fullback Jim Taylor and New York linebacker Sam Huff had a particularly violent personal war going on. "Come on . . . can't you hit any harder than that?" Taylor chided Huff and the rest of the Giants' defenders after nearly every run. And Huff and his associates made a most concerted effort to oblige him.

The only sustained drive for either team in the first quarter ended in a 26-yard field goal by Green Bay's Jerry Kramer. In the second quarter, the Giants' Phil King fumbled on the New York 28, the Pack recovered, and on the next play Paul Hornung threw to Boyd Dowler at the 7 on a halfback option. Only one more play was needed for Taylor to burst across the goal line. The score at halftime was Green Bay 10, New York 0.

The Giants' only score came in the third quarter, when Erich Barnes blocked a Green Bay punt and end Jim Collier fell on it in the end zone. Throughout the dismal afternoon New York's normally productive offense, crippled by the wind and cold, failed to score a point. Two more Kramer field goals made the final score Green Bay 16, New York 7.

For the fourth time in five years, the Giants had made it to the championship game and had lost. The glorious season, the final game against Green Bay, the numbing cold weather, an offense rendered ineffective: there was a bitter taste of déjà vu in that final game of 1962. From head coach Allie Sherman down to the reserve linemen,

---

Another Disappointment at the Hands of the Pack, 1962

Offense

New York Giants		Green Bay Packers
Del Shofner	LE	Max McGee
Roosevelt Brown	LT	Norm Masters
Darrell Dess	LG	Fuzzy Thurston
Ray Wietecha	C	Jim Ringo
Greg Larson	RG	Jerry Kramer
Jack Stroud	RT	Forrest Gregg
Joe Walton	RE	Ron Kramer
Y. A. Tittle	QB	Bart Starr
Phil King	LH	Paul Hornung
Frank Gifford	RH	Boyd Dowler
Alex Webster	FB	Jim Taylor

Defense

New York Giants		Green Bay Packers
Jim Katcavage	LE	Willie Davis
Dick Modzelewski	LT	Dave Hanner
Roosevelt Grier	RT	Henry Jordan
Andy Robustelli	RE	Bill Quinlan
Bill Winter	LLB	Dan Currie
Sam Huff	MLB	Ray Nitschke
Tom Scott	RLB	Bill Forester
Erich Barnes	LCB	Herb Adderley
Dick Lynch	RCB	Jesse Whittenton
Alan Webb	LS	Hank Gremminger
Jim Patton	RS	Willie Wood

Packers	3	7	3	3 —	16
Giants	0	0	7	0 —	7

Touchdowns—*Giants:* Collier; *Packers:* Taylor. Field goals—*Packers:* J. Kramer (3).
PATs—*Giants:* Chandler; *Packers:* J. Kramer.

Paul Hornung (5) hurdles for a few yards in the 1962 NFL championship game. Converging on the Packers' halfback are Andy Robustelli (81) and Dick Modzelewski (77), and on the ground to the right is Jim Katcavage. The Giants held the Pack to 244 total yards that day, outgaining Green Bay by 47 yards, but New York came up short in the scoring column, 16–7. (Fred Roe)

the Giants took the loss personally. "I never saw a team that tried so hard and lost," said Kyle Rote, which summed it up the best.

For the season, Tittle had his records, and other Giants did too. Allie Sherman was named Coach of the Year for the second consecutive year. For the twenty-first time in his career (including five years with the Rams), Robustelli recovered a fumble, tops in the NFL at the time. Chandler's 104 points for 1962 surpassed the Giants' record set in 1949 by Choo Choo Roberts. Alex Webster pushed his lifetime rushing total to 4,340 yards, highest ever for a New York Giants player. All-Pro players for the season included Erich Barnes, Rosey Brown, Darrell Dess, Jim Katcavage, Jim Patton, Y. A. Tittle, and Ray Wietecha.

There was a more ominous sign in the statistics of the 1962 season, however. For the first time in years, New York's aging defensive squad had not led the league in a single important defensive category. And some were saying the Giants were growing old.

Although Coach Sherman may have been concerned about the advanced age of his players (ten starters were over the age of thirty), he made only minor changes for the new year. The most prominent involved Rosey Grier, a fixture on the defensive line that had been intact for seven seasons. Grier was traded to the Los Angeles Rams in exchange for six-foot-four-inch, 280-pound defensive tackle John LoVetere and a draft pick.

A familiar figure on the offensive line, four-time Pro-Bowler Ray Wietecha, retired after a decade of service, and Greg Larson took over his job at center. Other new faces included third-string quarterback Glynn Griffing (who would spend just a single season in the NFL), linebacker Jerry Hillebrand, and tackles Lane Howell and Lou Kirouac. There was nothing new about the face of Hall of Fame–bound Hurryin' Hugh McElhenny, who put on a Giants uniform for the first time in 1963 after eleven years as a star halfback with San Francisco and Minnesota. McElhenny stayed with the Giants for just a single season, and of the twelve new players on the Giants' roster in 1963, only Hillebrand and LoVetere spent more than two seasons with the team.

The city of New York's other professional football team, the AFL Titans, was undergoing massive changes in 1963. W. A. "Sonny" Werblin, a onetime president of Music Corporation of America, purchased what was left of the bankrupt team and immediately changed its name to the New York Jets. The name change did little to help the club's fortunes in the AFL East during that year, but when the season closed and the New York franchise had posted another last-place finish, its new owner revitalized the struggling league by negotiating a major television contract with NBC. The contract assured each AFL team of approximately $900,000 in television revenues yearly, just a scant $100,000 shy of the CBS guarantee to National Football League franchises. Werblin's deal made the AFL viable, and the Giants were soon to feel the competition from his team. But not in 1963.

The biggest news in the NFL in 1963 was a gambling scandal involving Green Bay's Paul Hornung and a half-dozen Detroit players including All-Pro Alex Karras. Although Hornung and Karras had bet on their own teams, Commissioner Pete Rozelle suspended both indefinitely. But there was positive news as well. The NFL established its Hall of Fame in Canton, Ohio. Among the honored charter members was Tim Mara, in company with such legends as Jim Thorpe, Red Grange, Bronko Nagurski, George Halas, and Ernie Nevers (there were seventeen charter members in all).

For Y. A. Tittle, 1963 was to be his finest season. The New York offense was flooded with capable receivers: Del Shofner, Frank Gifford, Alex Webster, Joe Morrison, Joe Walton, and Aaron Thomas were joined by the newly acquired Hugh McElhenny, who had already caught many a pass from Tittle when both played for the San Francisco 49ers. Complementing the offense was Don Chandler, whose accurate placekicking enabled him to become the league's leading scorer in 1963.

But the brightest of the stellar attractions was the come-from-behind quarterback himself, who had to rescue the 1963 season with yet another miracle finish. Although Y. A. Tittle threw three touchdown passes for a 37–28 victory in the season premiere in Baltimore, his ribs were injured in the third quarter, and he was forced to spend the rest of the game, and the entire next game as well, on

---

Defense Triumphs, Chicago, 1963

Offense

New York Giants		Chicago Bears
Del Shofner	LE	John Farrington
Roosevelt Brown	LT	Herman Lee
Darrell Dess	LG	Ted Karras
Greg Larson	C	Mike Pyle
Bookie Bolin	RG	Roger Davis
Jack Stroud	RT	Bob Wetoska
Joe Walton	RE	Mike Ditka
Y. A. Tittle	QB	Bill Wade
Frank Gifford	FL	Johnny Morris
Phil King	HB	Willie Galimore
Joe Morrison	FB	Joe Marconi

Defense

Jim Katcavage	LE	Ed O'Bradovich
Dick Modzelewski	LT	Stan Jones
John LoVetere	RT	Fred Williams
Andy Robustelli	RE	Doug Atkins
Jerry Hillebrand	LLB	Joe Fortunato
Sam Huff	MLB	Bill George
Tom Scott	RLB	Larry Morris
Erich Barnes	LCB	Bennie McRee
Dick Lynch	RCB	Dave Whitsell
Dick Pesonen	LS	Richie Petitbon
Jim Patton	RS	Roosevelt Taylor

Bears	7	0	7	0 —	14
Giants	7	3	0	0 —	10

Touchdowns—*Giants:* Gifford; *Bears:* Wade (2). Field goal—*Giants:* Chandler.
PATs—*Giants:* Chandler; *Bears:* Jencks (2).

Irwin Shaw on Y. A. Tittle

From Esquire, *1965:*

He almost always seems to be in desperate trouble, and almost always seems to get out of it at the last fateful moment. Whether the record bears it out or not, the Giants always seem to be behind, and in the good days, at least, Tittle put them ahead when all hope seemed lost. It's the Alamo every Sunday, with Davy Crockett sighting down his long rifle with the powder running out, and Jim Bowie asking to be carried across the line with his knife in his hand.

Tight end Mike Ditka (89) catches a pass for the Chicago Bears amidst a swarm of Giants: Jim Katcavage (75), Dick Modzelewski (77), Dick Nolan (25), and Sam Huff (70). Ditka was an integral part of the 1963 Bears team that snatched the NFL title from the Giants. (Fred Roe)

the sidelines. Reserve quarterbacks Ralph Guglielmi and Glynn Griffing were of little help in game two, a 31–10 drubbing of the Giants at Pittsburgh. Fortunately for New York, Tittle recovered in time for the third game of the season.

In victories over the Eagles and Redskins, Tittle threw a total of five touchdown passes. The defense came alive as well, especially Dick Lynch, who intercepted three Jurgensen passes in New York's defeat of the Eagles.

The Giants' homecoming, perennially delayed by Yankee Stadium's baseball tenant, was the first critical game of the season. Jim Brown and the undefeated Cleveland team kept the Browns' perfect record intact and increased Cleveland's Eastern Conference lead over the Giants to

two games with a 35–24 victory. With nine games remaining in the 1963 schedule, New York's 3–2 record did not seem particularly hopeful.

During the next five games, however, Tittle shifted the Giants' offense into overdrive, averaging an astounding 39.6 points per game. The sweetest of the victories was a 33–6 shellacking of the Browns in the face of 84,000 stunned Cleveland spectators. Before a frustrated Jim Brown was ejected late in the fourth quarter for fighting with a New York defender, he had been held to a mere 40 yards rushing.

Of the final nine games in the 1963 season, the Giants lost only one: a 24–17 defeat by St. Louis in a game played at Yankee Stadium a few days after the assassination of President Kennedy. (NFL Commissioner Rozelle received broad criticism from many quarters for allowing the regular schedule to proceed on that bleak Sunday, for it had been set aside as a national day of mourning.) New York closed out the season with big wins over Dallas, Washington, and Pittsburgh, and the Giants captured their third consecutive Eastern Conference crown on the final Sunday of the season, finishing 11–3–0, one game ahead of the Browns.

Throughout the autumn of 1963, the air above Giants football games virtually hummed with forward passes. The team had amassed 3,558 total passing yards, a mere 47 shy of the Baltimore Colts, led by Johnny Unitas. More importantly, Tittle led the NFL with 36 touchdown tosses, breaking his one-year-old single-season record of 33. But New York's passing game was to be severely tested in the NFL championship game, slated for gelid, windy Chicago and the defense-conscious Bears.

The Bears had not appeared in a championship game since 1956, when they lost to the Giants. In the interim, the Bears' assistant coach George Allen had developed a zone defense for the pass that was tops in the league.

During the regular 1963 season, the Bears' pass defenders led the NFL by allowing the fewest completed passes and the fewest total yards through the air. They also led the league with 36 interceptions, two more than the second-place Giants. The tough Bears' defense gave up the fewest rushing first downs and the fewest total points in the league. Statistically, the game stacked up as a classic matchup: New York's record-breaking aerial attack set against the toughest pass defense anyone could remember. Nevertheless, oddsmakers polled by *Newsweek* magazine rated the Giants a ten-point favorite for the December 29 game.

As it had been in the two previous championship contests, the weather at kickoff time was brutal. More than 45,000 fans jammed into Wrigley Field on Chicago's North Side and shivered in the nine-degree cold. At first,

In this crucial 1963 game against the Cleveland Browns, Y. A. Tittle (14) lofts a pass to Frank Gifford. The Giants split their two games with the Browns that year, but ended up a game ahead at season's end, with a record of 11–3 and the NFL East title. The Cleveland defenders are Ross Fichtner (20), Bernard Parrish (30), and Jim Houston (82). (Fred Roe)

it seemed as if the hot-air machines installed near both benches might thaw the Giants' offense, which had been anything but warm in the 1961 and 1962 championship games, when Tittle drew first blood with a 14-yard scoring toss to Frank Gifford. With the score still 7–0 in the first quarter, Tittle then found Del Shofner in the end zone, but the usually sure-handed receiver saw the ball bounce off his frozen fingers. On the next play Bears' linebacker Larry Morris picked off a Tittle pass and ran it all the way to the Giants' 5-yard line. Chicago quarterback Bill Wade scampered across the goal line two plays later.

In the second quarter, the Giants drove deep into Bears territory but had to settle for a Chandler field goal, making the score 10–7, New York. There was no further scoring in the period, but on the Giants' next possession Tittle's knee was severely sprained when he was tackled by the Bears' Larry Morris just as he released a pass. Glynn Griffing was called on to finish the half for the injured Tittle.

During the halftime intermission, a doctor injected Tittle's knee with painkillers and wrapped it as tightly as possible, but the thirty-seven-year-old quarterback could barely walk as he took the field in the second half. Unable to set on his left leg, Tittle found his passing ability severely limited, and the fearsome Bears' defense took control of the game. Chicago's Ed O'Bradovich intercepted a screen pass and ran it back 62 yards to the Giants' 14. Following a critical first-down pass to Mike Ditka on third and 9, Wade scored on a quarterback sneak. Chicago had the lead 14–10 after the successful conversion.

In the frigid, defense-dominated battle, the score remained 14–10, but with just ten seconds remaining in the game, Tittle, who had been intercepted four times, still had one shot at pulling off a miracle finish. From the Bears' 39-yard line, he dropped back into the pocket and let fly with a desperation bomb to Del Shofner, who was streaking toward the end zone. The ball was overthrown, however, and landed in the hands of safety Richie Petitbon in the end zone for the Bears' fifth interception of the afternoon.

Overcome with exhaustion, pain, and grief, Tittle limped off the field and did not watch the final play of the game. While Bears quarterback Bill Wade grabbed the snap and fell to the ground to safeguard the Chicago victory, Tittle sat on the sidelines wrapped in a parka, openly weeping over the game that, on paper at least, his team should have won. The Giants gained 128 yards rushing to Chicago's 93, 140 yards passing to the Bears' 129, and had accumulated three more first downs than their opponent. But the five interceptions had been costly, and the NFL championship belonged to Chicago.

It had been a frustrating trio of championship games for the Giants from 1961 through 1963, disheartening to the players, coaches, and owners alike, and what they did not know as they left the unneighborly confines of Wrigley Field that day was that much harder times lay ahead.

A graphic illustration of the intensity of the combat between Green Bay fullback Jim Taylor (31) and New York middle linebacker Sam Huff (70) in the 1962 NFL title tilt. The two went at each other with savagery all day, and Taylor needed 31 carries to rack up 85 yards rushing. Watching the melee are Paul Hornung (5) and Dick Lynch (22). (Fred Roe)

KYLE ROTE DAY!

The Kyle Rote Day Committee Wishes to Thank the Following Organizations for Their Participation—

N. Y. FORD DEALER'S ASSOCIATION—1962 Thunderbird Landau Coupe

DALLAS, TEXAS, FANS — 1962 Ford Ranch Wagon

PAN AMERICAN WORLD AIRWAYS—Transportation to and from Europe

AMERICAN EXPRESS WORLD TRAVEL SERVICE—Accommodations in Europe

WNEW RADIO—RCA Color TV, Stereo, AM-FM Radio Combination

HEREFORD ASSOCIATION—Champion Hereford Steer

PHILCO CORP.—2 1-ton Room Air Conditioners

FAIRCHILD CAMERA CORP.—16 mm. Sound Movie Camera and Projector

SAN ANTONIO, TEXAS, FANS — 20 cu. ft. Home Freezer

E. LEITZ, INC.—35 mm. Leica Camera

BULOVA WATCH CO.—Accutron Wrist Watch

SAMSONITE CO.—10 pieces Samsonite Luggage

JOHNSTOWN, N. Y., FANS—Leather Goods for entire family

WESTMINSTER PRINTING CO.—All Printing for Kyle Rote Day

MACK KENNETH CO.—Fur Trimmed Women's Coat

P. BALLANTINE & SONS — U. S. Treasury Bond

THE NEW YORK FOOTBALL GIANTS, INC. —Silver Tea Service

THE PARK PLAZA HOTEL—Meeting Rooms

ESKA CORP.—Power Driven Snow Thrower

THE GARDEN EQUIPMENT CO. — Snow Plower and Lawn Sweeper

THE PARKER CO.—Lawn Sweeper

MORSE ELECTRIC PRODUCTS CO.—Morse Sewing Machine

MILES & RILEY, INC.—Cashmere Top Coat

TRIPLER'S—$200 Gift Certificate

THE B.V.D. CO.—Complete B.V.D. Wardrobe

AMF PIN SPOTTERS—Bowling Balls, Bags and Shoes for Rote Family

VAN HEUSEN SHIRT CO. — Pleasurewear wardrobe

SAVIN BUSINESS MACHINE CO.—Portable Dictation Machine

THE EMERSON CO.—Portable TV Set

THE RAWLINGS SPORTING GOODS CO. —Golf Clubs and Bag

HARRY ROLNICK—$100 Resistall Texas Hat

SECTION 5 CLUB—Gold Money Clip

J. P. STEVENS CO.—4 pairs Slacks for Mr. Rote and 3 Sons

GOLET ORIGINALS—Coat for Mrs. Rote

PEPSI COLA CO.—1 year Supply of Pepsi Cola

L. ABLESON & SONS—Blazers for 3 Rote Boys

SIMPSON CLOTHES—Sport Jacket

LOUIS MARX & CO.—Toys for Rote Children

CANADA DRY CORP.—Soda Cooler

FINKLE & CO.—Washer Drier Combination

NEPTUNE STORAGE CO.—Storing, Insuring and Transporting All Gifts

1961 (New York Giants)

Detroit Lions halfback Dan Lewis cannot free his leg from the grasp of Giants defensive back Allen Webb in this 1962 game at Yankee Stadium. New York won during that afternoon, 17–14. Some of the other Giants are Erich Barnes (49), Andy Robustelli (81), Tom Scott (82), and Jim Patton (20). (New York Giants)

Dick Pesonen stops Redskins fullback Don Bosseler in another 1962 game at Yankee Stadium. The Giants pummeled Washington that day, 49–34. About to add his bulk to the situation is Rosey Grier (76); in the background is Dick Lynch (22). (New York Giants)

Dick Lynch (22) leaps to block a St. Louis Cardinals field goal attempt which has just left the toe of Gerry Perry. The Giants squeaked by, 31–28, one of the conquests in New York's nine-game winning streak which closed out the 1962 season and earned them the NFL East title. No. 20 for the Giants is Jim Patton, and No. 82 is Tom Scott. (New York Giants)

Joe Morrison (40) grinds out some yardage against the Cowboys in 1963. Morrison averaged 4.8 yards a carry that season for the Giants, gaining 568 yards rushing and another 284 on pass receptions. Bringing him to earth is Dallas linebacker Jerry Tubbs (50). In a pile behind them are New York's Bookie Bolin (63) and John Meyers (78) of the the Cowboys. (New York Giants)

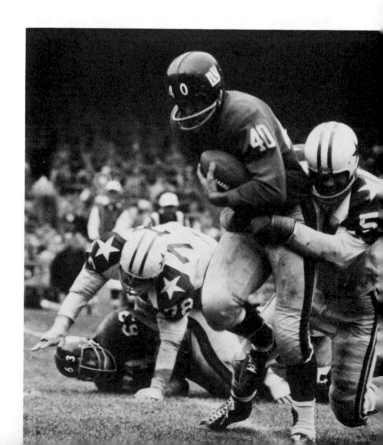

A newcomer to the Giants backfield in 1963, 34-year-old Hugh McElhenny picks up a few yards against the Cowboys. McElhenny came to New York in a trade with the Vikings after an illustrious nine-year career with the 49ers and two years with Minnesota, all of which earned him a berth in the Pro Football Hall of Fame. Trying to tackle him here is Dallas linebacker Harold Hays (56). (New York Giants)

On the sidelines, 1963. Head coach Allie Sherman confers with quarterback Y. A. Tittle and backfield coach Kyle Rote. Between the three, they would mold a Giants offense worthy enough to occupy the same field with the team's magnificent defense and help New York capture the NFL East crown that year. (New York Giants)

Seldom perceived as a scrambler, 36-year-old Y. A. Tittle (14) is forced to hotfoot it around end against the Browns at Yankee Stadium in 1963. Tittle glowed with special incandescense that year at passing, becoming the first player in Giants history to toss the ball for more than 3,000 yards in a season (3,145). His 36 touchdown passes during the year still stand as a club record. In pursuit here is Cleveland linebacker Jim Houston (82). (New York Giants)

Joe Walton carefully cradles a bullet from Y. A. Tittle in this 1963 contest with the Cowboys. Six of Walton's 26 receptions that year were for touchdowns. Looking on futilely is Dallas defensive back Jimmy Ridlon (42). (New York Giants)

Aaron Thomas (88) would have had this pass were it not for the interfering hand of St. Louis defensive back Bill Stacy (24). Thomas gained 469 yards on his 22 receptions in 1963, but his best years with the Giants were when he led the club in receiving in 1964 (43 for 624 yards) and 1967 (51 for 877 yards). (New York Giants)

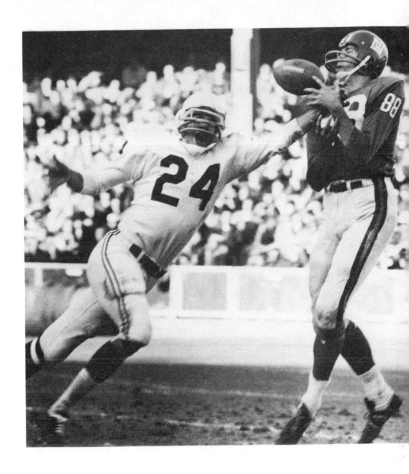

Dick Lynch corrals the ever-elusive Jim Brown in a 1963 game, but the Giants sustained one of their three losses for the year that day against Cleveland, 35–24. No. 13 of the Browns is quarterback Frank Ryan. (New York Giants)

Two men eminently responsible for the Giants' success in 1963, defensive behemoths Rosey Grier (76) and Sam Huff (70), take a breather on the New York sideline. (Fred Roe)

Just before a collision analagous to a freight train crashing into a Toyota. Miniscule Cowboy Eddie LeBaron (five-nine, 170 pounds) gets rid of the ball and grimacingly awaits the bone-rattling impact about to be dished out by Giants defensive tackle Big John LoVetere (six-four, 285 pounds). The Giants triumphed in this 1963 game, 37–21, at Yankee Stadium. (New York Giants)

Catches like this were the order of the day for Del Shofner in 1963. The adhesive-handed end gained more than 1,000 yards on pass receptions for the season, breaking the millenary barrier for the third consecutive year. Chasing Shofner is Eagles defensive back Irv Cross (27), better known these days as a television commentator on NFL broadcasts. The Giants annihilated Philadelphia in this meeting at Yankee Stadium, 42–14. (New York Giants)

Phil King bursts through the St. Louis line on the heels of a savage block by New York guard Darrell Dess (62). King was the Giants' most productive ground gainer in 1963, rushing for 613 yards and adding another 377 yards on 32 pass receptions. New York lost this game, 24–17, the last of only three losses that year. The Cardinals in the picture are Marion Rushing (52) and Joe Robb (84). (New York Giants)

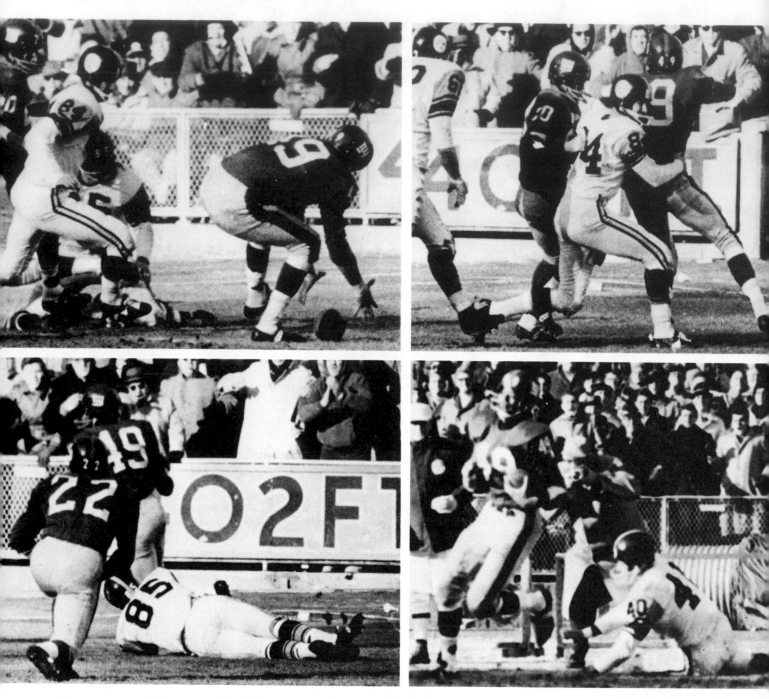

A key turnover in the last game of the 1963 regular season. Giants defensive back Erich Barnes (49) scoops up a Steelers fumble (upper left), writhes out of the grasp of Pittsburgh end Buddy Dial (upper right), races away from a diving Gary Ballman (lower left), and carries the ball for 30 yards (lower right). This fumble recovery was only one of the highlights in the 33–17 victory that assured the Giants of the NFL East championship on a cold December afternoon at Yankee Stadium. (New York Giants)

Life on the football field was a total and brutal commitment for 37-year-old Y. A. Tittle, a fierce and unyielding competitor. No words can portray his commitment more dramatically than this now-classic photo of a bloodied, frustrated, exhausted Tittle in the end zone after suffering an especially savage hit in a 1964 game at Pittsburgh. (Pittsburgh Post-Gazette)

Giants Milestones

Individual Giants records have been set by the following notable players. Each record, when set, became an important milestone in the team's history.

Career Records

Most Points Scored
Frank Gifford (1952–60, 1962–64): 484 (78 TDs, 2 FGs, 10 PATs)
Pete Gogolak (1966–74): 646 (126 FGs, 268 PATs)

Most Touchdowns
Alex Webster (1955–64): 56
Frank Gifford (1952–60, 1962–64): 78

Most Touchdowns Rushing
Alex Webster (1955–64): 39
Joe Morris (1982–): 40

Most Touchdown Passes
Charlie Conerly (1948–61): 173

Most Touchdowns Receiving
Kyle Rote (1951–61): 48

Most Yards Rushing
Tuffy Leemans (1936–43): 3,142
Frank Gifford (1952–60, 1962–64): 3,609
Alex Webster (1955–64): 4,638

Most Yards Passing
Charlie Conerly (1948–61): 19,488

Most Yards Receiving
Frank Gifford (1952–60, 1962–64): 5,434

Most Pass Completions
Charlie Conerly (1948–61): 1,418

Most Pass Receptions
Frank Gifford (1952–60, 1962–64): 367
Joe Morrison (1959–72): 395

Most Field Goals
Pete Gogolak (1966–74): 126

Most Extra Points
Ben Agajanian (1949, 1954–57): 157
Pete Gogolak (1966–74): 268

Most Punt Return Yards
Emlen Tunnell (1948–58): 2,206

Most Kickoff Return Yards
Clarence Childs (1964–67): 3,163

Most Pass Interceptions
Emlen Tunnell (1948–58): 74

Most Punting Yards
Don Chandler (1956–64): 23,019
Dave Jennings (1974–84): 38,792

Season Records

Most Points Scored
Choo Choo Roberts (1949): 102 (17 TDs)
Ali Haji-Sheikh (1983): 127 (35 FGs, 22 PATs)

Most Touchdowns
Choo Choo Roberts (1949): 17
Joe Morris (1986): 19
Joe Morris (1985): 21

Most Touchdowns Rushing
Bill Paschal (1943): 10
Joe Morris (1985): 21

Most Touchdown Passes
Benny Friedman (1929): 19
Charlie Conerly (1948): 22
Y. A. Tittle (1963): 36

Most Touchdowns Receiving
Frank Liebel (1945): 10
Homer Jones (1967): 13

Most Yards Rushing
Tuffy Leemans (1936): 830
Eddie Price (1951): 971
Ron Johnson (1970): 1,027
Joe Morris (1985): 1,336
Joe Morris (1986): 1,516

Most Yards Passing
Frank Filchock (1946): 1,262
Charlie Conerly (1948): 2,175
Y. A. Tittle (1962): 3,224
Phil Simms (1984): 4,044

Most Yards Receiving
Frank Liebel (1945): 593
Frank Gifford (1959): 768
Del Shofner (1961): 1,125
Homer Jones (1967): 1,209

Most Pass Completions
Y. A. Tittle (1962): 200
Fran Tarkenton (1971): 226
Phil Simms (1984): 286

Most Pass Receptions
Bill Swiacki (1949): 47
Frank Gifford (1956): 51
Del Shofner (1961): 68
Earnest Gray (1983): 78

Most Field Goals
Pat Summerall (1959): 20
Pete Gogolak (1972): 21
Ali Haji-Sheikh (1983): 35

Most Extra Points
Pat Summerall (1961): 46
Don Chandler (1963): 52

Most Punt Return Yards
Emlen Tunnell (1951): 489

Most Kickoff Return Yards
Clarence Childs (1964): 987

Most Pass Interceptions
Frank Reagan (1947): 10
Otto Schnellbacher (1951): 11
Jim Patton (1958): 11

Most Punting Yards
Dave Jennings (1979): 4,445

Game Records

Most Points Scored
Ron Johnson (1972): 24
Earnest Gray (1980): 24

Most Touchdowns
Ron Johnson (1972): 4
Earnest Gray (1980): 4

Most Touchdowns Rushing
Bill Paschal (1944): 3
Choo Choo Roberts (1949): 3
Mel Triplett (1956): 3
Charlie Evans (1971): 3
Joe Morris (1984; 1985, 4 times; 1986): 3

Most Touchdowns Passing
Y. A. Tittle (1962): 7

Most Touchdowns Receiving
Earnest Gray (1980): 4

Most Yards Rushing
Harry Newman (1933): 108
Tuffy Leemans (1938): 159
Bill Paschal (1943): 188
Choo Choo Roberts (1950): 218

Most Yards Passing
Paul Governali (1947): 341
Y. A. Tittle (1962): 505
Phil Simms (1985): 513

Most Yards Receiving
Choo Choo Roberts (1949): 201
Del Shofner (1962): 269

Most Pass Completions
Charlie Conerly (1948): 36
Phil Simms (1985): 40

Most Pass Receptions
Frank Gifford (1957): 11
Mark Bavaro (1985): 12

Most Field Goals
Joe Danelo (1981): 6

Most Extra Points
Pete Gogolak (1972): 8

Most Punt Return Yards
Emlen Tunnell (1951): 147

Most Kickoff Return Yards
Joe Scott (1948): 207

Most Pass Interceptions
Ward Cuff (1941): 3
(This record has been equaled by Howard Livingston, Frank Reagan (3 times), Emlen Tunnell (4 times), Art Faircloth, Otto Schnellbacher, Tom Landry, Dick Lynch (3 times), Jim Patton, and Spider Lockhart.)

Most Punting Yards
Carl Kinscherf (1943): 583

Longest Run from Scrimmage
Hap Moran (1930): 91 yards

Longest Pass Play
Earl Morrall to Homer Jones (1966): 98 yards

Longest Field Goal
Ben Agajanian (1957): 50 yards
Joe Danelo (1981): 55 yards
Ali Haji-Sheikh (1983, 2 times): 56 yards

Longest Punt Return
Emlen Tunnell (1951): 81 yards
Eddie Dove (1963): 83 yards

Longest Kickoff Return
Emlen Tunnell (1951): 100 yards
Clarence Childs (1964): 100 yards

Longest Interception Return
Erich Barnes (1961): 102 yards

Longest Punt
Len Younce (1943): 74 yards
Don Chandler (1964): 74 yards

From the time he handled player personnel as a teenager and was the first unofficial team photographer, Wellington Mara has always had a first-person relationship with the Giants team. Season after season he has been a familiar figure at practices as well as games. (Fred Roe)

12
From Boom to Bust

It was one of the more spectacular collapses in the history of the game. The proud Giants, champions of the East in 1959, 1961, 1962, and 1963, suddenly found themselves finishing dead last in two of their next three seasons. By the end of the three-year period, almost all the great old players from the championship Giants were gone: only Jim Katcavage, Del Shofner, and Joe Morrison survived the stretch. Head coach Allie Sherman, lionized in the early 1960s, was now regularly excoriated in Yankee Stadium as the Giants lolled around the cellar of the Eastern Conference.

While the Giants' prospects were plummeting, the fortunes of the NFL—and the rival AFL as well—were soaring. Franchises in the older league were guaranteed a million dollars annually in a two-year deal with CBS. Only the Dallas Cowboys and St. Louis Cardinals failed to show satisfying profits in 1964. To keep spectators tuned in to the multimillion-dollar broadcast schedule, CBS introduced the instant replay, a mixed blessing at best for the foundering Giants of the middle 1960s.

The Maras and Allie Sherman made some trades before the start of the 1964 season, but there were still a number of familiar faces around. The backfield of Y. A. Tittle, Alex Webster, and Joe Morrison was still there, and so were end Del Shofner and flanker Frank Gifford. Phil King had been traded to Pittsburgh, and two more unfortunate trades involved Sam Huff, who was sent to Washington, and Dick Modzelewski, dealt to Cleveland. For Huff, an important motivator for the entire defense and a favorite of the fans in his middle linebacking position, New York acquired Dick James, a little five-foot-nine-inch,

179-pound halfback and kick return specialist who had performed well in Redskins games with New York, but would last only a year with the Giants. Coach Sherman hoped to replace both Modzelewski and Huff with younger players, but none were found that were as capable as the aging veterans. Huff recalled that he was "deeply hurt" by the trade. So were the Giants, who almost immediately felt the loss of both players.

Newcomers joining the club were Cornell quarterback Gary Wood and two running backs: six-foot-three-inch, 235-pound Ernie Wheelwright from Southern Illinois, and six-foot, 180-pound Clarence Childs from Florida A&M.

The Cleveland Browns, ultimate champions of the East, finally fulfilled the experts' predictions. With rookie receiver Paul Warfield teaming with quarterback Frank Ryan to develop a deep pass threat to augment Jim Brown's rushing, the Browns suddenly developed into the team everyone thought they would be in the early 1960s. No small key to Cleveland's defensive success was the presence of former Giant Dick Modzelewski on the line.

While the Browns were opening their season by whipping Washington 27–13, the Giants were getting a shocking premonition of the year to come in their first game. They were destroyed, 38–7, by the Philadelphia Eagles, a team almost entirely rebuilt from the previous season but destined to finish the year with a 6 8 0 record. The loss of Huff and Modzelewski seemed to demoralize the New York defenders, who, at the close of the season, had surrendered more points than any other squad in the NFL.

The Giants almost won their second game against Pitts-

143

burgh, but the porous defense allowed a 27–24 loss to the mediocre Steelers. The New Yorkers also lost more than the game. In the course of play, Y. A. Tittle took a bruising hit in the ribs from the Steelers' John Baker, one from which the thirty-seven-year-old Bald Eagle would not bounce back. Two games later he returned to face Detroit, but it would never again by the same Y. A. Tittle who had led his team to three consecutive Eastern championships. He did not finish out the season as a starter, being replaced by Gary Wood, whose unimpressive statistics ranked him next to last among NFL quarterbacks. The famous photograph taken by Morris Berman at the Pittsburgh game, showing the fallen Tittle kneeling in front of the goalposts, bleeding from the head and struggling for breath, pretty much said it all about an illustrious career coming to an end.

The defense surrendered 399 points during the 1964 season, 20 more than the Chicago Bears (whose defense had also fallen apart) for first place in that ignoble category. Their final record was 2–10–2. For the first time in seventeen years, the Giants had ended up last in their conference. The team's leading rusher, with 402 yards, was rookie Ernie Wheelwright. One of the few bright spots during the year was provided by Clarence Childs, who led the league in kickoff returns, averaging 29 yards per return. Another was the consistent play of Erich Barnes, Rosey Brown, and Aaron Thomas, who were invited to the Pro Bowl.

Two old New York favorites, Frank Gifford and Alex

Thoughts About Tittle

Offensive tackle Roosevelt Brown: *"Y. A. worried about you like your wife worries about you. He had the interests of the whole team on his mind all the time."*

Offensive end Joe Walton: *"The greatest honor I've had in football is being a teammate and a friend of Y. A.'s."*

Defensive back Dick Lynch: *"The measure of anyone's ability is results, and Y. A.'s results speak for themselves."*

Frank Gifford, on Y. A.'s record-tying 7-touchdown day in 1962: *"We were so far ahead that Tittle didn't want to pass anymore, but we knew he had a shot at the record. In the huddle we told him, 'Throw the ball.' We said if he didn't pass, we weren't going to play. That's how much his teammates thought of Y. A."*

Fullback Alex Webster: *"He was the greatest."*

Webster, announced that they would not return for the 1965 season. Gifford, a versatile and productive fixture on the team since 1952, was on his way to the Pro Football Hall of Fame; and Alex Webster, the Giants' all-time leading rusher, left his bold imprint on the team's history and would, of course, return to guide it from the sidelines in 1969.

On January 22, 1965, reporters and television crews crowded around a dais set up in Mamma Leone's restaurant in New York for a lavish Giants press conference. At about noon, Y. A. Tittle stepped up on the platform and, in his down-home but articulate manner, began to speak.

"This is a moment I have dreaded," the great quarterback admitted. "I don't want to come back and be a mediocre football player again," he continued. "I was one last fall."

He announced his retirement and told of future plans. "What I'll be doing exactly hasn't been decided. I suppose I'll be looking at college players the Giants are interested in." It was clear to everyone there that day that an all-too-brief but glorious era of Giants football had come to an end. Tittle returned to his suburban San Francisco home to pursue a successful career as co-owner of an insurance agency and to perform various duties for his old team.

To the very day, the end of one era signaled the start of another. Just a few hours after Tittle announced his departure from football, many of the same reporters who had been covering the event at Mamma Leone's moved on to Toots Shor's restaurant, where the New York Jets had called a press conference to introduce the media to a senior from Alabama named Joe Namath, whom they had signed to a $400,000-plus contract, setting off a very expensive bidding war between the two leagues.

It was a unique date for pro football. The other newsworthy event of the day was described in this Associated Press report:

> The Dallas Bonehead Club said today that Jim Marshall went the wrong way again and wound up in Chicago instead of Dallas, where he was supposed to receive the Bonehead of the Year Football Trophy.
>
> Marshall, a defensive end for the Minnesota Vikings, was selected for running 66 yards the wrong way in a Viking–San Francisco 49er National Football League game. The boner resulted in a safety for the 49ers, but the Vikings won.

Wrong Way Marshall, who jubilantly threw the ball into the air after he thought he had scored a Vikings touchdown, did indeed take a plane to Chicago instead of Dallas, but it was all part of a publicity stunt. The Vikings, with Fran Tarkenton and the Purple People Eaters defense, could afford to joke. In its few years of existence, the young Minnesota franchise was steadily working its

Two New York defenders, Dick Pesonen (25) and Dick Lynch (22), bat away a pass intended for Washington's Joe Hernandez (80) from Sonny Jurgensen in this 1964 battle at Yankee Stadium. The Giants won the game, 13–10, which turned out to be one of only two games they would win during that dismal season. (New York Giants)

Despite increased pressure from the AFL, it was a good year for the draft. The Giants also selected Texas halfback Ernie Koy, Yale fullback Chuck Mercein, and cornerbacks Spider Lockhart of North Texas State and Willie Williams from Grambling.

On June 15, well before the start of the 1965 season, Jack Mara died after having served as team president for thirty-one years. His brother Wellington succeeded him, and Jack's son Timothy was named vice-president and continued to serve as treasurer. Wellington Mara also functioned as chairman of the board of directors, which also included Mrs. John V. "Jack" Mara, Timothy Mara, and Richard Concannon.

A little more than a month later, Wellington Mara and forty-two-year-old Allie Sherman signed a new ten-year contract for the head coach's services. The agreement superseded a five-year deal that had been made in 1963, thus giving the recently embattled coach a new vote of confidence, as well as a raise.

"I think any coach in the business would envy me today," Sherman gleefully announced at the ceremony. And in 1965, it seemed as if Sherman once again had the

way up the standings of the NFL West. For the Maras, however, it appeared that their franchise had, like Marshall, suddenly raced the wrong way.

In addition to Tittle, Andy Robustelli and Jack Stroud also retired. With the departures of Gifford and Webster at the end of the previous season, the Giants had lost many of their mainstays. Coach Allie Sherman hoped that the Giants' first-round draft choice, six-foot-three-inch, 233-pound Auburn running back Tucker Frederickson, would rejuvenate the Giants' backfield. The Maras and Sherman had considerable faith in Frederickson. Since the Giants had placed last in 1963, they were awarded the first pick in the NFL draft, and they chose Frederickson, passing up Joe Namath, Gale Sayers, Dick Butkus, Craig Morton, and John Huarte. In defense of the Frederickson pick, many agree that he might have had a legendary career in the NFL had he not been plagued by injuries.

Alex Webster

In 1969, Alex Webster became the eighth head coach in New York Giants football history. Big Red, as he was known to New York football fans, was well remembered for his performances on the field in a Giants uniform from 1955 through 1964. As a powerful running back, he was a key counterpoint to the passing of Charlie Conerly and subsequently Y. A. Tittle in the Giants' offensive scheme.

During his ten-year career as a Giants player, Webster played in six NFL championship games. In regular-season play he carried the ball more often (1,196 carries), gained more yardage (4,638), and scored more touchdowns rushing (39) than any Giant in history. His average gain rushing of 3.88 has been bettered only by Frank Gifford (4.30) and Mel Triplett (4.14). Only four other Giants have scored more points than his 336 (Pete Gogolak, Frank Gifford, Joe Danelo, and Joe Morrison), and Webster ranks seventh in all-time pass receptions (240 for 2,679 yards).

As a coach in New York, his career was shorter and less spectacular. Over five seasons (1969–73) his teams won 29, lost 40, and tied 1. His best year at the helm was 1970, posting a 9–5 record, good enough for second place in the NFC Eastern Conference, and it earned him recognition as Coach of the Year by UPI.

team on the right track, although a major last-minute adjustment was needed.

Just a few weeks before the season began, Sherman lost confidence in quarterback Gary Wood. He traded away Erich Barnes and Darrell Dess in a three-way deal for Detroit quarterback Earl Morrall. The thirty-one-year-old Morrall was a ten-year veteran of the NFL, with stints in San Francisco and Pittsburgh as well as at Detroit. He was no youngster, but the Giants' recent experiences with Y. A. Tittle and even Charlie Conerly left them with little prejudice against aging quarterbacks. Kicker Don Chandler was also traded away, a move that put the Giants into a year-long search for a good placekicker, which eventually led to the signing of the AFL's Pete Gogolak.

The new Giants' offense performed relatively well throughout the 1965 season. Only twice in the fourteen-game schedule were the Giants held to fewer than 14 points, but once again the defense was weak.

In the season opener, it appeared as if New York was faced with another disastrous year when the Giants were slaughtered, 31–2, by Dallas. But Morrall settled the team down with victories over Philadelphia and Pittsburgh before bowing, 40–14, to Fran Tarkenton's Vikings. During the erratic season, the Giants gave evidence of a credible if not explosive offense, but they also had a defense that gave up 31 or more points a game no fewer than six times.

The Roots of Destruction

All-Pro Players Lost by the Giants Between 1962 and 1964

Traded

　Defensive back Erich Barnes (to Cleveland after the 1964 season)

　Offensive lineman Darrell Dess (to Washington after the 1964 season)

　Linebacker Sam Huff (to Washington after the 1963 season)

　Defensive tackle Dick Modzelewski (to Cleveland after the 1963 season)

　Defensive tackle Rosey Grier (to L.A. after the 1962 season)

Retired (after the 1964 season)

　Flanker Frank Gifford

　Defensive end Andy Robustelli

　Offensive lineman Jack Stroud

　Quarterback Y. A. Tittle

　Running back Alex Webster

Joining the Giants' roster in 1964 was wide receiver Homer Jones from Texas Southern. Nicknamed "Rhino" although he had the speed of a gazelle, Jones collected a plethora of team pass-catching records during his six-year career in New York. To this day, he still has the standards for most yards gained on receptions in a season (1,209, in 1967), the highest average gain per reception over a career (22.6 yards) and for a single season (24.7). And he is credited with the Giants' longest TD reception (98 yards, from Earl Morrall in 1966 against the Steelers). (Pro Football Hall of Fame)

A sportswriter dubbed the young offensive backfield, which included such promising youngsters as Frederickson, Koy, and Mercein, the "Baby Bulls."

Near midseason a most promising phenomenon joined the starting lineup, a lightning-fast six-foot-two-inch, 211-pound flanker from Texas Southern named Homer Jones. After his entry into the lineup, Jones gained 709 yards on just 26 receptions.

Although they were anything but the polished champions of the previous years, the Giants managed to finish the 1965 season with a 7–7 record, good enough for a second-place tie with Dallas in the Eastern Conference. In contrast to the Giants' many contributions to the Pro Bowl in previous seasons, only Rosey Brown and Tucker Frederickson were invited at the end of the year, Frede-

NFL Films Born in New York

NFL Films, the largest producer of 16mm motion pictures in the world, was in effect born in New York—to be precise, at the 1962 New York Giants–Green Bay Packers championship game that year. A now-familiar producer of game-by-game highlights for network, local, and syndicated sports shows, as well as for cable productions such as HBO's "Inside the NFL," the company was started by Ed Sabol of Blair Productions in Philadelphia. Soon joined by his son Steve, the elder Blair won a contract to cover the Giants-Packers game. The coverage was an overwhelming success, and the production company run by Ed and Steve Sabol was soon filming the entire NFL schedule. The well-crafted features have won nearly three dozen Emmy Awards.

rickson's first and only appearance. In retrospect, Allie Sherman summed up the team's relatively strong comeback in 1965: "We were lucky," he said.

He must have been right. In 1966 the proverbial roof caved in.

The 1966 season was a historic one for the NFL and the New York Giants as well. That year Wellington Mara signed kicker Pete Gogolak just as the soccer-style kicker's option ran out with the AFL's Buffalo Bills. The controversial acquisition threatened an all-out personnel war between the two leagues, which had previously restricted their skirmishing to the enormously expensive draft battles.

"I have no qualms about signing him," said Giants owner Wellington Mara at the May 17, 1966, ceremony marking the acquisition of Gogolak. Mara defended an action many thought would greatly intensify the wars between the two leagues: "We honor the contracts of other organizations just like we honor the ones in our own league," he said. "We would not have talked to Gogalak, or any other player, prior to his becoming a free agent." The reaction was fierce, however. Newly elected AFL Commissioner Al Davis set up a blue-ribbon task force to raid NFL teams for their established stars, and before long many were seriously considering moving to the AFL.

A peace treaty was signed before the war got out of hand, however. Dallas Cowboys President Tex Schramm and Kansas City Chiefs owner Lamar Hunt worked out the general terms of an AFL/NFL merger, and the agreement was announced on June 8, less than a month after Mara had signed Pete Gogolak. Super Bowl I was to be played at the end of the season, a common draft would

be held in January 1967, and the two circuits would begin playing a common schedule in 1970.

In the final year of the NFL/AFL draft wars, the Giants selected a defensive back from Arizona State named Henry Carr. In all, twenty new faces appeared on the Giants' roster in 1966, many acquired in what proved to be a futile attempt to shore up the sagging defense. Only defensive tackle Jim Moran and defensive back and end Freeman White remained on the team for more than a year or two. Tucker Frederickson sat out the entire year with a knee injury.

The first game of the season against Pittsburgh demonstrated what many had predicted: the Giants were a middling team with a decent offense led by Earl Morrall and a weak defense. Still, few would have predicted the 34–34 tie in the opener would be the Giants' second-best effort of the entire season. There was one highlight in the first game, however: a 98-yard touchdown pass from Morrall to Homer Jones.

The true nature of the disappointing year was demonstrated in front of 60,000 Dallas fans on the NFL's second

Joe Morrison

Dave Klein, in Quarterback *magazine:*

Joe Morrison is not real. He exists in the minds of every too slow, too small, too old former athletes who stand on street corners in every city in this country dreaming of what might have been, of how it should have been for them.

Joe Morrison is not fast enough to be a running back in the National Football League. Furthermore, he is not big enough, either, and he runs straight up and he is thirty-three years old and he should not be able to make it as a flanker or a tight end. And you could probably stop him for a 6-yard loss in the park Sunday morning, before everybody showers and changes and goes to the Stadium to see the Giants play.

Forget it, Joe. Hey, somebody tell this guy to get packing. Go home to Ohio. . . . Leave the playing of this bone-snapping game to the younger men. . . . Get serious, Joe. Before you get killed.

But Joe Morrison was serious. And he played fourteen years for the Giants, from 1959 through 1972 (only Mel Hein, who played fifteen, has a longer service record with the club). His 65 touchdowns added up to 390 points, the fourth highest total in Giants history, and only Frank Gifford scored more touchdowns (78). No Giant has caught more passes than Morrison (395), and the 4,993 yards he gained catching passes is exceeded only by Frank Gifford's 5,434. And he is the club's seventh-ranking rusher ever with 2,474 yards.

Sunday. Knowing that he would need a massive offensive effort to help his weak defense, Sherman began the game by establishing an unbalanced offensive lineup with a single running back behind Morrall. Four receivers flooded the right side of the line in the hope of forcing the Dallas secondary into one-on-one coverage of receiver Homer Jones.

For two plays, the unorthodox lineup worked, but then Dallas called a time-out and made adjustments to develop a two-man defense for Jones. It worked. The speedy receiver was limited to four receptions and one touchdown, the Giants' only score of the long afternoon. Dallas quarterback Don Meredith and receiver Bob Hayes, owner of the world record for the 100-yard dash, had a field day dissecting the Giants' defense. As the Cowboys' points piled up, happy Texas fans even began applauding Meredith when he threw an incomplete pass. The final score was 52–7.

The Giants' defense set an NFL record in 1966 by allowing 501 points. In a freak accident during a training session in the second half of the season, Earl Morrall fractured his wrist and was lost for the year. Backup quarterbacks Gary Wood and Tom Kennedy couldn't get the offense moving fast enough to overcome the huge point totals Giants' opponents piled up. On November 27, the Washington Redskins defeated the Giants, 72–41, establishing a new NFL record for the most points scored by a team in a single regular-season game (the Chicago Bears had run up 73 when they shut out the Redskins in the 1940 title game). The total of 113 points in a game

was also a record. The Giants' only victory of the entire year had been over Washington earlier in the season. Other defensive embarrassments were losses of 55–14 to Los Angeles, 49–40 to Cleveland, and 47–28 to Pittsburgh. The Giants' defense gave up 47 points or more five times.

By the end of the season, fans at Yankee Stadium had seen enough. On the final day of the regular NFL schedule, New York spectators carried thousands of blue-and-white banners with "Good-bye, Allie" printed on them into Yankee Stadium and then watched their team fall to Dallas, 17–7. As they had before, the fans began singing "Good-bye, Allie" to the tune of "Good Night, Ladies."

New York's head coach, with eight full years remaining in his ten-year contract with the team, could do little but watch helplessly as New York finished the season with a record of 1–12–1, the worst showing in Giants history. In response to the criticism, Wellington Mara told *Time* magazine: "Allie's going to be the coach next year, and, I hope, for many years to come." But rumors were sweeping Wall Street, the magazine pointed out, that the Mara family was interested in selling the team that had been part of the family since the earliest days of the NFL.

The rumors were unfounded, but Wellington Mara knew that a major change was needed. Only defensive back Spider Lockhart was invited to the Pro Bowl at the end of the season. For the once-proud New York Giants, who just a few seasons earlier had perennially sent a small army of players to the Pro Bowl game, there was only one way to go.

GIANTS DEFENSE

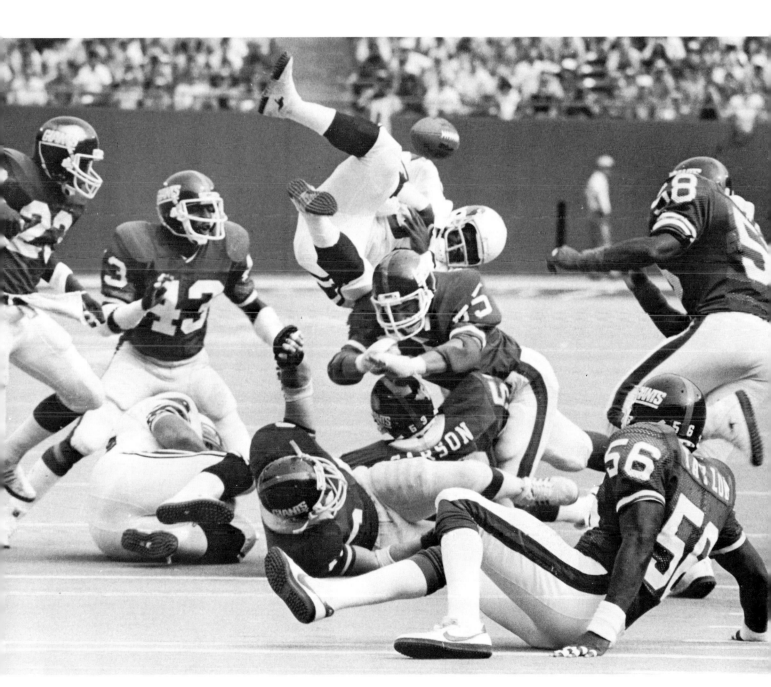

The modern Giants "Dee-fense" separates Cardinal running back Ottis Anderson from the ball. The Giants, left to right, are Perry Williams (23), Terry Kinard (43), Jim Burt (on the ground, with his helmet toward the camera), Harry Carson (53), Gary Reasons (55), Lawrence Taylor (56), and Carl Banks (58).

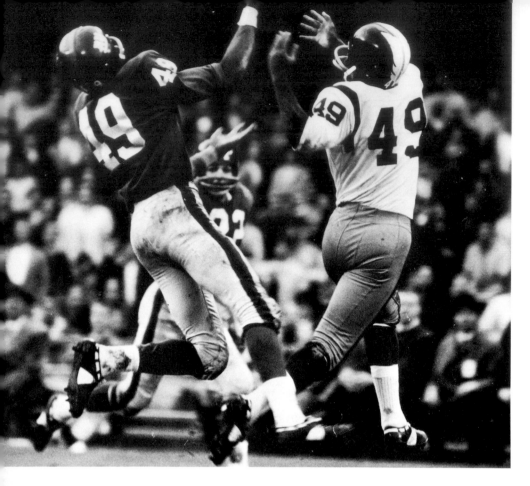

Erich Barnes (49) defending against Washington's Bob Mitchell.

The 1960s' Giants defense stops Dallas cold. Giants, from the left, are Dick Modzelewski (77), Jim Katcavage (75), Andy Robustelli (81), and Rosey Grier (76).

Washington's Ralph Guglielmi (3) is stopped by Dick Modzelewski (77) and Rosey Grier (76), as Sam Huff (70) moves in.

Dick Lynch (22) levels a Cleveland receiver.

Lawrence Taylor (56) & Co. force Dallas quarterback Gary Hogeboom into a fumble. No. 54 is Andy Headen.

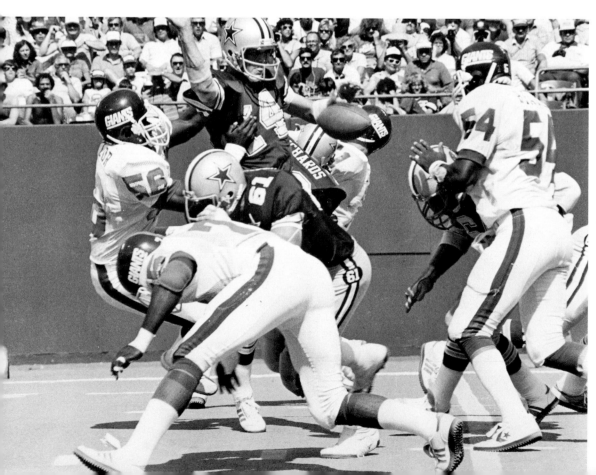

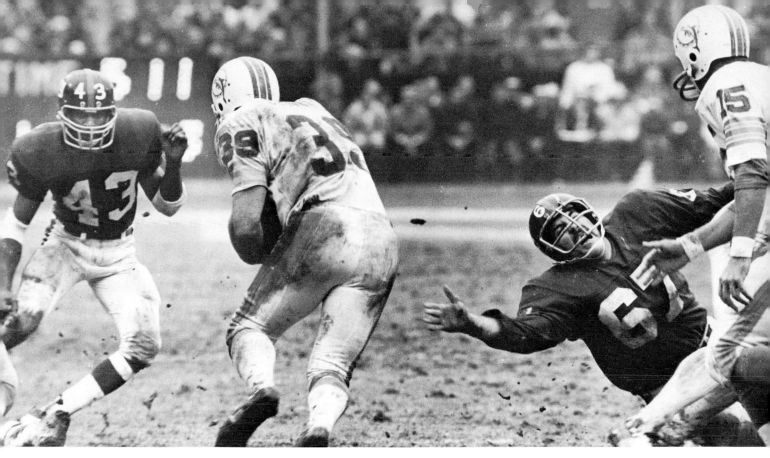

Spider Lockhart (43) gets ready to tackle Miami fullback Larry Csonka (39). To the right are Ron Hornsby (67) and Dolphins quarterback Earl Morrall (15).

George Martin (75) sacks Dallas quarterback Danny White (11), as Bill Currier (29) watches and Byron Hunt (57) moves in to help.

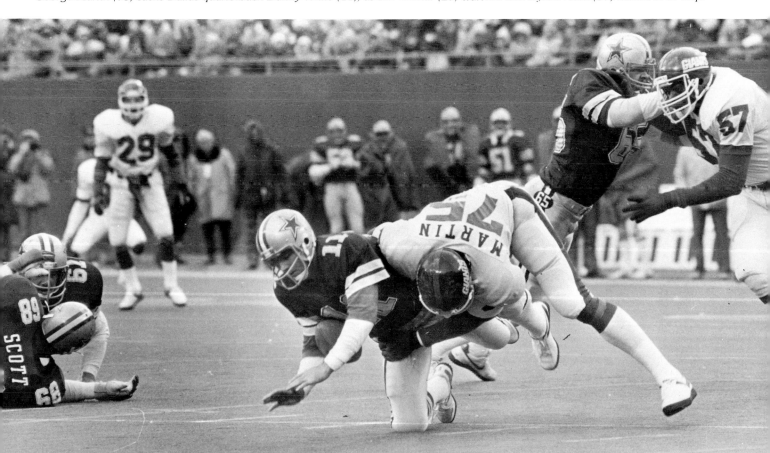

Lawrence Taylor (56) crunches Philadelphia's Ron Jaworski.

Jim Patton (20) moves forward to take on Cleveland great Jim Brown (32).

Terry Jackson (24) and a Cardinal ball carrier in mid-air.

Bill Currier (29) and Lawrence Taylor (56), behind the ball carrier, bring down Tony Dorsett of the Cowboys.

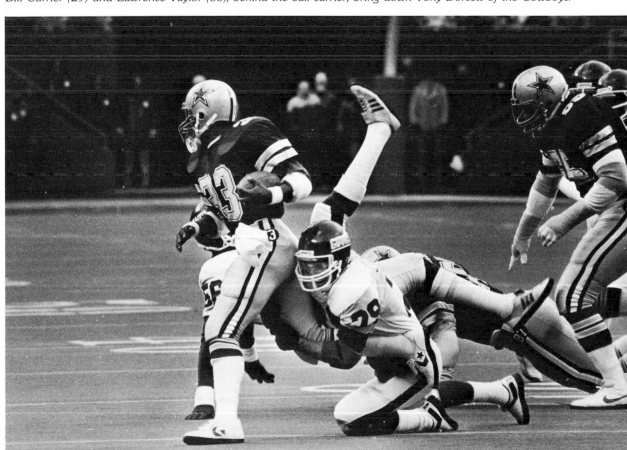

Jim Katcavage (75) and Charlie Janarette (73) knock the ball loose from Washington's Ralph Guglielmi (3).

The defense in 1964 may have looked as vicious as ever, but it was not. Shown here is linebacker Tom Scott (82) upending Dallas running back Don Perkins as Andy Robustelli (81), in his last year as a Giants lineman, and Bill Winter (31) converge on the play. The Cowboys prevailed, 31–21, in a game that was part of an altogether forgettable season. (New York Giants)

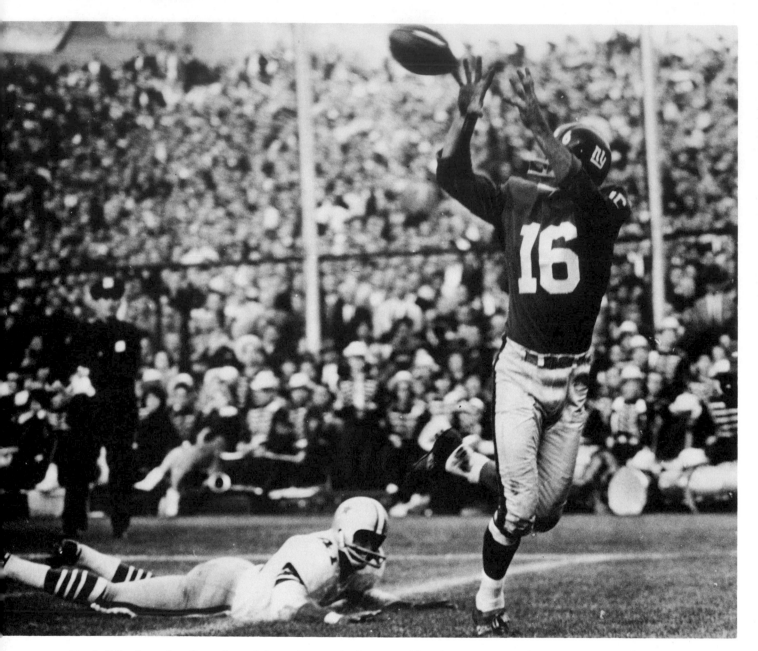

Frank Gifford, another Giants legend shown here in the last year of his playing career, gathers in a pass in a 1964 game against the Cowboys. From the Polo Grounds and Yankee Stadium to the Pro Football Hall of Fame and the Monday Night Football broadcast booth, Gifford has truly left his imprint on the game of professional football. (New York Giants)

In the right place at the right time, Erich Barnes (49) opens his arms to gather in an interception against the Cardinals. Barnes came to the Giants in 1961 in a trade that sent Lindon Crow to the Los Angeles Rams. That same year, Barnes returned an interception 102 yards for a touchdown, an all-time Giants record and an NFL standard he shares with several other players. No. 20 on the Giants is Jim Patton, and the intended receiver for St. Louis is Sonny Randle (88). (Fred Roe)

Carl "Spider" Lockhart also joined the Giants in 1965, beginning an eleven-year career with the team. An outstanding free safety, Lockhart was a thirteenth-round draft pick out of North Texas State. Here he races away from a Chicago Bear after picking off one of the many interceptions he made for New York (41 in all, third most in club history). (New York Giants)

Another acquisition in 1965 was running back Tucker Frederickson (24), shown here trying to wriggle out of the grasp of an Eagle defender. A first-round draft pick out of Auburn, Frederickson was one of the most highly regarded running backs in some time, but knee injuries plagued his pro football career and never allowed him to play up to his enormous potential. He did manage to lead the club in rushing in 1965 (659 yards) and 1968 (486 yards). (Fred Roe)

A key addition to the Giants in 1965 was 31-year-old quarterback Earl Morrall (11), obtained from the Detroit Lions. Morrall completed 155 passes for 2,446 yards, including 22 touchdowns, and brought the Giants out of the cellar of the NFL East, where they finished the year before, into a tie for second place. (New York Giants)

Ernie Koy (23) takes a pitchout from Earl Morrall in this 1965 game against the Eagles. Koy, from Texas, was another in the rich rookie draft of that year to secure a starting position. His best year with the Giants was in 1967, when he led the team in rushing with 704 yards. (New York Giants)

A bone-jarring tackle by defensive back Clarence Childs separates St. Louis Cardinals flanker Billy Gambrell (3) from the football in this 1966 game. Childs wore a Giants uniform from 1964 through 1967, before being traded to the Chicago Bears. (New York Giants)

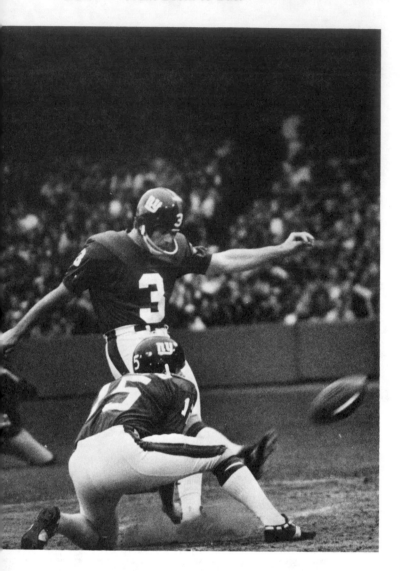

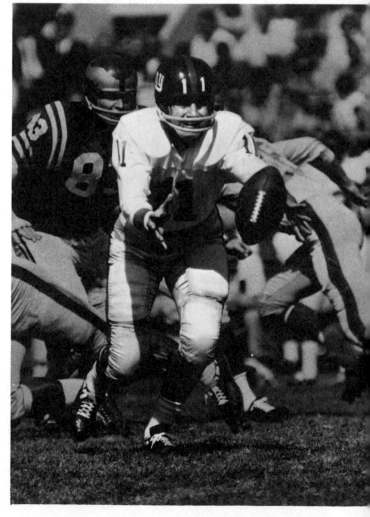

The Giants lured soccer-style kicker Pete Gogolak away from the AFL in 1966 to begin a career in New York that would last through the 1974 season. When it ended, Gogolak was—and still is—the Giants' all-time leading scorer, with 646 points (126 FGs, 268 PATs). No Giants kicker has booted more field goals or extra points than Gogolak. Holding here is Tom Blanchard (15). (New York Giants)

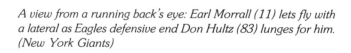

A view from a running back's eye: Earl Morrall (11) lets fly with a lateral as Eagles defensive end Don Hultz (83) lunges for him. (New York Giants)

Giants running back Danny Lewis (41) follows the interference provided by guard Bookie Bolin (63) against the Eagles at Yankee Stadium in the mid-1960s. (New York Giants)

A view from the quarterback's eye: Giants defenders Jim Patton (20) and Jerry Hillebrand (87). This particular quarterback happens to be Rudy Bukich of the Chicago Bears. (New York Giants)

A meeting of a pair of future Hall of Famers. Linebacker Sam Huff addresses the leg of Cleveland's Jim Brown. Watching the tussle is New York's Jim Patton (20). (New York Giants)

13

The Tarkenton Years

In February 1967, the sports pages of newspapers across the country carried stories about the resignation of Minnesota Vikings head coach Norm Van Brocklin, apparently over a feud with star quarterback Fran Tarkenton, who also announced his intention to quit the team. Van Brocklin explained his side of the controversy to Dick Cullum, a Minneapolis sportswriter.

"Tarkenton talked to players about his own situation," Van Brocklin said. "He made friends and supporters. This split the squad. If either one of us had quit and the other had returned, the squad would have continued to be split."

Wellington Mara took little time to capitalize on Van Brocklin's misfortune. Offering first-round draft choices in 1967 and 1968 and a second-round choice in 1967, as well as a fourth player to be named later, Mara acquired the 27-year-old quarterback from Van Brocklin's old team. The Giants' last-place finish the preceding season had given them first choice in the draft and the pick of graduating quarterbacks such as Bob Griese and Steve Spurrier, but Mara decided not to wait for a rookie quarterback to develop. "In New York, you've got to have a winner," he said. "We intend to have one."

With the trade complete, New Yorkers could boast of having two of the premier quarterbacks in professional football, Joe Namath of the Jets and Fran Tarkenton, now with the Giants. The comparisons came quickly. An article in the *New York Times* was called "The Swinger and the Square," referring, of course, to Namath's fondness for New York night life and the fact that Fran Tarkenton, the son of a Pentecostal minister, declined to drink, smoke, or

swear and was a quiet-living family man. On the football field, however, he was a proven crowd-pleaser. An accurate and highly mobile passer, Tarkenton had been nicknamed "The Scrambler," an appellation he vigorously disliked (see sidebar). But there was no denying the fact that, practically single-handedly, Tarkenton transformed the Giants from losers to contenders. From 1967 through 1970, the Giants managed second-place finishes every year.

The Giants' return to respectability following the dismal 1966 season coincided with the inauguration of the Capitol and Century divisions of the NFL Eastern Conference and the Coastal and Central divisions of the NFL West. The National Football League welcomed its newest franchise, the New Orleans Saints, to the Capitol Division of the Eastern Conference. To make room in the East and increase the Western Conference from an unwieldy total of seven teams to a more manageable eight, the Atlanta Falcons were moved to the Western Conference.

The "four C's" arrangement would last only three years, until the league was reorganized once again in 1970 as part of the final integration of the NFL and the AFL into the National and American Football Conferences. The history of the "four C's" organization was brief, but the Giants managed to keep it lively by changing divisions every year, beginning as a member of the Century Division in 1967, moving to the Capitol Division the following season, and returning to the Century circuit in 1969. In 1970, the team finally settled down to become part of the National Conference's Eastern Division, where it remains today.

157

Quarterback Fran Tarkenton (10), a new face in the backfield in 1967, is flanked here by veteran Joe Morrison (40) and newcomer Bill Triplett (38). Acquired from Minnesota, Tarkenton took command on the field and guided the Giants from a 1–12–1 season in 1966 to a 7–7 record and a second-place finish in the NFL East's Century Division in 1967. (New York Giants)

An important acquisition for the defense in 1967 was Vince Costello, a six-foot, 228-pound veteran middle linebacker gotten from Cleveland in a trade. Costello brought talent to his position that had not been seen in New York since the heyday of Sam Huff. The Giants also obtained, for a draft choice, six-foot-six-inch, 250-pound rookie defensive specialist Bob Lurtsema from the Baltimore Colts.

The Giants had something else going for them in the 1967 season. When visited by middleweight boxing champion Nino Benvenuti in Rome, Pope Paul VI recalled a visit the previous year by Allie Sherman. On June 2, using the prizefighter as an emissary, the Pope sent his personal blessing to the Giants and their head coach.

On the down side, kicker Pete Gogolak, acquired from the AFL by Wellington Mara over much controversy in 1966, was inducted into the army on January 25, 1967. The Giants scrambled for kickers during the first five games of the season, but eventually an agreement was worked out permitting Gogolak to play. A series of weekend passes allowed him to fly to New York on Friday evenings, arriving easily in time for Sunday games.

After the first ten games of the season, the Giants had won five, including a 38–34 heart-stopper over the Century Division–leading Cleveland Browns. As it had in the previous three seasons, the defense continued to give up large point totals, but the offense blossomed with Tarkenton at the helm. Aaron Thomas, Joe Morrison, Ernie Koy, and Tucker Frederickson were frequently on the receiving end of Tarkenton passes, but the most exciting receiver was still Homer Jones. The speedy end habitually discarded the intended pattern and roamed through the opposition's secondary trying to get free. Often enough, with the scrambling Tarkenton and the roving Jones, both ends of the passing connection were so unpredictable that it was nearly impossible to plan a defense against them.

The highlight of the Giants' season came on the NFL's eleventh Sunday in a game against the Eagles. Philadelphia head coach Joe Kuharich plotted to stop New York's now-potent aerial attack by blitzing Tarkenton from the outside to "cut off his escape routes," and by double- and even triple-teaming Homer Jones. It didn't work. New York scored the first seven times it had the ball, including two touchdown receptions by Jones.

New York's 44–7 victory over the Eagles set the stage for a dramatic confrontation in week twelve, when the Giants traveled to Cleveland to play the first-place Browns. A victory would give the Giants a share of the Century Division lead, but it was not to happen. Cleveland no longer had star running back Jim Brown, but halfback Leroy Kelly was taking up much of the slack. Ex-Giant Erich Barnes added a new punch to the defensive secondary. Cleveland's rugged but sometimes inconsistent defense toughened up enough to hold the Giants to 14 points, and with the 24–14 loss, the Giants fell two games behind Cleveland.

New York finished the season with a 30–7 loss to Detroit and a 37–14 victory over St. Louis. Their final 7–7–0 mark was good enough for second place in the Century Division, a marked improvement over 1966. The defense, somewhat improved, especially in the second half of the season, still was the Giants' big weakness. Tarkenton had thrown for 3,088 yards and 29 touchdowns, becoming only the second Giants quarterback to pass for more than 3,000 yards (Tittle did it in 1962 and 1963). Three touchdown passes by backup quarterback Earl Morrall and one by Ernie Koy gave the Giants an NFL-leading 33 scoring tosses. (Washington's Sonny Jurgensen led the league in the individual passing statistics, however, with 3,747 total yards and 31 touchdowns.) Aaron Thomas caught 51 passes, 9 for touchdowns, but Homer Jones led the NFL with 13 touchdown receptions. He had a total of 49 catches and led the league with a 25-yard-per-reception average. Tarkenton, Jones, and Koy were invited to the Pro Bowl, and the freewheeling Jones also got All-Pro acknowledgment.

Considering that they had started from the cellar at the end of the previous season, it had been an excellent year for the Giants. The "Good-bye, Allie" chorus at Yankee Stadium had been quieted.

A number of former Giants greats retired prior to the 1968 season, including Sam Huff, Del Shofner, and Don Chandler, although only Shofner ended his career in New York. The team's draft picks had been depleted by the Tarkenton trade, and there were few new young faces on the Giants' squad.

There was talk of an intracity confrontation between the Giants and the Jets (see sidebar). And the idea seemed exciting enough because in 1968, the Jets' franchise came of age. After Sonny Werblin sold his interest in the team to four partners, Joe Namath led the Jets to the AFL championship and a 16–7 victory over Baltimore in Super Bowl III. As Broadway Joe triumphantly proclaimed in the locker room following the Super Bowl victory, "The AFL and the Jets have arrived." The victory over heavily favored Baltimore was even sweeter because, at a Super Bowl banquet earlier in the week, the Jets' quarterback had "guaranteed" a victory for New York.

Compared to the other New York team, the Giants' performance in 1968 was only average, but the season was not without its thrills. Behind the passing of Fran

The Scrambler

The Giants' new quarterback, Fran Tarkenton, wrote a series of articles for Sports Illustrated *when he first arrived in New York. In the first piece (published on July 17, 1967), he discussed his dislike for the moniker he had acquired playing in New York while still with the Vikings. He did not like to be called "The Scrambler."*

Sure, I scramble. When everything else breaks down, I don't hesitate to roam out of the pocket. . . . These wild sideline-to-sideline scrambles have become my trademark, and people have forgotten the simple truth of the matter, which is that I'm basically a pocket passer.

After we beat the Giants in 1964 there was a lot of stuff in the papers about my scrambling. It seems to me that the name stuck after that. I don't think there was a reporter covering the game who didn't tell about the time I popped out of the pocket, roamed 40 yards behind the line of scrimmage and finally completed a pass downfield for a 10-yard gain. And how many times do you think I scrambled in that ball game? Once.

After the tag "The Scrambler" had become mine, all mine, the public misconceptions about me seemed to multiply. I'd play a game away from home and I'd scramble maybe two or three times, which is my average, and after the game all the reporters would come in and say, "Why didn't you play your usual style?" and "How come you threw so much from the pocket?" And I would try to say, "I threw from the pocket because that's my style."

"No it isn't," they would say. "You're a scrambler."

"O.K.," I would say. "I'm a scrambler." Anything to get to the shower.

Tarkenton, the Giants won their first four games with an offensive onslaught that produced 34 points each against Pittsburgh and Philadelphia, 44 points against Washington, and 33 against New Orleans.

Talk of a title in the Capitol Division, now dominated by the Dallas Cowboys, began to sweep New York. But the hopes faded when the Giants lost three of their next four games, including a 24–21 loss to Atlanta, which gave the Falcons one of their only two victories of the season. To have a chance of catching the division-leading Cowboys, the Giants needed to pull off a miracle in week nine by defeating the Cowboys, who, at that point, had suffered only one defeat.

If the Giants were to pull off an upset, they would have to do it the hard way, in Dallas. The New Yorkers got off to a solid start by scoring first when Tarkenton, searching for Homer Jones in the end zone and finding him well covered, scrambled for a 22-yard touchdown run. Later in

the game, with the score tied at 14, Tarkenton sensed a Cowboys blitz and called an audible at the line. He sent Jones slanting in toward the middle of the field and quickly threw a soft lob in his direction, arcing the ball over the onrushing Dallas defenders. Jones caught it and raced 60 yards for a touchdown. In all, Tarkenton completed 16 out of 24 passes for 187 yards and 2 touchdowns against one of the toughest defenses in the NFL, and the Giants beat mighty Dallas, 27–21.

Going into week ten of the NFL schedule, the Giants had just one more loss than the Cowboys. A sweep of the remaining five games, including the final game of the season which would bring Dallas to Yankee Stadium, would ensure the Giants of at least a tie for first place in the Capitol Division.

New York continued in high gear in week eleven, winning a 7–6 defensive squeaker against Philadelphia; the same day, incidentally, that NBC television infamously

Rookie running back Ronnie Blye (22) from Notre Dame carries several Washington tacklers, including Jim Carroll (60), for a few yards in this 1968 game. The Giants won that game at Yankee Stadium, 48–21, on their way to a second consecutive 7–7, second-place season. (New York Giants)

Bart Starr of the Packers, a true nemesis who addled New York defenses until he retired after the 1971 season, unloads a long one here. No. 57 is Giants linebacker Vince Costello, acquired from the Browns in 1967. (New York Giants)

Giants vs. Jets

Early in 1968 there were high hopes that New York's two professional football teams could at last play a game together. Wellington Mara and the Jets' Sonny Werblin agreed in principle to play a preseason game at Yankee Stadium in 1968 and another exhibition contest at Shea Stadium, which the Jets shared with major-league baseball's New York Mets, the following season.

But the plans came to a halt when New York Mets President Donald Grant issued these stipulations for the use of Shea Stadium:

1. The game had to be scheduled at least five days before the next Mets' home game.

2. The mayor of New York had to make certain that the field would not be damaged.

3. All profits from the game had to be given to charity.

4. No further requests could be made in the future for nonbaseball events that could in any way damage the field during baseball season.

In a joint statement, Mara and Werblin called the demands a "one-shot, don't ever bother us again" proposal and terminated the plans.

But the Giants and Jets did get together in 1969 at the Yale Bowl in New Haven to decide the in-town champ out of town.

decided to discontinue coverage of the close New York Jets–Oakland Raiders game in the final two minutes so the network's presentation of the movie *Heidi* could be seen in its entirety.

While Joe Namath was passing the Jets to the Super Bowl, the Giants began to fall apart. Many fans had hoped that the final game of the regular NFL season would be a battle between the Giants and the Cowboys for the Capitol Division crown, but for the Giants, the 1968 season ended abruptly. They lost all four of their remaining games, including the final matchup with Dallas, when the standings had already been decided.

The Giants had to settle for another 7–7–0 record, good again for second place in the Capitol Division, but not good enough to give Dallas a scare of any sort. Statistically, Tarkenton had another good season, completing 182 passes in 337 attempts for 2,555 yards and 21 touchdowns.

Homer Jones led the Giants' receivers with 45 catches and 7 touchdowns, and again led the NFL with an average gain of 23 yards per reception. But the Giants' rushing attack was just average, with leading ground gainer

Tucker Frederickson achieving only 486 yards. Defensive back Spider Lockhart and center Greg Larson were standouts, and they, along with Tarkenton and Jones, went to the Pro Bowl.

During the 1969 preseason, a much-anticipated exhibition game between the newly crowned world champion New York Jets and the New York Giants finally took place. Following through on a Mara-Werblin promise of the previous year to "remain committed to an early beginning of this series, if not in New York then in another city," the venue was changed to New Haven's Yale B___ where, on August 17, the Jets won easily, 34–___

Coach Allie Sherman talks a little strategy with a fiercely loyal fan, New York senator Robert Kennedy, who had played some football himself during his undergraduate days at Harvard. (New York Giants)

When the Giants lost their next and last preseason game to Pittsburgh in a cold and nearly empty stadium in Montreal, the event marked the end of a winless warm-up to the regular schedule. Wellington Mara had seen enough. With the approval of most New York fans, he removed Allie Sherman as head coach.

"I expect Allie and I will be two of the highest-paid spectators in Yankee Stadium," Mara joked, referring to the five remaining years on Sherman's ten-year contract. Then Mara named former Giants fullback Alex Webster as the new head coach of the team.

The selection of Webster to replace Sherman was a popular choice among Giants fans, who remembered well the steady backfield performances Big Red Webster turned in on the championship teams of the early 1960s. But Webster, with just a week remaining before the start of the regular season, faced a formidable task in rejuvenating the team.

To augment the cast of regulars in 1969 was running back Junior Coffey, a five-year veteran acquired in a trade from Atlanta. The first-round draft pick was a six-foot-six-inch, 239-pound defensive end from San Diego State, Fred Dryer.

At a news conference called before the regular season began, Webster was asked what kind of record he would like to have in his first year as a coach. "Fourteen and oh," he replied.

The new head coach's wish was still a possibility after the first game of the season, when the Giants sneaked past Minnesota, 24–23, in an offensive thriller. But the offense died the following week, and Detroit beat the New Yorkers, 24–0. The Giants won their next two games, giving their new head coach a nice 3–1 start, but then a series of injuries and lackluster performances by stars such as Homer Jones took their effect. With Jones off his usual touchdown pace and the backfield as slow as ever, the Giants lost seven in a row.

Even in the depths of the losing streak, New York fans and players stood behind Webster. Allie Sherman had been controversial among Giants players as well as among their fans, and the entire team seemed to have more fun playing for Webster. The Giants salvaged a respectable season by winning their last three games, including the finale against the Century Division–champion Cleveland Browns. New York's 6 8 0 record was good enough, once again, to place second in the division.

The greatest mystery of the year was the performance of Homer Jones, who registered only a single touchdown reception all season. Joe Morrison, Don Herrmann, Aaron Thomas, Ernie Koy, and newcomer Junior Coffey all managed to pull in at least three scoring tosses. As usual, Fran Tarkenton had an excellent year, completing 220 passes for 2,918 yards and 23 touchdowns.

A new man in charge. The Giants' former star running back Alex Webster took over the head coaching duties from Allie Sherman in 1969. Over five years, Webster compiled a record of 29–40–1 and proved to be more beloved as a player than as a coach. However, he did earn Coach of the Year honors in 1970, his one winning season in New York (9–5). (New York Giants)

But perhaps the biggest news was hardly noticed at first. Back on January 26, 1969, just two weeks after the Jets had won Super Bowl III, a short article from UPI was buried in the sports pages of a number of New York dailies. According to New Jersey State Senator Frank J. Guarini, the Giants' management was actively considering moving the team away from Yankee Stadium. Guarini said he had met with Tim Mara and Giants General Manager Ray Walsh to discuss the possibility of building a new stadium for the team in the Hackensack Meadowlands of New Jersey. "They indicated serious interest," Guarini told the UPI reporter, and agreed to "take a tour of the meadows probably within a week."

The 1970 season finally integrated the playing schedules of the old NFL and rival AFL, now combined into the National and American conferences of the National Football League. The teams were all the same from the 1969 season, but the Baltimore Colts, Cleveland Browns, and Pittsburgh Steelers were moved over to the AFC so that each conference would have thirteen

Summer camp in 1969. Tight end Butch Wilson (86) takes a turn on the blocking sled. Looking on is former Dallas receiver Pete Gent (35), who had been released by the Cowboys after the previous season. Before the 1969 season started, Gent turned in his pads and helmet for a typewriter and sat down to write the best-selling football novel North Dallas Forty. *No. 81 is Freeman White. (New York Giants)*

bers. The Giants became a member of the Eastern Division of the National Conference.

Another historic first occurred the same season as ABC television began broadcasting a series of thirteen games during prime viewing time on Monday nights. Commentators for the first year of "Monday Night Football" were Keith Jackson, Don Meredith, and Howard Cosell. It was not until the second season that Jackson was replaced by the Giants' former halfback and flanker Frank Gifford. With about $8 million from ABC, the three television networks were now spending approximately $150 million ___ for the right to broadcast NFL football.

___ ___ veteran wide receiver Clifton

McNeil from San Francisco and traded Homer Jones, who had been a disappointment for the past season and a half, to Cleveland in exchange for halfback Ron Johnson and defensive tackle Jim Kanicki. Johnson, just a youngster of twenty-two, would prove to be a valuable acquisition over the years. Another soon-to-be valuable addition was rookie tight end Bob Tucker from Bloomsburg State in Pennsylvania.

The 1970 season turned out to be the Giants' best since the championship years in the early 1960s. Although they finished second again, the year was filled with excitement.

Some claimed the Giants had an easy schedule, but after the New Yorkers lost the first three games of the regular season to Chicago, Dallas, and even lowly New Orleans, it looked as if no schedule would be easy enough for Webster and the Giants. But then Tarkenton, along with Ron Johnson, Clifton McNeil, and Tucker Frederickson, the latter for once relatively free of injuries, turned things around, and the Giants won six games in a row, their longest winning streak since the days of Y. A. Tittle. They even beat both the Jets and the Cowboys.

In the upset over Dallas at Yankee Stadium on November 8, kicker Pete Gogolak had field goals of 40, 42, and 54 yards, the last an all-time Giants record. But it was Ron Johnson's running, as much as anything else, that helped the Giants achieve the victory and beat the fierce Dallas pass rush. Time after time, Johnson and other backs ran draw plays, slipping past the Dallas defenders racing toward Tarkenton.

With the exception of the early minutes of the third quarter, when the Cowboys recovered a Tucker Frederick-

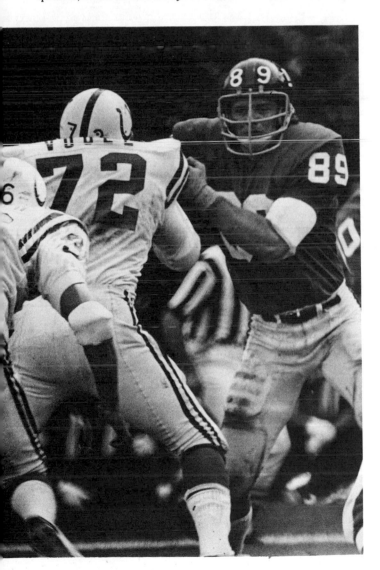

son fumble deep in Giants territory and took advantage of it with a field goal, the New York defense held Dallas scoreless throughout the second half. And in the final minutes of the game, the Giants' rushing attack had finally opened up the passing game to Tarkenton. Three completions for a total of 49 yards set the pace for New York's final winning drive, capped by a 13-yard scoring toss from Tarkenton to Johnson with just three minutes remaining, and the Giants had a 23–20 triumph. It had been a fine day for Johnson, who rushed 23 times for 136 yards and gained 59 more with 4 pass receptions.

The victory placed the Giants (5–3) in a tie for second place with Dallas in the NFC East, a game behind St. Louis, which led the conference with a 6–2 record. New York chalked up its sixth consecutive victory the following week against Washington, but the string was broken in week ten by a 23–20 loss to Philadelphia. However, the Giants bounced back with three victories in a row, capped by a 34–17 win over the Cardinals. Going into the final week of the regular season, the New York Giants had won nine out of their last ten games, good enough for a first-place tie with Dallas. For the first time since 1963, they were just one game away from a conference championship.

An impressive come-from-behind season ended sadly, however, on the last Sunday of the football year when the Giants fell, 31–3, to Los Angeles, while the Cowboys whipped Houston, 52–10. A 9–5–0 record placed New York, for the fourth consecutive time, second in their division, but it was their best effort since 1963. The Giants' offense led the NFC in total first downs, first downs by passing, and pass completions. Ron Johnson rushed for 1,027 yards, the first time any Giants' player had run for a thousand yards or more in a single season. Tarkenton and Johnson were invited to the Pro Bowl.

The 1971 season is one that almost all New York football fans would like to forget. For the Giants, it was both unsuccessful and tumultuous.

During the preseason and before a Sunday night game with the Oilers in Houston, the Giants announced that Fran Tarkenton had retired over a salary dispute. "I really

Establishing himself as a defensive end of much repute in his rookie season, Fred Dryer from San Diego State fends off a block by Baltimore's Bob Vogel. Dryer, the Giants' first-round draft choice in 1969, played in New York through the 1972 season before being traded to the Los Angeles Rams. (New York Giants)

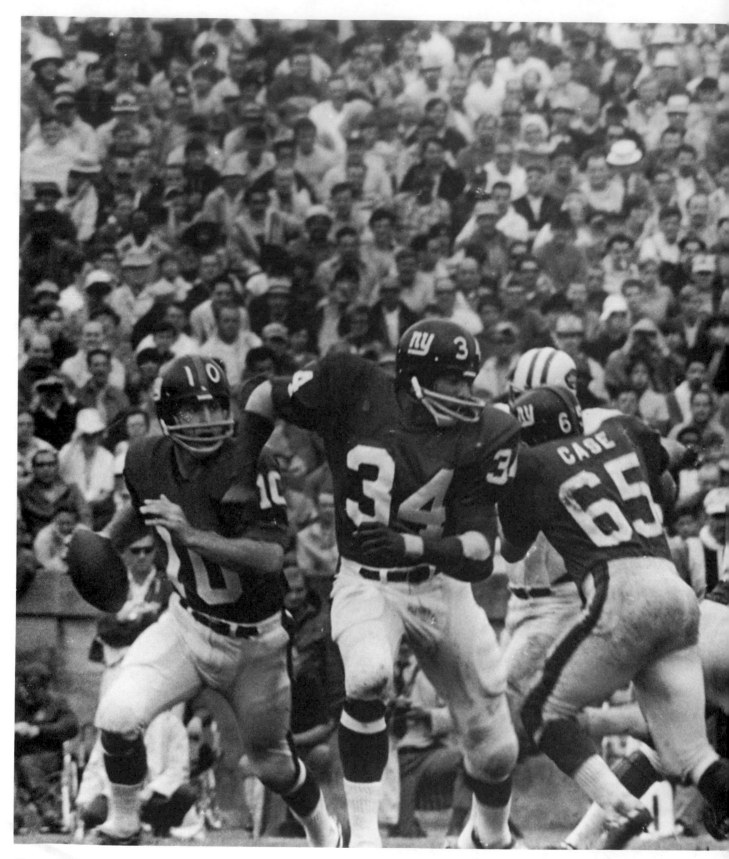

He was known everywhere as "The Scrambler," and no one ever did it better than Fran Tarkenton (10), rolling out here against the St. Louis Cardinals. Blocking for him are fullback Junior Coffey (34) and guard Pete Case (65). (New York Giants)

The nimble Fran Tarkenton did not always get away with scrambling, as is evidenced here, with Washington linebacker Chris Hanburger (55) trying to disrobe the Giants' quarterback while bringing him to earth. (New York Giants)

think Fran's retiring," the *New York Times* reported Wellington Mara as saying. "We've been discussing salary for some time, but I don't think Fran's bluffing." Earlier, Mara had explained that the All-Pro quarterback had been seeking a half-million-dollar loan from the Giants, much of it for his educational foundation devoted to vocational training for underprivileged people.

Tarkenton told Mara that he would play in the game against Houston if he was needed, but would then step aside. Head coach Alex Webster declined the offer and named backup quarterback Dick Shiner as starter.

"There is no rancor," Mara said, referring to his relationship with Tarkenton. "But I haven't seen him since." After the Tarkenton-less Giants were routed by Houston, 35–6, the star quarterback headed toward his home in Atlanta.

His absence lasted only four days. "When I did what I did in Houston, it seemed to me I was doing the right thing," Tarkenton said upon his return to training camp. "But now I admit it was a hasty move." Tarkenton signed a 1971 contract that was estimated to be worth $125,000. Both the quarterback and his head coach agreed that Tarkenton's leadership would not be affected by the incident.

For some New York fans, there was far worse news just two weeks later. On August 26, Wellington Mara and New Jersey Governor William T. Cahill announced that the Giants had signed a thirty-year lease to play all home games beginning in 1975 in a new stadium being built in the Meadowlands, actually a 750-acre parcel of land in the town of East Rutherford, New Jersey.

Mara said that the Meadowlands stadium would give

the Giants their first real home in history and would be more convenient to many of their fans. "New York is not losing a team but gaining a sports complex," he added. While it was true that the Meadowlands would be easier to reach for many fans living in Westchester County, Connecticut, and the New Jersey environs, some residents of New York City regarded the move as little less than treason.

The most vociferous of all was New York Mayor John Lindsay, who took the news in much the same way a general in wartime might feel about a deserter. "The Giant management crossed the line that distinguishes a sport from a business," he said. "I am today directing the corporation counsel to initiate proceedings to restrict the right of the Giants to call themselves by the name of the city they have chosen to leave." Just to make sure no one missed the point, Lindsay characterized Mara's decision as "selfish, callous, and ungrateful." He further announced that he would meet with NFL Commissioner Pete Rozelle to investigate the possibility of bringing a new or existing professional football franchise to the city; that he would plan a suit in federal court to attack football's exemption from antitrust laws should a new franchise fail to develop; and that he would ask New York Representative Emanuel Celler, chairman of the House Judiciary Committee, to conduct a broad investigation into the matter. In the unkindest cut of all, he suggested that New York might prohibit the Giants from playing in Yankee Stadium while their new park was being built. "We made them a successful operation," he added, "and now they want to leave. If they want to play in a swamp, let them play in a swamp right now."

The Giants' first-round draft choice in 1971 was a halfback from West Texas State, Symonds "Rocky" Thompson, who could do little to improve the standing of an injury-laden team. Most missed was the running sensation of 1970, Ron Johnson, who sat out much of the year with a thigh injury, and Tucker Frederickson reinjured his knee. Defensively, a number of injuries hampered the secondary, and veteran defensive back Bennie McRae, acquired from the Chicago Bears, at the age of thirty, seemed to have lost much of his effectiveness.

The Giants lost all their preseason games in 1971 and, after winning two out of their first three regular-season contests, lost all but two of their remaining games. The 4–10–0 record put them in last place in the NFC East. The defense surrendered 64 more points than any other team in the conference. With only 11 touchdown passes all year going into the final game, Tarkenton was benched in favor of backup quarterback Randy Johnson. New York lost the season finale to Philadelphia, 41–28. For the first time in history, no New York Giants player was invited to the Pro Bowl.

Fran Tarkenton never again played in a Giants uniform. It was the end of an era in which, except for the chaotic final season, the Giants were respectable enough to be contenders, but just not quite good enough to win a division title. And there were to be some hard times ahead in the remainder of the 1970s.

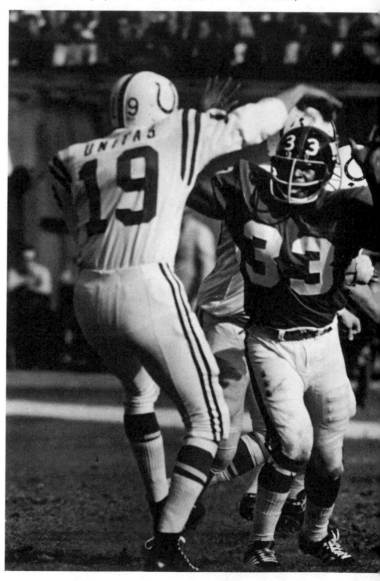

The legendary Johnny Unitas, here in the twilight of his Baltimore Colts career in the early 1970s, still has his inimitable form as he gets one off against the Giants. Applying the pressure is New York safety Joe Green (33). (New York Giants)

Ron Johnson (30), shown here carrying against the Redskins, was acquired from Cleveland in 1970 and promptly became the first New York Giant to rush for more than 1,000 yards in a season (1,027). Two years later he broke his own record by gaining 1,182 yards, a Giant mark that stood until Joe Morris rushed for 1,336 in 1985. In the background is quarterback Fran Tarkenton (10). (New York Giants)

Bob Hyland (70) attended to the duties of center for much of the period from 1971 through 1975, after coming to the Giants in a trade with the Chicago Bears. (New York Giants)

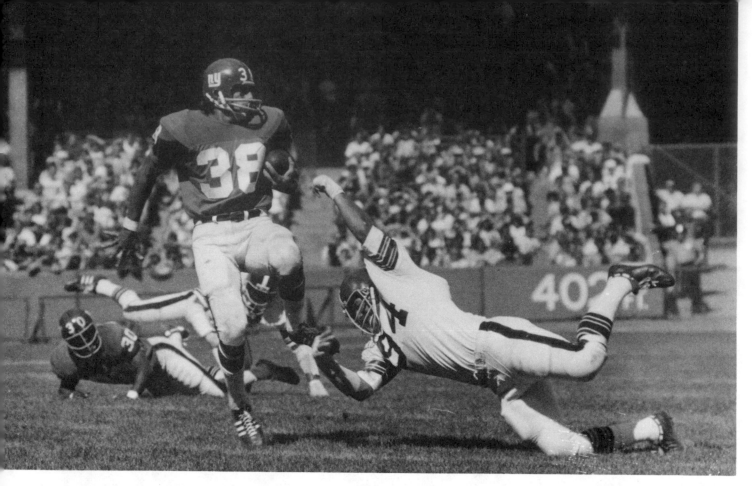

The Giants had to scout tiny Bloomsburg State in Pennsylvania to come up with tight end Bob Tucker (38), signing him as a free agent in 1970. Here he shows some fancy footwork, but pass catching was his truest talent. To illustrate the serendipity of it, Tucker became the first tight end in NFL history to lead the league in pass receptions (59 in 1971), won All-Pro honors the following year, and is third in career receptions for the Giants (327 for 4,376 yards and 22 touchdowns). (New York Giants)

Putting the crunch on Dallas quarterback Roger Staubach is New York linebacker Ralph Heck (55), who had a six-year NFL career with Philadelphia and Atlanta before joining the Giants in 1969. (New York Giants)

14

Orphans of the NFL

A few years after it was all over, sportswriter Red Smith looked back on the chaotic seasons between 1972 and 1976 and referred to the team as the "New York–New Haven–Long Island–New Jersey Giants."

The renovation of Yankee Stadium, begun in 1973, forced the team into a public search for a temporary park, which led to stays in Connecticut's Yale Bowl as well as a season sharing Long Island's Shea Stadium with the Jets before the Giants finally settled into their permanent home in New Jersey in 1976. They were the most highly visible orphans in the NFL, and it apparently had a deleterious effect on the players. The Giants managed a winning season in 1972 but finished last the next two years and next to last in 1975.

The New York Giants began their four-year scramble for a place to play without their scrambling quarterback Fran Tarkenton. Before the final game of the 1971 season, Tarkenton asked to be traded, providing a list of five acceptable teams to Wellington Mara and Coach Alex Webster.

The well-publicized problems faced by the Giants were in obvious contrast to the stability developing in the NFL as a whole. With the difficulties of interleague rivalries finally behind them, NFL owners and officials could settle down to refining the rules, a process that, in just a few seasons, brought the game very close to its present state.

In an attempt to diminish the effectiveness of zone defenses and thus open up the passing game, new rules for 1972 decreased the distance between the hash marks by 6 yards. At least partially in response to a dilemma faced by the Giants in 1973, the U.S. Congress passed a bill that prohibited blackouts of home games sold out seventy-two hours in advance.

Major changes were put into effect in 1974: to cut down on long field goals, the goalposts were moved back ten yards to the back line of the end zones, and missed kicks from outside the 20 were awarded to the opposing team at the original line of scrimmage, rather than at the 20. In the same year, the first of several rulings on the defense now called "bump and run" were put into effect, allowing defenders a single hit on receivers heading downfield. Reserve teams, dubbed "taxi" squads, were abolished in 1975.

Word of the Giants' upcoming real estate problems surfaced during a New York Yankees off-season promotion tour in January 1972. As officials from the Yankees' business office toured cities in Connecticut, New Jersey, and upstate New York to drum up ticket sales, they brought news of a major facelift of Yankee Stadium to be performed during 1973 and 1974. The arrangement, first suggested by New York Mayor John Lindsay, involved the purchase of the structure and grounds of the stadium by the City of New York from Rice University and the Knights of Columbus, previous owners. While their stadium was being rebuilt, the Yankees would be able to share Shea Stadium with the Mets, but few New York officials seemed concerned with helping the Giants. The Maras' problems were also compounded by difficulties in raising funds for the Meadowlands, so significant that there was now litigation and the possibility of a major delay in the start of construction work.

"Officially, we haven't been informed about any of

this," Wellington Mara said to reporters in early 1972 regarding the renovation of Yankee Stadium. "We've talked a little among ourselves about what we would do, but we haven't made any sort of real plans. You might say we'll cross that bridge when we come to it, but under the circumstances that might be a poor choice of words."

At around the same time he was talking to the press about Yankee Stadium, Mara was burning up the phone lines to Minnesota, hammering out a trade with Vikings' General Manager Jim Finks. The agreement sent Fran Tarkenton back to Minnesota in exchange for eleven-year veteran quarterback Norm Snead (who had been in and out of the Vikings' offensive lineup the previous season), offensive end Bob Grim, running back Vince Clements, and two draft choices.

Jack Gregory, a defensive end, was acquired from Cleveland. Notable rookies from the draft included a pair of monstrous defensive tackles: six-foot-one-inch, 255-pound John Mendenhall from Grambling, and six-foot-six-inch, 260-pound Larry Jacobson from Oklahoma. Tucker Frederickson retired following the 1971 season, unable to overcome knee injuries that had ruined a potentially great career.

Economic and political problems were still swirling around the team's proposed new home in New Jersey, only in the planning stages, when Giants management took the first step in the move by setting up training camp at New Jersey's Monmouth College. At Monmouth, head coach Alex Webster let everyone—veterans and rookies alike—know that his days as a nice guy were over. Hard training and discipline replaced the rather easygoing approach that Big Red had adopted before the lackluster 1971 season.

Perhaps in part because of Webster's new hard-nosed approach, the Giants responded with a season better than anyone expected. After losing their first two games to Detroit and Dallas, the Giants won the next four. Leading the way was quarterback Norm Snead, who, by the end of the season, could boast of the highest pass completion average in the NFL. Halfback Ron Johnson returned to the lineup in good shape following a nearly season-long recovery from a leg injury in 1971. And tight end Bob Tucker was playing his position as well as anyone in the league. Following a 27–13 loss to the first-place Washington Redskins in week nine of the NFL schedule, New York bounced back to defeat St. Louis, 13–7, giving the Giants a record of 6–4, three games behind the 9–1 Washington Redskins.

The Giants were two games behind Dallas in a bid for an NFC wild card berth when they returned to Yankee Stadium on November 26 to play the less than lustrous Philadelphia Eagles (2–7–1). The Giants indicated what kind of afternoon it would be when they scored touch-

---

Cosell and Rozelle on the Move to the Meadowlands

On June 19, 1972, "Monday Night Football" commentator Howard Cosell launched a verbal tirade against the Giants' announced move to the New Jersey Meadowlands.

"The Giants have sold every available seat for fifteen straight years," Cosell reported. By moving across the Hudson River, he continued, the Giants were harming the people of New York City, who had supported them so loyally over the years, and they were contributing to the city's image as an "unlivable" place.

One of the members of the "Monday Night Football" viewing audience was Senator Marlow W. Cook, Republican of Kentucky. The senator was so moved by Cosell's remarks that less than a week later he brought NFL Commissioner Pete Rozelle to Washington to answer his pointed questions about the proposed move.

"The new Giants Stadium will be 6.9 miles from Times Square," Rozelle testified. "Yankee Stadium is 6.6 miles. The same fans will have tickets. Some will have a somewhat longer ride, but others will have a shorter ride. The same fans will watch all Giant road games on the same New York television stations."

---

downs on their first two plays from scrimmage. The 62–10 triumph was the highest score ever posted by the Giants and the most points ever surrendered by the Eagles (see sidebar). More importantly, Dallas lost to San Francisco the same day, putting New York only a single game behind the NFC's leading contender for the wild card playoff spot. Since the Giants were scheduled to travel to Dallas for the final game of the season, they now had, as sportscasters are wont to say, control over their destiny in the NFC East.

Four days after the humiliation of the Eagles, New Jersey governor William T. Cahill officially broke ground for the Giants' new Meadowlands stadium in East Rutherford. The ceremony took place in bitter cold weather at a site surrounded by mountains of garbage and rusty automobile carcasses, and the speeches were continuously interrupted by a group of demonstrators opposed to the project. A spokesman for the "Save the Meadowlands" committee argued that the ceremony itself was illegal, since litigation was still pending to stop the entire project. Wellington Mara and ex-Jets owner Sonny Werblin, now chairman of the Meadowlands project, put on brave faces and smiled for photographers.

Norm Snead, shown here throwing through the snow, came to the Giants in a trade in 1972 that sent Fran Tarkenton back to the Minnesota Vikings. Snead captained the offensive attack through that and the following season. His best effort came in 1972, when he completed 60 percent of his passes, tops in the NFC, while gaining 2,307 yards passing. (New York Giants)

In the final game of the season, the Giants beat Dallas, 23–3, and would have earned a wild card spot in the playoffs had they not lost the two previous games to the Cincinnati Bengals and Miami Dolphins. Nevertheless, New York's 8–6–0 season was judged to be reassuringly good considering the team's poor showing in 1971. Norm Snead had completed 196 of 325 passes for a 60 percent completion rate, tops in the NFL. Overall he was ranked second in the NFC, right behind Fran Tarkenton of the 7–7–0 Vikings. Halfback Ron Johnson rushed for 1,182 yards, a new Giants record, and led the NFL with nine touchdowns rushing. Bob Tucker was Snead's top receiver with 55 catches, followed by 45 for Johnson. Tucker and defensive end Jack Gregory made All-Pro, and Gregory along with Snead and Johnson went to the Pro Bowl.

For New York's professional football fans, much of the excitement in 1973 took place before the start of the season. For Wellington Mara and the rest of the Giants' management it became a nightmare as they were forced into a highly public search for a ballpark in which to play their home games.

Although Mayor John Lindsay had proposed that the city of New York buy Yankee Stadium before refurbishing it, a group of investors, many from Cleveland, eventually acquired the stadium. Nevertheless, the city decided to proceed with its plans for a major renovation.

There is evidence that the ensuing eviction of the Giants was also part vendetta, a little something for their plans to move to New Jersey in a few years. The executive director of the NFL stated earlier that it should have been possible to schedule all seven Giants home games in Yankee Stadium by November 4, but city officials insisted that the work would have to begin by October 1 for the park to be ready by the start of the 1976 baseball season, about two and a half years away. City Hall informed the Giants that the team would have to be out of Yankee Stadium after the first two home games in 1973.

Dave Anderson of the *New York Times* reported that a high-placed but unnamed New York City official was overheard to say: "We're not going to do the Giants any favors. We're going to throw them out as soon as the Yankees' season ends."

In March, the Maras learned that the Yale Corporation had decided against allowing the Giants to play in New

Haven's Yale Bowl for the 1973 and 1974 seasons. The main difficulty reportedly revolved around the NFL's blackout rule for home games, which would have prevented Hartford's television station WTIC from covering the games. Just a day or two later, Princeton University in New Jersey also turned down the Giants' request to play in that school's Palmer Stadium for two years.

By the end of April, the NFL was forced to release its official schedule without naming the site of Giants home games. Faced with a mounting crisis, Commissioner Pete Rozelle suggested that, "as part of a continuing experiment," the blackout restriction could be rescinded for the five games the Giants might play in the Yale Bowl. The plan was heartily approved by the Yale Corporation, but chairman John Pastore of the U.S. Senate's Communications Subcommittee, which was studying alleged unfair practices by the television networks, labeled the plan "un-

satisfactory." On May 24, the Giants announced that they would play five home games in the Yale Bowl, but that the question of television coverage remained "unresolved."

The situation was finally put to rest in the fall session of the U.S. Congress. Legislation was passed and signed into law by President Richard Nixon lifting the home city blackout on games sold out at least seventy-two hours in advance of kickoff time.

On July 11, Jersey City Mayor P. T. Jordan signed a two-year contract allowing the Giants to practice in that city's Roosevelt Stadium. It was now certain that the team still called the New York Giants would practice in New Jersey and play all but two of its home games in Connecticut.

With the excitement of the spring and summer over, the Giants got ready for the 1973 season. Their first draft pick (in the second round) was linebacker Brad Van Pelt from

Defensive end Jack Gregory (81) makes the Cowboys' Roger Staubach painfully aware of his presence, although the Dallas quarterback managed to get rid of the ball. Gregory was obtained from the Cleveland Browns in 1972. On twenty-one other occasions during his first season with the Giants, opposing quarterbacks were not as fortunate as Staubach and were victims of Gregory's sacks. Gregory played for the Giants through the 1978 season. No. 62 for Dallas is John Fitzgerald. (New York Giants)

Michigan State. In marked contrast to the regular season, the Giants went 6–0 in the preseason, including a 45–30 victory over the Jets on August 19 in the Yale Bowl.

In the closing weeks of the preseason and the early weeks of the regular schedule, yet another ballpark problem arose. New Jersey authorities were having difficulty floating bonds to cover the costs of building the Meadowlands stadium. On November 1, Wellington Mara told reporters that he had given the New Jersey Sports and Exposition Authority until December 1 to show that the money for the stadium could be raised. But following the general elections in November, New Jersey's new Gover-

---

A Record-Setting Rout

The Giants, their collective eye still on a playoff berth as a wild card, rampaged into Yankee Stadium on November 26, 1972, to play the Philadelphia Eagles. With quarterback Norm Snead, running back Ron Johnson, and receiver Bob Tucker all in top form, it was hardly a contest. On New York's first possession, they scored on a 15-yard pass from Snead to Tucker. The next time the Giants had the ball, they made another score, this one on a 35-yard run by Johnson.

On the first play of the second quarter, Snead passed to fullback Joe Orduña for a 5-yard touchdown. Not much later, Pete Gogolak nailed a 25-yard field goal. Tucker then made his second touchdown reception of the day on a 29-yard pass from Snead, and Johnson added yet another touchdown on a 1-yard run. At halftime, the score was 38–10, New York.

Later in the game, reserve quarterback Randy Johnson took over for Snead, and a host of other Giants' replacements took to the field. For Philadelphia, it was just one of those days. In the final eighteen minutes of the game, Randy Johnson hit Don Herrmann twice in the end zone with touchdown tosses and even ran in once for a score. The final score, 62–10, set team scoring records for the Giants and the Eagles as well. Philadelphia had never before given away so many points in a single game. Pete Gogolak also set a team game record when he kicked his eighth extra point. Ron Johnson rushed for 123 yards before he was pulled in the third quarter. Bob Tucker caught 8 passes for 100 yards.

A group of disgruntled Philadelphia fans planned to use the game as evidence in their lawsuit against the Eagles. The season ticket holders went to court demanding their money back because they alleged that the Philadelphia team failed to provide football entertainment at a big-league level.

nor-elect Brendan T. Byrne clouded the issue even more by announcing that he would not necessarily support Governor Cahill's backing of the project, at least not without a renegotiated contract with the Giants. Word of the governor elect's stance was met with enthusiasm in Albany, where New York's Governor Nelson Rockefeller renewed his efforts to block the building of the stadium and force the Giants to remain in New York City.

Wellington Mara, barely over the crises of the summer, now had to throw more energy into the Meadowlands project, supposedly settled more than two years earlier. But on November 27, Byrne, a month and a half away from taking office, announced that he had come to terms with the Maras and the Giants. Governor Cahill was lavish in his praise of the new agreement, and the Maras must have breathed a great sigh of relief.

There was no relief on the playing field for the Giants, however. After an impressive preseason, the Giants won the opening game of the year in Yankee Stadium by defeating Houston, 34–14. In the second week, the team played its final game in Yankee Stadium, battling Philadelphia to a 23–23 tie. But then the Giants went on the road, so to speak, and the nomadic life-style seemed to destroy them. They lost eleven of the remaining twelve games, managing but a single victory in the Yale Bowl over the St. Louis Cardinals. One of the biggest losers was Alex Webster, who resigned as head coach before the final game of the season, a 31–7 loss to Fran Tarkenton and the Vikings in the Yale Bowl.

Ron Johnson had another good year, rushing for 902 yards and scoring 9 touchdowns, 6 rushing and 3 on pass receptions. Norm Snead completed 56 percent of his passes, but far too many of them fell into the hands of opposing players. He was intercepted 22 times against only 7 touchdown tosses. Backup quarterback Randy Johnson, who announced that he was quitting the team, played in many of the games. The defense, which had shown signs of coming alive in 1972, gave up a total of 362 points, just 31 shy of the NFC-leading Eagles. No one from the team was invited to the Pro Bowl.

The 1973 Giants had not had much of a season, but there was no lack of help in shaping it. The president of the United States, the U.S. Congress, the governor of New York, the mayor of New York City, numerous courts, two Ivy League universities, the commissioner of the NFL, and two New Jersey governors all had their hands in Giants affairs that year.

On January 16, 1974, Andy Robustelli, who had been named Giants director of operations a month earlier, opened a press conference at New York's 21 Club to introduce the team's new head coach, forty-seven-year-old Bill Arnsparger. Although he had never played football professionally, Arnsparger brought solid credentials to his first head coaching position. Most recently, he had spent four years masterminding the Miami Dolphins' championship defenses as assistant coach to Don Shula.

"He's got the job of coaching football," Robustelli said at the conference. "He's going to tell me what he needs, and I'm going to try and get it for him."

After the new head coach had completed his remarks, he was asked if he would be "satisfied with a .500 season." His answer came quickly: "No."

Arnsparger's first goal was to rebuild the aging offensive line, which had not done enough to protect Norm Snead the previous season. Work began at the NFL draft held two weeks later. In the first round, Arnsparger selected All-American offensive guard John Hicks from Ohio State. To a chorus of boos from the crowd watching the proceedings during the second round, he chose another offensive lineman, Tom Mullen, from Southwest Missouri State. Despite the reaction of the audience, both newcomers were good enough to step into the starting lineup.

Unfortunately, the reinforced offensive line was not enough to help the Giants to a respectable season. In the first seven games of the fourteen-game schedule, the New

The top draft choice for the Giants in 1973, although it came in the second round, was linebacker Brad Van Pelt, an All-American from Michigan State. Van Pelt was named All-Pro five times in his eleven-year Giants career before being traded after the 1983 season. (Fred Roe)

Arnsparger's Résumé

Bill Arnsparger's Impressive Credentials

He may have had limited success as the head coach of the Giants, but Bill Arnsparger brought as fine a pedigree to his first head coaching position as anyone could want.

- *While still in high school, he played football under Blanton Collier.*
- *He played offensive tackle at Miami of Ohio under Woody Hayes.*
- *His first coaching job was as a graduate assistant to Hayes at Miami.*
- *When Hayes went to Ohio State in 1951, he brought Arnsparger along.*
- *From 1954 to 1961, he worked at Kentucky under Blanton Collier. Don Shula was also on the staff.*
- *In 1964 he became an assistant to Don Shula with the Baltimore Colts.*
- *When Shula took over the Miami Dolphins, Arnsparger was the only coach he brought with him from Baltimore.*
- *At Miami, he masterminded some of the toughest defenses the professional game had yet seen and was Shula's defensive coach in two Super Bowl victories.*

Yorkers were 1–6, scoring just 68 total points, to 141 for their opponents.

The Giants' road loss to the Washington Redskins in week six was indicative of the first half of the 1974 season. The previous Sunday, the Redskins and their eighteen-year-veteran quarterback, Sonny Jurgensen, had engineered a come-from-behind victory against the Miami Dolphins. Before 53,879 roaring spectators, Jurgensen (who, ironically, had been acquired from Philadelphia for Norm Snead) picked apart the Giants' secondary, completing the 249th, 250th, and 251st touchdown passes in his professional career. For the third consecutive game, Snead and the New York offense were unable to get anything going and the final score was 24–3, Washington.

A 21–7 loss to Dallas in the Yale Bowl the following Sunday proved conclusively that the Giants' offense was in deep trouble. The solution, Arnsparger thought, was to be provided by thirty-two-year-old Craig Morton, a former Dallas quarterback, who was traded to New York from the Birmingham Americans of the new World Football League (WFL). After acquiring Kenny Stabler, the Birmingham team traded Morton to a struggling WFL franchise in Houston. Gambling that Morton would be able to get out of his WFL contract, the Giants acquired him from Dallas in midseason, and Snead was traded to San Francisco.

Morton, who after only three days with the club relieved interim quarterback Jim Del Gaizo in the eighth game of the season, immediately put new vitality into the Giants' offense. The team that had scored just 68 points in the first half of the season managed to put 127 points on the board during the second half, but even the much-improved offense under Craig Morton was not enough to rescue a poor season. The defense was unable to hold opponents to less than 16 points in any of the last ten games. The final 2–12–0 record was made even poorer by the fact that the Giants lost every home game in 1974. The record for nearly two full seasons at the Yale Bowl was 1–11.

Although work on the new Giants Stadium in the New Jersey Meadowlands was progressing, it was clear that the park would not be ready by the 1975 season. Officials at the Yale Corporation were surprised when, on December 19, Abraham Beame, still in his first year as mayor of New York City, announced that the Giants would be playing their home games in Shea Stadium during the 1975 season. Beame apparently did not share former Mayor John Lindsay's feelings toward the team. He also announced that the Giants were given an option to play in refurbished Yankee Stadium during 1976 in the event the Meadowlands stadium was still unfinished.

"We understand it is a stopgap measure," said a spokesman for the NFL, which was now faced with the difficult task of scheduling Giants games in a stadium shared by the Mets and Yankees as well as the Jets.

The Giants, who had traded their number-one draft choice in 1975 to Dallas the previous season in exchange for Craig Morton, selected in the second round offensive tackle Al Simpson from Colorado State. Simpson would be used extensively on special teams during the 1975 season and remain with the Giants only for one more year.

The Houston Texans, the WFL team that owned Craig

Wide receiver Bob Grim holds onto a Norm Snead pass despite the efforts of St. Louis defender Larry Willingham (8) in this 1972 game. Grim came to New York along with Snead when Fran Tarkenton was dealt to the Vikings. The Giants beat the Cardinals in both their encounters in 1972 to post an 8–6, third-place standing in the NFC East. (New York Giants)

Morton's 1975 contract, folded. Stating that he had no further commitments with the WFL, the former Dallas quarterback signed a three-year contract with New York in April. In May, the Giants acquired linebacker Bob Schmidt, a free agent after playing the 1974 season with the WFL's Portland franchise.

On July 23 came the sad word that former Giants great and Hall of Famer Emlen Tunnell had died of a heart attack. At the time of his death, he was working as a scout for the Giants' organization.

For nearly a year, NFL Players Association president Ed Garvey had been battling with owners and Commissioner Pete Rozelle over the "Rozelle rule," which limited the movements of free agents playing out their options. The dispute led to a brief strike during the 1975 preseason, but seemed, still unresolved, about to threaten the regular season in 1975. On September 13, just one day before their final exhibition game, the New England Patriots went out on strike. Within the next four days, officials for both the Giants and the Jets, as well as the Washington Redskins and the Detroit Lions, found their players also walking away from them as a response to the controversy over the Rozelle rule. On September 18, just four days before the start of the regular season, a peace pact was signed allowing the regular season to commence without a final decision on the controversial rule, but courtroom battles over free agent status continued well into 1976.

Opening at Shea Stadium

When the Giants met Dallas on October 12, 1975, at Shea Stadium in New York, it had been two years since the Giants played in New York City. It was an inauspicious homecoming. On the game's first play from scrimmage, New York quarterback Craig Morton fumbled, setting up a 24-yard field goal by Dallas's Toni Fritsch. Two first-half drives by the Giants ended in Dallas interceptions. In the third period the New Yorkers went ahead, 7–3, but another Morton fumble, this time at his own 32, set up a second Dallas field goal, making the score 7–6, New York.

The Giants' defense performed well all day, limiting Dallas quarterback Roger Staubach to 8 completions in 22 attempts and sacking him 3 times. But late in the game, another error by Morton led to a Dallas victory. The Cowboys' Mark Washington intercepted a Morton pass headed into the end zone and ran the ball all the way back to the New York 17-yard line. A short scoring toss from Staubach sealed the Cowboys' come-from-behind victory, 13–7.

In the meantime, the Giants started the 1975 season on a high note. More than 65,000 fans watched the Eagles take an early lead in the September 21 season opener in Philadelphia, but the Giants bounced back with two short scoring rushes by Ron Johnson and a 41-yard George Hunt field goal to give New York a 16–7 lead in the third quarter. The Giants' defense performed well, sacking Eagles quarterback Mike Boryla three times and intercepting him twice. In the fourth quarter, he was replaced by Roman Gabriel, who managed a 2-yard touchdown toss, but it wasn't enough. The final score was 23–14, New York.

The joy of a season-opening win was short-lived, however. The Giants were slaughtered, 49–13, the following Sunday in Washington and lost, 26–14, in week three at St. Louis. Things looked far from rosy as the New Yorkers prepared for their home opener at Shea Stadium against Dallas on October 12 (see sidebar).

Following a 13–7 loss to the Cowboys, the Giants upset previously undefeated Buffalo in a 17–14 Monday night thriller the next week, despite 128 rushing yards gained by O. J. Simpson, but fell, 20–13, to St. Louis the following Sunday. In week seven, Craig Morton and the rest of the offensive squad put on a fine show, defeating San Diego 35–24 in the Giants' first victory at Shea Stadium. But the team fell from contention in the NFC East by losing the next five games in a row. Only victories in the final two games over New Orleans and San Francisco enabled the Giants to post an improved record of five wins against nine losses.

Although the team improved, there were few bright spots in the year-end statistics. Fullback Joe Dawkins, with just 438 yards, was the team's leading rusher. Quarterback Craig Morton, with only 13 touchdown passes and 11 interceptions, was ranked eighth in the NFC. The defense gave up a total of 306 points, third worst in the conference.

There was, at least, some good news. Although the entire Meadowlands sports complex was running millions of dollars over the projected $302 million budget (it also included a horseracing track and an arena), the new Giants Stadium in New Jersey was finally taking shape. There were signs, at least, that the orphans of the NFL were about to have a real home, the first in their history.

New York's Ron Johnson struggles to break loose from the grasp of Miami's Mike Kolen (57) in this 1972 game. The season was Johnson's finest with the Giants as he gained 1,182 yards rushing, then an all-time Giants standard. New York lost this game, however, 23–13. No. 84 of the Giants is wide receiver Dick Houston. (Fred Roe)

Guard John Hicks (74), adding a little something to the head of Washington's Diron Talbert, was New York's first-round draft pick in 1974. The former Ohio State All-American made the NFL All-Rookie team and was one of the Giants' finest blockers through the 1977 season. (New York Giants)

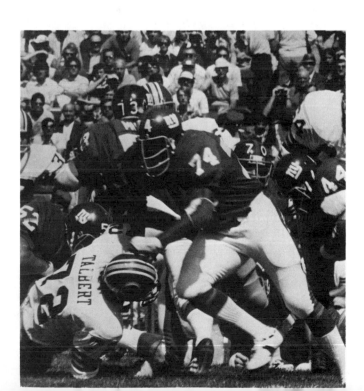

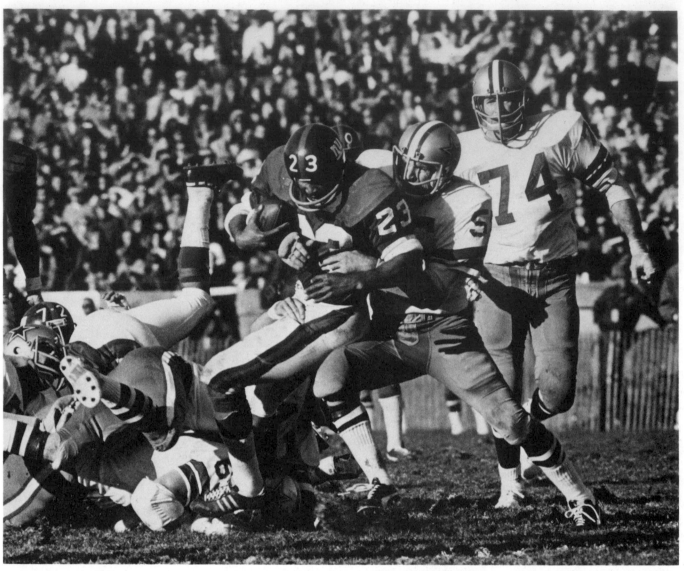

Johnny Roland (23) struggles for a few yards in this 1973 meeting with the Cowboys, but cannot get out of the clutches of Dallas linebacker Lee Roy Jordan. Roland was in the last year of his career, coming to the Giants that year after seven fine seasons with the Cardinals. He gained 142 yards for the Giants in a lackluster 2–11–1, last-place season. No. 74 on Dallas is Hall of Famer Bob Lilly. (New York Giants)

About to make a spectacular catch is wide receiver Walker Gil-lette (84), who was picked up on waivers from the Cardinals in 1974. His best year with New York was 1975, when he led the team with 43 receptions for 600 yards. He left the squad after the 1976 season. (New York Giants)

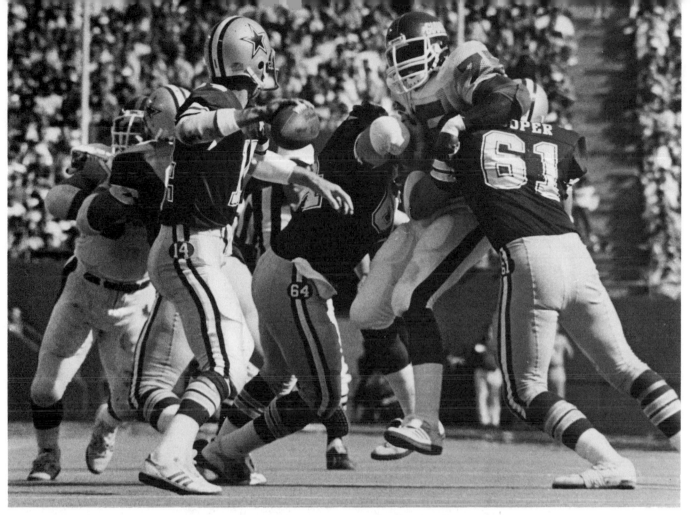

It takes two Cowboys to keep New York defensive end George Martin away from passer Danny White. Martin, an eleventh-round draft choice from Oregon in 1975, proved to be one of New York's most devastating pass rushers over the next decade. He holds the NFL record for most touchdowns by a defensive lineman, six, the last a 78-yard interception return in 1986 against Denver. (Fred Roe)

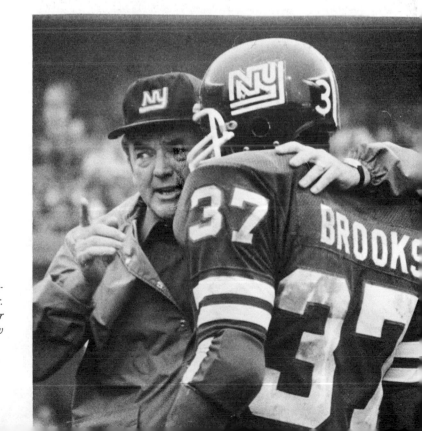

Bill Arnsparger, the new head coach in 1974, confers with defensive back Bobby Brooks, also a Giants newcomer that year. Arnsparger replaced Alex Webster and remained at the helm for three seasons, posting a disappointing record of 7–28. (New York Giants)

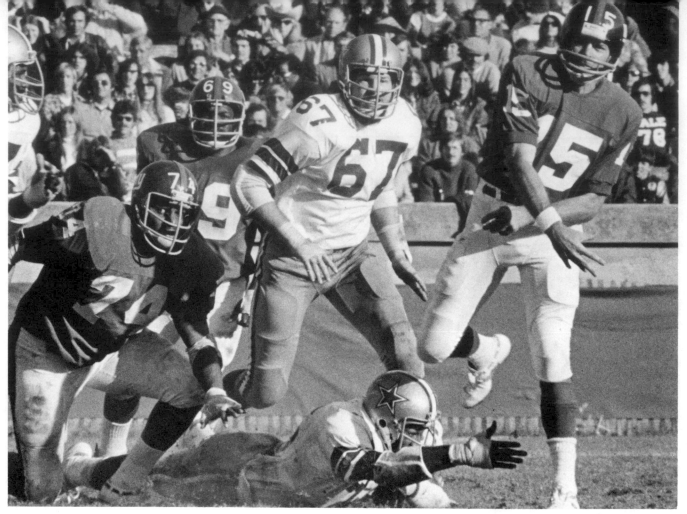

Veteran quarterback Craig Morton (15), acquired in October 1974 from Dallas, was the hope on which the restoration of the Giants passing game was based. Here he fires one off against Dallas as New York's John Hicks (74) and Willie Young (69) as well as Pat Donovan (67) of the Cowboys watch. Morton quarterbacked the club for three seasons. His best year was 1975, when he completed 186 passes for 2,359 yards and 11 touchdowns. (New York Giants)

One of the great surprise finds of 1974 was not a headless football player but punter Dave Jennings, shown here limbering up. Signed as a free agent from St. Lawrence University in New York, Jennings quickly became one of the NFL's premier punters, earning All-Pro honors five times in his eleven-year Giants career. He holds the NFL record for the most punts in a career (1,090) as well as for the most consecutive punts without having one blocked (623), and the club standards for most punts (931), most punts in a season (104), most yards punting (38,792), and the highest average in a game (55.3 yards, 4 punts). (Fred Roe)

Joe Dawkins, acquired from Denver in 1974, leaps over the New Orleans Saints' line for a first down. Dawkins led the Giants in rushing for two seasons before moving on to Houston. The Giants won this game, 28–14. (New York Giants)

Doug Kotar, obtained from the Steelers during training camp of his rookie year in 1974, landed a starting job in the Giants' backfield right away. Kotar remained with the Giants through the 1981 season, gaining a total of 3,378 yards on 900 carries, enough to rank him as the fifth all-time Giant rusher. His best year was 1976, when he gained 731 yards, averaging four yards per carry. (New York Giants)

Pressuring Dallas quarterback Roger Staubach is defensive end Dave Gallagher, who came to New York in 1975, in a trade that sent Bob Grim to the Chicago Bears, and remained through two seasons. (New York Giants)

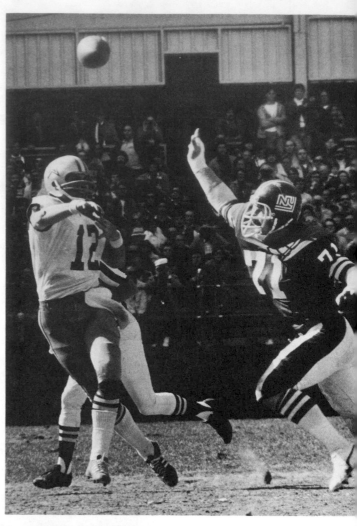

Bobby Brooks (37) puts the shoulder to Eagles wide receiver Charlie Smith in this 1975 game. Moving in to help are George Martin (75) and Brian Kelly (55); Stan Walters is the horizontal Eagle in the foreground. (New York Giants)

Rondy Colbert (35) enters the open prairie after fielding a New Orleans punt, on his way to a 65-yard touchdown return. A rookie in 1975 out of Lamar University, he proved to be an adept defensive back as well as a fine kick returner. No. 28 of the Giants is Robert Giblin. (New York Giants)

15

A Stadium of One's Own

The United States celebrated its two hundredth birthday in 1976, and the festivities were a nationwide pageant. The New York Giants, on the other hand, were only entering their fifty-second year of existence, but they were able to celebrate that milestone with a brand-new home. No more baseball parks or college bowls; they now had a football stadium of their own replete with their name on it in enormous boldface letters: GIANTS STADIUM.

But that was about all the organization had to celebrate, having just come off three losing seasons in which they had posted a collective record of 9–32–1. Bill Arnsparger was beginning his third year as head coach and predicted that "1976 is the year we break .500, the first real step on our way back up."

In recent years the Eastern Division had been fairly well dominated by Tom Landry's Dallas Cowboys, showcasing Roger Staubach and a defense approaching legendary status; Don Coryell's St. Louis Cardinals, who featured the two-fisted attack of Jim Hart's passing and the running of Jim Otis and Terry Metcalf; and George Allen's Washington Redskins, with their punishing defense and conglomerate of very old but still very good pros, not the least of whom was Billy Kilmer. The Giants had not been in a class with them for some time now.

The league itself was undergoing some changes. Welcomed into the fold were the Tampa Bay Buccaneers and Seattle Seahawks, bringing the number of franchises to twenty-eight. The thirty-second clock became a feature in all NFL stadiums. And the World Football League was no longer any threat, gone to the same burial ground as so many other rival leagues that preceded it.

The biggest name to join the Giants in 1976 was Larry Csonka, the bone-crushing fullback who had battered his way through several Super Bowls for the Miami Dolphins in the early 1970s and who had spent the 1975 season playing for the WFL's Memphis franchise, now defunct. The Giants signed Csonka after giving him, according to Dan Jenkins in *Sports Illustrated,* "most of Wall Street." Then just before the start of the regular season, the Giants reacquired quarterback Norm Snead, now thirty-six, from the San Francisco 49ers.

From the draft, the Giants had picked up defensive tackle Troy Archer from Colorado, defensive lineman–turned-linebacker Harry Carson from South Carolina State, and running back Gordon Bell out of Michigan.

Anticipating a last-minute scramble to get the Meadowlands stadium ready for the 1976 season opener, the NFL schedule-makers put the Giants on the road for the first four games of the year. The New York coaching staff dearly wanted to win the first game of the season, hoping to upset a strongly favored Redskins in Washington. And the Giants almost pulled it off. With only about a minute and a half remaining in the game, they led, 17–12. But their offense stalled, and fleet Larry Brown fielded a New York punt and broke loose on a 40-yard return. Two Billy Kilmer passes later, the Redskins had the score and eradicated the Giants' bid for an upset with a 19–17 come-from-behind victory.

The road show moved on to Philadelphia, Los Angeles, and St. Louis, but the story in each city was unfortunately much the same, at least in terms of the final score.

When the Giants finally traveled to New Jersey to make

186

a long-anticipated debut in their new stadium, they brought with them a record of 0–4. Despite that, 76,042 fans jammed Giants Stadium to watch the new tenants take on the powerful Dallas Cowboys. There was, of course, color and controversy as the new home of the Giants was christened that October afternoon (see sidebar). Notable were the new Giants' helmets with the long-familiar *NY* removed from the side and replaced simply by the word *Giants*.

When the game began, Roger Staubach and the rest of the Cowboys demonstrated why they were the only undefeated and untied team in the NFL as they moved smartly downfield with nine consecutive first downs and two touchdowns on their first two possessions. The second Dallas score was a 40-yard Staubach-to–Drew Pearson touchdown strike.

"We played very well in the first quarter," Red Smith quoted Dallas head coach Tom Landry as saying, "and then we began to work on our running game, which hasn't been going very well lately." While the Cowboys spent the remainder of the contest practicing their rushing attack, New York managed to make the final score look respectable. After a Dallas field goal made the score 17–0 at halftime, New York finally scored in the third quarter on a 30-yard pass from Craig Morton to wide receiver Jimmy Robinson, who had been signed as a free agent prior to the start of the season. Halfway through the final quarter, Dallas put its third touchdown on the board soon after intercepting a Morton pass. Minutes later, Morton was sacked for the fifth time during the afternoon and left the game with a minor leg injury. Replacement Norm Snead completed four consecutive passes to give the Giants their final score of the day. But it wasn't enough. The handsome new stadium was besmirched with a 24–14 Dallas win. And for the first time in club history, the Giants opened their season with five consecutive losses.

Two more losses, a 24–7 lacing by Fran Tarkenton's Super Bowl–bound Vikings and a 27–0 shutout by the world champion Pittsburgh Steelers, doomed head coach Bill Arnsparger.

On October 25, director of operations Andy Robustelli announced that Arnsparger had been fired and that forty-five-year-old assistant coach John McVay had been moved up to the top slot. "He is not an interim coach in the strict sense of the word," Robustelli said, implying there was more than a little pressure on the new head coach.

Wellington Mara, after living through the relocation controversy and the disappointments of his team in recent years, sounded a bit world-weary when he said: "I feel we've reached the point where it's imperative to see if the people we have can respond to a personality other than Bill."

Opening Day Color and Controversy

"I haven't missed a Columbus Day parade in years," said New Jersey governor Brendan T. Byrne, trying to explain why he chose to attend a local parade rather than the pregame dedication ceremonies at brand-new Giants Stadium in the Meadowlands. But there were other explanations.

"He didn't come because he didn't want to get booed," the New York Times *quoted an unnamed official from the New Jersey Sports and Exposition Authority. "He got booed pretty badly when the race track opened last month."*

Former governor William T. Cahill, one of the guiding forces behind early plans for the sports complex, answered "no comment" when he was asked to speculate why the current governor chose not to attend. Outside the stadium, several hundred demonstrators carried placards demanding that the sports authority pay a larger share of taxes.

Although a few fans were disappointed that their seat locations made it impossible to see either of two huge electronic scoreboards, most agreed that the three-tiered stadium, dedicated solely to football, was a comfortable place to watch a game. In the audience and participating in the pregame festivities were former Giants from the 1956 championship team, including Charlie Conerly, Kyle Rote, Rosey Grier, and Alex Webster. Bob Hope, Peggy Cass, and other celebrities were also in attendance.

Said Sonny Werblin, former Jets owner and now chairman of the New Jersey sports authority: "I'm as excited as I can be because everybody said that it would never happen." Robert Meyner, another former New Jersey governor, waxed even more enthusiastic: "Even from the time of William Penn and Ben Franklin, we were considered a state between New York and Philadelphia. I'm pleased to see it's worked out, and it augurs well for the identity of New Jersey."

But the Giants did not get off on the old right foot. While a group of fans displayed a banner reading "Brand New Stadium—Same Old Giants," the New Yorkers lost to Dallas, 24–14.

McVay's number one objective was to get the faltering Giants' offense rolling again, and his ability to work with offensive teams was undoubtedly part of the reason he was given the head coaching position. When he had directed the WFL's Memphis Southmen two seasons earlier, his team led that league in most offensive categories and won seventeen games.

This opening day crowd of 76,042 christened brand-new Giants Stadium in the Meadowlands of East Rutherford, New Jersey, on October 10, 1976. Ground was broken for the edifice back in November 1972. (New York Giants)

But in McVay's debut at Giants Stadium on October 31, the offenseless New Yorkers were shut out, 10–0, by the Philadelphia Eagles, a team destined to win only four games that year. Craig Morton was sacked six times. Things were not much better at Dallas the following week, as the 0–7 Giants became the 0–8 Giants in a game they should have won. The defense had not allowed Dallas a touchdown all afternoon, and with the score 9–3 favoring Dallas and one minute left to play, the Giants had the ball on the Cowboys' 6-yard line. There, with a Dallas defender all over potential receiver Bob Tucker in the end zone, Craig Morton was hit hard before he could get rid of the football. He fumbled and Dallas got it—and the game. Then, as the NFL moved into the second half of its schedule, the Giants dropped to 0–9 by losing to Denver, 14–13.

New York finally won its first game of the year in NFL week ten. With Norm Snead now at quarterback, the Giants upset Washington, 12–9, marking not only the first win for the team in Giants Stadium, but also John McVay's first victory as head coach and the first victory in fifteen attempts for the Giants over a George Allen–coached team.

McVay and the Giants won two of the remaining four

Doug Kotar (44) carries for the Giants as Bill Ellenbogen (65) moves in to lay a block on Dallas defensive tackle Larry Cole. (New York Giants)

Some action from the first game played in Giants Stadium.

Rookie defensive end Troy Archer, the Giants' number one draft choice from Colorado in 1976, snares Roger Staubach for a loss. (New York Giants)

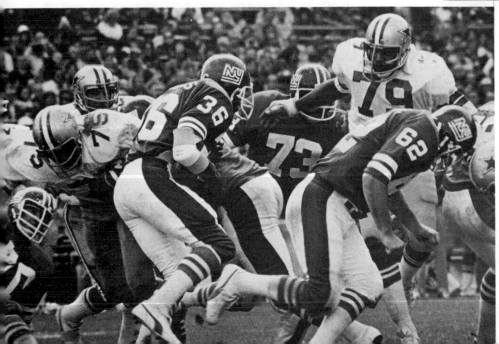

Larry Watkins (36) hits the line against Dallas, but awaiting him is monstrous defensive end Harvey Martin (79). Other Giants are Tom Mullen (73) and Ron Mikolajczyk (62); No. 75 on the Cowboys is Jethro Pugh. (New York Giants)

games, giving them a final 1976 record of 3–11. One of the few standouts on the squad was linebacker Brad Van Pelt, who had been the team's second-round draft choice in 1973. As he would for the next five years in succession, Van Pelt was invited to the Pro Bowl, and it was the first time any Giants player had been selected since 1972. Running back Doug Kotar, who had been acquired from Pittsburgh in 1974, led the team with 731 yards rushing. Larry Csonka, sidelined much of the time with injuries, gained 569 yards. Bob Tucker again led the receivers with 42 catches. On December 14, John McVay signed a two-year contract to continue as head coach, his record of 3–4 considerably but not excitingly better than what the Giants had been experiencing.

The Giants traded Craig Morton to Denver in 1977 for quarterback Steve Ramsey, but the major acquisition, management felt, was free agent Joe Pisarcik, who had spent three years with the Canadian Football League's Calgary franchise. The six-foot-four-inch, 220-pound athlete arrived at training camp as the number *five* quarterback, but he eventually won the job. The first-round draft choice was defensive lineman Gary Jeter of USC.

The Giants opened the 1977 season on September 18 in a game against Washington before a then-record crowd of 76,086 at Giants Stadium. Midway through the first period, New York defensive end George Martin intercepted a Billy Kilmer pass and rumbled 30 yards for a touchdown. The score stayed at 7–0 until the third quarter, when a 64-yard New York drive was capped by an apparent touchdown that was called back by a penalty. The New Yorkers had to settle for a 22-yard Joe Danelo field goal. With the score at 10–0 at the start of the final quarter, the Washington offense exploded. A 3-yard touchdown run by Mike Thomas, a short scoring toss from Billy Kilmer to John Riggins, and a 51-yard Mark Moseley field goal gave the Redskins 17 unanswered points and a 17–10 lead late in the final period. But the Giants came back in one of their finest finishes of the time. Quarterback Jerry Golsteyn, a youngster out of Northern Illinois who had been New York's twelfth-round draft choice in 1976, led a 74-yard touchdown drive on four plays, knotting the score at 17. With less than two minutes remaining, defensive tackle Troy Archer stripped the ball from Washington running back Mike Thomas, and Giants middle linebacker Harry Carson recovered the fumble. With seven seconds remaining, Joe Danelo kicked the winning field goal.

The 20–17 upset marked the second time in a row the Giants had surprised the George Allen–coached Redskins. The season had begun on a high note, but unfortunately it ended in a familiar refrain, as the New Yorkers won only four of their remaining thirteen games.

The club's record of 5–9 was an improvement over the

Distant Replay

The ambulance that stood by in New York's Central Park was not needed, despite the ninety-degree heat, as the stars from the Colts' and Giants' 1958 championship game played touch football on July 7, 1978, a game that was to be broadcast later in the season by CBS television. Colts players included Johnny Unitas, Alan Ameche, Gino Marchetti, Lennie Moore, Ray Berry, Jim Parker, Art Donovan, and Steve Myhra. The Giants' players hoping for revenge were Charlie Conerly, Frank Gifford, Kyle Rote, Alex Webster, Rosey Brown, Ray Wietecha, Dick Modzelewski, and Pat Summerall.

Myhra brought a six-pack of beer to the Colts' bench for pregame refreshments, but soon referee Sonny Jurgensen had the players, six to a side, on the field. After just a few plays from scrimmage, Unitas threw a scoring spiral to Lennie Moore in the end zone. Jurgensen declared the score 7–0 without a point-after attempt.

Conerly's first pass was intercepted. "Same old Charlie," cracked Alex Webster. To round out the scoring in the first half, Unitas hit Raymond Berry on two touchdown bombs, and Gifford took over quarterbacking responsibilities for Conerly, now nearly sixty years old.

In the third quarter, the Giants resorted to subterfuge to get on the scoreboard. Kyle Rote hid on the sidelines and just before the ball was snapped ran into the end zone, where he pulled in a toss from Gifford. Later, Gifford threw another touchdown pass, this time to Webster, and for a time it looked as if the Giants might pull off an upset by tying the game. But with less than one minute left to play in the second thirty-minute half, Unitas intercepted a Gifford pass and ran it back all the way for a touchdown. And the Colts had won again.

3–11 1976 season, but it had been a year marred by dropped passes—Pisarcik and Golsteyn managed only 135 completions in 311 attempts. The defense ranked third in the conference against the rush and showed definite promise. Brad Van Pelt was the only Giants player named All-Pro and invited to the Pro Bowl in 1977.

To many the highlight of the 1978 preseason came on July 7, when many of the stars of the unforgettable 1958 Giants-Colts championship game were reunited for a game of touch football for the benefit of CBS cameras. The Colts, who won their first championship in the NFL's first sudden-death overtime period twenty years earlier, won the geriatric contest as well (see sidebar).

The Giants' first-round draft choice was a six-foot-six-inch, 275-pound offensive tackle from Stanford, Gordon

This sequence records the Giants' first touchdown in their new stadium. Wide receiver Jimmy Robinson gathers in a pass from Craig Morton, wheels around, and races off to the end zone, eluding a diving tackle by the Cowboys' Aaron Kyle (25). Unfortunately for the Giants, the Cowboys scored more touchdowns that day and a field goal to boot, and won 24–14. (New York Giants)

King. A surprise from the fifth round was little five-foot-ten-inch, 197-pound cornerback Terry Jackson from San Diego State. The Giants would need all the help they could get, because the NFL season was expanded from fourteen to sixteen games in 1978, while the preseason was cut from six games to four.

The first game of the regular season was against Tampa Bay and their rookie quarterback, Doug Williams. When Williams stepped onto the field, he became the first black quarterback in NFL history to start a game. But his debut was spoiled when he was intercepted in the first minute of play by Giants rookie Terry Jackson, who ran 32 yards for the touchdown. Throughout the remainder of the first half, however, Tampa Bay's offense outplayed the Giants' offense, which recorded its initial first down only midway in the second quarter. But by the end of the half, the Giants had arisen, and when Joe Danelo kicked a 42-yard

field goal the Giants had a 10–10 tie at the intermission.

In the second half, Joe Pisarcik, who replaced Jerry Golsteyn, connected with Johnny Perkins on a long scoring toss. Both teams made one more field goal, which left the Giants with a 19–13 victory. Pisarcik had been reasonably impressive, completing 9 out of 15 passes.

For the first eight games of the season, Pisarcik led the Giants to a respectable 5–3 record, including big wins over Kansas City and San Francisco and a 17–6 upset over the first-place Redskins in front of a record 76,192 cheering fans at the Meadowlands. But after the big win over Washington, the team fell apart, losing all but one of the year's final eight games.

Perhaps the lowest point of the season in a disappointing football decade was reached in NFL week twelve, when the Giants were leading the Eagles, 17–12, with just twenty seconds left to play and the ball in New York's

Some veterans of past football wars who wore the Giants colors with special brilliance are honored at the new Giants Stadium. From left to right: Ben Agajanian, Andy Robustelli, Rosey Grier, Herb Rich, Jim Katcavage, Kyle Rote, Charlie Conerly, and Jack Stroud. (New York Giants)

New to the Giants defense in 1976 was linebacker Harry Carson (53) from South Carolina State, shown here later in his career, hauling down Redskins running back Joe Washington. By the end of the 1986 season, Carson had made eight trips to the Pro Bowl and had been cited as an All-Pro five times. His best single effort was in a 1982 Monday night game against Green Bay, when he racked up an incredible twenty solo tackles and five assists. The supine Giant in the background is Lawrence Taylor (56). (Fred Roe)

possession. To run out the clock and win the game, the Giants only had to snap the ball and fall on it. Instead, they tried a handoff. The ball was fumbled, and a Philadelphia defender recovered it, running it back for the winning touchdown.

The only victory in the second half of the season was in a game against St. Louis on December 10, 1978, at Giants Stadium, but after the streak of six losses had ruined a 5–3 start to the season New York fans were dissatisfied, to put it somewhat mildly. The biggest applause at the 17–0 shutout of the Cardinals that day was reserved for the pilot of a chartered airplane who flew above the stadium trailing a banner that read: "15 Years of Lousy Football—We've Had Enough." Fans huddling in the cold at Giants Stadium picked up the message and began chanting, "We've had enough, we've had enough, we've had enough."

In the game, running back Doug Kotar became the first Giants player to rush for more than a hundred yards in a single game all year, and the offense, for the fourth consecutive time, scored 17 points. "We're still stuck on seventeen, but that's all right as long as we get shutouts," said head coach John McVay. "I guess this means I can take my wife out to dinner now. I can be seen in public." McVay was fired eight days later.

One day after the final game of the season, a 20–3 loss to the Eagles, director of operations Andy Robustelli announced that he would resign on December 31. "What made this year so hard to accept," admitted Wellington Mara, "was the knowledge that we were losing Andy." Robustelli resigned only partly because of the Giants' dismal record. With a successful travel agency and extensive real estate holdings in the Caribbean, he had many responsibilities outside the Giants' organization.

Harry Carson and punter Dave Jennings were named All-Pro and invited to the Pro Bowl, and Brad Van Pelt went to the All-Star classic in Hawaii for the third year in a row.

Wellington Mara expressed the hope of luring Joe Paterno away from Penn State to become the Giants' new head coach but said that he would follow "the rules of common decency" and not contact him until after Penn State's appearance in the Cotton Bowl. Mara was unsuccessful in his bid for the college coach, but major help was in fact on the way.

In the early months of the year, it hardly looked as though 1979 would set the Giants on the comeback trail. Soon after the new year began, Giants Vice-President Tim Mara, a nephew of Wellington and half owner of the club, announced that the Giants would hire a new director of operations by February 1. But when that day came and went, there were rumors that the Maras, both 50 percent owners of the club, were not in agreement over the choice.

On February 8, the disagreement that had been quietly smoldering heated up. Wellington Mara called a press conference and announced that he would appoint a new head coach before the two owners would agree on a replacement for director of operations Andy Robustelli. "As president I have the full decision-making responsibility," Wellington said.

There was a definite reason why Wellington Mara called the press conference that did not surface at the time. "I thought that as a result of the difficult time we were having in agreeing on a general manager and the delay it was going to cause us, we would lose our top choices for a new coach. They probably would not be available by the time a general manager was hired. I was afraid we would end up with a second-rate coach." Later Wellington observed that of the three top prospects he was talking about (Andy Robustelli's choices as well), two have since taken their teams to Super Bowls.

Tim Mara disagreed and called in NFL Commissioner Pete Rozelle to act as an arbitrator (which had already been tried a few weeks earlier, before the squabble became public knowledge). "I just wish my father, God rest him, had given fifty-one percent to either Jack [Tim's father] or myself," Wellington remarked.

"I want to have a winner. Well wants to have a winner, his way," Tim Mara said, "but Well's way has had us in the cellar the last fifteen years."

Fortunately, the family feud lasted only a few days longer before the Maras, still without the head coach Wellington had threatened to hire, agreed on the selection of George Young as the new general manager. Young had been hired by Don Shula on two separate occasions to act as his director of personnel with Baltimore and later

Miami. Shula described him as his "right-hand man," and it didn't take long for Young, hired February 14, to solve the Giants' head coaching problem.

In a matter of days, both of the Maras were interviewing Young's choice for the new head coach. They approved, and at a February 22 press conference at Giants Stadium, thirty-seven-year-old Ray Perkins was formally introduced to the media. "This situation was made for me," the former wide receiver for the Baltimore Colts remarked. During the 1978 season, Perkins had been offensive coordi-

Midway through the 1976 season, with the Giants shamefacedly sporting a record of 0–7, a clapping John McVay was brought in to replace Bill Arnsparger as head coach. His record for the remainder of the season was 3–4. He remained in command through 1978, but could not come up with a winning season and logged a collective record of 14–23. (New York Giants)

nator for the San Diego Chargers and had helped develop an anemic squad into the top passing team in the NFL.

Perkins may have thought the job was made for him, but it only lasted through the 1982 season. Bad luck and a rash of injuries hurt the team and spurred him to accept the head coaching job at the University of Alabama in 1983.

But the truly significant acquisition of 1979 came at the NFL draft held in May. At the Waldorf Astoria Hotel in New York, a number of spectators booed as the Giants selected a relatively unknown quarterback from Morehead State University, six-foot-two-inch, 216-pound Phil Simms. The fans were hoping that their team, desperately in need of offense, would be able to select Washington State's quarterback Jack Thompson. But Thompson went to the Bengals, and when the Giants' turn came four selections later, spectators in Manhattan were surprised as the choice of the Giants' brain trust was announced. Who was Phil Simms? And why was he chosen ahead of established college stars like Kellen Winslow and Charles Alexander?

But the pros knew what the amateurs didn't. Simms had labored at Kentucky's Morehead State University, and even though the team had a 2–6–1 record and its ball-control offense left Simms with relatively modest statistics, most professional scouts expected the blond quarterback not to last into the second round.

Those who were unhappy with the Giants' first-round draft choice were only partly placated by their second selection, a six-foot-three-inch, 195-pound wide receiver from Memphis State, Earnest Gray. The speedy receiver (4.5 seconds for the 40-yard dash) had averaged 29.5 yards per reception in his junior year, breaking an NCAA record, and a year later was named to several All-America teams and invited to both the Senior Bowl and the East-West Game.

With Simms sitting on the bench, the Giants lost their first four games of 1979. A diversion in the early season came at a Monday Night affair in which the Giants' number 78, misidentified by Howard Cosell's crew as Gordon Gravelle, missed some blocks (actually number 78 was Gus Coppens). According to the *New York Times*, Cosell so excoriated number 78 that Gravelle's wife was mortified enough to lodge a complaint.

"Cosell is a pompous, senile idiot," Gravelle concluded following the broadcast. Cosell explained later that he had never actually mentioned Gravelle's name on the air and, according to the *New York Times*, Howard Cosell attributed it as being "all Frank Gifford's fault anyway."

The Giants' fifth game, against New Orleans, brought their fifth loss, but Simms appeared briefly in a relief role that was impressive enough to win him a start in game six. With Simms at quarterback, the Giants won four straight

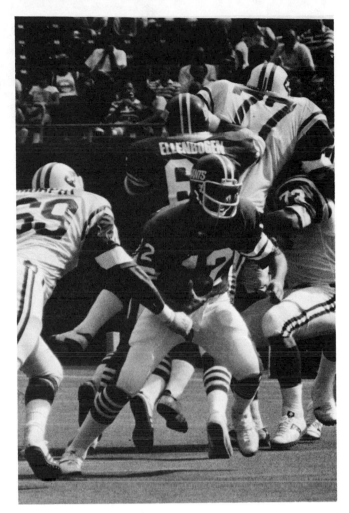

A New York intracity battle was waged in New Jersey as the Giants and Jets met at Giants Stadium during the 1977 preseason. In this scene, quarterback Jerry Golsteyn (12) tries to pick up some yardage on a quarterback draw while guard Bill Ellenbogen appears to be blocking in a way that might catch a referee's attention. The Jets won on that day, 27–23. (New York Giants)

contests, and six out of the next eight before dropping the final three games of the season to Dallas, St. Louis, and Baltimore.

The Giants ended the year with a 6–10 record, identical to that of the previous season. But for the first time, there seemed to be new hope in the New Jersey Meadowlands. Simms was a unanimous choice for All-NFL Rookie honors, and runner-up to the Cardinals' Ottis Anderson for NFC Rookie of the Year. Wide receiver Earnest Gray was also named to the All-NFL Rookie team. As they had in 1978, Brad Van Pelt, Harry Carson, and Dave Jennings went to the Pro Bowl.

The 1980s, it was deeply hoped, would be very different from the seventies. "I would not mind a return to the style of the early 1960s," Wellington Mara mentioned when asked about the Giants' prospects for the coming decade. A lot of Giants fans felt the same way.

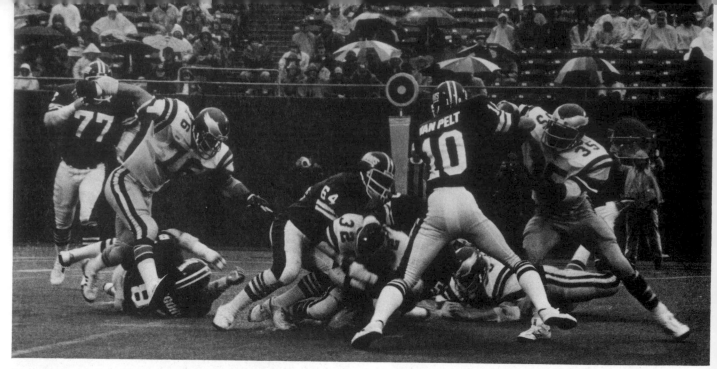

Defensive tackle John Mendenhall (64) wrestles Philadelphia running back Herb Lusk (32) to the Astroturf in this early 1977 match. Mendenhall, a third-round draft choice from Grambling in 1972, was a mainstay on the Giants' front line for most of the 1970s and earned All-Pro honors in 1974. Linebacker Brad Van Pelt (10) is also shown fighting off the block of Eagles fullback Mike Hogan (35). The Eagles won, 28–10, on a rain-soaked field. (New York Giants)

Defensive end Jack Gregory (81) snags 49ers quarterback Jim Plunkett as Troy Archer (77) lunges to provide the leveling factor in a 1977 encounter. The 49ers watching are Jean Barrett (77) and Randy Cross (51); the Giant on the ground is Gary Jeter. The Giants won the game, 20–17. (New York Giants)

Dallas quarterback Roger Staubach seems either to be saying something nasty or crying out for mercy as New York's John Mendenhall (64) and George Martin (75) zero in on the fallen Cowboy. But the Super Bowl–bound Cowboys won on that day, 24–10. (New York Giants)

Cleveland's Greg Pruitt gets loose with the ball and scampers around end moments after almost having his jersey torn from him. In pursuit are New York linebacker Dan Lloyd (54) and defensive back Bill Bryant (21). The Browns won this 1977 game, 21–7. (New York Giants)

Fullback Larry Csonka (39), signed by the Giants in 1976 after the demise of the WFL, carries the ball across an icy field and prepares to meet Chicago Bears linebacker Doug Buffone (55) in the last game of the 1977 season. Csonka played only two seasons for New York. No. 87 for the Giants is tight end Gary Shirk. (New York Giants)

During that same slippery afternoon in 1977, Walter Payton (34) carried the ball for the Bears only to have his foot ensnared by George Martin (75) and his body engulfed by Brian Kelley (55). The Bears eked out a 12–9 win in overtime on that wintry day. Some of the other Giants in the picture are Troy Archer (77), Jack Gregory (81), John Mendenhall (64), and Harry Carson (53). (New York Giants)

At Canton, Ohio, in July 1978, former Giants great Tuffy Leemans smiles from the official escort car on his way to the ceremony to formally induct him into the Pro Football Hall of Fame. He died six months later. (New York Giants)

George Young was hired in February 1979 to replace Andy Robustelli, who had resigned his post as the Giants' director of operations. Young, the new general manager and vice-president, had previously spent eleven years with the Baltimore Colts and Miami Dolphins, and was rightfully known as Don Shula's "right hand." Young's first job was to find a new coach for the club, and his overriding mission was to turn the Giants into a contender. He succeeded at this, as New York earned its way into the playoffs in 1981, 1984, 1985, and 1986. (New York Giants)

Ray Perkins, hired by George Young in 1979, became the eleventh head coach in New York Giants history. Replacing John McVay, Perkins had been the offensive coordinator for the San Diego Chargers the season before and was credited with the fine development of their quarterback Dan Fouts. Perkins remained in the Giants general's chair through the 1982 season, compiling an overall record of 23–30 before accepting the head coaching job at the University of Alabama. (New York Giants)

Ready to take the snap in 1978 against San Francisco is Joe Pisarcik (9), signed as a free agent the year before after having played three years in the CFL for Calgary. He made the NFL All-Rookie team in 1977, had a more productive season in 1978, but lost the starting job to Phil Simms the following year. The Giants' center is Jim Clack (56) and No. 63 is tackle Doug Van Horn. (New York Giants)

Watching from the sidelines in 1979 is the new starting quarterback for the Giants, Phil Simms (11), along with his predecessor, Joe Pisarcik. Simms, a first-round draft pick that year out of little Morehead State in Kentucky, got the nod after the first five games of the season and, except for the times he has been injured, has held down the job ever since. (Fred Roe)

Another newcomer of note in 1979 was Earnest Gray (83), the fleet wide receiver who was a second-round draft choice from Memphis State, shown here moving out with determination. He would quickly prove to be one of the finest pass catchers in Giants history, and in 1983 set a New York record of 78 receptions in a single season, ten more than the previous record set by Del Shofner in 1961. (Fred Roe)

Tight end Gary Shirk (87) stretched for a Simms pass in 1979 and managed to haul it in despite the efforts of New York Jets defensive back Johnny Lynn (29). Simms completed 134 passes for 1,743 yards in his first year and was runner-up for Rookie of the Year. (Fred Roe)

A view of the area between the uprights, that coveted space where Joe Danelo's kick is about to enter. This kick, booted in 1979, was Danelo's eighteenth consecutive field goal, a Giants record which still stands today. The previous record of fourteen straight was set by Pat Summerall in 1961. Danello joined the Giants in 1976 and handled the kicking chores through the 1982 season, ending up as the third all-time Giants scorer with 482 points (104 FGs, 170 PATs). He also still holds the record for the most field goals kicked in a single game—six, against Seattle in 1981. (New York Giants)

16

Some New Blood

The decade of the eighties began with a lot of firsts in sports. The United States, for the first time in the history of the modern Olympics, chose to boycott the summer games in Moscow; the Philadelphia Phillies won their very first World Series on the arm of Steve Carlton and the bat of Mike Schmidt; and the New York Islanders captured their first Stanley Cup with one of the youngest teams ever to take the hockey title. "Doctor of Dunk" Darrell Griffith led Louisville to its first NCAA basketball national championship; and Georgia, behind the running of spectacular freshman Herschel Walker, took its first NCAA national title in football. But unfortunately there was nothing all that new around Giants Stadium in 1980.

Coach Ray Perkins and General Manager George Young hoped for a noticeable improvement over the club's fourth-place finish the year before in the five-team NFC East. So did Wellington Mara, hounded by the fans' discontent, which seemed to become more vocal and vitriolic with each loss.

The first Giant to be drafted in the 1980s was cornerback Mark Haynes from Colorado, who was highly regarded by all pro scouts and had earned invitations to both the Senior and Hula bowls after the 1979 college football season. Curtis McGriff, an immense defensive tackle from Alabama, made the team as a free agent and was eventually elected to the NFL All-Rookie squad.

Phil Simms, now in his second year, showed signs of brilliance. In the September 7 season opener at St. Louis, he threw five touchdown passes in the Giants 41–35 victory. Earnest Gray, the Memphis State receiver drafted right after Simms in 1979, caught four of the touchdown

tosses, establishing an all-time Giants single-game record.

But after the victory over the Cardinals, the Giants began to self-destruct, losing eight games in a row and falling far out of contention in the NFC East. The losing streak was finally broken by a 38–35 victory over Dallas on November 9 in the Meadowlands, a game in which Simms threw for 351 yards and three touchdowns. Remarkably, he would have had five touchdown passes and a total of 402 yards through the air if two of his strikes had not been called back because of penalties. But during the very next game in San Francisco, the young quarterback was sacked by the 49ers ten times, tying a club record, in a 12–0 loss.

Simms had to sit out the final three games of the 1980 season due to a shoulder injury. His replacement was rookie quarterback Scott Brunner, a sixth-round draft choice who had had but one season as a starting quarterback at Delaware, then an NCAA Division II school. Under Brunner, the Giants managed one victory in their final three games, but many were impressed by the poise of the relatively inexperienced rookie.

What was not impressive was the 4–12 record of the Giants. It left them in last place in the NFC East, a notch lower than in Coach Perkins's first season at the helm the year before.

There was a remarkable turnaround in 1981, and it started in controversy. In January, some players went on record objecting to the public criticism they had received from Ray Perkins. But the biggest flap came in April, just a few days before the NFL college draft.

"I haven't been part of any type of discussion," Brad Van Pelt said, "but I know about it." The Giants' All-Pro linebacker was referring to a threat among New York veterans to walk away from the team if Giants management agreed to pay planned first-round draft choice Lawrence Taylor the $750,000-per-year salary his agent was reportedly demanding (see sidebar).

But by the time the NFL draft began on April 28, all was apparently forgiven. The six-foot-three-inch, 245-pound linebacker from North Carolina signed with the Giants and began a magnificent career of terrorizing all of New York's opponents.

Lawrence Taylor was certainly the standout among the new bodies donning Giants uniforms in 1981, but the rebuilding efforts hardly stopped there. Other significant draftees were defensive tackle Bill Neill from Pittsburgh, guard Billy Ard from Wake Forest, and linebacker Byron Hunt from SMU. Free agents who came aboard and remained at least three seasons were linebacker Joe McLaughlin, running back Leon Bright, defensive tackle Jim Burt, safety Larry Flowers, defensive end Dee Hardison, and center Ernie Hughes. Veteran running back Rob Carpenter was obtained from Houston after the fifth game of the season, and safety Bill Currier was acquired from New England.

The rebuilt Giants lost the season opener against Philadelphia, 24–10, in a contest played at Giants Stadium. Although he completed 20 out of 37 passes for 241 yards, Phil Simms was sacked six times.

The New York defense, feeling the leadership of rookie linebacker Lawrence Taylor, helped the Giants win their next two games against the Redskins and Saints, allowing only 7 points in each of the two victories. But consecutive losses to Dallas and Green Bay dropped New York's

Throwing here against the Los Angeles Rams is Scott Brunner, a sixth-round draft choice from Delaware in 1980. He took over the quarterbacking for the Giants late in the 1981 season after an injury sidelined Phil Simms, and he did the majority of passing for New York over the following two seasons as injuries continued to plague Simms. Brunner's best year was 1983, when he completed 190 passes for 2,516 yards and 9 touchdowns. Some of the other Giants are tackle Gordon King (72), guard Billy Ard (67), and guard J. T. Turner (68). (Fred Roe)

record to 2–3. Running back Rob Carpenter made his Giants debut in the second half of game six with the St. Louis Cardinals at the Meadowlands and, rushing for 103 yards on just 14 carries, helped his new teammates to a 34–14 win.

The hero of the next game in Seattle was placekicker Joe Danelo, a graduate of Washington State, who had now been the Giants' regular kicker for six years. With his wife, his parents, and two dozen friends in the stands, Danelo kicked six out of six field goals, including a 54-yarder, helping the Giants to a 32–0 shutout of the Seattle Seahawks. No other Giant has ever kicked six field goals in a single game. Carpenter had his second straight 100-yard rushing game, and Harry Carson and Lawrence Taylor led the revitalized defense. When the Giants won an overtime thriller in Atlanta, 27–24, the following week, their surprising 5–3 record clearly put them in the hunt for a playoff spot.

Three consecutive losses over the next three weeks, however, seemed to doom their chances. In the final contest of that three-game stretch, a heartbreaking overtime loss to the Redskins, quarterback Phil Simms suffered a separated shoulder and was lost for the season.

Minus their starting quarterback and in the throes of a three-game losing streak, the Giants traveled to Philadelphia to play the winningest team in the NFL, the 9–2 Eagles. In a stirring 20–10 upset, Rob Carpenter rushed for 111 yards, and Danelo kicked two field goals.

Five turnovers to the Super Bowl–champion San Francisco 49ers in week thirteen resulted in a 17–10 loss and diminished the odds for a successful bid for the wild card in the NFC East. But there was still hope. Teams in the other two NFC divisions, except for the leader of each, were doing badly (as it would turn out, none of the runners-up in either of those divisions would produce a record better than 8–8), and a 9–7 season might just do it. So the Giants were faced with three must-win situations in the final games of the regular season. The team, especially the defense—and, most particularly, Lawrence Taylor—rose to the assignment. A 10–7 victory over the Los Angeles Rams and a 20–10 triumph over the St. Louis Cardinals set the stage for the now-famous 1981 season finale.

Before New York's final game of the season, a Saturday affair at Giants Stadium against the Dallas Cowboys, who had already clinched the NFL East title (while fellow division-member Washington had secured the first wild card berth in the NFC), the complicated wild card picture took this shape: the Giants would become eligible for the playoffs only if they defeated Dallas and if the New York Jets beat the Green Bay Packers on the last weekend of the regular season. If those events took place, the Giants would enjoy postseason play for the first time since 1963,

Welcome, Lawrence Taylor

Lawrence Taylor's career in New York almost ended before it began when certain Giants players threatened a walkout over his agent's salary demands in the days leading up to the 1981 NFL draft. The consensus All-American linebacker from North Carolina talked about it to the New York Times.

"I heard the talk that some of the Giants would walk out if I got a lot of money," the North Carolina linebacker said. "I didn't want people to get mad at me. So I sent the Giants a telegram Monday saying I would rather not be drafted by them.

"Monday night I got calls from some of the players, on the offense and defense, and some of the coaches. They said there was nothing to the story, and there would be no walkout. They said they wanted me here. That made me feel better."

Taylor arrived in New York on April 28, the same day the draft began. He seemed to enjoy his initial exposure to the Big Apple.

"I'll enjoy New York," he said. "You've got a pretty good selection of TV up here. I watched 'The Three Stooges.' I like them." It would not be long before Taylor, clad in Giants uniform number 56, began making opposing offensive linemen, quarterbacks, and running backs look a little like stooges themselves.

an eighteen-year famine. And it would mark the first time in history that both New York teams would enter the playoffs during the same year (the Jets were a wild card from the AFC).

"When you hit the Cowboys early, and keep hitting them, they'll lose interest," said Giants All-Pro linebacker Harry Carson, "particularly if it's a game they're not totally committed to." It was a good point. The Giants were riding high into the game, with obvious good reason; the Cowboys, on the other hand, had no real playoff advantage to gain in winning at the Meadowlands that Saturday afternoon. Still, they were the Dallas Cowboys, coached by Tom Landry, featuring the running of Tony Dorsett, the passing of Danny White, receivers like Drew Pearson, Tony Hill, and Billy Joe Dupree, and defensive stalwarts in the class of Randy White, Ed "Too Tall" Jones, Harvey Martin, Charlie Waters, and Dennis Thurman.

When the Cowboys and Giants took to the field on December 19 at the Meadowlands, the temperature was twenty-five degrees with a twenty-mile-per-hour wind producing a windchill of somewhere just above zero. It was a defensive struggle in the first half, one as bitter as the weather. The New York defenders, led by linebackers Harry Carson, Brian Kelley, and Lawrence Taylor, held Dallas to 41 yards of total offense in the first half. But New York was frustrated as well when two first-half drives fizzled in missed field goals by Danelo of just 21 and 27 yards. The first half ended in a scoreless tie.

New York finally scored in the third quarter on a 20-yard Brunner pass to tight end Tom Mullady. But the Cowboys came right back with a touchdown of their own, set up by a 44-yard pass from Danny White to Tony Hill. The score was knotted at 7 until Brunner's only interception of the day was shortly converted to a Dallas field goal.

With less than three minutes remaining in the game, Staubach completed a 23-yard pass to Drew Pearson, who held the ball high above his head after the whistle blew. Suddenly, New York cornerback Terry Jackson reached up and knocked the ball out of Pearson's hand.

"Don't ever do that again," an official yelled at Jackson, but the defender had his reasons for the move.

"Drew was showing us they had the game wrapped up," Jackson said later. "I was showing him we were still in it."

With just over two minutes to play and Dallas owning a 10–7 lead and the ball, Tony Dorsett fumbled at his own 45, and New York defensive end George Martin recovered. With thirty seconds remaining in the fourth quarter, kicker Joe Danelo, the two short ones he missed earlier in the game still fresh in his mind, faced a stiff wind and booted a 40-yarder to tie the score at 10 and send the

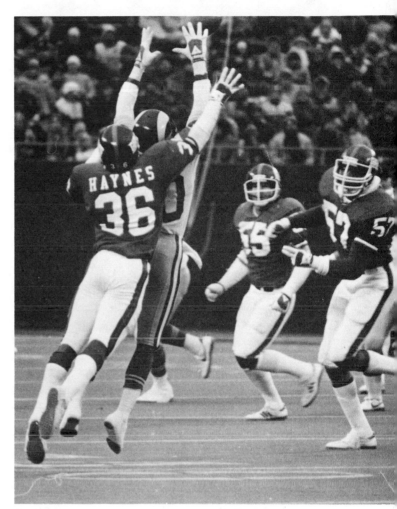

Mark Haynes covers a Ram receiver like a proverbial blanket. The Giants' first-round draft choice in 1980, the cornerback hailed from Colorado and made his mark impressively in New York with three All-Pro berths and second-team All-Pro mention in his first five years with the team. Nos. 55 and 57 on the Giants are, respectively, linebackers Brian Kelley and Byron Hunt. (Fred Roe)

An Ill-timed Punch

When the first postseason play the Giants had enjoyed since 1963 ended on January 3, 1982, in San Francisco, no one on the team felt worse than defensive end Gary Jeter. After the New York defense had forced San Francisco into a third-and-18 situation in the fourth quarter, Jeter threw a punch at 49ers lineman Dan Audick. The ensuing unnecessary roughness penalty was just what San Francisco, leading 24–17, needed. Instead of a difficult third-down situation at New York's 41, the penalty gave them a first down at the Giants' 26. It took only three more plays to give the 49ers a two-touchdown lead.

"He was holding me," Jeter said afterward. "The play was over and he kept pushing me down field. . . . All linemen hold, but he was holding the whole game."

"The Jeter penalty was a big break," head coach Ray Perkins said, "but there were a lot of big plays in the game." He was asked if he had talked to Jeter about the penalty. "No," he said, "not yet."

game into overtime.

In the sudden-death extra period, New York got a big break when Lawrence Taylor stripped Tony Dorsett of the ball and then recovered the fumble. But when the Giants went for a 33-yard field goal, Danelo's kick hit the upright and bounced away. Then during the next series of downs, New York rookie linebacker Byron Hunt intercepted a Danny White pass and ran the ball to the Dallas 24-yard line. With the playoffs again on the line, Danelo this time connected on a 35-yard, game-winning field goal.

The celebration, if there was to be one, had to wait another day, however, because the Jets and Packers were scheduled to meet the following afternoon. But on Sunday, December 20, the champagne bottles were opened in the press box lounge at Giants Stadium, where the team's staff and many of the players had gathered to watch the game. In an act of intracity brotherhood, the Jets trounced the Packers, and the Giants were on their way to the playoffs.

"They had a buffet set up for us. The bar stayed open the whole time," Giants free safety Beasley Reece told *Sports Illustrated.* "Kids were running around all over the place. Everyone was trying to play it loose, pretending to eat and not show too much concern, but I can assure you that all eyes were glued to that TV set. When [Jets quarterback] Richard Todd got intercepted early you could feel a chill come over the room. Someone got a plate of food for me," Reece continued, "but until the Jets went ahead 28–3, I couldn't tell if it was roast beef or cole slaw that I was eating. That's how tight I was."

Giants punter Dave Jennings watched the game at home. "I'm glad it wasn't thrilling," he said. "I wasn't ready for two in a row like that."

But Jennings and the rest of the Giants had to be ready to face the defending NFC-Champion Eagles at Philadelphia in just seven days. With the passing of Ron Jaworski to receivers like Harold Carmichael and the running of Wilbert Montgomery, the Dick Vermeil–coached Eagles posed a formidable roadblock.

But for the 71,611 fans in Philadelphia, the first period of the game was an unrelenting nightmare. In the opening minutes of the game, New York was forced to punt. The Eagles' Wally Henry fielded the kick, but a bone-jarring tackle by Lawrence Taylor separated him from the ball.

The First Monday Night, Giants Stadium

When Giants alumnus Frank Gifford and the rest of the ABC television crew covered the first Monday Night Football game ever to be staged at Giants Stadium on September 20, 1982, it was hardly a happy occasion for football fans, except, perhaps, those from Green Bay. According to the NFL Players' Association, there would be no more games after it until a new contract was signed to replace the one that had expired on July 15. To add to the misery of New York football fans, the Giants blew a 19–7 lead in the third quarter and lost to the Packers by the score of 27–19.

To top off everything, not one but two of the East Coast's famous power failures occurred during the game, causing delays totaling twenty-four minutes and darker-than-normal conditions during another portion of the game. New York's disheartening loss was the final game played in the NFL for eight weeks.

New York's Beasley Reece recovered at the Philadelphia 25. Five Carpenter runs and a short Scott Brunner pass to back Leon Bright gave the Giants the first score of the game, but on the point-after attempt the snap was fumbled.

On its next possession, New York marched 62 yards in eleven plays and scored on Brunner's second touchdown pass of the first quarter, a 10-yard bullet to wide receiver John Mistler. The extra point gave the Giants a 13–0 lead. On the ensuing kickoff, Wally Henry bobbled the catch, then was hit by New York's Mike Dennis. The ball skittered into the end zone, where it was recovered by Mark Haynes for the third Giants touchdown in the first period.

With the score 20–0 at the start of the second quarter, the Eagles were forced to play catch-up football for the rest of the game. But with two and a half minutes remaining in the first half, they finally got on the board. A Scott Brunner pass was intercepted at the Giants' 24-yard line, and shortly after, Ron Jaworski threw a 15-yard touchdown pass to Harold Carmichael. But Rob Carpenter and

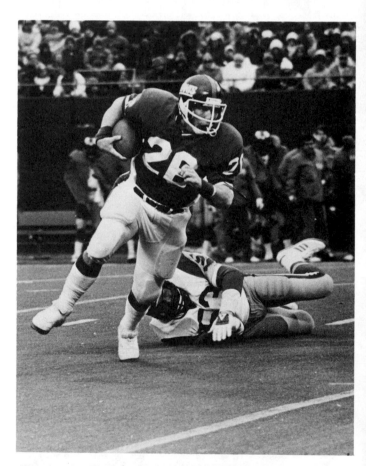

Charging the Eagles' defense is Rob Carpenter (26), acquired from the Oilers in 1981. Carpenter led New York in rushing in 1981 with 748 yards and in 1984 when he gained 795. (Fred Roe)

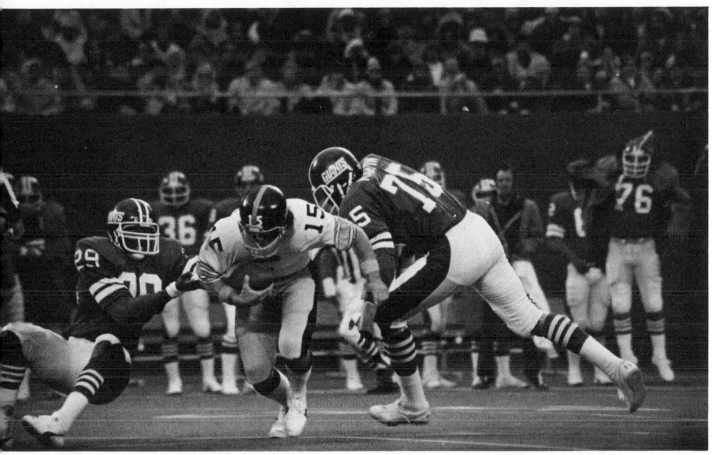

Dragging Pittsburgh's Mike Kruczek (15) to the ground is safety Beasley Reece (29), who joined the Giants in 1977 as a free agent. About to add his 255 pounds to the situation is defensive end George Martin (75). (Fred Roe)

the Giants retaliated immediately. Carpenter carried the ball for 40 yards on four plays, and Brunner capped the drive with a 22-yard scoring strike to tight end Tom Mullady. The score at halftime was 27–7, New York.

The Giants did not score again in the game, but there was no need to. With an oppressive defense and ball-control offense, led by Rob Carpenter runs, the Giants held the Eagles to a touchdown in each of the remaining two quarters. The surprising New York Giants, minus their starting quarterback, had won the first round of the 1981 playoffs by beating the favored Philadelphia Eagles, 27–21. Carpenter finished the game with 161 yards on 33 carries, 65 yards more than Brunner gained through the air. On the defensive squad, Harry Carson had nine tackles, Lawrence Taylor had eight and a sack, and defensive end Gary Jeter had seven and a sack.

The Giants' next obstacle was the San Francisco 49ers, who had dominated the NFC West that year with a record of 13–3. Coached by offensive wizard Bill Walsh, the 49ers had one of the game's most devastating passing attacks. Quarterbacked by Joe Montana and with receiv-

ers the caliber of Freddie Solomon, Dwight Clark, and Charles Young, they had the inherent potential of breaking any game wide open. In addition, the San Francisco defense was the second stingiest in the league that year, having given up only 250 points (the Giants surrendered only 257, third best behind the Eagles' 221).

A chilly, steady rain fell on Candlestick Park's natural grass on the day of the game, a condition that could affect the Giants' blitzing defense as harshly as it could San Francisco's passing game.

Bill Walsh's plan to control New York's intimidating defense centered around minimizing the effectiveness of Lawrence Taylor. "They blitz him or somebody on almost every play," Walsh said. So the 49ers' head coach instructed his best blocker, guard John Ayres, to cover Taylor on all pass plays. But on runs, he told his tight end, Charles Young, to anticipate Taylor's moves and lie in wait for him. It would ultimately prove to be a successful strategy.

The 49ers got out to an early lead, driving to New York's 8-yard line in the first quarter. From there Montana found Charles Young in the end zone. But the Giants bounced back sensationally when Scott Brunner lofted a bomb to Earnest Gray, a picture-perfect 72-yard touchdown pass play. The 7–7 tie taken into the second quarter did not last long, however. A Montana-to-Dwight Clark pass netted 39 yards and set up a Ray Wersching field goal. Rookie safety Ronnie Lott then snatched a Brunner pass to return the ball to the 49ers, and Montana quickly took advantage of the turnover by unloading a 58-yard touchdown pass to Freddie Solomon.

New York's second-quarter misfortunes continued on its next possession when Leon Bright fumbled the ball over to the 49ers in Giants territory. Again San Francisco capitalized, this time when running back Ricky Patton broke loose for 25 yards and another touchdown. Joe Danelo did manage a 48-yard field goal before the half ended to reduce the 49ers' lead to 24–10.

Not easily recognizable here, as he is balanced precariously— and probably painfully—on his head, is linebacker Lawrence Taylor, in the process of sacking Jets quarterback Richard Todd. The Giants' first-round draft choice (number two in the entire draft) in 1981, Taylor had been a consensus All-American at North Carolina before beginning his illustrious pro career in New York. He has earned All-Pro honors and has gone to the Pro Bowl every year since entering the NFL. (Fred Roe)

The Giants came even closer in the third period when Brunner hit Johnny Perkins with a 59-yard touchdown pass. The New York defense held throughout the period, not ceding a single point. And near the end of it, the Giants, trailing 24–17, worked their way downfield all the way to the San Francisco 4-yard line. But there, instead of a score, came what Ray Perkins later described as "the point where the game turned." Brunner dropped back and rifled one over the middle to Earnest Gray, who, for a moment, appeared to have the game-tying touchdown in his hands; but another pair of hands belonging to a 49ers defender got there at about the same time and knocked the ball away.

"I just tried to put it in there low," Brunner said later. "It would have been a great catch if he'd made it, but their cornerback, Eric Wright, came in from behind and stripped the ball." As a result of the incomplete third-down pass, the Giants were forced to settle for a field goal. But they did not even get that when Danelo's 21-yard attempt banged off the upright.

"That was a big factor not getting any points on that drive down there," Coach Perkins recalled. "Especially not getting a touchdown and then missing the field goal. If we'd got a touchdown there for 24–24, we would have had the momentum going for us."

The Giants were still not out of it, especially with the defense shutting down Joe Montana and his colleagues. But just as they forced the 49ers into an apparent third-and-18 situation at the Giants' 41, with only a touchdown separating the two teams in the fourth quarter, a crucial mistake changed San Francisco's extremely difficult situation into one of special good fortune. After the second-down play had been whistled dead, a flag was suddenly thrown. Defensive end Gary Jeter had lost his temper and taken a swing at a 49ers player (see sidebar). The resulting penalty gave the 49ers a first down. They scored three plays later. Not too many moments after that, when Ronnie Lott picked off a Brunner pass for the 49ers and ran it back for a touchdown, the demise of the Giants that day was fully accepted. The final score was 38–24, San Francisco.

The Giants in effect had just been a few big plays shy of attending the NFC championship game, and they could look back on a reasonably impressive year. Their 9–7 regular-season record, although third in the NFC East behind Dallas and Philadelphia, had been good enough to capture the newly created second wild card spot in the NFC. It was the first season above .500 since 1972. Rob Carpenter led New York rushers with 748 yards. Simms and Brunner had combined for more than 3,000 yards passing. Although he did not yet lead New York's defenders in tackles or quarterback sacks, Lawrence Taylor was the big defensive story for the Giants. The Associated

A more easily identifiable Lawrence Taylor—here eminently so to Steelers quarterback Terry Bradshaw—adds another sack to his statistics. One of the league's most fearsome pass rushers, Taylor had 9½ sacks in his rookie year. His best season was 1986, when he downed enemy quarterbacks 20½ times. The other Giants shown here are George Martin (75) and Byron Hunt (57). (Fred Roe)

Press named him Rookie of the Year and Defensive Player of the Year as well. The professional players themselves named him NFC Defensive Rookie of the Year and NFC Linebacker of the Year. By unanimous vote, he was selected, along with veteran linebacker Harry Carson and cornerback Mark Haynes, for the Pro Bowl. The same three, with punter Dave Jennings (second team), were named All-Pro.

The Giants needed to savor the 1981 season. Two difficult years loomed ahead.

The strike-shortened 1982 NFL season started disastrously for the Giants when Phil Simms, the promising but injury-prone quarterback, tore the ligaments in his knee during the second quarter of a preseason game with the Jets. Doctors determined that surgery was necessary and that Simms would be lost for the entire season. It was the third consecutive year the young quarterback was benched by injuries.

The offense would again have to be led by Scott Brunner, who, despite relatively unimpressive statistics, had helped the Giants reach the second round of the playoffs the previous season. Hoping to add some punch to the backfield, the Giants chose two running backs in the first two rounds of the college draft, Butch Woolfolk of Michigan and Joe Morris from Syracuse. Soon after Simms went down with his preseason knee injury, the Giants acquired reserve quarterback Jeff Rutledge from the Los Angeles Rams to back up Brunner. In July, Doug Kotar, New York's starting halfback for most of the previous seven seasons, announced his retirement.

Despite amassing 378 yards of offense, including two Brunner touchdown passes to wide receiver Earnest Gray, the Giants made some critical mistakes, which led to a

16–14 defeat by the Atlanta Falcons in the season opener at Giants Stadium. When the Giants lost their second game, a Monday Night fiasco against Green Bay (see sidebar), the NFL Players' Association had already announced its strike.

When the Giants came back to the Meadowlands to face the eventual Super Bowl–champion Washington Redskins at the end of the eight-week players' strike, the NFL had dramatically altered the usual rules for postseason play.

Because of the shortened season, the concept of divisions within each conference was suspended. Rather than ending the season with six conference champions and four wild card teams, it was decided that the eight top clubs in *each* fourteen-team conference would be invited to postseason play. With an extra week added to the original prestrike schedule, each club would now play a total of nine regular-season games. The new playoff rules gave teams such as the Giants, who had gotten off to a bad start, a chance to come back and get into the playoffs.

The Giants were not ready to take advantage of the reprieve granted them by the temporary postseason rules, however, and they fell to Washington, 27–17, to restart

Jeff Rutledge was obtained from the Rams in 1982 as a backup quarterback, a role in which he has continued to play well over the ensuing years. His best games were in 1983, when he started for an injured Phil Simms and threw 29 completions for 349 yards against Seattle and 24 for 324 yards against the defending NFL champion Redskins. (Fred Roe)

Jim Burt, famed for his tight-fitting jersey numbered 64, wrestles with a Kansas City blocker with an aim toward decimating Chiefs quarterback Bill Kenney (9). Signed as a free agent in 1981, the six-foot-one, 260-pound Burt soon developed into one of the finest nose tackles in the game. (Fred Roe)

the NFL season. But the next game, nicknamed the "Lawrence Taylor Show," finally put the Giants into the win column.

In that nationally televised Thanksgiving Day contest at Pontiac, Michigan, against the Detroit Lions, Taylor put on an amazing defensive display. After sitting out much of the first half because of a minor knee ailment, the sophomore sensation entered the game with the Giants trailing, 6–0. First, he blitzed the Lions' quarterback and forced a hurried throw that was intercepted by Harry Carson and set up a Joe Danelo field goal. On the next Detroit possession, he hit running back Billy Sims hard enough to jar the ball loose. Brad Van Pelt recovered, setting up another Danelo field goal, which tied the score at 6. The next time the Lions had the ball, he made an almost unbelievable one-handed sack of Detroit quarterback Gary Danielson, forcing a punt. In the fourth quarter, with the game tied and the Lions on the Giants' 4-yard

TIME OUT

On the sideline, in the rain, part of the Giants defense. Seated, left to right: Jim Patton, Sam Huff, and Emlen Tunnell. Standing: Henry Moore and Bill Svoboda.

In the locker room: Buzz Guy, Dick Modzelewski, and Dick Lynch.

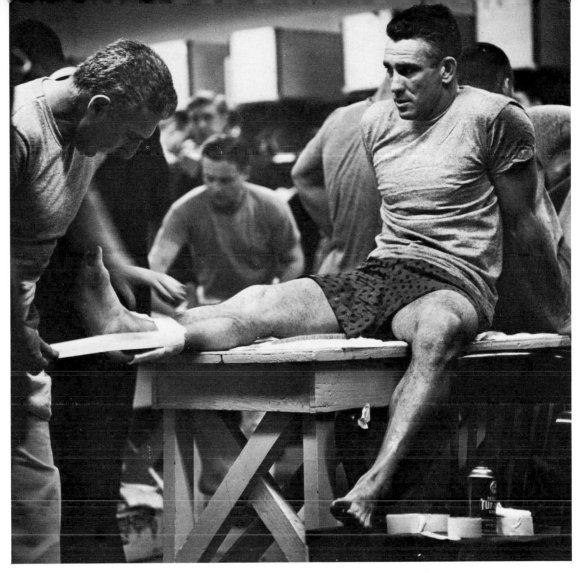

Sid Moret, left, tapes Charlie Conerly's ankle in the Giants' lockerroom. In the background is John Dziegiel.

The trainer's table.

Three Giants quarterbacks—Mark Reed, Scott Brunner, and Phil Simms—drop back to pass during practice outside Giants Stadium.

Del Shofner, center, goes out for a pass during practice at Yankee Stadium, covered by Dick Lynch, left, and Jim Patton.

Pain etched on his face, Del Shofner is helped off the field by trainer John Johnson and his assistant, Julius "Whitey" Horai.

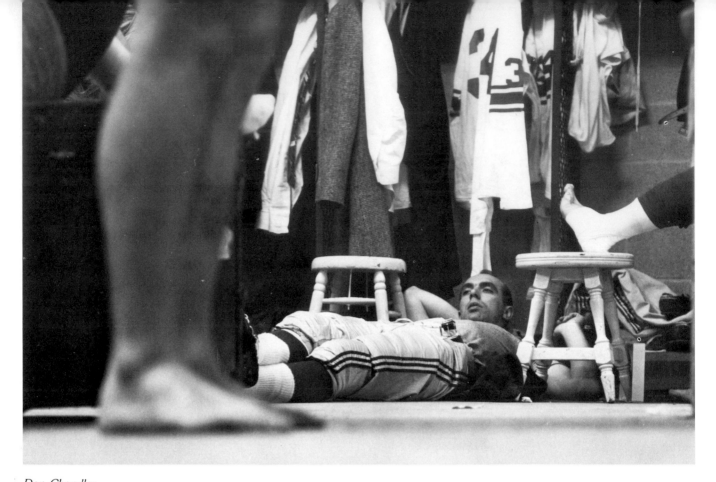

Don Chandler.

Charlie Conerly, Andy Robustelli, and other team members run through a practice drill at Yankee Stadium.

Tom Landry, right, and Andy Robustelli planning Giants defenses.

Coach Jim Lee Howell.

The Giants bench during a game. Left to right: Ray Beck, Sam Huff (drinking), Frank Gifford, Bill Austin, Andy Robustelli, Don Chandler.

line, Taylor intercepted a Danielson swing pass at the 3 and ran the ball back 97 yards for a touchdown. It was the third longest interception return in club history. Taylor had almost single-handedly won the game for the Giants, 13–6.

The Giants won their next two games, against Houston and Philadelphia, and were back in the race for a spot in the playoffs. But on December 15, just four days before a major showdown against Washington, news from Tuscaloosa, Alabama, surprised most football fans in New York.

On that day, Paul "Bear" Bryant, at the time the winningest coach in the history of collegiate football, announced that he was retiring as head man at the University of Alabama. On the very same day, the Giants' head coach Ray Perkins, who had been an All-American end in 1966 under Bryant at Alabama, announced that he would leave New York to take over Bryant's job. Perkins explained that he had been born and raised in Mississippi and had dreamed for years of returning to the South and coaching at his alma mater. "It's just something I've wanted to do very, very much," he added.

Butch Woolfolk, shown here streaking away from a fallen Cowboy, was the Giants' first-round draft pick in 1982. A highly regarded running back from Michigan, he immediately broke into the starting lineup in that abbreviated season and won NFC Offensive Rookie of the Year honors. He led the Giants in rushing during the 1982 and 1983 seasons before being traded away midway through the 1984 season. (Fred Roe)

Fifth Coach in Eleven Years

The fact that the New York Giants had played through a decade of frustrating and tumultuous times was brought home by veteran linebacker Brian Kelley as he prepared to greet his fifth head coach.

"I think he's going to be a personable coach," Kelley said of Bill Parcells on December 15, 1982, the day the announcement was made. "I think he's the kind you can talk to, and he's going to be very efficient."

Parcells, the Giants' defensive coordinator in 1981 and 1982, was well respected by the players, especially on the defensive squad.

"He can get on you when he wants to, but if he does, it's because you're doing something wrong," said Lawrence Taylor.

"Bill Parcells was first on my list," said General Manager George Young, "and it was a very short list."

And so was welcomed the twelfth head coach in Giants history, who, despite the opening tributes, had to know that job security was not the principal perk when he thought about the four coaches who had held the same job in the decade before his appointment.

On Tuesday, the night before the big announcements, Giants General Manager George Young was on the phone to Wellington Mara, who was attending an NFL owners' meeting in Dallas. Young had learned of Perkins's decision on Monday and had already decided on his replacement. Young also called Tim Mara to discuss his choice with the other half of the Giants' ownership.

"George told me that he wanted to name Bill Parcells the next coach," Tim Mara explained. "And he told me that he wanted to announce it the same day that Ray Perkins made his announcement, so that there wouldn't be weeks of speculation as to who was going to be the next coach."

By promoting the former defensive coordinator to the head position, George Young was making certain that the Giants avoided the publicity and infighting that had led up to his own and head coach Ray Perkins's appointments a few seasons earlier.

"For better or worse," wrote the *Times*'s Dave Anderson, "George Young—not the coach, not the owners, not even Lawrence Taylor—has emerged as the foundation of the Giants' future."

When the whirlwind of announcements subsided, the Giants got back to preparing for the decisive meeting with the Redskins on December 19. With a three-game winning streak already behind them, the Giants were assured of a spot in the playoffs if they beat Washington and then won their remaining two games.

Before more than 50,000 fans at Washington, the Giants built up a 14–3 lead by halftime. But on a broken play in the third quarter, the Redskins scored a touchdown. And with four seconds remaining in the game, Washington's Mark Moseley kicked his NFL-record twenty-first straight field goal from 42 yards out, giving the Redskins a dramatic 15–14 victory.

On December 26, New York played its next-to-last game of the season in St. Louis. With just forty seconds left to go in the game and the Giants ahead, 21–17, the Cardinals drove 70 yards in four plays, scoring the winning touchdown with just seconds on the clock. The sec-ond heart-wrencher in succession all but ruined any Giants' hope for a playoff spot.

Seasoned computer analysts explained a long series of events that could make a Giants' playoff berth conceivable if New York won the final game of the season, but as the team traveled to Philadelphia for the year's finale, victory was considered nothing more than a mathematical possibility in a convoluted scenario.

The Giants won the season closer, 26–24, on a Joe Danelo field goal with two seconds left to play. "It was kind of nice to win one in the last few seconds [rather] than the other way around," said Ray Perkins of his final game as the New York Giants' head coach.

New York had won the game, but the complicated

Joe Morris (20), who has become the Giants' premier running back, moves out behind a block by Billy Ard. Morris was New York's second-round draft choice in 1982 out of Syracuse, but did not get full-time duty until after the departure of Butch Woolfolk in 1984. The following year, his first full season as a starter, Morris set two all-time Giants rushing records by gaining 1,336 yards and scoring 21 touchdowns. He also became only the second Giant to rush for more than 200 yards in a game (204 against Pittsburgh; previously, Choo Choo Roberts had 218 against the Chicago Cardinals in 1950). (Fred Roe)

Bill Parcells, talking here with linebacker Brian Kelley, was named the twelfth head coach in New York Giants history in 1983. A former head coach at the Air Force Academy, Parcells served as defensive coordinator with the Giants before taking the top job. After a disastrous, injury-riddled first year (3–12–1), he rewrote the scenario and turned in three consecutive winning seasons and three trips to the playoffs (1984–86). (Fred Roe)

script required for a playoff spot failed to materialize. "Coming into this game," said quarterback Scott Brunner, "we didn't hold any high hopes that we would get into the playoffs. We just wanted to send Ray Perkins away with a win."

New York's 4–5 record was not good enough for a playoff berth, but the fact didn't quite seem as important as in previous years. After all, it was not a real season anyway, rather a kind of patched-up scramble to earn some money for players, coaches, and owners. Lawrence Taylor, Harry Carson, Dave Jennings, and Mark Haynes were again recognized with invitations to the Pro Bowl and All-Pro honors.

On the first and second rounds of the 1983 draft, the Giants selected safety Terry Kinard from Clemson and defensive end from Louisiana State Leonard Marshall. Way down in the ninth round they picked placekicker Ali Haji-Sheikh, who had been a walk-on at Michigan and now in New York would eventually win the job from Joe Danelo.

But major problems developed shortly after the final preseason game when new head coach Bill Parcells announced that Scott Brunner was to be the starting quarterback instead of Phil Simms or backup quarterback Jeff Rutledge.

"To say I'm disappointed is the understatement of the

world," said Simms, the team's number-one draft choice in 1979 (who had just lost his starting job to the sixth-round choice of 1980).

With Brunner as the starting quarterback, New York won two out of its first five games, and Simms was extraordinarily unhappy in his role as a backup. On October 3, he asked to be traded.

"I think it would be best for me and everyone concerned if it happened," he said. "If I stay, I'll work hard. But how long can I wait? We're pretty deep into our season. They've made a commitment to Scott Brunner. They have to play him. It's been six weeks since I've had a good look at anything."

Six days later, Simms replaced Brunner in the third quarter in a game against Philadelphia at Giants Stadium. A few minutes later, the more than 73,000 fans must have experienced a collective and unpleasant sense of déjà vu. There was Phil Simms, in obvious pain, leaving the field of play, lost for the season. It was the fourth year in a row that the promising but ill-fated young quarterback was beset with season-ending injuries.

The Giants lost to the Eagles that day and went on to win only one of their remaining ten games. The dismal 3–12–1 record sank New York into the cellar of the NFC East and gave new coach Bill Parcells a less than gleeful introduction to his new job.

There had been some noteworthy performances that gave hope for the future. Ali Haji-Sheikh had toted up 127 points, the most ever by any Giant, with his 35 field goals and 22 extra points. He also set a team mark when he booted a 56-yard field goal against Green Bay; then he did it again a few weeks later while facing the Lions. Another rookie, defensive back Terry Kinard, had lived up to his credentials and was a welcome addition. The linebacking trio of Lawrence Taylor, Brian Kelley, and Harry Carson contributed 88, 71, and 68 solo tackles, respectively. Earnest Gray caught 78 passes for 1,139 yards, the first receiver to go over the 1,000-yard mark since Homer Jones in 1968. Taylor and Haji-Shiekh were named All-Pro, and both, along with Harry Carson and Mark Haynes, went to the Pro Bowl.

The quarterback situation was still shaky as the Giants looked to the 1984 season. Rushing left a little to be desired, although Butch Woolfolk had gained 857 yards and Rob Carpenter another 624. "Some changes are needed," Parcells said. "And we're going to make some. We are a much better team than last year's record indicates." In 1984, he was going to prove the truth of that statement. Better times—much better times—were just ahead.

Defensive end Leonard Marshall (70) is two-timed by Chicago Bears blockers Jimbo Covert (74) and Mark Bortz (62). New York's second-round draft pick in 1983 hailing from LSU, Marshall set a club record with 15½ sacks in 1985 and was named All-Pro and the NFC Lineman of the Year that season. (Fred Roe)

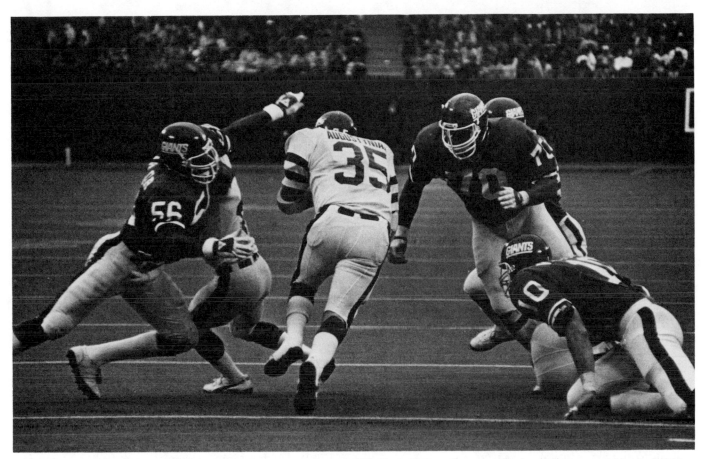

The Giants defense began to take on devastating proportions in 1983. Here All-Pros Lawrence Taylor (56), Leonard Marshall (70), and Brad Van Pelt (10) converge on Jets running back Mike Augustyniak. Defensive end Marshall, a second-round draft choice from Louisiana State, joined the two veteran linebackers in 1983. (Fred Roe)

Ali Haji-Sheikh (6) appeared to be the answer to any and all of the Giants' kicking problems when he arrived in 1983. In his rookie season, he set an all-time NFL record by booting 35 field goals and was honored as an All-Pro. He also set the following team records: most points scored (127), most field goals attempted (42), highest conversion percentage (83.3), and the longest field goal (56 yards, twice). His career was stymied by a hamstring injury in 1985 and he left the Giants after that season. (Fred Roe)

17

Playoffs Bound

The year 1984 signaled the sixtieth anniversary of New York Giants football. A full six decades had elapsed since that day before the 1925 season when Tim Mara put his signature on the franchise papers and his money on the proverbial line to give life to his belief that the city of New York was ready to host the then rather controversial sport of professional football.

The Irish bookmaker had, of course, made a good bet; by 1984 the team had a history as illustrious as any in the National Football League. There had been seventeen first-place finishes in divisional play, fourteen trips to the NFL championship game, three league crowns, and eleven second-place seasons. At the end of sixty years, the Giants would be able to boast a regular-season record of 407–343–32, having outscored their opponents 14,062 points to 13,140.

From the Polo Grounds to Yankee Stadium to Giants Stadium, the story had been played out on plains of grass, in muddy quagmires, on snow-packed frozen fields, and finally on a carpet of Astroturf. Players had become legends through their deeds on those fields: Hinkey Haines, Steve Owen, Benny Friedman, Ray Flaherty, Red Badgro, Ken Strong, Mel Hein, Ed Danowski, Tuffy Leemans, Johnny Dell Isola, Bill Swiacki, Arnie Weinmeister, Eddie Price, Emlen Tunnell, Kyle Rote, Frank Gifford, Andy Robustelli, Rosey Brown, Rosey Grier, Charlie Conerly, Sam Huff, Alex Webster, Del Shofner, and Y. A. Tittle; and now there were the glistenings of some novas of the eighties like Lawrence Taylor, Harry Carson, Leonard Marshall, Phil Simms, and Joe Morris.

It was only appropriate, then, that the Giants start their seventh decade with a chance at a divisional crown, something they had once done regularly, but also something they had not accomplished since 1963. New York sportswriters were cautious in their optimism; after all, the Dallas Cowboys, Washington Redskins, and St. Louis Cardinals were highly regarded in the always-tough NFC East. But Wellington Mara expressed some feeling of comfort at the club's prospects; they were turning it around, he felt, and a resolution of the quarterbacking situation and a little more support from the running game might just make the difference.

First to be culled from the draft that year, however, was linebacker Carl Banks from Michigan State. Another first-rounder, the selection obtained from the Redskins for the Giants' second- and fifth-round choices, was mountainous (six foot five inches, 275 pounds) offensive tackle William Roberts of Ohio State. Other draftees who made the squad were quarterback Jeff Hostetler from West Virginia, linebacker Gary Reasons of Northwest Louisiana State, offensive tackle Conrad Goode from Missouri, wide receiver Lionel Manuel from Pacific, and offensive guard David Jordan of Auburn. Two free agents caught on: wide receiver Bobby Johnson from Kansas and wide receiver/punt returner Phil McConkey of Navy. Recovered and off injured reserve were cornerback Perry Williams and offensive tackle Karl Nelson. Five of the newcomers—Banks, Reasons, Johnson, Nelson, and Williams—would earn NFL All-Rookie team honors at the end of the '84 season.

Annual All-Pro Brad Van Pelt, now discontented, got his wish and was traded to the Minnesota Vikings, who, in turn, could not sign him and traded him to the Los

Angeles Raiders. As part of the first deal, nine-year veteran running back Tony Galbreath came to the Giants and would prove to be a most valuable "third-down player," coming in then to pose a threat as both a runner and pass receiver.

During the preseason, Bill Parcells shifted the quarterbacking duties between a now-healthy Phil Simms and Jeff Rutledge, both of whom looked very good in three decisive wins over the New England Patriots, New York Jets, and Pittsburgh Steelers. In fact they even stood out in the loss to the Colts, who were playing their very first game at their new home in Indianapolis.

For the opener of the regular season, Parcells decided on Simms to lead New York against the Eagles at Giants Stadium, and at the end of that sixty minutes of play the quarterbacking situation was resolved. The blond hurler from Morehead State, now in his sixth year in the NFL and coming off several injury-riddled seasons, put on an aerial display for the hometown fans that had never been witnessed at the Meadowlands before, in fact had not

The Giants' first pick in the 1984 draft brought linebacker Carl Banks from Michigan State. As a rookie, he joined All-Pros Lawrence Taylor and Harry Carson in the linebacking corps and has been a mainstay ever since. (Fred Roe)

been seen in the Giants' domain since Y. A. Tittle dazzled the fans at Yankee Stadium with his passes one day in 1962. Hitting Zeke Mowatt, Byron Williams, and Bobby Johnson with touchdown strikes in the first half, and adding another to Johnson in the final period to secure a 28–27 victory over the Philadelphians, Simms had the most productive day passing for the Giants in twenty-two years. The 409 yards (23 completions in 30 attempts) he gained passing that afternoon stood, at that point, second in Giants annals only to the 505 Tittle chalked up against the Redskins back in 1962. Simms had hit Byron Williams five times for 167 yards and Bobby Johnson eight times for 137 yards, and he also completed passes to Zeke Mowatt, Rob Carpenter, Earnest Gray, Butch Woolfolk, Tony Galbreath, and Joe Morris. Although they did not need it that day, Simms also connected on a 66-yard touchdown that was called back because of a penalty.

Next to arrive in New York were the Dallas Cowboys, coming off a 12–4 season in 1983, the same year they decisively beat the battered Giants twice. The scenario was considerably different in 1984, however, and again it was Phil Simms who set the tenor of the day. A 62-yard bomb to wide receiver Byron Williams, then a 16-yard bullet to rookie Lionel Manuel, gave New York a 14–0 lead in the first period.

Dallas then got going, moving all the way to the New York 6, but there Lawrence Taylor broke through and separated Cowboys quarterback Gary Hogeboom from the football as he desperately looked for an open receiver. Linebacker Andy Headen scooped up the fumble and carried it 81 yards for a Giants touchdown and a club record, 9 yards farther than the fumble return by Wendell Harris against Pittsburgh in 1966.

The Cowboys never got into the game. Simms connected with Zeke Mowatt for another score in the third quarter, and the Giants ended the day with a 28–7 rout of their longtime nemesis from Texas. Taylor had three sacks, two of which resulted in fumbles that the Giants recovered, and a total of nine solo tackles.

It was down in Washington, however, that the Giants were brought back to the reality of the NFL East. The Redskins, who lost only two of sixteen regular-season games the year before and had gone all the way to the Super Bowl (where they lost to the Los Angeles Raiders, 38–9), still showcased the running of John Riggins, the passing of Joe Theismann, and one of the most overwhelming defenses in the league.

But the Giants might have made it three in a row if not for a disastrous fourth quarter. Going into that period, New York held a 14–13 lead, the result of a 1-yard Rod Carpenter plunge for a touchdown after a concerted Giants' drive in the first quarter and a Simms-to-Johnson TD toss in the third quarter.

It appeared the Giants were moving toward another score in the last period, but Carpenter fumbled the ball away, and the Redskins turned around and marched until Mark Moseley booted a 21-yard field goal to give them the lead. Two mistakes later—a Simms pass picked off and returned for a touchdown and a Lionel Manuel fumble snatched up and lugged for another 6 points—and the Redskins had a 17-point quarter and a 30–14 win.

The following week Simms and Taylor combined to provide the winner's edge, slipping by Tampa Bay, 17–14, principally on Simms's touchdown passes to Johnson and Mowatt and Ali Haji-Sheikh's first field goal of the season. At the same time, Taylor terrorized the Bucs' quarterback, Steve DeBerg, sacking him four times. The Giants were 3–1 and looking good, but there was still a lot of concern about the running game. Bill Parcells mentioned, "Carpenter had good games against Dallas and Tampa [87 and 70 yards rushing respectively], but that's about all we've shown in four games. We're going to have to do better than that if we want to get in the playoffs this year."

Coach Parcells should have saved that statement for the following week. Out in Anaheim, against the Rams, the Giants gained only 8 yards rushing all day, 6 of them picked up by Carpenter on nine attempts and two by Woolfolk on three runs. The entire game was played so poorly by the Giants that the club's public relations staff wrote of it later: "Every NFL team has a highlight film. For the Giants this one game could have constituted an entire season's lowlight film." Not only was the rushing game nonexistent, New York had three safeties recorded against them (all, incidentally, in the third quarter), setting an ignominious NFL record. Haji-Sheikh missed two extra points and a field goal; the offense allowed Simms to be sacked five times; the defense let Eric Dickerson run for 120 yards, and 84 more were gained by other Los Angeles rushers; and the Giants' special team watched Henry Ellard return a New York punt 83 yards for one of the Rams' touchdowns. The final score was the Rams 33, the Giants 12.

The next week it was the Super Bowl–bound San Francisco 49ers who came to Giants Stadium and displayed what would earn them diamond-encrusted rings a few months down the line. With three touchdowns in less than eight minutes of the first quarter, including a 59-yard bomb from Joe Montana to Renaldo Nehemiah and a 79-yard punt return by Dana McLemore, the game was securely in the hands of the 49ers with fifty-two minutes still remaining, and ended with another 21-point Giants deficit, 31–10. Wellington Mara noted that there appeared now more to worry about than merely the paltry running game (95 yards total that day, not counting Simms's 22 on scrambles). Scoring, punt return coverage, protection for Simms, and a reenergized defense were

Hauling in a touchdown pass against the Eagles is Lionel Manuel (86), who was drafted in 1984 and took over as a starting wide receiver late that season. In 1985, despite missing four games because of an injury, he led the team in pass receptions (49) and yards gained receiving (859). The frustrated Eagles defender is Roynell Young. (Fred Roe)

obviously some of the things being discussed at the Giants' coaches' meetings.

A win over Atlanta and a surprise drubbing by the Eagles left the Giants with a 4–4 record at midseason, certainly better than the 2–5–1 standing of the year before but disappointing after the hope engendered through the first two games of the season.

To start the second half of the season, the Giants found one of the things they had been lacking. Joe Morris, with the build and tenacity of a pit bulldog, was given the starting assignment at running back in place of Butch Woolfolk. The five-foot-seven-inch, 195-pound dynamo from Syracuse, in his third year with the Giants, exploded for three touchdowns rushing against the Redskins, tying a club record (no Giant had run for three touchdowns since Mel Triplett did it against the Chicago Cardinals back in 1956). His 68 yards on 15 carries produced the kind of average Bill Parcells had been looking for from Woolfolk and had not been able to find. But it was not just Joe Morris who enabled New York to decimate the Redskins that day, 37–13. Phil Simms got some protection and completed 18 of 29 passes for 339 yards, including touchdowns to Earnest Gray and Bobby Johnson.

When combined with a victory over the Cowboys the following week, 19–7, the Giants, now with a 6–4 record, were right back in the race for the division title. It was, incidentally, the first time since 1963 that the Giants swept their two games with Dallas.

A surprise loss to Tampa Bay and a win over the Cardinals gave the Giants a 7–5 record and part of a three-way tie with the Cowboys and Redskins for the NFC East crown. These were followed by triumphs over the Kansas City Chiefs and New York Jets, and suddenly the Giants were the talk of New York and New Jersey. The talk turned a bit vexatious, however, when New York managed to lose the last two games of the year to the Cardinals and the New Orleans Saints, both of whom they were favored to defeat. But, as it turned out, it did not

really matter as far as the playoffs went. The Redskins had clinched the NFC East before the last game of the season, and the Giants were in contention for a wild card berth with division mates Dallas and St. Louis, all three teams having records of 9–6. If New York beat the Saints, it would have the wild card bid by dint of its divisional record; if the Giants lost (they did, 10–3), both Dallas and St. Louis would have to lose that weekend as well, which, considerately, they did.

The Los Angeles Rams were the NFC's other wild card and, because of their better record (10–6), were the designated host. So two days before Christmas the Giants trotted onto the field in Anaheim, where they had been demolished and demoralized almost three months earlier.

Once again, the Rams were counting on the running of All-Pro Eric Dickerson, augmented by the passing of Jeff Kemp. "We can beat them if we control Dickerson," Bill

Wide receiver Bobby Johnson (88) widens the gap with a stiff arm against the Cowboys after grabbing a Phil Simms pass. Johnson came aboard as a free agent in 1984 and won a starting berth in his first year, and earned NFL All-Rookie honors after leading the Giants with 795 yards gained on receptions. (Fred Roe)

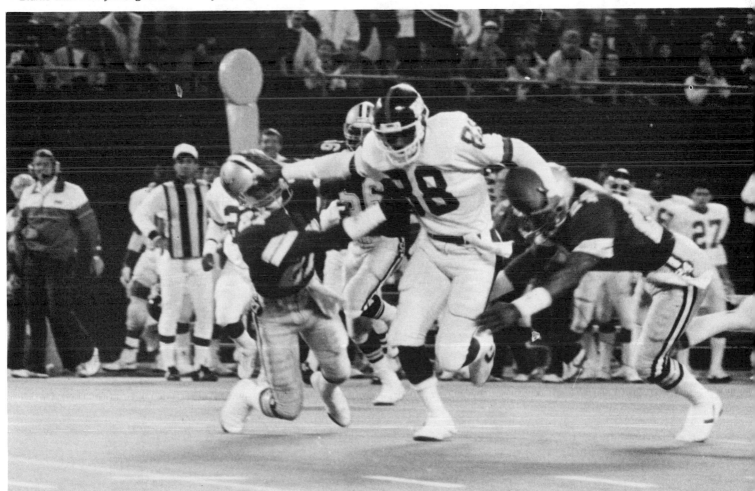

Another new linebacker in 1984 was Gary Reasons (55), a fourth-round draft choice from Northwestern Louisiana State, shown here wrestling an Eagles ballcarrier to the turf. Reasons broke into the starting lineup in 1985 and ended that season as the third-leading tackler on the team. (Fred Roe)

Parcells said the week before the game. "We've got to put more than twelve points on the scoreboard if we want to win," Wellington Mara added, referring to the 33–12 loss to Los Angeles earlier in the season.

The Giants did both that sunny day in southern California . . . barely. They held Dickerson to one touchdown, caused him to fumble once, and deprived him of important first-down yardage several times. And they scored 16 points. The first tally was a 37-yard field goal by Ali Haji-Sheikh after Simms passed the Giants into position on their first possession. Shortly after that Dickerson fumbled the ball to the Giants, and Simms connected on two passes to bring the ball to the Los Angeles 1-yard line, where Rob Carpenter dove in for a touchdown.

At halftime the Giants held a 10–3 lead, then increased it by 3 points with a 39-yarder from the toe of Haji-Sheikh in the third quarter. Dickerson ran 14 yards for a Rams touchdown in the same period, but then Haji-Sheikh made it 16–10 with a 36-yard field goal. The Rams came within three with a field goal of their own in the final period, but as time was winding down Lawrence Taylor burst through and sacked Jeff Kemp, causing a fumble that was recovered by the Giants' Andy Headen. And that was it for the day, 16–13, Giants, and a trip up the Pacific coast to face the San Francisco 49ers, winner of the NFC West and sporting a 15–1 record.

During the regular season, the 49ers had followed the Rams with a decisive defeat of the Giants, and New York was looking to deal them the same kind of turnaround justice as they had Los Angeles. But Bill Walsh's San Francisco team was flying high. It had scored an average of 30 points a game during the regular season, and its defense, the best in the entire NFL, had given up 227, an average of only 14 per game.

Just as they had back in October, the 49ers grabbed the gold at the very start. Joe Montana, that year's All-Pro quarterback, guided a 71-yard drive early in the first quarter, capping it with a 21-yard touchdown pass to Dwight Clark. On New York's ensuing possession, a pass from Phil Simms bounced off the hands of intended receiver Lionel Manuel into those of 49ers defender Ronnie Lott. Moments later, Montana found tight end Russ Francis in the end zone, and San Francisco had a 14–0 first-quarter lead.

But unlike their outlook during the previous encounter, the Giants had no thoughts of surrender. In the second quarter, Gary Reasons intercepted a Montana pass, which the Giants shortly converted into three points on a booming 46-yard field goal by Haji-Sheikh. In the same period, with San Francisco backed up to its own 5-yard line, the result of a splendid punt by Dave Jennings, Montana had another pass picked off, this one by linebacker Harry Carson, who toted it in for a touchdown.

But the two point-producing interceptions did not deter Montana. He went to the air again and moved his team down the field later in the quarter. Montana culminated the drive with a 29-yard touchdown pass to Freddie Solomon, and the 49ers had a 21–10 lead at the end of the first half.

The Giants' defense solidified in the second half and held the ordinarily prolific San Francisco offense score-less. New York had a fair share of opportunities to score during the last two periods of the game, but something went wrong each time—an interception deep in 49er territory here, a missed field goal there—and, like their opponents, the Giants were unable to post a point in the second half.

Simms threw 25 completions that day for 218 yards; Montana completed the same number for 309 yards, and 3 of them were for touchdowns. Montana was also the game's leading rusher with 63 yards on 3 scrambles. And so the 49ers went on to the Super Bowl and won the NFL championship, and the Giants went home with the consolation of having appeared in two postseason games in 1984 and prideful of the fact that they had given San Francisco a scare and a game as no other team would be able to do in that year's playoffs.

When the season's statistics were tabulated, Phil Simms

Running back Tony Galbreath, here making a diving catch of a Phil Simms pass, came to the Giants as part of the trade that sent Brad Van Pelt to the Minnesota Vikings before the 1984 season. A threat as a running back and as a receiver, Galbreath became a highly productive third-down specialist for the Giants after having played five seasons with the New Orleans Saints and three with Minnesota. (Fred Roe)

had set two New York passing records, his 286 completions being 60 more than former title-holder Fran Tarkenton (226 in 1971), and the 4,044 yards gained passing far outdistancing the 3,224 toted up by Y. A. Tittle in 1962. Both linebacker Lawrence Taylor and cornerback Mark Haynes were named All-Pro. Joe Morris and Rob Carpenter gave evidence that the running game was taking on some form and substance. It was enough to make even the more skeptical of fans optimistic for 1985.

The Giants convened at Pace University in Pleasantville, New York, on July 15 to begin the football fiscal year of 1985, ninety-seven veterans and hopefuls sweating under the hot summer sun to earn one of forty-five berths on the team. Heading the list of newcomers was first-round draft choice George Adams, a running back from Kentucky, and second-round pick Stacy Robinson, a wide receiver from North Dakota State. Neither would land starting jobs that year, but tight end Mark Bavaro from Notre Dame would later in the season.

Other rookies who made the 1985 Giants included Herb Welch, a defensive back from UCLA; Lee Rouson, a running back out of Colorado; and center Bart Oates from Brigham Young and the USFL. Other players from the USFL were punter Sean Landeta and running back Maurice Carthon.

The Giants were scheduled for five preseason games because they were to kick off the season in the now-annual Pro Football Hall of Fame exhibition game in Canton, Ohio, to benefit that organization. And to reassure those who were thinking optimistically, the Giants won all five, defeating the Houston Oilers, Denver Broncos, Green Bay Packers, New York Jets, and Pittsburgh Steelers.

The opener of the regular season brought the Eagles to Giants Stadium, and New York extended its thus-far perfect season with an easy 21–0 victory. Two touchdowns in the first quarter, both set up by Phil McConkey's kick

Playoff Showdown, 1985

New York Giants		Chicago Bears	
Offense			
WR	Bobby Johnson	WR	Willie Gault
WR	Lionel Manuel	WR	Dennis McKinnon
TE	Mark Bavaro	TE	Emory Moorehead
T	Brad Benson	T	Jimbo Covert
T	Karl Nelson	T	Keith Van Horne
G	Billy Ard	G	Mark Bortz
G	Chris Godfrey	G	Tom Thayer
C	Bart Oates	C	Jay Hilgenberg
QB	Phil Simms	QB	Jim McMahon
RB	Joe Morris	RB	Walter Payton
FB	Rob Carpenter	FB	Matt Suhey
Defense			
E	Curtis McGriff	E	Dan Hampton
E	Leonard Marshall	E	Richard Dent
NT	Jim Burt	T	Steve McMichael
LB	Byron Hunt	T	William Perry
LB	Gary Reasons	LB	Otis Wilson
LB	Harry Carson	LB	Mike Singletary
LB	Lawrence Taylor	LB	Wilber Marshall
CB	Elvis Patterson	CB	Mike Richardson
CB	Perry Williams	CB	Leslie Frazier
SS	Kenny Hill	SS	Dave Duerson
FS	Terry Kinard	FS	Gary Fencik

Giants	0	0	0	0 —	0
Bears	7	0	14	0 —	21

Touchdowns—*Bears:* Gayle, McKinnon (2).
PATs—*Bears:* Butler (3).

Trivium

The New York Giants played their first "road game" at Giants Stadium on December 2, 1984, a contest hosted by the relatively new tenant New York Jets. The visitors shocked the perversely partisan Jets fans by running up a 17–0 lead by the third quarter and then triumphing, 20–10, with the show being stolen by Phil Simms's passing (18 of 28 for 252 yards), Joe Morris's running (17 carries, 83 yards), and the voracious defense of Gary Reasons (17 solo tackles) and Leonard Marshall (2 quarterback sacks).

returns of 40 and 37 yards, marked the tone of the game. The Giants scored again in the fourth quarter, although it was meaningless after the defense had totally dominated the Eagles. Joe Morris had the second-best day of his career, earning 88 yards on the ground, including 2 touchdowns. Leonard Marshall sacked Eagle quarterback Ron Jaworski 3 times, and Lawrence Taylor did the same 2½ times. And everybody agreed it was a good way to start the season.

The glamor faded the next week, however, with a 23–20 loss to the Green Bay Packers. And besides the loss of the game, there was another of major proportions.

The Giants had had a number of important casualties going into the second game of the season. All-Pro cornerback Mark Haynes, although now healthy, had been a contract holdout and had yet to don a Giants uniform for 1985. Tight end Zeke Mowatt was lost for the season after knee surgery. Fullback Rob Carpenter, with a bad knee of his own, had not played a minute of football thus far. And Ali Haji-Sheikh, beleaguered by a hamstring problem earlier in the season although he had been playing, had been worrisome to the Giants' coaching staff. Now the worries turned to despair when, after kicking a 52-yard field goal in Green Bay, Haji-Sheikh aggravated the injury to an extent that would put him on injured reserve for the rest of the 1985 season. Going into their third game of the season, the Giants now had to scurry to fill a key position.

The St. Louis Cardinals, having won their first two games of the season, were on top in the NFC East when they came to Giants Stadium, but when they left were in a three-way tie with the Giants and the Dallas Cowboys. Simms scorched them with three touchdown passes, and new placekicker Jess Atkinson added a pair of field goals to the 27–17 victory. The Giants' defense was brutal enough to prompt Cardinal running back Ottis Anderson, nursing multiple bruises and scratches after the game, to tell a sportswriter asking how he felt, "I'm going to leave my body to science next week."

The defense was overwhelming the following week in Philadelphia as well, allowing the Eagles only 3 points and 168 yards of total offense all afternoon. But the Philadelphians got a touchdown late in the fourth quarter when Herman Edwards snatched a deflected Simms pass and ran it in for a touchdown to send the game into overtime. And it was there that the defense won it for the Giants, when, on the second play of the additional period, corner-

Drafted in 1985 from Notre Dame, tight end Mark Bavaro gains a few yards for the Giants against the Tampa Bay Buccaneers. Bavaro made the NFL All-Rookie team that year, and the following season he led the Giants with 66 pass receptions and 1,001 yards gained receiving. The Bucs defender is linebacker Keith Browner. (Fred Roe)

back Elvis Patterson, playing for holdout Mark Haynes, intercepted a pass from Ron Jaworski and carried it 29 yards for a touchdown.

The Cowboys came to town the next week for a special, nationally televised Sunday night game, broadcast by the trio ordinarily seen on Monday nights, Frank Gifford, O. J. Simpson, and Joe Namath (Howard Cosell having put to rest his football microphone after the previous season). Since it joined the league in 1960, Dallas had been a most annoying factor in the Giants' world. This was to be their forty-sixth encounter, and in their preceding meetings the Cowboys had triumphed 30 times, lost only 13 games, and tied the other 2. And when they enplaned for Texas Monday morning they had claim to 31 victories in the series, the result of a beneficent gift by the Giants.

In the third quarter, the Giants had a comfortable 26–14 lead. And, despite an uncharacteristic lapse on the part of the defense, which allowed Dallas 10 points, New York would still have won had it not been for two fourth-quarter fumbles by Phil Simms that resulted in two Rafael Septien field goals, the game winner a 31-yarder with just over two minutes remaining. The 30–29 setback dropped the 3–2 Giants into a tie for second place in the division with the Cardinals and gave the Cowboys (4–1) undis-

And They Lost?

Phil Simms had his finest day as a Giant on October 13, 1985, and the second most productive passing game of any quarterback in the history of the National Football League, when he filled the air with footballs against the Cincinnati Bengals. The 513 yards Simms gained passing stands second only to the 554 Norm Van Brocklin of the Rams picked up against the New York Yankees in 1951. His 40 completions rank second only to the 42 Richard Todd chalked up for the Jets against the 49ers in 1980. And his 62 attempts were exceeded only by the 68 passes thrown by George Blanda of the Houston Oilers against Buffalo in 1964.

Rookie tight end Mark Bavaro caught 12 of Simms's passes, a Giants record, surpassing the record of 11 shared by Frank Gifford, Del Shofner, Doug Kotar, Billy Taylor, and Gary Shirk.

The Giants' offense set a team record of 34 first downs in the game and an NFL all-time standard of 29 passing first downs.

New York's defense held the Bengals to a mere 199 yards of total offense in the game, including minus-3 yards of total offense in the second half.

Still, the Giants lost that day to the Bengals, 35–30.

Prominent Debut

Placekicker Eric Schubert made his debut with the Giants against Tampa Bay on November 3, 1985. He had been cut by the team back in August, but, after Ali Haji-Sheikh's hamstring injury did not get better and the release of Jess Atkinson, who had replaced him, he got a telephone call from coach Bill Parcells three days before the game with the Buccaneers. The gist of it was to get over to Giants Stadium and put on a uniform.

Schubert, who at the time was working as a high school substitute math teacher in Wanaque, New Jersey, did as suggested and reported for duty. That Sunday, in his premier appearance, Schubert kicked five field goals to become the first player in NFL history to boot that many in his pro football debut. The kicks of 24, 36, 24, 41, and 33 yards were only one shy of the club record of six set by Joe Danelo in 1981.

And the 15 points were a substantial contribution to New York's 22–20 victory that afternoon.

puted possession of first place. The fumbles tainted the most productive passing game Phil Simms had ever had as a Giant, 432 yards on 18 completions, including 2 touchdowns to Lionel Manuel and a 70-yarder to rookie George Adams, which was also the longest TD pass of Simms's pro career.

If turnovers were a problem against Dallas, they were a disaster the following week at Cincinnati. Against the Bengals, two fumbles and two interceptions "accounted for a possible swing of 28 points," Bill Parcells noted with grim astonishment after the game, which the Giants lost, 35–30. What made it more incredible was that it occurred in the same game that Phil Simms virtually rewrote the Giants' record book with his passing (see sidebar), and the team's defense only gave up 199 total yards all day.

After that, however, New York cleansed the butter from its collective fingers and won the next four games in succession, defeating the Washington Redskins, the New Orleans Saints, the Tampa Bay Buccaneers, and the Los Angeles Rams. And it was partly the result of a suddenly energized running game, featuring Joe Morris.

At the end of week ten in the NFL, the Giants had a record of 7–3 and shared the division lead with the Dallas Cowboys. The top spot was still shared the following week when both the Giants and Cowboys lost. Despite 3 rushing touchdowns from Joe Morris (56, 41, and 8 yards), tying the club record, New York was, in the words of one Giants coach, "fleeced out of it by Redskin flim-flam." He was referring to a fake punt and two unexpected onside

Records Broken, 1985

Individual

Most Touchdowns Scored	Joe Morris	21
Most Yards Rushing, Season	Joe Morris	1,336
Most 100-Yard Rushing Games, Season	Joe Morris	7
Most Rushing Touchdowns, Season	Joe Morris	21
Most Touchdowns Rushing, Game (tie)	Joe Morris	3
Most Passes Attempted, Game	Phil Simms	62
Most Passes Completed, Game	Phil Simms	40
Most Passing Yards, Game	Phil Simms	513
Most Games 300 Yards Passing	Phil Simms	11
Most Pass Receptions, Game	Mark Bavaro	12
Most Punt Returns, Season	Phil McConkey	53
Most Fair Catches, Season	Phil McConkey	18
Most Fumbles, Season	Phil Simms	16
Most Own Recoveries, Season (tie)	Phil Simms	5
Most Own Recoveries, Game (tie)	Phil Simms	2

Team

Most Yards Gained, Season	5,884
Most Yards Rushing, Season	2,451
Most Touchdowns Rushing, Season	24
Most First Downs, Season	356
Most First Downs Rushing, Season	138
Most First Downs, Game (vs. Cincinnati)	34
Most First Downs Passing, Game (vs. Cincinnati)	29*
Most Rushing Attempts, Season	581
Most Passes Attempted, Game (vs. Cincinnati)	62
Most Passes Completed, Game (vs. Cincinnati)	40
Most Yards Passing, Game (vs. Cincinnati)	513

*NFL record

Passing Records

Against the Cincinnati Bengals, October 13, 1985, Phil Simms set one NFL and four Giants passing records.

NFL
Most Consecutive Games, 400 or More Yards Passing
Phil Simms (432 and 513, total of 945 yards)
Dan Fouts (San Diego, 1982, 444 and 435, total of 879)

Giants
Most Passing Yardage, Game
Phil Simms (513)
Y. A. Tittle (505 in 1962)

Most Pass Completions, Game
Phil Simms (40)
Charlie Conerly (36 in 1948)

Most Pass Attempts, Game
Phil Simms (62)
Charlie Conerly (53 in 1948)

Most Games 300 or More Yards Passing, Career
Phil Simms (10)
Y. A. Tittle (9)

kickoffs, the latter two converted into touchdowns that stood as significant contributions to the 23–21 win.

It was the first of a six-game loss-win roller coaster ride for the Giants, which also saw the team slipping in and out of a tie with Dallas for the division lead. When the season finally closed, the Giants, with a record of 10–6, were actually in a three-way tie with the Cowboys and the Redskins. During that stretch, Joe Morris became only the second Giant in history to rush for over 1,000 yards in a season (Ron Johnson did it in 1970 and 1972), and the 21 rushing touchdowns he scored were not only the most

in the entire NFL but the player closest to him, Eric Dickerson of the Rams, had only 12.

The division title was awarded to Dallas because it had a better record within the division, and the wild card berth was earned by New York because it had a better divisional record than the Redskins. And so for the second year running the Giants were slated for postseason play as a wild card team.

Their first opponent was the defending Super Bowl–champion San Francisco 49ers, who had ended their season with a 10–6 record, a game behind the Los Angeles Rams in the NFC West. The oddsmakers, perhaps remembering the 49ers' 18–1 record of the year before and the flashy rings the players sported as a result, gave San Francisco the edge. Sportswriters noted the volatile offense of the 49ers: the passing of Joe Montana to receivers Dwight Clark and sensational rookie Jerry Rice, and the presence of running back Roger Craig, who had just become the first player in NFL history to gain more than 1,000 yards each on rushing and on pass receptions.

What many pundits overlooked, however, was the New York defense, second best in the entire NFL, and the undisputed leader in quarterback sacks (68). Another thing was the Giants' thirst for revenge after the two losses

Wide receiver Stacy Robinson beats San Diego Chargers cornerback Terry Lewis on the way to establishing himself as a full-fledged Giants starter. Robinson was a second-round draft pick from North Dakota State in 1985. (Fred Roe)

the year before, in which they had given up 31 points in the regular season and 21 in the postseason to the same San Francisco team.

Vengeance was theirs. New York allowed only 3 points that cold December afternoon at Giants Stadium, sacked Joe Montana 4 times, and prompted Phil Simms to say after the game, "That was the best I've ever seen our defense play." The offense was not bad either, putting 17 points on the board. Simms threw 2 touchdown passes to tight ends Mark Bavaro and Don Hasselbeck, and Eric Schubert kicked a 47-yard field goal. Joe Morris rushed for 141 yards on 28 carries. It earned the Giants the right to travel to Chicago to play the Bears, the team with the best record in the NFL (15–1).

The Bears, of course, had the NFL's all-time leading rusher, Walter Payton. They also had the best total defense in the league; a quarterback named Jim McMahon

who got in trouble for wearing inscribed headbands and was considered something of an enfant terrible, but who had also come into his own as a passer and team leader; and a 308-pound behemoth called "the Refrigerator," William Perry, who played defensive tackle and occasionally filled in in the backfield as a rusher, pass receiver, and blocker for Payton. The latter prompted Lawrence Taylor, when asked if he was worried about trying to tackle a 308-pound ballcarrier, to remark, "I don't want to think about the Refrigerator. Or the stove. I'm going to throw all my appliances out of the house."

The site was Soldier Field on Chicago's lakefront, former home of the College All-Star Game, a stadium known for its bitter cold and ice-needle winds in January. Before the game, Bill Parcells admitted the team his Giants were to face was the most formidable one in the league. It was to be a battle of the two best defenses in the game.

With an appropriate if unappreciated pun, the Giants got off on the wrong foot when punter Sean Landeta, trying to kick from his own 5-yard line, only barely grazed the ball. Bears defender Shaun Gayle, who scooped it up and ran it in for the game's first touchdown, called it "a foul tip."

That was, in effect, enough to win the game for Chicago. The Bears' defense totally shut down the Giants. Led by All-Pro defensive end Richard Dent (3½ sacks), the Refrigerator, and a host of other fierce and fired-up tacklers, Chicago held New York scoreless and to only 181 net yards gained all afternoon. Joe Morris was held to a mere 32 yards, and Phil Simms, sacked 6 times, completed only 14 of 35 passes. The final score was the Bears 21, the Giants 0.

Coach Bill Parcells had been correct; the Bears were the most formidable team in the NFL in 1985. They proved that as they blithely went on to win the Super Bowl, barely contested. But the Giants had had a fine year, the best since 1963. Chicago's head coach, Mike Ditka, said later, "The Giants may have been the best all-around team we played all year."

Club records fell by the score in 1985 (see sidebar). The Giants had found a running game and a passing game. They were a young team—twenty-five active players with three years or less NFL experience, fifteen of whom were starters—with untold promise. Among their accomplishments in 1985: they had consecutive winning seasons for the first time in twenty-two years; had five players named to the Pro Bowl, the most in twenty-two years (Phil Simms, Joe Morris, Leonard Marshall, Harry Carson, and Lawrence Taylor); had their second straight 7–2 record in games played at Giants Stadium; and had given the fans good reason to look forward to the 1986 season.

Joe Morris tries to break a tackle by diving San Francisco safety Carlton Williamson in the first game of the 1985 playoffs at Giants Stadium. Morris gained 141 yards rushing that day as the Giants defeated the defending Super Bowl champion 49ers, 17–3. (Fred Roe)

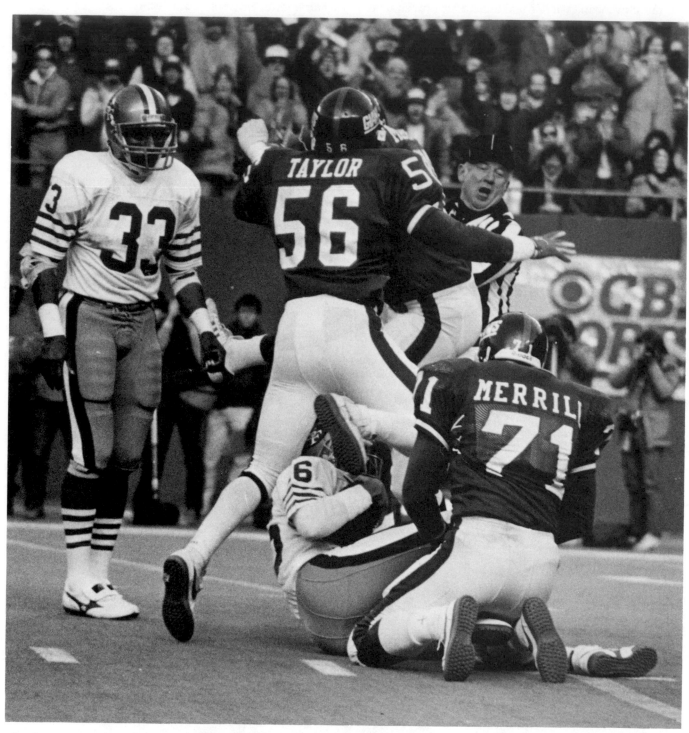

On the ground is San Francisco quarterback Joe Montana, one of the four times he was sacked in the 1985 playoff game at Giants Stadium. Hovering over him are linebacker Lawrence Taylor (56) and defensive end Casey Merrill (71). No. 33 on the 49ers is running back Roger Craig. (Fred Roe)

The proverbial frosting on the cake, tight end Don Hasselbeck (85) holds the ball aloft in triumph after scoring the Giants' final touchdown of the day on a 3-yard pass from Phil Simms in the 1985 playoffs against the 49ers. The win that afternoon enabled the Giants to go to Chicago and meet the Bears in the NFC title game. (Fred Roe)

An ever-devastating force the Giants had to contend with against the Bears in the 1985 playoffs was the NFL's all-time most productive rusher, Walter Payton (34), shown here stiff-arming Lawrence Taylor (56). Payton picked up 93 yards rushing that afternoon. Blocking New York defensive back Perry Williams (23) is guard Mark Bortz (62). (Fred Roe)

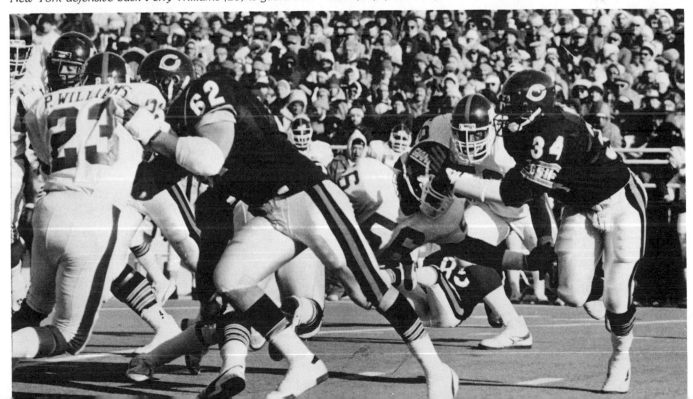

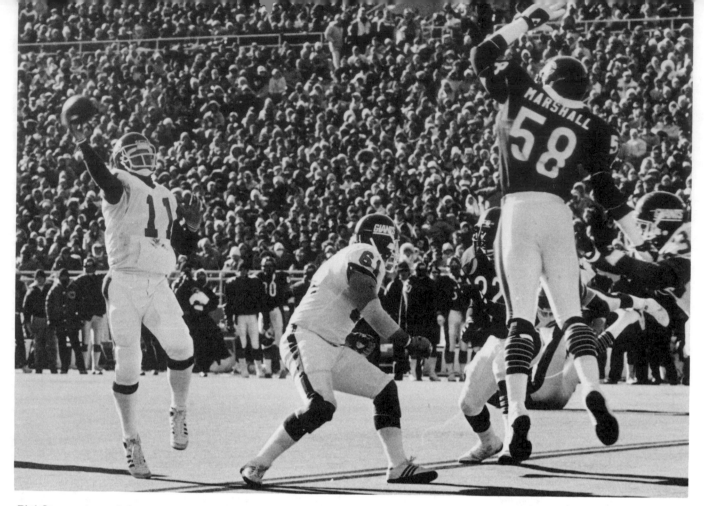

Phil Simms tries to loft one over leaping Chicago Bears linebacker Wilber Marshall (58) in the 1985 NFL playoffs at Soldier Field in Chicago. Simms had a disillusioning day under the relentless attack of what was the NFL's top defense that year and completed only 14 of 35 passes (149 net yards passing, 129 of which were gained on New York's final two possessions of the game). No. 61 on the Giants is guard Chris Godfrey. (Fred Roe)

Safety Terry Kinard corrals the Bears' Keith Ortego, who was returning one of New York's all-too-frequent punts in their playoff game in 1985. Kinard, the Giants' first-round draft choice of 1983 from Clemson, led the Giants secondary in tackles both in 1984 and 1985. (Fred Roe)

The trench, the battleground where so many games are won and lost. This one is in Chicago, where the Giants succumbed to the Bears in the 1985 playoffs. The Giants waging war here are linebacker Gary Reasons (55), nose tackle Jim Burt (64), and defensive end Leonard Marshall (70); the Bears are tight end Emery Moorehead (87), tackle Jimbo Covert (74), and guard Mark Bortz (62). (Fred Roe)

Jim Burt (64) hangs on the back of Bears fullback Calvin Thomas while safety Kenny Hill (48) addresses his ankle. Adding a shoulder to the effort is linebacker Harry Carson (53). But the Super Bowl–bound Bears gained 147 yards rushing to the Giants' 32, as they worked their way through the 1985 playoffs. (Fred Roe)

One of the key factors in the Giants' demise in the 1985 postseason—besides, of course, the Bears' awesome defense—was a healthy Jim McMahon, here throwing one of his 11 completions of the day. The final score was Bears 21, Giants 0. Two of Chicago's touchdowns came on McMahon passes. The Giants are defensive end George Martin (75) and linebacker Andy Headen (54). (Fred Roe)

18
Year of Triumph

It certainly did not look like a year of triumph for the Giants when they left Texas Stadium in Irving after the first game of the regular season. On Monday night, September 8, 1986, before a national television audience, New York fell to the Cowboys and found themselves starting out in the cellar of the NFL East.

New York's highly regarded defense gave up 31 points that night, the most they would yield the entire season. But the offense made a game of it. Trailing 14–0 in the second quarter, the Giants bounced back with touchdown passes from Phil Simms to Bobby Johnson and Stacy Robinson. They even took the lead, 21–17, in the third quarter, when Joe Morris bulled in from the 2-yard line, and again in the final period, 28–24, after Simms connected once more with Johnson on a 44-yard touchdown pass. New York's problem, however, was Herschel Walker, making his NFL debut after Tony Dorsett left the game with a sprained ankle. The most famous player from the dormant USFL averaged 6.4 yards on each of his 10 carries and scored touchdowns on two of them, the last a 10-yard burst up the middle with little more than a minute left in the game to give the Cowboys a 31–28 victory.

The fans who were worrying about New York's once-vaunted but now seemingly leaky defense had their concerns wiped away at Giants Stadium the following Sunday. To kick off the season in New Jersey, the Giants defenders held the high-powered offense of the San Diego Chargers to a single touchdown and their ordinarily prolific quarterback, Dan Fouts, to a mere 19 completions in 43 attempts. They also intercepted five passes.

Phil Simms gained exactly 300 yards on his 18 completions, one of them a touchdown toss to Lionel Manuel, and Joe Morris rushed for 83 yards, with one of his carries taking him into the end zone for his second touchdown of the season. Those scores, along with two field goals, were enough to give New York its first win of the year, 20–7. The most intimidating figure on the field that day was safety Terry Kinard, who was credited with six tackles, two interceptions, and a fumble recovery, which earned for him the honor of being named the NFC defensive player of the week.

Next on the agenda was a game in Anaheim, California, against another volatile offense, that of the Los Angeles Raiders, which featured the passing of Jim Plunkett and the running of Marcus Allen. But the defense was again up to the challenge, allowing the Raiders only three field goals, holding Allen to a mere 40 yards rushing, and sacking Plunkett three times. Phil Simms threw two touchdown strikes to Lionel Manuel in the second half, and that was enough to post a 14–9 win. Joe Morris registered his first 100-yard game of the season that afternoon when he picked up 110 yards on 18 carries.

Back at Giants Stadium the following week New York fans were astonished to find their team trailing the ordinarily lackluster New Orleans Saints 17–0 in the first half. Unfortunately for New Orleans, there was enough time remaining for the Giants offense to tote up 20 points and for the defense to definitively shut down the Saints. New place kicker Raul Allegre booted two field goals, and Phil Simms added two touchdowns to his stats, hitting Mark Bavaro with a 19-yarder and Zeke Mowatt on a 4-yarder.

At the quarter mark of the season, New York could boast a three-game winning streak and a record of 3–1—good enough, however, only for a second-place tie with the Cowboys behind the undefeated Redskins.

For their next assignment the Giants traveled to St. Louis to face the team which Jimmy the Greek had predicted in the preseason would win the Super Bowl but which had so far failed to win a regular-season game. A crowd of just over 40,000 watched the ill-starred Cards extend their losing record to 0–5, as the Giants, with a 13–6 victory, moved to 4–1. The defense was especially effective that day, allowing St. Louis only 241 net yards and two field goals and sacking Neil Lomax seven times. Carl Banks was credited with 10 tackles and two sacks, and Lawrence Taylor and Leonard Marshall each had six tackles and two sacks.

If the Giants offense was a little on the quiet side in St. Louis, it came roaring back in the more obliging confines of Giants Stadium the next Sunday. There, the Philadelphia Eagles, under new coach Buddy Ryan (best known for designing and guiding the defense of the Super Bowl–champion Chicago Bears the preceding year), were witness to New York's most productive offensive output of the season. In fact, the 35 points they tallied would be

the most all year until the hapless Green Bay Packers showed up for the last game of the season. In addition, the defense was the stingiest it would be until the playoffs, giving up only a lone field goal.

Joe Morris got things going by breaking loose on a 30-yard touchdown run, and Phil Simms followed with a four-yard scamper to give the Giants a 14–3 lead at halftime. In the third quarter, Simms hit wide receiver Solomon Miller for another touchdown. Then, a few minutes later, after a Giants drive stalled at the Eagles' 13, Raul Allegre lined up to kick the field goal. But his foot never touched the ball. Holder Jeff Rutledge surprised everybody in the stadium by grabbing the ball and then flipping it to linebacker Harry Carson, in the game supposedly to block, for a 13-yard touchdown. Simms added the fifth and final touchdown of the day with a 37-yarder to running back Lee Rouson. The final: Giants 35, Eagles 3. Lawrence Taylor, proving why he was a perennial All-Pro, was credited with nine tackles and four sacks.

There was some additional good news from down Dallas way. The Cowboys stunned the hitherto undefeated Redskins, 30–6, and so New York, now 5–1, moved into a tie for first place in the NFC East.

Residence at the top was short-lived, however. The

As he did so often in 1986, Mark Bavaro gathers in a Phil Simms pass, this one against the San Diego Chargers. Bavaro caught five passes for 89 yards that September afternoon, as the Giants dealt San Diego a 20–7 defeat. No. 54 on the Chargers is linebacker Billy Ray Smith. (Fred Roe)

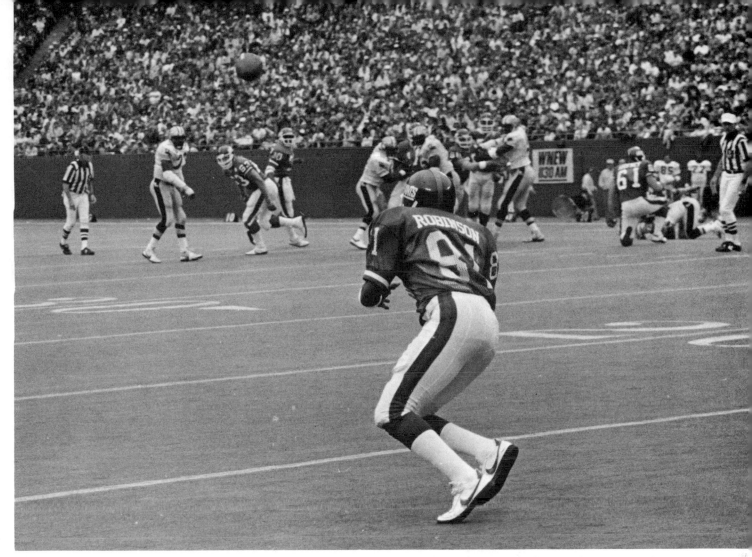

Stacy Robinson, very alone, awaits another Simms toss in the game against New Orleans. Robinson gathered in four of Simms' passes that day for 66 yards, as the Giants rallied to beat the Saints, 20–17. (Fred Roe)

Giants traveled out to the Kingdome in Seattle, where Phil Simms experienced one of his most disappointing games in some time. Sacked seven times, he netted only 190 yards passing and was intercepted four times. The Giants managed a 9–7 lead at intermission, but the Seahawks regained the lead with a field goal, then converted an interception into a touchdown, the ball eventually lugged in by Curt Warner. The final score found the Seahawks on top, 17–12, and the Giants back in a second-place tie in their division with the Dallas Cowboys, a game behind the Redskins.

The stage was now set for a most important confrontation, a nationally televised meeting on Monday, October 27, between New York and the Redskins at the Meadowlands—a game that caused many football fans who were also following the seventh game of World Series between the Red Sox and the Mets to spin their dials back and forth all night. Raul Allegre got the Giants off on the right foot, so to speak, by kicking a 37-yard field goal in the first quarter. Joe Morris added six more points when he car-

ried the ball 11 yards into the end zone. Another Allegre field goal and the Giants had a 13–3 halftime lead.

It appeared that the game might be taking on blow-out proportions in the third quarter when Phil Simms connected with Bobby Johnson on a 30-yard touchdown pass to extend the lead to 20–3. But an unintimidated Jay Schroeder brought the Redskins back with a phenomenal passing performance (420 yards), racking up 17 unanswered points and tying the game late in the final period.

The Giants, however, launched a drive of their own, starting from their 19-yard line. With a little more than a minute and a half left in the game, they reached the Redskins 13-yard line. There, Joe Morris broke loose and carried the ball in for the winning score. The final: Giants 27, Redskins 20. And in the NFC East there was now a three-way tie for the lead, because Dallas had destroyed the Cardinals that weekend. Each of the leaders was now sporting a record of 6–2.

Accolades were merited in various corners that Monday night. Joe Morris, who gained 181 yards on 31 rushes and

Jeff Rutledge (17) and Harry Carson (53) admire the football they teamed up to use on a fake field goal against the Eagles that resulted in a touchdown. Holder Rutledge grabbed the snap, rolled up and out, and lobbed the ball to the ordinarily linebacking Carson, who was in to block, for a 13-yard touchdown. Carson earned his way to the Pro Bowl in 1987 for the eighth time in nine years. (Fred Roe)

added another 59 on pass receptions, was named the NFC offensive player of the week. Phil Simms completed 20 of 30 passes without a single interception. And the defense was highlighted by Carl Banks's 10 solo tackles, while Lawrence Taylor was credited with six tackles and three sacks.

Six days later the Giants faced another formidable obstacle on the path to the playoffs. Dallas was coming to town in the hope of knocking New York back into second place in their division. The Giants, needless to say, wanted revenge for their opening-night embarrassment at the hands of the Cowboys, and they were all too aware of the heated three-team division race in which they were involved, one where a single loss might later prove to be disastrous for their playoffs hopes.

Once again Allegre got the Giants off to a three-point lead in the first period with a 25-yarder. The Cowboys snatched it back the following quarter when Steve Pelluer, quarterbacking for Danny White, who had left the game with a broken thumb after a Harry Carson sack, pitched a touchdown to Mike Renfro. But the Giants responded with a march that culminated in an eight-yard touchdown run by Joe Morris, and it was 10–7 at the half.

Phil Simms was having his worst day of the year, however (at day's end his stats would register just six completions in 18 attempts, for a negligible 67 yards), and so it was left to the Giants defense and the running power of Joe Morris to maintain control of the game.

Another touchdown by Morris in the fourth quarter, this one a six-yard run, gave New York a 10-point lead, but it was countered by a 23-yard touchdown run by Tony Dorsett. Then the Giants gave the ball up to the Cowboys, who began a drive that they hoped would win the game in the closing minutes. Fortunately for New York, Dallas was slowed by several penalties, and when Rafael Septien attempted a desperate 63-yard field goal, it fell short. The final score was Giants 17, Cowboys 14.

Morris had certainly done his job, rushing for 181 yards and two touchdowns for the second week in a row. And the defense had held Tony Dorsett to 45 yards rushing and Herschel Walker to 34. Harry Carson was the feature, being responsible for 13 tackles.

New York was not alone at the top, however, Washington having slipped past Minnesota, 44–38, in overtime. But what the Giants could boast of was a share of the best record in the NFC, 7–2, along with Washington, the Chicago Bears, and the Los Angeles Rams.

The Giants were a heavy favorite to beat the Eagles, their next opponent—after all, there had been a 32-point margin in their first encounter. But many of the Giants may have been looking beyond the Eagles to what lurked in the ensuing four weeks: Minnesota (5–4 and in definite contention for a wild-card berth), Denver (8–1, the best record in the NFL), San Francisco (5–3–1 and battling for a playoff bid), and another confrontation with Washington.

But whatever the reason, the Giants looked lackluster in the first period that early November afternoon in Philadelphia. Neither team showed any sort of offense during the first fifteen minutes, but Joe Morris broke loose for an 18-yard touchdown run in the following quarter, and Raul Allegre added a field goal to give the Giants a 10–0 lead at the half. Another Morris touchdown, a 3-yard run in the third period, brought the score to 17–0, and everything seemed wrapped up and ready to take home. But in the final period the Eagles came to life, as Randall Cunningham teamed with wide receiver Mike Quick on a 75-yard touchdown pass, then led an 87-yard march that culminated in another touchdown when he snuck the ball in from the 1. That was the scoring for the day, however, and the New Yorkers escaped with a 3-point victory and a lesson in both mortality and vulnerability.

Another lesson and another escape awaited them the following Sunday at the Metrodome in Minneapolis in what would prove to be one of the Giants' two most exciting games of the season. The Vikings, two games behind the Bears in the NFC Central and in a desperate duel with at least two teams from the East and West for a wild-card spot, truly needed to win this game. They were geared to stop the run: "controlling Morris is the key to stopping the Giants—that and getting some points on the board against that defense," said Minnesota's new head coach, Jerry Burns.

And the Vikings did control Morris, holding him to a mere 49 yards on 18 carries. What they neglected to take into consideration was the talented toe of Raul Allegre and the arm of Phil Simms. In the first quarter Allegre kicked his first field goal of the day, a 41-yarder. The Vikings responded in kind. Then Allegre booted a 37-yarder, but the Vikings came back with another of their own. The former Colts' kicker then sent the Giants to the locker room with a 9–6 lead by kicking his third field goal of the day. Minnesota took the lead in the third period on a Tommy Kramer touchdown pass, but the Giants recaptured it with Allegre's fourth field goal and a 25-yard

touchdown pass from Simms to Bobby Johnson.

Another Minnesota touchdown pass in the fourth quarter gave the lead back to the Vikings, 20–19. And with less than two minutes remaining in the game, it appeared that the Giants' last drive was stalled at their own 48-yard line on fourth down with a distant 16 yards to go for a first down. But Simms dropped back, found Bobby Johnson, and delivered the ball to him for a 22-yard gain. Five plays later, with 12 seconds on the clock, Allegre was perfect with a 33-yarder, and the Giants made their escape, 22–20.

Allegre's five field goals was one short of the club record set by Joe Danello against Seattle in 1981, and he was now 15 of 21 for the season. "I feel like I'm involved in the team now," he said after the game. "I feel like I've made a contribution." Also contributing substantially that day, and much of the reason Allegre got close enough to kick his five field goals, was Phil Simms, who completed

Bobby Johnson makes a diving catch of a 30-yard touchdown pass from Phil Simms to help the Giants overcome the Redskins in their late October encounter, which the Giants won 27–20. The Washington defenders in futile pursuit are cornerback Vernon Dean (32) and safety Curtis Jordan (22). (Fred Roe)

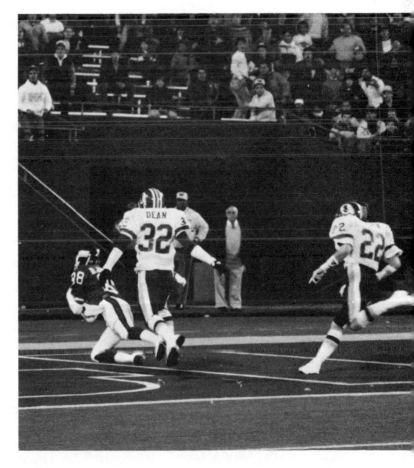

25 of 38 passes for 310 yards. Mark Bavaro and Bobby Johnson caught four each, for 81 and 79 yards, respectively.

Denver was still on top of the AFC West with a record of 9–3 when they came to the Meadowlands to meet the Giants. John Elway was getting rave reviews for his work at quarterbacking the Broncos, and running back Sammy Winder was on his way to leading the AFC in touchdowns scored. The game would prove to be the second of the Giants' two most heart-stopping encounters of the 1986 season, and the cast of heroes would be just about the same.

New York never trailed in the game, but with less than two minutes to go they were tied, 16–16, and facing a third-and-21 situation at their own 18-yard line. Once again Simms rifled it to Bobby Johnson for a first down. He followed that with a 46-yard pass play to Phil McConkey. Then, with six seconds remaining, Allegre again took center stage and drilled a 34-yarder to give the Giants a 19–16 triumph.

Allegre was successful with four field goals that afternoon, and Simms, although he registered only 11 of 20 passes for 187 yards, was perfect when he needed to be. Joe Morris rushed for 106 yards. But perhaps the play of the day occurred when 255-pound, thirty-three-year-old defensive end George Martin picked off an Elway swing pass and galloped 78 yards for a touchdown. It was Martin's sixth touchdown, an NFL record for a defensive lineman. The smiling veteran of many football wars during his twelve-year career with the Giants said of the feat, "When I caught the ball, it was a bright sunny day. By the time I got to the end zone it was partly cloudy." Other defensive stalwarts of the day included Carl Banks, who made 11 tackles, and Harry Carson who chalked up 10.

With the season now three-quarters of the way over, New York had a record of 10–2, by far their best record since the championship years several decades earlier. But they still were not alone at the top of their division, for Washington was battling them win for win. The only other teams in the NFL to sport as good a record were the

Joe Morris erupts through the Redskins line, and Phil Simms, in the background, signals touchdown, one of two Morris scored that day. Morris gained 181 yards rushing while the Giants racked up the first of three victories over the Redskins during the 1986 season. (Fred Roe)

Coach of the Year Bill Parcells makes a point from the sideline—and whatever points he made during the 1986 season were certainly effective, as the Giants rolled up a record of 19–2 and took the NFL title. Looking on are Harry Carson (53), Phil Simms (11), and Jeff Rutledge (17). (Fred Roe)

defending NFL champion Bears and the surprising New York Jets.

Meeting San Francisco marked the Giants' third Monday night game of the season, and at the end of the first half it appeared to the national television audience that New York's five-game win streak was about to come to an end. A remarkably recovered Joe Montana, whose back surgery in September left questions as to whether he would ever play football again, led the 49ers on three sustained drives that resulted in a field goal and two touchdowns. And the San Francisco defense was devouring Joe Morris (he would only gain 14 yards on 13 carries that evening).

The second half was another story, a more-than-total reversal. Suddenly it was Phil Simms engineering the drives. The first ended with a 17-yard touchdown pass to Morris, the next with a 34-yard scoring toss to Stacy Robinson. The third, set up by 49-yard completion to Robinson, was a simple 1-yard plunge by Ottis Anderson, the longtime NFL running back vet acquired from St. Louis a few weeks earlier. While all this was going on, the Giants defense shut down Montana and his fellow 49ers completely. The final score: 21–17, Giants.

This victory set up a showdown, with the Redskins, tied with the Giants with an 11–2, record, and both comfortably ahead of the 7–6 Cowboys. Washington had the home-field advantage, and in that city of extraordinarily loyal and fervid fans it was indeed a distinct advantage.

Nothing happened in the first quarter, at least as far as the scoreboard was concerned. In the second period, Phil Simms clicked with two scores, a 9-yard touchdown toss to Mark Bavaro, and one for 7 yards to Bobby Johnson, enough to give the Giants a 14–7 edge at intermission. In the second half Raul Allegre added a field goal and Simms teamed with Phil McConkey for his third TD pass of the day. And the defense was simply overwhelming. A desperate Jay Schroeder was forced to throw 51 passes, six of which were intercepted by the Giants, and on four other occasions he was sacked. The Redskins' rushing attack was held to 73 yards, and the usually volatile George Rogers picked up only 22 yards on 10 carries. It was a masterful game for both offense and defense, and, with the 24–14 victory, the Giants for the first time in 1986 had sole occupancy of the top floor of the NFC East.

The following two weeks were exercises in ennui. A 27–7 beating of the hapless St. Louis Cardinals (4–11–1 in 1986, to prognosticator Jimmy the Greek's ultimate chagrin) and a 55–24 annihilation of the even more hapless Green Bay Packers (4–12) ended the Giants' regular season with a nine-game win streak and the most victories, fourteen, in the team's long history.

It was the New York Giants' first divisional title since 1963, and the long drought was finally over. It was also a record-breaking year of major proportion (see sidebar).

Joe Morris had virtually rewritten the rushing-record log by gaining 1,516 yards on 341 carries and was the second most productive runner in the entire NFL, trailing only Eric Dickerson of the Rams. Phil Simms, who completed 259 of 468 passes for 3,487 yards and 21 touchdowns, ranked fourth among passers in the NFC with a rating of 74.6. Mark Bavaro was the club's leading receiver with 66 receptions for 1,001 yards. Sean Landeta was the top punter in the NFC with an average of 44.8 yards for his 79 punts. And Raul Allegre was the fifth highest point scorer in the NFC, his total of 105 coming from 24 of 32 field goals and 33 of 33 points-after-touchdowns. Lawrence Taylor led the league with 20½ sacks. The team's top tacklers in 1986 were Carl Banks, with 120 (87 solos and 33 assists), and Harry Carson, with 118 (87 solos and 31 assists).

Bill Parcells was named NFL Coach of the Year, and Lawrence Taylor NFL Defensive MVP. And a total of eight Giants earned their way to the Pro Bowl: Mark Bavaro, Brad Benson, Jim Burt, Harry Carson, Sean Landeta, Leonard Marshall, Joe Morris, and Lawrence Taylor.

With the best record in the NFC, and more wins within their division than the Chicago Bears, who also posted a 14–2 record, the Giants earned the home-field advantage for both playoff games—provided, of course, they triumphed in the first. They had to get by the San Francisco 49ers, whom they had come from behind to beat 21–17 during the regular season.

Joe Montana said before the game that the 49ers were ready, hungry to redeem themselves. Coach Bill Walsh was a little wary and expressed his concern about the Giants' awesome defense, which he had seen firsthand. The Giants were a favorite, no doubt about it, but there was a lot of talk about the high-flying, ever-explosive 49ers, who had beaten three top teams (Jets, Patriots, and Rams) to round out their regular season.

The game, however, was a portrait of systematic destruction, with the final score 49–3. New York's offense was as imposing as its defense, a monstrous combination that led Bill Parcells to say: "not a perfect game, but it was pretty close to it." It did not look that way at the start, however, when Joe Montana connected with Jerry Rice on a short pass and Rice broke loose, streaking for the

Records Set or Tied in 1986

Team

Most victories, regular season	14
Most consecutive victories	9
Most victories at home, regular season	8
Most points scored first period (vs. Green Bay, (12/20)	21
Most field goals attempted, game (vs. Minnesota, 11/16)	6

Individual

Most yards rushing, season:	Joe Morris	1,516
Most rushing attempts, season:	Morris	341
Most games 100 yards rushing, career:	Joe Morris	16
Most games 100 yards rushing, season:	Joe Morris	8
Highest rushing average, career:	Joe Morris (818—3,555)	4.35
Most rushing touchdowns, career:	Joe Morris	40
Most rushing touchdowns, game:	Joe Morris	3
Most 300-yard passing games, career:	Phil Simms	15
Most 300-yard passing games, season:	Phil Simms	4
Most receptions, tight end, season:	Mark Bavaro	66
Most receiving yards, tight end, season:	Mark Bavaro	1,001
Most quarterback sacks, season:	Lawrence Taylor	20½
Most field goals attempted, game:	Raul Allegre	6
Highest punting average, career:	Sean Landeta (160—7,011)	43.8
Most opponent fumbles recovered, game:	Harry Carson	2
Most defensive touchdowns, lineman, career:	George Martin	6

Attendance

Largest home attendance, season	594,433
Largest road attendance, season	471,835
Largest home attendance, game (vs. Washington, 1/11)	76,633

Divisional Playoff Game

New York Giants   49
San Franciso 49ers   3

January 4, 1987
Giants Stadium
Attendance: 76,034

Scoring

Giants	7	21	21	0	49
49ers	3	0	0	0	3

NY	Bavaro, 24-yard pass from Simms (Allegre PAT)
SF	Wersching, 26-yard field goal
NY	Morris, 45-yard run (Allegre PAT)
NY	Johnson, 15-yard pass from Simms (Allegre PAT)
NY	Taylor, 34-yard interception return (Allegre PAT)
NY	McConkey, 28-yard pass from Simms (Allegre PAT)
NY	Mowatt, 29-yard pass from Simms (Allegre PAT)
NY	Morris, 2-yard run (Allegre PAT)

Individual Statistics

	Giants			49ers		
Rushing:	Morris	24	159 yds	Craig	5	17 yds
	Rouson	8	28 yds	Rathman	3	8 yds
	Carthon	6	17 yds	Cribbs	12	4 yds
	Simms	1	15 yds			
	Anderson	4	2 yds			
	Manuel	1	–5 yds			
Passing:	Simms	9–19	136 yds	Montana	8–15	98 yds
	Rutledge	1–1	23 yds	Kemp	7–22	64 yds
Receiving:	Bavaro	2	47 yds	Craig	4	22 yds
	Rouson	2	22 yds	Rice	3	48 yds
	Mowatt	1	29 yds	Clark	3	52 yds
	McConkey	1	28 yds	Francis	3	26 yds
	Johnson	1	15 yds	Margerum	1	12 yds
	Galbreath	1	9 yds	Cribbs	1	2 yds
	Carthon	1	7 yds			
	Morris	1	2 yds			

goal line with the Giants secondary in pursuit, only to fumble the ball in midstride, with the Giants recovering it in their own end zone. After the game one of the 49ers was asked what would have been the outcome if Rice had not fumbled. His reply was that the final score would have been 49–10. The Giants began with a touchdown pass from Phil Simms to Mark Bavaro in the first quarter and ended with New York's seventh touchdown in the third quarter. The defense limited the 49ers to a single field goal all day, holding Joe Montana to a mere 98 yards passing before he left the game with a concussion, and his replacement, Jeff Kemp, to 64. The entire San Francisco rushing attack gained only 29 yards all afternoon.

The Giants were on their way to the NFC title game.

An all-time-record crowd turned out at Giants Stadium to watch New York take on the Washington Redskins for the third time of the season. The Redskins, a wild-card entry in the playoffs, got to the conference championship by defeating the Los Angeles Rams, 19–7, and then upsetting the defending title holders, the Chicago Bears, 27–13.

Despite defeating the Redskins twice during the regular season, Bill Parcells was far from overconfident: "The Redskins are the best team we played this year," he told New York sports reporters. "I thought they would beat the Rams in the wild-card game, and they did. I thought they would have a good shot against the Bears, and they beat them. A month ago Lawrence Taylor told me it was going to be us and the Redskins for the championship, and he was right."

As the two teams convened on the field in the Meadowlands, a poster showing a heart pierced by a Giants blue arrow said it all:

> The arrow that points to Pasadena
> Passes through the heart of Washington

Streaking in to deliver one of his league-leading 20½ sacks in 1986 is Lawrence Taylor (56). The total was also a club record. The unlucky quarterback here is Steve Pelluer of the Dallas Cowboys, whom the Giants beat that day, 17–14. (Fred Roe)

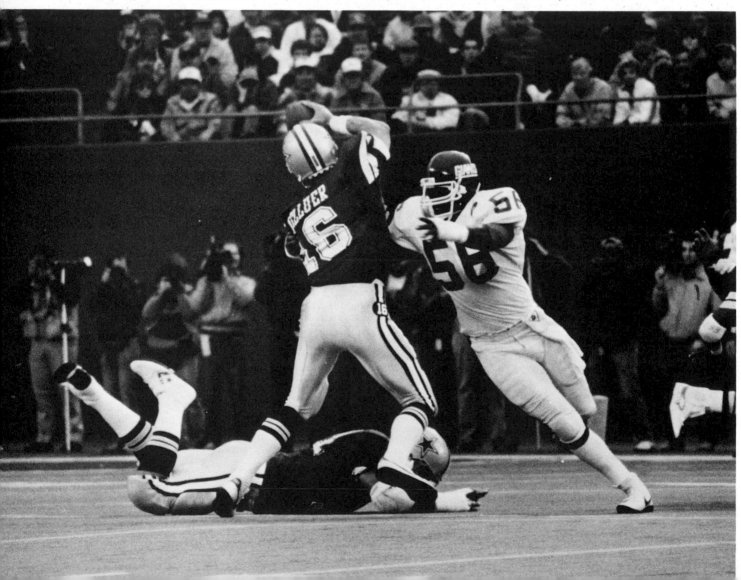

Where it happened, beneath the sunny skies of southern California.

It was not all glamour for Phil Simms in Super Bowl XXI. Occasionally he had to run for his life. But fortunately for Giants fans it was only on rare occasions. Number 61 on the Giants is guard Chris Godfrey.

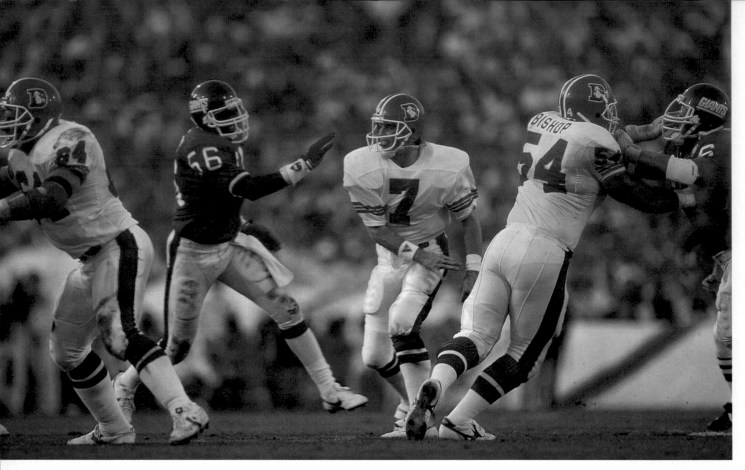

A fearsome image to any quarterback is the NFL's top sacker of 1986, Lawrence Taylor (56). A little late here, he still menaces Denver quarterback John Elway.

Zeke Mowatt is all alone in the end zone and the football, tossed by Phil Simms, is headed right on the proverbial mark. The reception marked the Giants' first touchdown of the afternoon and gave them a 7–3 lead in the first quarter.

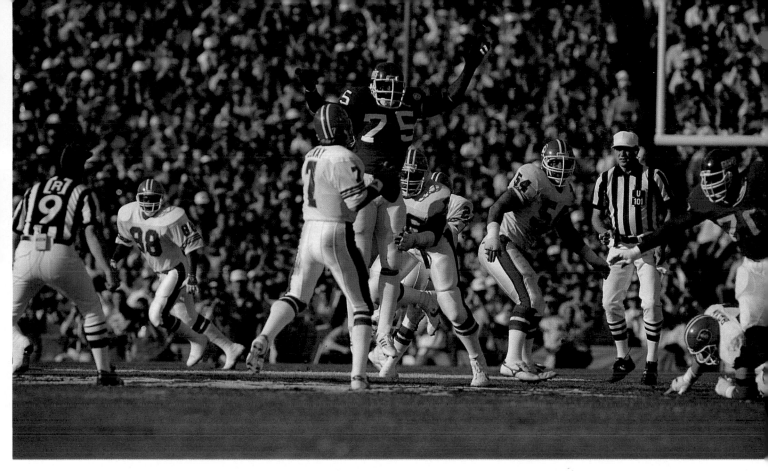

George Martin, New York's 33-year-old honored veteran defensive end leaps high to thwart a John Elway pass. Angling in from the side is Leonard Marshall (70).

Leaping even higher to thwart another Elway pass is linebacker Carl Banks.

Wide receiver Stacy Robinson (81) spins out after taking a pass from Phil Simms. Looking for someone to block is tight end Mark Bavaro (89).

Mark Bavaro caught a few himself that Super Bowl Sunday, four in fact for 51 yards, but this one ricocheted off Bavaro to Phil McConkey (80), seen here trailing the play, who made a diving catch in the end zone.

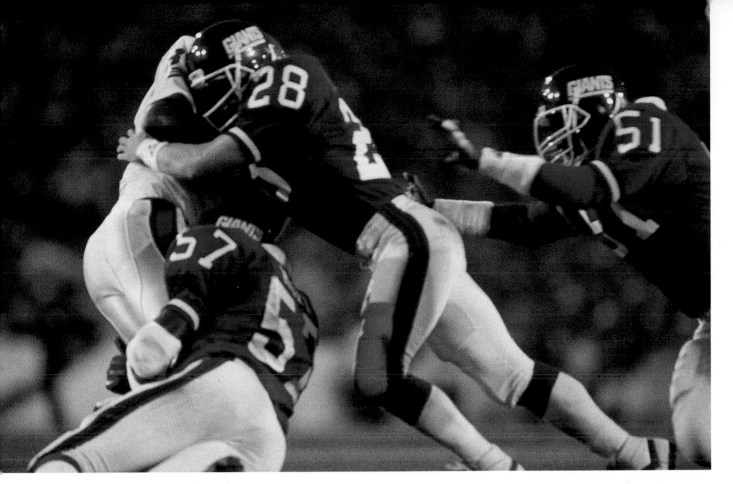

Denver felt the brunt of the Giants defense most of the day. Here Denver's Gene Lang meets up with several New York defenders: linebacker Byron Hunt (57), safety Tom Flynn (28), and linebacker Robbie Jones.

Joe Morris (20) has abundant running room here as he picks up several of the 67 yards he gained in his first Super Bowl appearance. He also scored a touchdown to help the cause.

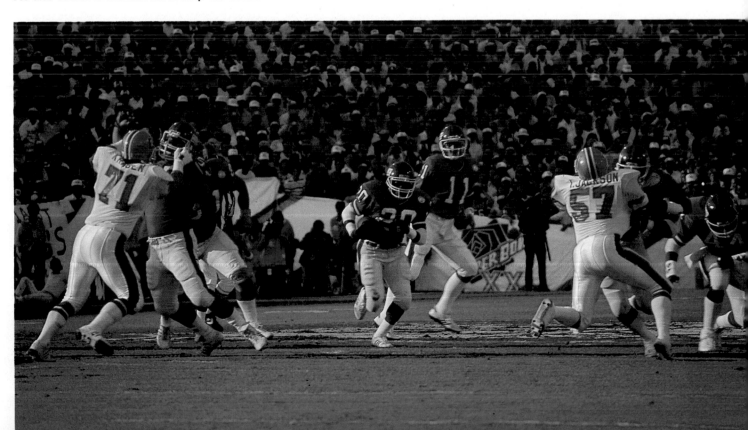

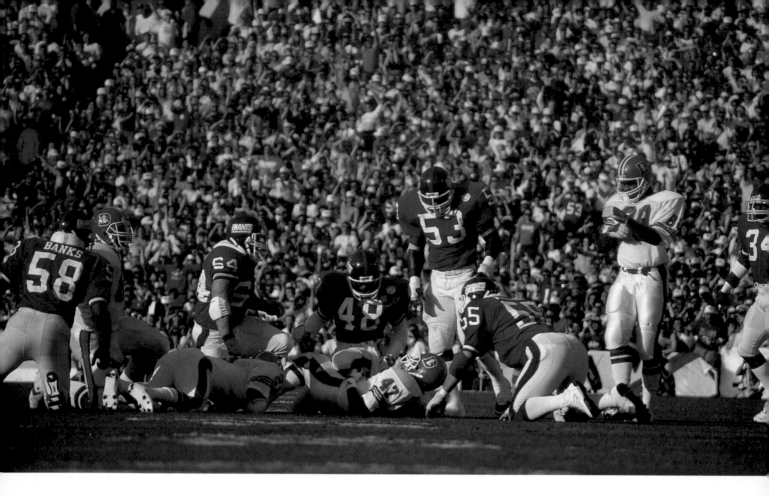

The Giants defense was in evident attendance at the Rose Bowl Super Bowl Sunday, to which various Broncos could attest. Top: running back Gerald Willhite looks up at the menacing crowd: Carl Banks (58), Jim Burt (64), Kenny Hill (48), Harry Carson (53), Gary Reasons (55), and Elvis Patterson (34). Below: Denver's Sammy Winder is smothered by Carl Banks; hovering nearby are George Martin (75), Leonard Marshall (70), Erik Howard (74), Kenny Hill (48), Perry Williams (23), and Harry Carson (53).

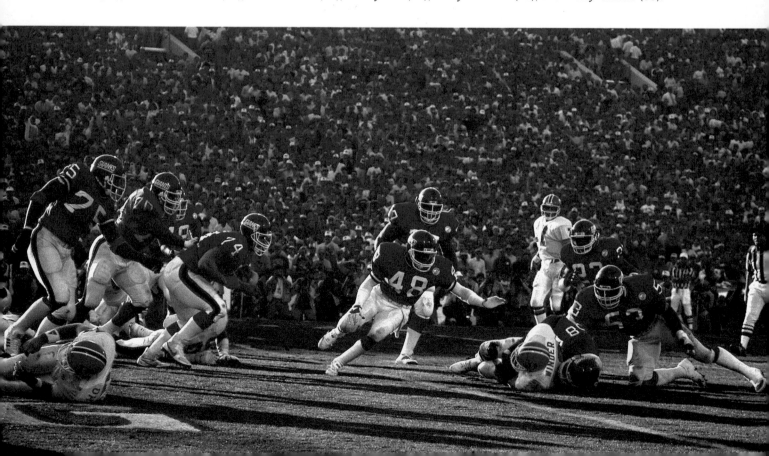

It is nearing time for the now-traditional Gatorade baptism. The fans want it, Harry Carson is lurking near the vat, and Bill Parcells knows it is coming.

Phil Simms was the game's MVP, no surprise after he completed a remarkable 22 of 25 passes, 10 in a row, both Super Bowl records.

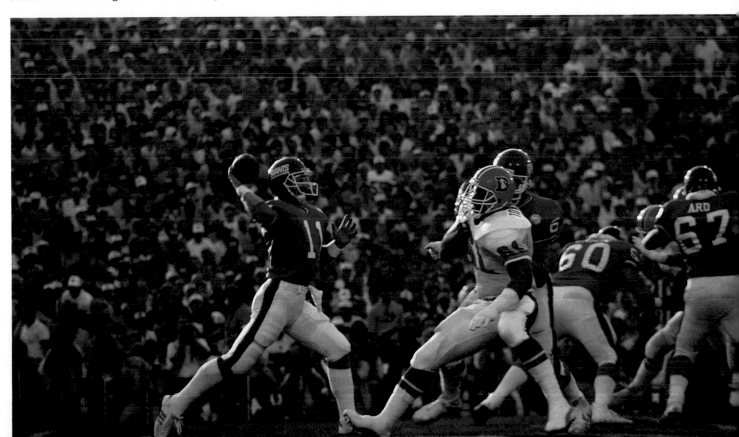

It is all over. The Giants are the NFL champs, triumphing easily in Super Bowl XXI, 39–20, the club's first title since they won it back in 1956 when they had such memorables as Frank Gifford, Kyle Rote, Alex Webster, and Charley Conerly. Celebrating at the top is ever-effervescent Phil McConkey; behind is Chris Godfrey (61). Below is equally effervescent Jim Burt having shed his jersey and pads announcing to the world that the Giants indeed are number one.

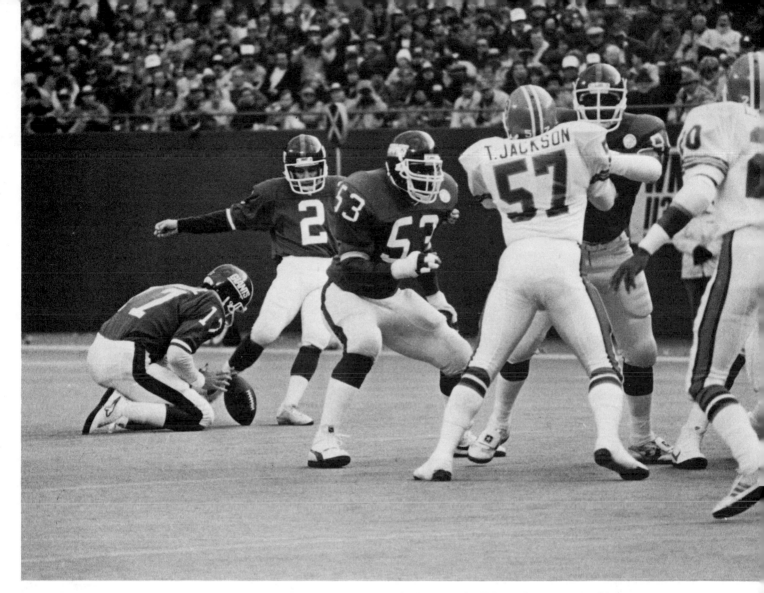

Raul Allegre puts toe to ball and drills one of the four field goals he kicked against the Denver Broncos. The 12 points he put on the board were instrumental in the Giants' 19–16 win that day, the winning margin of 3 points coming on his 34-yarder with less than a minute remaining in the game. Allegre's 105 points scored was seventh best in the NFL in 1986. No. 53 on the Giants is Harry Carson, and the holder is Jeff Rutledge. (Fred Roe)

The afternoon was a cold one, and to say it was blustery is an understatment. Winds gusted at about 30 miles per hour, and Bill Parcells knew that it would wreak havoc on both the passing and kicking games. He felt the advantage lay clearly with the team that could run, score first, and force the other team to throw the football. And he had extraordinary faith in his defense—the best in the NFL in 1986, most agreed. So when the Giants won the coin toss, the instructions were to kick off instead of receive and put the wind at their backs. It was a surprise to the more than 76,600 fans in the stands, and it was a tactic that, if it had backfired, would come back to forever haunt the head coach and his staff.

It did not, of course, backfire. And the defense lived up to their coach's expectations. The Giants stopped the Red-skins summarily, and the Washington punt into that stiff Meadowlands wind carried only 23 yards. The Giants moved the ball to a position where Raul Allegre, blessed by the same wind, kicked a 47-yard field goal. Again the Giants held, and again the Redskins had to punt. This one the wind held to 27 yards. Starting from excellent field position, Simms moved the Giants down to the Washington 11-yard line, where he culminated the drive with a touchdown pass to Lionel Manuel.

In the second period, Washington had the wind, but they bobbled away the advantage. First Gary Clark got behind the Giants secondary and Jay Schroeder threw a picture-perfect bomb that stunned Redskins' fans when it went through the ordinarily sure hands of the team's top receiver of 1986. Then, after the Redskins moved the ball

NFC Championship Game

New York Giants   17
Washington Redskins   0

January 11, 1987
Giants Stadium
Attendance: 76,633

Scoring

Giants	10	7	0	0	17
Redskins	0	0	0	0	0

NY   Allegre, 47-yard field goal
NY   Manuel, 11-yard pass from Simms (Allegre PAT)
NY   Morris, 1-yard run (Allegre PAT)

Individual Statistics

	Giants			**Redskins**		
Rushing:	Morris	29	87 yds	Bryant	6	25 yds
	Carthon	7	28 yds	Rogers	9	15 yds
	Anderson	1	3 yds	Schroeder	1	0 yds
Passing:	Simms	7–14	90 yds	Schroeder	20–50	195 yds
Receiving:	Carthon	3	18 yds	Monk	8	126 yds
	Manuel	2	36 yds	Bryant	7	45 yds
	Bavaro	2	36 yds	Warren	3	9 yds
				Griffin	1	8 yds
				Didier	1	7 yds

to the New York 34-yard line (but were held short of a first down), on the snap for the field-goal attempt the ball went through the hands of holder Jay Schroeder and bounced to the Washington 49-yard line. From there Simms hit tight end Mark Bavaro for a 30-yard gain and eventually moved the Giants to the Washington 1. From there Joe Morris carried it in on a slant.

The halftime score of 17–0 remained unaltered through the following two periods. The Giants defense was as niggardly as Bill Parcells had hoped (and believed) it would be. The Redskins were held to 40 yards rushing and 150 yards passing. Jay Schroeder completed only 20 of 50 passes and was sacked four times. As he explained afterwards, "We lost the game in the first quarter. We got behind, couldn't make the plays, and their defense was in

control." And indeed he was correct.

Next stop on the Giants' barreling express would be the Rose Bowl, in Pasadena, California; the event, Super Bowl XXI.

By the time the Giants deplaned in sunny southern California, they were booked as 9½ point favorites over the AFC champion Denver Broncos. After conquering the AFC West with a record of 11–5 (one of those losses, of course, to the Giants), the Broncos disposed of the AFC East champs, the New England Patriots, 22–17, and then slipped past the AFC Central champion Cleveland Browns, 23–20, in overtime.

After a week of hype and hoopla, mammoth press conferences and media blitzes, and a pregame show that

George Martin (75) celebrates with nose tackle Jerome Sally after Martin picked off a Denver pass and carried the ball 78 yards for a Giants touchdown. It was Martin's sixth TD as a defender, an NFL record. In his 12th year as a Giant, Martin was the oldest member of the Super Bowl champs. (Fred Roe)

would have impressed even P. T. Barnum, the captains of the Giants and the Broncos stood at midfield of the fabled Rose Bowl for the coin toss to launch the game that would determine the NFL champion of the 1986 season.

Denver won the toss and, with no cyclonic winds in southern California, chose to receive. John Elway moved the team deftly, even scrambled for a first down on third and seven, and Rich Karlis, with a 48-yard field goal, put the first score of Super Bowl XXI on the board.

The Giants responded with an impressive march of their own. With Phil Simms completing passes to Lionel Manuel, Mark Bavaro, Joe Morris, and Stacy Robinson, plus a pair of 11-yard runs by Morris, the Giants moved from their own 22 to the Denver 6. From there Simms rifled one over the middle to Zeke Mowatt in the end zone and the Giants took the lead.

In what was turning out to be a very offense-oriented game, Elway marched his Broncos back down the field. On third and goal from the 4, he surprised the Giants and just about everybody in the Rose Bowl by running a draw up the middle from the shotgun formation for a touchdown.

In the second quarter, however, scoring was not the name of the game. Denver was able to move the ball, but kicker Rich Karlis, who had booted 20 of 28 field goals during the regular season, for one of the best percentages in the league, missed a 24-yarder and a 34-yarder. The only score of the period came when old vet George Martin broke through and chased Elway down in the end zone for a safety. At the half the Broncos clung to a fragile 10–9 lead.

Whatever Bill Parcells had to say in the locker room

while Walt Disney Productions entertained the halftime crowd with an extravaganza in which more than 2,000 performers took part, or whatever super-adrenalin osmotically infiltrated the Giants players during the intermission, it produced a vibrant and violent Giants team that virtually controlled the second half.

After Lee Rouson returned the opening kickoff to the 37, the Giants were stymied on fourth down and one at their own 46-yard line. But from punt formation, the Giants suddenly shifted on the Broncos' special team, and Jeff Rutledge moved up to take the snap from center and quarterback-sneaked the first down. After that, Simms completed four passes, the last of which a 13-yard strike to Mark Bavaro for a touchdown, and the Giants had a lead they would never relinquish.

In the same period Raul Allegre added a 21-yard field goal. And Simms, who was playing one of the finest games of his career, shattered the Broncos with a fleaflicker 44-yard pass to Phil McConkey that brought the ball to the Denver 1. From there Joe Morris carried it in for the score on the next play. The New York defense was equally aroused, not giving up a single first down, much less a score. By the end of the third quarter the Giants had a comfortable 26–10 lead.

To start the fourth quarter, New York cornerback Elvis Patterson picked off an Elway pass. And just to show that bad times sometimes run in streaks, a Simms pass to Mark Bavaro in the end zone fell incomplete, but Denver was called for pass interference, which gave the Giants a first down on the Denver 1. Further proof of that maxim came three plays later when a Simms pass bounced off the hands of Bavaro in the end zone but was deflected into those of a surprised but elated Phil McConkey.

Denver's Rich Karlis managed a 29-yard field goal to bring the score to 33–13, Giants, but his onside kickoff failed. The Giants quickly took advantage of it and moved the ball down to the Denver 2-yard line, most of the yards coming on an 18-yard run by Lee Rouson and a 22-yard bootleg by Simms. Ottis Anderson then bulled it in for the Giants' last score of the day.

With just over two minutes left, John Elway connected with Vance Johnson on a 47-yard touchdown play, but the game was far out of reach by that time. When the gun finally sounded in the gray twilight of the Rose Bowl, the score stood New York Giants 39, Denver Broncos 20.

The Vince Lombardi Trophy, symbol of professional football's ultimate triumph, belonged to the Giants. For the first time since 1956, the Mara family could claim an NFL championship. And Giants fans in New York, New Jersey, Connecticut—and everywhere else for that matter —were ecstatic.

Phil Simms, who set two Super Bowl records by completing an incredible 22 of 25 passes, 10 of which were consecutive, was the obvious choice for Super Bowl XXI's MVP award. Triumph came, however, on the legs and shoulders of an entire team that combined an explosive offense with a magnificent defense and iced it with determination and spirit.

With more than a hundred million people in the United States witnessing the team's splendid victory, and with coverage by television or radio for fans in countries as diverse as China and England, it can surely be said that the Giants had added a handsome and rich landmark to the odyssey that began that Sunday back in 1925 when Tim Mara, on the sidewalk outside Our Lady of Esperanza Church, said, "I'm gonna try to put pro football over in New York today."

Super Bowl XXI

New York Giants   39
Denver Broncos   20

January 25, 1987
Rose Bowl
Pasadena, California
Attendance: 101,063

Scoring

Giants	7	2	17	13	39
Broncos	10	0	0	10	20

DN	Karlis, 48-yard field goal
NY	Mowatt, 6-yard pass from Simms (Allegre PAT)
DN	Elway, 4-yard run (Karlis PAT)
NY	Martin, tackled Elway in end zone for safety
NY	Bavaro, 13-yard pass from Simms (Allegre PAT)
NY	Allegre, 21-yard field goal
NY	Morris, 1 yard run (Allegre PAT)
NY	McConkey, 6-yard pass from Simms (Allegre PAT)
DN	Karlis, 28-yard field goal
NY	Anderson, 2-yard run (kick failed)
DN	V. Johnson, 47-yard pass from Elway (Karlis PAT)

Individual Statistics

	Giants			Broncos		
Rushing:	Morris	20	67 yds	Elway	6	27 yds
	Simms	3	25 yds	Willhite	4	19 yds
	Rouson	3	22 yds	Sewell	3	4 yds
	Galbreath	4	17 yds	Long	2	2 yds
	Carthon	3	4 yds	Winder	4	0 yds
	Anderson	2	1 yd			
	Rutledge	3	0 yds			
Passing:	Simms	22–25	268 yds	Elway	22–37	304 yds
				Kubiak	4–4	48 yds
Receiving:	Bavaro	4	51 yds	V. Johnson	5	121 yds
	Morris	4	20 yds	Willhite	5	39 yds
	Carthon	4	13 yds	Winder	4	34 yds
	Robinson	3	62 yds	Jackson	3	51 yds
	Manuel	3	43 yds	Watson	2	54 yds
	McConkey	2	50 yds	Sampson	2	20 yds
	Rouson	1	23 yds	Mobley	2	17 yds
	Mowatt	1	6 yds	Sewell	2	12 yds
				Long	1	4 yds

Brad Benson, the Giants Pro Bowl–bound tackle, was named NFC offensive player of the week after his performance in the second Washington game of the season, in which he blocked then NFL sack leader Dexter Manley (17½ at the time) all day and held him to no sacks and just three tackles. The Giants won the game, 24–14. It was the first time in NFL history that a lineman was so honored. (Fred Roe)

Phil McConkey is about to make a key catch here for a 46-yard gain with less than a minute to go against the Broncos. With the game tied, Simms' pass to McConkey set up the game-winning field goal by Raul Allegre. No. 45 on Denver is cornerback Steve Wilson. (Fred Roe)

A little playful celebration on the sideline between Jim Burt (64) and Lawrence Taylor (56), two of the Giants sterling defenders, after stopping one of the many opponents they stopped all year. Both players went to the Pro Bowl for their efforts. (Fred Roe)

Mark Bavaro (89) snares a Phil Simms pass and carries it in for one of the two touchdowns he scored in the last game of the season against Green Bay. The Giants posted their season-high point total that December day, as they routed the Packers, 55–24. The other Giants in the picture are center Bart Oates (65) and tackle Karl Nelson (63). (Fred Roe)

The hometown fans at Giants Stadium are informed of an honor well earned just before the team and Lawrence Taylor took on the San Francisco 49ers in their first playoff appearance. (Fred Roe)

What helped Joe Morris (20) gain 1,516 yards rushing in the regular season, 246 yards in two playoff games, and another 67 in the Super Bowl were shattering blocks like this one delivered by tandem running back Maurice Carthon. Morris gained 159 yards rushing as the Giants destroyed the 49ers, 49–3, in the NFC divisional playoff game. Other Giants in the picture are Phil Simms (11), Karl Nelson (63), and Mark Bavaro (89). The luckless recipient of Carthon's block is safety Carlton Williamson. (Fred Roe)

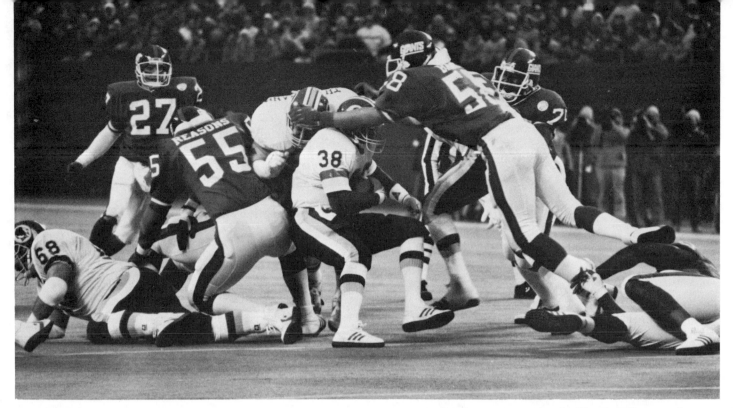

To say the least, the Giants defense was up for the Redskins in the NFC championship game. Here linebacker Carl Banks (58) pummels Washington running back George Rogers (38) to the turf. New York held the Redskins scoreless and limited them to 40 yards rushing and only 190 yards total offense all day. Other identifiable Giants are safety Herb Welch (27) and linebacker Gary Reasons (55). (Fred Roe)

Zeke Mowatt (84) gathers in a Simms pass and goes in for the Giants' sixth touchdown of the day against the 49ers. A seventh was added a little later, and, with a 49–3 victory, the Giants were in a position to take on the Washington Redskins for the NFC title. San Francisco defenders are Carlton Williamson (27) and Don Griffin (29). (Fred Roe)

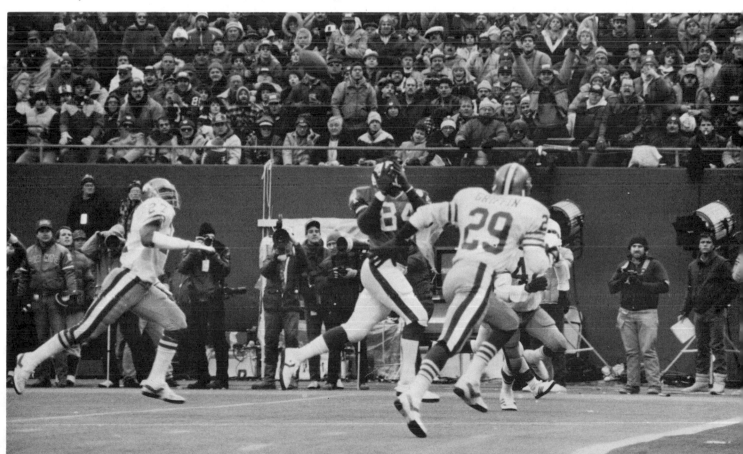

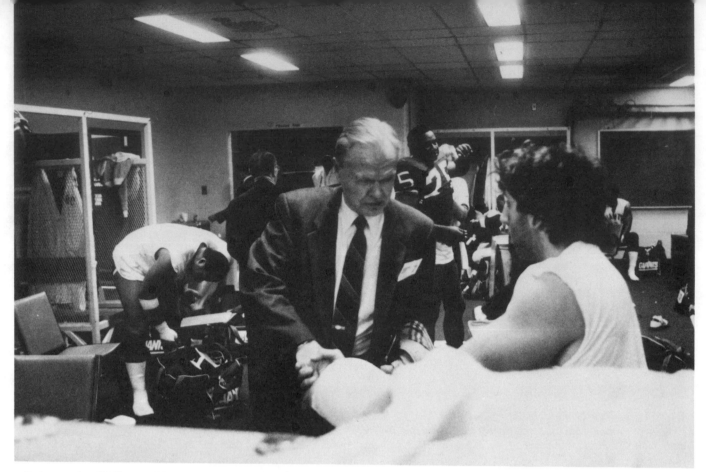

Club president Wellington Mara congratulates Mark Bavaro in the locker room after the Giants prevailed in the NFC East, taking the title and looking forward now to their first Super Bowl appearance. (Fred Roe)

Lionel Manuel (86) is all by himself in the end zone, happily taking possession of an 11-yard Phil Simms pass in the first quarter of the NFL title tilt with Washington. The Giants added another touchdown and a field goal to give them a 17–0 triumph and a ticket to Super Bowl XXI. (Fred Roe)

An enthusiastic, ebullient Jim Burt joins his fans in the stands after the Giants' decisive conquest of the Washington Redskins, which gave them their first conference championship since 1963. (Fred Roe)

Appendix

ANNUAL RECORDS

Team
Scoring
Rushing
Passing
Receiving
Interceptions

CAREER RECORDS

Scoring
Rushing
Receiving
Interceptions

INDIVIDUAL RECORDS

Service
Scoring
    Total Points
    Touchdowns
    Points after touchdown
    Field goals
    Safeties
Rushing
Passing
Receiving
Interceptions
Punting
Kickoff returns
Fumbles
    By Giants
    Total recoveries
    Giants' fumbles recovered
    Opponents' fumbles recovered
    Yards returned

COACHING

MISCELLANEOUS RECORDS

Attendance
"Best Days"
All-Pro honor roll
Retired jersey numbers
First-round draft choices

ANNUAL RECORDS

Team

	Won	Lost	Tied	Points	Opp. Points	Standing		Won	Lost	Tied	Points	Opp. Points	Standing
1925	8	4	0	122	67	4	1959†	10	2	0	284	170	1
1926	8	4	1	147	51	6	1960	6	4	2	271	261	3
1927*	11	1	1	197	20	1	1961†	10	3	1	368	220	1
1928	4	7	2	79	129	6	1962†	12	2	0	398	283	1
1929	13	1	1	312	77	2	1963†	11	3	0	448	280	1
1930	13	4	0	308	98	2	1964	2	10	2	241	399	7
1931	7	6	1	154	90	5	1965	7	7	0	270	338	3
1932	4	6	2	93	113	5	1966	1	12	1	263	501	8
1933†	11	3	0	244	101	1	1967	7	7	0	369	379	2
1934*	8	5	0	147	107	1	1968	7	7	0	294	325	2
1935†	9	3	0	186	96	1	1969	6	8	0	264	298	2
1936	5	6	1	115	163	3	1970	9	5	0	301	270	2
1937	6	3	2	128	109	2	1971	4	10	0	228	362	5
1938*	8	2	1	194	79	1	1972	8	6	0	331	247	3
1939†	9	1	1	168	85	1	1973	2	11	1	226	362	4
1940	6	4	1	131	133	3	1974	2	12	0	195	299	5
1941†	8	3	0	238	114	1	1975	5	9	0	216	306	4
1942	5	5	1	155	139	3	1976	3	11	0	170	250	5
1943†	6	3	1	197	170	1 (tie)	1977	5	9	0	181	265	4
1944†	8	1	1	206	75	1	1978	6	10	0	264	298	5
1945	3	6	1	179	198	3	1979	6	10	0	237	323	4
1946†	7	3	1	236	162	1	1980	4	12	0	249	425	5
1947	2	8	2	190	309	5	1981	9	7	0	295	257	3
1948	4	8	0	297	388	3	1982‡	4	5	0	164	160	4
1949	6	6	0	287	298	3	1983	3	12	1	267	347	5
1950†	10	2	0	268	150	1 (tie)	1984	9	7	0	299	301	2
1951	9	2	1	254	161	2	1985	10	6	0	399	283	2
1952	7	5	0	234	231	2	1986*	14	2	0	371	236	1
1953	3	9	0	179	277	5							
1954	7	5	0	293	184	3							
1955	6	5	1	267	223	3							
1956*	8	3	1	264	197	1							
1957	7	5	0	254	211	2							
1958*	9	3	0	246	183	1							

*NFL champion.
†First in division or conference.
‡Nine-game season.

Scoring

		TDs	PATs	FGs	Total
1932	Ray Flaherty	5	0	0	30
1933	Ken Strong	6	13	5	64
1934	Ken Strong	6	8	4	56
1935	Dale Burnett	6	0	0	36
1936	Tillie Manton	1	15	0	21

		TDs	PATs	FGs	Total
1937	Ward Cuff	4	0	2	30
1938	Ward Cuff	2	18	5	45
1939	Ward Cuff	2	6	7	39
1940	Ward Cuff	2	9	5	36
1941	Ward Cuff	2	19	5	46
1942	Ward Cuff	2	18	3	39
1943	Bill Paschal	12	0	0	72
1944	Bill Paschal	9	0	0	54
1945	Frank Liebel	10	0	0	60
1946	Ken Strong	0	32	4	44
1947	Ken Strong	0	24	2	30
1948	Bill Swiacki	10	0	0	60
1949	Gene Roberts	17	0	0	102
1950	Ray Poole	0	30	5	45
1951	Ray Poole	0	30	12	66
1952	Ray Poole	0	26	10	56
1953	Frank Gifford	7	2	1	47
1954	Ben Agajanian	0	35	13	74
1955	Ben Agajanian	0	32	10	62
1956	Frank Gifford	9	8	1	65
1957	Ben Agajanian	0	32	10	62
1958	Pat Summerall	0	28	12	64
1959	Pat Summerall	0	30	20	90
1960	Pat Summerall	0	32	13	71
1961	Pat Summerall	0	46	14	88
1962	Don Chandler	0	47	19	104
1963	Don Chandler	0	52	18	106
1964	Don Chandler	0	27	9	54
1965	Tucker Frederickson	6	0	0	36
	Homer Jones	6	0	0	36
1966	Pete Gogolak	0	29	16	77
1967	Homer Jones	14	0	0	84
1968	Pete Gogolak	0	36	14	78
1969	Pete Gogolak	0	33	11	66
	Joe Morrison	11	0	0	66
1970	Pete Gogolak	0	32	25	107
1971	Pete Gogolak	0	30	6	48
1972	Pete Gogolak	0	34	21	97
1973	Pete Gogolak	0	25	17	76
1974	Pete Gogolak	0	21	10	51
1975	George Hunt	0	24	6	42
1976	Joe Danelo	0	20	8	44
1977	Joe Danelo	0	19	14	61
1978	Joe Danelo	0	27	21	90
1979	Billy Taylor	11	0	0	66
1980	Joe Danelo	0	27	16	75
1981	Joe Danelo	0	31	24	103
1982	Joe Danelo	0	18	12	54
1983	Ali Haji-Shiekh	0	22	35	127
1984	Ali Haji-Shiekh	0	32	17	83
1985	Joe Morris	21	0	0	126
1986	Raul Allegre	0	33	24	105

Rushing

		Yds.	Atts.	TDs
1932	John McBride	302	84	1
1933	Harry Newman	437	130	3
1934	Harry Newman	483	141	3
1935	Elvin Richards	449	153	4
1936	Tuffy Leemans	830	206	2
1937	Hank Soar	442	120	2
1938	Tuffy Leemans	463	121	4
1939	Tuffy Leemans	429	128	3
1940	Tuffy Leemans	474	132	1
1941	Tuffy Leemans	332	100	4
1942	Merle Hapes	363	95	3
1943	Bill Paschal	572	147	10
1944	Bill Paschal	737	196	9
1945	Bill Paschal	247	59	2
1946	Frank Filchock	371	98	2
1947	Gene Roberts	296	86	1
1948	Gene Roberts	491	145	0
1949	Gene Roberts	634	152	9
1950	Eddie Price	703	126	4
1951	Eddie Price	971	271	7
1952	Eddie Price	748	183	5
1953	Sonny Grandelius	278	108	1
1954	Eddie Price	555	135	2
1955	Alex Webster	634	128	5
1956	Frank Gifford	819	159	5
1957	Frank Gifford	528	136	5
1958	Frank Gifford	468	115	8
1959	Frank Gifford	540	106	3
1960	Mel Triplett	573	124	4
1961	Alex Webster	928	196	2
1962	Alex Webster	743	207	5
1963	Phil King	613	161	3
1964	Ernie Wheelwright	402	100	0
1965	Tucker Frederickson	659	195	5
1966	Chuck Mercein	327	94	0
1967	Ernie Koy	704	146	4
1968	Tucker Frederickson	486	142	1
1969	Joe Morrison	387	107	4
1970	Ron Johnson	1,027	263	8
1971	Bobby Duhon	344	93	1
1972	Ron Johnson	1,182	298	9
1973	Ron Johnson	902	260	6
1974	Joe Dawkins	561	156	2
1975	Joe Dawkins	438	129	2
1976	Doug Kotar	731	185	3
1977	Bob Hammond	577	154	3
1978	Doug Kotar	625	149	1
1979	Billy Taylor	700	198	7
1980	Billy Taylor	580	147	4
1981	Rob Carpenter	748	190	5
1982	Butch Woolfolk	439	112	2
1983	Butch Woolfolk	857	246	2
1984	Rob Carpenter	795	250	7
1985	Joe Morris	1,336	294	21
1986	Joe Morris	1,516	341	14

Passing

		Atts.	Comps.	Yds.	TDs	Ints.
1932	John McBride	74	36	363	6	9
1933	Harry Newman	136	53	973	11	17
1934	Harry Newman	93	35	391	1	12
1935	Ed Danowski	113	57	794	10	9
1936	Ed Danowski	104	47	515	5	10
1937	Ed Danowski	134	66	814	8	5
1938	Ed Danowski	129	70	848	7	8
1939	Ed Danowski	101	42	437	3	6
1940	Ed Miller	73	35	505	4	7
1941	Tuffy Leemans	66	31	475	4	5
1942	Tuffy Leemans	69	35	555	7	4

		Atts.	Comps.	Yds.	TDs	Ints.
1943	Tuffy Leemans	87	37	360	5	5
1944	Arnie Herber	86	36	651	6	8
1945	Arnie Herber	80	35	641	9	8
1946	Frank Filchock	169	87	1,262	12	25
1947	Paul Governali	197	85	1,461	14	16
1948	Charlie Conerly	299	162	2,175	22	13
1949	Charlie Conerly	305	152	2,138	17	20
1950	Charlie Conerly	132	56	1,000	8	7
1951	Charlie Conerly	189	93	1,277	10	22
1952	Charlie Conerly	169	82	1,090	13	10
1953	Charlie Conerly	303	143	1,711	13	25
1954	Charlie Conerly	210	103	1,439	17	11
1955	Charlie Conerly	202	98	1,310	13	13
1956	Charlie Conerly	174	90	1,143	10	7
1957	Charlie Conerly	232	128	1,712	11	11
1958	Charlie Conerly	184	88	1,199	10	9
1959	Charlie Conerly	194	113	1,706	14	4
1960	George Shaw	155	76	1,263	11	13
1961	Y. A. Tittle	285	163	2,272	17	12
1962	Y. A. Tittle	375	200	3,224	33	20
1963	Y. A. Tittle	367	221	3,145	36	14
1964	Y. A. Tittle	281	147	1,798	10	22
1965	Earl Morrall	302	155	2,446	22	12
1966	Gary Wood	170	81	1,142	6	13
1967	Fran Tarkenton	377	204	3,088	29	19
1968	Fran Tarkenton	337	182	2,555	21	12
1969	Fran Tarkenton	409	220	2,918	23	8
1970	Fran Tarkenton	389	219	2,777	19	12
1971	Fran Tarkenton	386	226	2,567	11	21
1972	Norm Snead	325	196	2,307	17	12
1973	Norm Snead	235	131	1,483	7	8
1974	Craig Morton	237	122	1,510	9	13
1975	Craig Morton	363	186	2,359	11	16
1976	Craig Morton	284	153	1,865	9	20
1977	Joe Pisarcik	241	103	1,346	4	14
1978	Joe Pisarcik	301	143	2,096	12	23
1979	Phil Simms	265	134	1,743	13	14
1980	Phil Simms	402	193	2,321	15	19
1981	Phil Simms	316	172	2,031	11	9
1982	Scott Brunner	298	161	2,017	10	9
1983	Scott Brunner	386	190	2,516	9	22
1984	Phil Simms	533	286	4,044	22	18
1985	Phil Simms	495	275	3,829	22	20
1986	Phil Simms	468	259	3,487	21	22

		No.	Yds.	TDs
1946	Ray Poole	24	307	3
1947	Ray Poole	23	395	4
1948	Bill Swiacki	39	550	10
1949	Bill Swiacki	47	652	4
1950	Bill Swiacki	20	280	3
1951	Joe Scott	23	356	2
1952	Bill Stribling	26	399	5
1953	Kyle Rote	26	440	5
	Eddie Price	26	233	1
1954	Bob Schnelker	30	550	8
1955	Frank Gifford	33	437	4
1956	Frank Gifford	51	603	4
1957	Frank Gifford	41	588	4
1958	Frank Gifford	29	330	2
1959	Frank Gifford	42	768	4
1960	Kyle Rote	42	750	20
1961	Del Shofner	68	1,125	11
1962	Del Shofner	53	1,133	12
1963	Del Shofner	64	1,181	9
1964	Aaron Thomas	43	624	6
1965	Joe Morrison	41	574	4
1966	Homer Jones	48	1,044	8
1967	Aaron Thomas	51	877	9
1968	Homer Jones	45	1,057	7
1969	Joe Morrison	44	647	7
1970	Clifton McNeil	50	764	4
1971	Bob Tucker	59	791	4
1972	Bob Tucker	55	764	4
1973	Bob Tucker	50	681	5
1974	Joe Dawkins	46	332	3
1975	Walker Gillette	43	600	2
1976	Bob Tucker	42	498	1
1977	Jim Robinson	22	422	1
1978	Jim Robinson	32	620	2
	Johnny Perkins	32	514	3
1979	Gary Shirk	31	471	2
1980	Earnest Gray	52	777	10
1981	Johnny Perkins	51	858	6
1982	Tom Mullady	27	287	0
1983	Earnest Gray	78	1,139	5
1984	Zeke Mowatt	48	698	7
	Bob Johnson	48	795	6
1985	Lionel Manuel	49	859	6
1986	Mark Bavaro	66	1,001	4

Receiving

		No.	Yds.	TDs
1932	Ray Flaherty	21	350	5
1933	Dale Burnett	12	212	3
1934	Morris Badgro	16	206	1
1935	Tod Goodwin	26	432	4
1936	Dale Burnett	16	246	3
1937	Tuffy Leemans	11	157	1
1938	Hank Soar	13	164	2
	Dale Burnett	13	145	1
1939	Hank Soar	12	134	0
1940	Leland Shaffer	15	121	2
1941	Ward Cuff	19	317	2
1941	Ward Cuff	16	267	2
1943	Bill Walls	14	231	2
1944	O'Neal Adams	14	342	1
1945	Frank Liebel	22	593	10

Interceptions

		No.	Yds.
1940	Doug Oldershaw	4	48
	Leland Shaffer	4	14
1941	Ward Cuff	4	152
	George Franck	4	94
1942	Merle Hapes	3	49
	Hank Soar	3	31
1943	Dave Brown	6	64
1944	Howard Livingston	9	172
1945	Howard Livingston	3	65
1946	Frank Liebel	5	117
1947	Frank Reagan	10	203
1948	Frank Reagan	9	145
1949	Emlen Tunnell	10	251
1950	Otto Schnellbacher	8	99
1951	Otto Schnellbacher	11	194

		No.	Yds.
1952	Tom Landry	8	99
1953	Emlen Tunnell	6	117
1954	Emlen Tunnell	8	108
	Tom Landry	8	71
1955	Emlen Tunnell	7	76
1956	Emlen Tunnell	6	87
1957	Emlen Tunnell	6	87
1958	Jim Patton	11	183
1959	Dick Nolan	5	57
	Lindon Crow	5	54
	Jim Patton	5	13
1960	Jim Patton	6	100
1961	Dick Lynch	9	60
1962	Jim Patton	7	125
1963	Dick Lynch	9	251
1964	Dick Lynch	4	68
1965	Carl Lockhart	4	117
	Dick Lynch	4	38
1966	Carl Lockhart	6	20
1967	Carl Lockhart	5	38
1968	Willie Williams	10	103
1969	Bruce Maher	5	112
1970	Willie Williams	6	114
1971	Willie Williams	5	58
1972	Carl Lockhart	4	56
	Willie Williams	4	42
	Richmond Flowers	4	30
	Pete Athas	4	11
1973	Pete Athas	5	52
1974	Chuck Crist	3	20
1975	Bobby Brooks	4	38
1976	Rick Volk	2	14
	Brad Van Pelt	2	13
	Jim Steinke	2	0
1977	Bill Bryant	3	54
1978	Terry Jackson	7	115
1979	Brian Kelley	3	41
	Harry Carson	3	28
	Terry Jackson	3	10
1980	Mike Dennis	5	68
1981	Beasley Reece	4	84
1982	Terry Jackson	4	75
1983	Terry Jackson	6	20
1984	Mark Haynes	7	90
1985	Elvis Patterson	6	88
1986	Terry Kinard	4	52
	Perry Williams	4	31

CAREER RECORDS
Scoring

	Seasons	TDs	PATs	FGs	Total
Pete Gogolak	1966–74	——	268	126	646
Frank Gifford	1952–60, 62–64	78	10	2	484
Joe Danelo	1976–82	——	170	104	482
Joe Morrison	1959–72	65	——	——	390
Alex Webster	1955–64	56	——	——	336
Ken Strong	1933–35, 39, 44–47	13	141	35	324
Pat Summerall	1958–61	——	136	59	313
Kyle Rote	1951–61	52	——	——	312

	Seasons	TDs	PATs	FGs	Total
Ward Cuff	1937–45	19	98	31	305
Joe Morris	1982–	42	——	——	252

Rushing

	Seasons	Atts.	Yds.	Avg.	TDs
Alex Webster	1955–64	1,196	4,638	3.9	39
Ron Johnson	1970–75	1,066	3,836	3.6	33
Frank Gifford	1952–60, 62–64	840	3,609	4.3	34
Joe Morris	1982–	818	3,555	4.3	40
Doug Kotar	1974–81	900	3,378	3.8	20
Eddie Price	1950–55	846	3,292	3.9	20
Tuffy Leemans	1936–43	919	3,132	3.4	17
Joe Morrison	1959–72	677	2,474	3.7	18
Mel Triplett	1955–60	553	2,289	4.1	11
Tucker Frederickson	1965, 67–71	651	2,209	3.4	9

Receiving

	Seasons	No.	Yds.	Avg.	TDs
Joe Morrison	1959–72	395	4,993	12.6	47
Frank Gifford	1952–60, 62–64	367	5,434	14.8	43
Bob Tucker	1970–77	327	4,376	13.4	22
Kyle Rote	1951–61	300	4,797	16.0	48
Aaron Thomas	1962–70	247	4,253	17.2	35
Alex Webster	1955–64	240	2,697	11.2	17
Del Shofner	1961–67	239	4,315	18.1	35
Homer Jones	1964–69	214	4,845	22.6	35
Ron Johnson	1970–75	189	1,813	9.6	15
Bob Schnelker	1954–60	183	3,232	17.7	29

Interceptions

	Seasons	No.	Yds.	Avg.	TDs
Emlen Tunnell	1949–58	74	1,240	16.8	4
Jim Patton	1955–66	52	712	13.7	2
Carl Lockhart	1965–75	41	475	11.6	3
Dick Lynch	1959–66	35	568	16.2	4
Willie Williams	1965, 67–73	35	462	13.2	0
Tom Landry	1950–55	31	360	11.6	3
Frank Reagan	1941, 46–48	20	376	18.8	0
Howie Livingston	1944–47	20	375	18.8	1
Otto Schnellbacher	1950–51	19	293	15.4	2

INDIVIDUAL RECORDS
Service

Most Seasons, Active Player
- 15   Mel Hein, 1931–45
- 14   Charlie Conerly, 1948–61
- 14   Joe Morrison, 1959–72
- 13   Rosey Brown, 1953–65
- 13   Jim Katcavage, 1956–68
- 13   Greg Larson, 1961–73

Most Consecutive Seasons, Active Player
(Same as above)

Most Consecutive Games Played, Lifetime
- 172 Mel Hein, 1931–45
- 131 Dave Jennings, 1974–82
- 126 Emlen Tunnell, 1948–58
- 124 Ray Wietecha, 1953–62

Most Seasons, Head Coach (*See also* Coaching)
- 23 Steve Owen, 1931–53
- 8 Allie Sherman, 1961–68
- 7 Jim Lee Howell, 1954–60

Scoring

TOTAL POINTS

Most Points, Lifetime
- 646 Pete Gogolak, 1966–74 (268 PAT, 126 FG)
- 484 Frank Gifford, 1952–60, 62–64 (78 TD, 10 PAT, 2 FG)
- 482 Joe Danelo, 1976–82 (170 PAT, 104 FG)
- 390 Joe Morrison, 1959 71 (65 TD)

Most Points, Season
- 127 Ali Haji-Shiekh, 1983 (22 PAT, 35 FG)
- 126 Joe Morris, 1985 (21 TD)
- 107 Pete Gogolak, 1970 (32 PAT, 25 FG)
- 106 Don Chandler, 1963 (52 PAT, 18 FG)
- 104 Don Chandler, 1962 (47 PAT, 19 FG)

Most Points, Rookie Season
- 127 Ali Haji-Shiekh, 1983 (22 PAT, 35 FG)

Most Points, Game
- 24 Earnest Gray, vs. St. Louis., Sept. 7, 1980
- 24 Ron Johnson, vs. Philadelphia, Oct. 2, 1972
- 20 Joe Danelo, vs. Seattle, Oct. 18, 1981

Most Consecutive Games Scoring
- 61 Pete Gogolak, 1969–73
- 57 Ben Agajanian, 1949, 54–57
- 46 Pat Summerall, 1958–61

Most Seasons Leading League
- 1 Ken Strong, 1933 (tied)
- 1 Gene Roberts, 1949 (tied)
- 1 Don Chandler, 1963

TOUCHDOWNS

Most Touchdowns, Lifetime
- 78 Frank Gifford, 1952–60, 62–64
- 65 Joe Morrison, 1959–71
- 56 Alex Webster, 1955–64

Most Touchdowns, Season
- 21 Joe Morris, 1985
- 17 Gene Roberts, 1949
- 15 Joe Morris, 1986
- 14 Homer Jones, 1967
- 14 Ron Johnson, 1972
- 12 Bill Paschal, 1943
- 12 Del Shofner, 1962
- 12 Ron Johnson, 1970

Most Touchdowns, Rookie Season
- 12 Bill Paschal, 1943

Most Touchdowns, Game
- 4 Earnest Gray, vs. St. Louis, Sept. 7, 1980
- 4 Ron Johnson, vs. Philadelphia, Oct. 2, 1972
- 3 By many players

Most Consecutive Games Scoring Touchdowns
- 10 Frank Gifford, 1957–58
- 7 Bill Paschal, 1944
- 7 Kyle Rote, 1959–60
- 6 Frank Gifford, 1953

Most Seasons Leading League
- 2 Bill Paschal, 1943 (tied), 1944 (tied)
- 1 Gene Roberts, 1949
- 1 Homer Jones, 1967
- 1 Joe Morris, 1985

POINTS AFTER TOUCHDOWN

Most Points After Touchdown Attempted, Lifetime
- 277 Pete Gogolak, 1966–74
- 176 Joe Danelo, 1976–82
- 159 Ben Agajanian, 1949, 54–57

Most Points After Touchdown Attempted, Season
- 56 Don Chandler, 1963
- 48 Don Chandler, 1962
- 46 Pat Summerall, 1961

Most Points After Touchdown Attempted, Game
- 8 Pete Gogolak, vs. Philadelphia, Nov. 26, 1972
- 7 By many players

Most Points After Touchdown, Lifetime
- 268 Pete Gogolak, 1966–74
- 170 Joe Danelo, 1976–82
- 157 Ben Agajanian, 1949, 54–57

Most Points After Touchdown, Season
- 52 Don Chandler, 1963
- 47 Don Chandler, 1962
- 46 Pat Summerall, 1961

Most Points After Touchdown, Game
- 8 Pete Gogolak, vs. Philadelphia, Nov. 26, 1972
- 7 Len Younce, vs. Green Bay, Nov. 21, 1948
- 7 Ray Poole, vs. Baltimore, Nov. 19, 1950
- 7 Pat Summerall, vs. Washington, Nov. 5, 1961
- 7 Don Chandler, vs. Washington, Oct. 28, 1962
- 7 Pete Gogolak, vs. St. Louis, Dec. 7, 1969

Most Consecutive Points After Touchdown
- 133 Pete Gogolak, 1967–72
- 126 Pat Summerall, 1958–61

Most Points After Touchdown (no misses), Season
- 46 Pat Summerall, 1961
- 36 Pete Gogolak, 1968
- 35 Ben Agajanian, 1954

Most Points After Touchdown (no misses), Game
- 8 Pete Gogolak, vs. Phila., Nov. 26, 1972
- 7 By five players (*see* Most Points After Touchdown, Game)

Most Seasons Leading League
- 1 Ward Cuff, 1938
- 1 Pat Summerall, 1961
- 1 Don Chandler, 1963

FIELD GOALS

Most Field Goals Attempted, Lifetime
- 219 Pete Gogolak, 1966–74

176   Joe Danelo, 1976–82
112   Pat Summerall, 1958–61

Most Field Goals Attempted, Season
42   Ali Haji-Sheikh, 1983
41   Pete Gogolak, 1970
38   Joe Danelo, 1981
34   Pat Summerall, 1961
31   Pete Gogolak, 1972
29   Pat Summerall, 1959
29   Don Chandler, 1963

Most Field Goals Attempted, Game
6   Joe Danelo, vs. Seattle, Oct. 18, 1981
6   Ben Agajanian, vs. Philadelphia, Nov. 14, 1943
6   Pete Gogolak, vs. Philadelphia, Nov. 25, 1973
6   Ali Haji-Sheikh, vs. Washington, Dec. 17, 1983

Most Field Goals, Lifetime
126   Pete Gogolak, 1966–74
104   Joe Danelo, 1976–82
59   Pat Summerall, 1958–61

Most Field Goals, Season
35   Ali Haji-Sheikh, 1983
25   Pete Gogolak, 1970
24   Joe Danelo, 1981
21   Joe Danelo, 1978
21   Pete Gogolak, 1972

Most Field Goals, Game
6   Joe Danelo, vs. Seattle, Oct. 18, 1981
5   Ali Haji-Sheikh, vs. Washington, Dec. 17, 1983
5   Eric Schubert, vs. Tampa Bay, Nov. 3, 1985
5   Raul Allegre, vs. Minnesota, Nov. 16, 1986
4   Don Chandler, vs. Philadelphia, Nov. 18, 1962
4   Don Chandler, vs. Chicago, Dec. 2, 1962
4   Don Chandler, vs. Cleveland, Oct. 27, 1963
4   Pete Gogolak, vs. St. Louis, Oct. 9, 1966
4   Pete Gogolak, vs. Cleveland, Dec. 4, 1966
4   Joe Danelo, vs. Washington, Nov. 14, 1976
4   Joe Danelo, vs. Philadelphia, Jan. 2, 1983
4   Raul Allegre, vs. Denver, Nov. 23, 1986

Most Consecutive Games Kicking Field Goals
18   Joe Danelo, 1977–79
15   Ali Haji-Sheikh, 1983
14   Pat Summerall, 1960–61
9   Pete Gogolak, 1972
7   Pat Summerall, 1958–59
7   Pat Summerall, 1959
7   Ali Haji-Sheikh, 1984

Longest Field Goal (in yards)
56   Ali Haji-Sheikh, vs. Green Bay, Sept. 26, 1983
56   Ali Haji-Sheikh, vs. Detroit, Nov. 7, 1983
55   Joe Danelo, vs. New Orleans, Sept. 20, 1981
54   Pete Gogolak, vs. Dallas, Nov. 8, 1970
54   Joe Danelo, vs. Seattle, Oct. 18, 1981
53   Don Chandler, vs. Dallas, Dec. 1, 1963
52   Joe Danelo, vs. San Francisco, Sept. 24, 1978
52   Joe Danelo, vs. San Francisco, Nov. 29, 1981
52   Ali Haji-Sheikh, vs. Green Bay, Sept. 15, 1985
51   Joe Danelo, vs. Dallas, Nov. 6, 1977
51   Joe Danelo, vs. Dallas, Oct. 5, 1980
50   Ben Agajanian, vs. Washington, Oct. 13, 1957
50   Joe Danelo, vs. Washington, Nov. 14, 1976

50   Joe Danelo, vs. New Orleans, Oct. 29, 1978
50   Joe Danelo, vs. Philadelphia, Sept. 22, 1980

Highest Completion Percentage, Lifetime (50 attempts)
67.5   Ali Haji-Sheikh, 1983–85 (54–80)
59.0   Joe Danelo, 1976–82 (104–176)
57.1   Pete Gogolak, 1966–74 (126–219)
54.8   Ben Agajanian, 1949, 54–57 (46–84)

Highest Completion Percentage, Season (14 attempts)
83.3   Ali Haji-Sheikh, 1983 (35–42)
75.0   Ray Poole, 1951 (12–16)
72.4   Joe Danelo, 1978 (21–29)
69.0   Pat Summerall, 1959 (20–29)
67.9   Don Chandler, 1962 (19–28)

Highest Completion Percentage, Game (4 attempts)
100.0   Joe Danelo, vs. Seattle, Oct. 18, 1981 (6–6)
100.0   Don Chandler, vs. Chicago, Dec. 2, 1962 (4–4)
100.0   Ali Haji-Sheikh, vs. Dallas, Nov. 4, 1984 (4–4)
100.0   Eric Schubert, vs. Tampa Bay, Nov. 3, 1985 (4–4)
83.3   Ali Haji-Sheikh, vs. Washington, Dec. 17, 1983 (5–6)
80.0   Don Chandler, vs. Philadelphia, Nov. 18, 1962 (4–5)
80.0   Don Chandler, vs. Cleveland, Oct. 27, 1963 (4–5)
80.0   Pete Gogolak, vs. St. Louis, Oct. 9, 1966 (4–5)
80.0   Pete Gogolak, vs. Detroit, Nov. 17, 1974 (4–5)
80.0   Joe Danelo, vs. Philadelphia, Jan. 2, 1983 (4–5)
80.0   Joe Danelo, vs. Washington, Nov. 14, 1976 (4–5)
80.0   Ali Haji-Sheikh, vs. Seattle, Dec. 11, 1983 (4–5)

Most Seasons Leading League
3   Ward Cuff, 1938 (tied), 1939, 1943 (tied)
1   Ken Strong, 1944
1   Pat Summerall, 1959
1   Ali Haji-Sheikh, 1983

SAFETIES

Most Safeties, Lifetime
3   Jim Katcavage, 1958, 61, 65
1   By many players

Most Safeties, Season
1   By many players

Most Safeties, Game
1   By many players

Rushing

Most Attempts, Lifetime
1,196   Alex Webster, 1955–64
1,066   Ron Johnson, 1970–75
919   Tuffy Leemans, 1936–43

Most Attempts, Season
341   Joe Morris, 1986
298   Ron Johnson, 1972
294   Joe Morris, 1985
271   Eddie Price, 1951
263   Ron Johnson, 1970
260   Ron Johnson, 1973

Most Attempts, Game
43   Butch Woolfolk, vs. Philadelphia, Nov. 20, 1983
38   Harry Newman, vs. Green Bay, Nov. 11, 1934
36   Ron Johnson, vs. Philadelphia, Oct. 2, 1972
36   Joe Morris, vs. Pittsburgh, Dec. 21, 1985

33 Rob Carpenter, vs. Philadelphia, Dec. 27, 1981
32 Eddie Price, vs. Chi. Cardinals, Nov. 25, 1951
30 Bill Paschal, vs. Washington, Dec. 3, 1944
30 Eddie Price, vs. N.Y. Yankees, Dec. 16, 1951
30 Ron Johnson, vs. Philadelphia, Sept. 23, 1973

Most Yards Gained, Lifetime
4,638 Alex Webster, 1955–64
3,836 Ron Johnson, 1970–75
3,609 Frank Gifford, 1952–60, 62–64
3,555 Joe Morris, 1982–
3,378 Doug Kotar, 1974–81
3,292 Eddie Price, 1950–55

Most Yards Gained, Season
1,516 Joe Morris, 1986
1,336 Joe Morris, 1985
1,182 Ron Johnson, 1972
1,027 Ron Johnson, 1970
971 Eddie Price, 1951
928 Alex Webster, 1961

Most Yards Gained, Game
218 Gene Roberts, vs. Chi. Cardinals, Nov. 12, 1950
188 Bill Paschal, vs. Washington, Dec. 5, 1943
181 Joe Morris, vs. Washington, Oct. 27, 1986
181 Joe Morris, vs. Dallas, Nov. 2, 1986
179 Joe Morris, vs. St. Louis, Dec. 14, 1986
171 Eddie Price, vs. Philadelphia, Dec. 9, 1951

Most Games, 100 Yards or More Rushing, Lifetime
16 Joe Morris, 1982–
11 Eddie Price, 1950–55
10 Ron Johnson, 1970–73
5 Rob Carpenter, 1981
5 Tuffy Leemans, 1936–43
5 Bill Paschal, 1943–47
4 Gene Roberts, 1947–50
4 Alex Webster, 1955–64
4 Doug Kotar, 1974–78

Most Games, 100 Yards or More Rushing, Season
8 Joe Morris, 1986
7 Joe Morris, 1985
5 Rob Carpenter, 1981
4 Eddie Price, 1951
4 Eddie Price, 1952
4 Ron Johnson, 1970
4 Ron Johnson, 1972
3 Tuffy Leemans, 1936
3 Eddie Price, 1950
2 Bill Paschal, 1943
2 Bill Paschal, 1944
2 Ward Cuff, 1944
2 Gene Roberts, 1949
2 Ron Johnson, 1973
2 Doug Kotar, 1976
2 Billy Taylor, 1979

Longest Run from Scrimmage
91 Hap Moran, vs. Packers, Nov. 23, 1930
80 Eddie Price, vs. Philadelphia, Dec. 9, 1951
79 Frank Gifford, vs. Washington, Nov. 29, 1959
77 Bill Paschal, vs. Clev. Rams, Nov. 4, 1945

Highest Average Gain, Lifetime
4.35 Joe Morris, 1982– (818–3,555)

4.30 Frank Gifford, 1952–60, 62–64 (840–3609)
4.14 Mel Triplett, 1955–60 (553–2289)
3.89 Eddie Price, 1950–55 (846–3292)
3.88 Alex Webster, 1955–64 (1196–4638)
3.75 Doug Kotar, 1974–81 (900–3378)

Highest Average Gain, Season (qualifiers)
5.58 Eddie Price, 1950 (126–703)
5.15 Frank Gifford, 1956 (159–819)
4.95 Alex Webster, 1955 (128–634)

Highest Average Gain, Game (10 attempts)
13.30 Frank Reagan, vs. Los Angeles, Dec. 5, 1946 (10–133)
12.23 Tuffy Leemans, vs. Green Bay, Nov. 20, 1938 (13–159)
11.43 Ernie Koy, vs. Washington, Oct. 1, 1967 (14–160)

Most Touchdowns, Lifetime
40 Joe Morris, 1982–
39 Alex Webster, 1955–64
34 Frank Gifford, 1952–60, 62–64
33 Ron Johnson, 1970–75

Most Touchdowns, Season
21 Joe Morris, 1985
14 Joe Morris, 1986
10 Bill Paschal, 1943
9 Ron Johnson, 1972
9 Bill Paschal, 1944
9 Gene Roberts, 1949
8 Frank Gifford, 1958
8 Ron Johnson, 1970

Most Touchdowns, Game
3 Bill Paschal, vs. Pitt. Cardinals, Oct. 22, 1944
3 Gene Roberts, vs. N.Y. Bulldogs, Sept. 30, 1949
3 Mel Triplett, vs. Chi. Cardinals, Oct. 7, 1956
3 Charlie Evans, vs. San Diego, Nov. 7, 1971
3 Joe Morris, vs. Washington, Oct. 28, 1984
3 Joe Morris, vs. Washington, Nov. 18, 1985
3 Joe Morris, vs. Cleveland, Dec. 1, 1985
3 Joe Morris, vs. Houston, Dec. 8, 1985
3 Joe Morris, vs. Pittsburgh, Dec. 21, 1985
3 Joe Morris, vs. St. Louis, Dec. 14, 1986

Most Consecutive Games Rushing for Touchdowns
7 Bill Paschal, 1944
5 Bill Gaiters, 1961
4 Ken Strong, 1934
4 Bill Paschal, 1943
4 Ron Johnson, 1970

Most Seasons Leading League
2 Bill Pascal, 1943–44
1 Tuffy Leemans, 1936
1 Eddie Price, 1951

Passing

Most Passes Attempted, Lifetime
2,833 Charlie Conerly, 1948–61
2,492 Phil Simms, 1979–
1,898 Fran Tarkenton, 1967–71
1,308 Y. A. Tittle, 1961–64

Most Passes Attempted, Season
533 Phil Simms, 1984
495 Phil Simms, 1985
468 Phil Simms, 1986

409   Fran Tarkenton, 1969
402   Phil Simms, 1980
389   Fran Tarkenton, 1970

Most Passes Attempted, Game
62   Phil Simms, vs. Cincinnati, Oct. 13, 1985
53   Charlie Conerly, vs. Pittsburgh, Dec. 5, 1948
52   Jeff Rutledge, vs. Seattle, Dec. 11, 1983

Most Passes Completed, Lifetime
1,418   Charlie Conerly, 1948–61
1,326   Phil Simms, 1979–
1,051   Fran Tarkenton, 1967–71
731   Y. A. Tittle, 1961–64

Most Passes Completed, Season
286   Phil Simms, 1984
275   Phil Simms, 1985
259   Phil Simms, 1986
226   Frank Tarkenton, 1971
221   Y. A. Tittle, 1963
220   Fran Tarkenton, 1969

Most Passes Completed, Game
40   Phil Simms, vs. Cin., Oct. 13, 1985
36   Charlie Conerly, vs. Pittsburgh, Dec. 5, 1948
31   Scott Brunner, vs. San Diego, Oct. 2, 1983
30   Randy Johnson, vs. Philadelphia, Dec. 19, 1971

Most Consecutive Passes Completed
12   Y. A. Tittle, vs. Washington, Oct. 28, 1962

Highest Passing Efficiency, Lifetime (1000 attempts)
55.89   Y. A. Tittle, 1961–64 (731–1308)
55.37   Fran Tarkenton, 1967–71 (1051–1898)

Highest Passing Efficiency, Season (qualifiers)
60.31   Norm Snead, 1972 (196–325)
60.22   Y. A. Tittle, 1963 (221–367)
58.55   Fran Tarkenton, 1971 (226–386)
58.25   Charlie Conerly, 1959 (113–194)

Highest Passing Efficiency, Game (20 attempts)
80.00   Y. A. Tittle, vs. Philadelphia, Nov. 10, 1963 (16–20)
80.00   Fran Tarkenton, vs. San Diego, Nov. 7, 1971 (16–20)
80.00   Norm Snead vs. New England, Sept. 22, 1974 (28–35)
77.27   Bob Clatterbuck, vs. Pittsburgh, Dec. 5, 1954 (17–22)

Most Yards Gained, Lifetime
19,488   Charlie Conerly, 1948–61
17,585   Phil Simms, 1979–
13,905   Fran Tarkenton, 1967–71
10,439   Y. A. Tittle, 1961–64

Most Yards Gained, Season
4,044   Phil Simms, 1984
3,829   Phil Simms, 1985
3,487   Phil Simms, 1986
3,224   Y. A. Tittle, 1962
3,145   Y. A. Tittle, 1963
3,088   Fran Tarkenton, 1967

Most Yards Gained, Game
513   Phil Simms, vs. Cin., Oct. 13, 1985
505   Y. A. Tittle, vs. Washington, Oct. 28, 1962

Most Games, 300 Yards or More Passing, Lifetime
15   Phil Simms, 1979–
9   Y. A. Tittle, 1961–64

4   Fran Tarkenton, 1967–71
4   Scott Brunner, 1980–83

Most Games, 300 Yards or More Passing, Season
4   Y. A. Tittle, 1962
4   Phil Simms, 1984
4   Phil Simms, 1985
3   Y. A. Tittle, 1961

Longest Pass Completion (in yards)
98   Earl Morrall (to Homer Jones), vs. Pittsburgh, Sept. 11, 1966
94   Norm Snead (to Rich Houston), vs. Dallas, Sept. 24, 1972
89   Earl Morrall (to Homer Jones), vs. Philadelphia, Oct. 17, 1965
88   Frank Reagan (to George Franck), vs. Washington, Oct. 12, 1947

Most Touchdown Passes, Lifetime
173   Charlie Conerly, 1948–61
103   Fran Tarkenton, 1967–71
96   Y. A. Tittle, 1961–64

Most Touchdown Passes, Season
36   Y. A. Tittle, 1963
33   Y. A. Tittle, 1962
29   Fran Tarkenton, 1967

Most Touchdown Passes, Game
7   Y. A. Tittle, vs. Washington, Oct. 28, 1962
6   Y. A. Tittle, vs. Dallas, Dec. 16, 1962
5   Fran Tarkenton, vs. St. Louis, Oct. 25, 1970
5   Phil Simms, vs. St. Louis, Sept. 7, 1980

Most Consecutive Games Touchdown Passes
13   Y. A. Tittle, 1963–64
10   Charlie Conerly, 1948–49
9   Earl Morrall, 1965–66

Fewest Passes Intercepted, Lifetime (1000 attempts)
68   Y. A. Tittle, 1961–64 (1308)
72   Fran Tarkenton, 1967–71 (1898)

Fewest Passes Intercepted, Season (qualifiers)
3   Gary Wood, 1964
4   Charlie Conerly, 1959
4   Ed Danowski, 1937

Fewest Passes Intercepted, Game (most attempts)
0   Scott Brunner, vs. St. Louis, Dec. 16, 1982 (51 attempts)
0   Fran Tarkenton, vs. Dallas, Oct. 11, 1971 (46 attempts)
0   Fran Tarkenton, vs. Dallas, Dec. 15, 1968 (43 attempts)
0   Y. A. Tittle, vs. Washington, Oct. 28, 1962 (39 attempts)

Most Passes Intercepted, Lifetime
167   Charlie Conerly, 1948–61
103   Phil Simms, 1979–
72   Fran Tarkenton, 1967–71
68   Y. A. Tittle, 1961–64

Most Passes Intercepted, Season
25   Frank Filchock, 1946
25   Charlie Conerly, 1953
23   Joe Pisarcik, 1978

Most Passes Intercepted Game
5   Harry Newman, vs. Portsmouth, Sept. 24, 1933
5   Frank Filchock, vs. Washington, Oct. 13, 1946

5 Charlie Conerly, vs. Chi. Cardinals, Oct. 14, 1951
5 Charlie Conerly, vs. Detroit, Dec. 13, 1953

Lowest Percentage Passes Intercepted, Lifetime (1000 attempts)
3.79 Fran Tarkenton, 1967–71 (72–1898)

Lowest Percentage Passes Intercepted, Season (qualifiers)
1.96 Fran Tarkenton, 1969 (8–409)
2.06 Charlie Conerly, 1959 (4–194)
2.10 Gary Wood, 1964 (3–143)

Most Seasons Leading League
2 Ed Danowski, 1935, 1938
1 Harry Newman, 1933
1 Charlie Conerly, 1959
1 Y. A. Tittle, 1963
1 Norm Snead, 1972

Receiving

Most Pass Receptions, Lifetime
395 Joe Morrison, 1959–72
367 Frank Gifford, 1952–60, 62–64
327 Bob Tucker, 1970–77

Most Pass Receptions, Season
78 Earnest Gray, 1983
68 Del Shofner, 1961
64 Del Shofner, 1963
59 Bob Tucker, 1971

Most Pass Receptions, Game
12 Mark Bavaro, vs. Cincinnati, Oct. 13, 1985
11 Frank Gifford, vs. San Francisco, Dec. 1, 1957
11 Del Shofner, vs. Washington, Oct. 28, 1962
11 Doug Kotar, vs. St. Louis, Oct. 3, 1976
11 Billy Taylor, vs. Tampa Bay, Nov. 2, 1980
11 Gary Shirk, vs. New Orleans, Sept. 20, 1981
10 Alex Webster, vs. Dallas, Dec. 16, 1962
10 Tucker Frederickson, vs. Washington, Nov. 15, 1970
10 Ron Johnson, vs. New England, Sept. 22, 1974

Most Consecutive Games, Pass Receptions
45 Bob Tucker, 1970–73
32 Homer Jones, 1965–67
26 Homer Jones, 1968–69
25 Earnest Gray, 1982–84
23 Kyle Rote, 1956–58
23 Joe Morrison, 1964–65

Most Yards Gained, Lifetime
5,434 Frank Gifford, 1952–60, 62–64
4,993 Joe Morrison, 1959–72
4,845 Homer Jones, 1964–69

Most Yards Gained, Season
1,209 Homer Jones, 1967
1,181 Del Shofner, 1963
1,139 Earnest Gray, 1983
1,133 Del Shofner, 1962

Most Yards Gained, Game
269 Del Shofner, vs. Washington, Oct. 28, 1962
212 Gene Roberts, vs. Green Bay, Nov. 13, 1949
201 Gene Roberts, vs. Chi. Bears, Oct. 23, 1949

Longest Pass Reception (in yards)
98 Homer Jones (from Earl Morrall), vs. Pittsburgh, Sept. 11, 1966

94 Rich Houston (from Norm Snead), vs. Dallas, Sept. 24, 1972
89 Homer Jones (from Earl Morrall), vs. Philadelphia, Oct. 17, 1965
88 George Franck (from Frank Reagan), vs. Washington, Oct. 12, 1947

Highest Average Gain, Lifetime
22.6 Homer Jones, 1964–69 (214–4845)
18.1 Del Shofner, 1961–67 (239–4315)
17.7 Bob Schnelker, 1954–60 (183–3232)
17.2 Aaron Thomas, 1962–70 (247–4253)

Highest Average Gain, Season (qualifiers)
24.7 Homer Jones, 1967 (49–1,209)
23.5 Homer Jones, 1968 (45–1,057)
21.8 Homer Jones, 1966 (48–1,044)

Highest Average Gain, Game (4 minimum)
50.3 Gene Roberts, vs. Chi. Bears, Oct. 23, 1949 (4–201)
49.0 Homer Jones, vs. Washington, Oct. 1, 1967 (4–196)
37.5 Frank Liebel, vs. Detroit, Nov. 18, 1945 (4–150)

Most Touchdowns, Lifetime
48 Kyle Rote, 1951–61
47 Joe Morrison, 1959–71
43 Frank Gifford, 1952–60, 62–64

Most Touchdowns, Season
13 Homer Jones, 1967
12 Del Shofner, 1962
11 Del Shofner, 1961

Most Touchdowns, Game
4 Earnest Gray, vs. St. Louis, Sept. 7, 1980
3 Frank Liebel, vs. Philadelphia, Dec. 2, 1945
3 Gene Roberts, vs. Chi. Bears, Oct. 23, 1949
3 Gene Roberts, vs. Green Bay, Nov. 13, 1949
3 Bob Schnelker, vs. Washington, Oct. 10, 1954
3 Del Shofner, vs. Washington, Nov. 5, 1961
3 Del Shofner, vs. Philadelphia, Dec. 10, 1961
3 Joe Walton, vs. Washington, Oct. 28, 1962
3 Del Shofner, vs. Dallas, Nov. 11, 1962
3 Del Shofner, vs. Washington, Nov. 25, 1962
3 Joe Walton, vs. Dallas, Dec. 16, 1962
3 Rich Houston, vs. Green Bay, Sept. 19, 1971
3 Ron Johnson, vs. Philadelphia, Oct. 2, 1972
3 Billy Taylor, vs. St. Louis, Dec. 9, 1979
3 Earnest Gray, vs. Green Bay, Nov. 16, 1980

Most Consecutive Games, Touchdown Receptions
7 Kyle Rote, 1959–60
5 Frank Liebel, 1945
5 Del Shofner, 1963
5 Homer Jones, 1966
5 Joe Morrison, 1966
5 Aaron Thomas, 1967

Most Seasons Leading League
1 Tod Goodwin, 1935
1 Bob Tucker, 1971
1 Earnest Gray, 1983

Interceptions

Most Interceptions by, Lifetime
74 Emlen Tunnell, 1948–58
52 Jim Patton, 1955–66
41 Carl Lockhart, 1965–75

Most Interceptions by, Season

11	Otto Schnellbacher, 1951
11	Jim Patton, 1958
10	Frank Reagan, 1947
10	Emlen Tunnell, 1949
10	Willie Williams, 1968

Most Interceptions by, Game

3	Ward Cuff, vs. Philadelphia, Sept. 13, 1941
3	Howard Livingston, vs. Brooklyn, Oct. 15, 1944
3	Frank Reagan, vs. Detroit, Nov. 2, 1947
3	Frank Reagan, vs. Green Bay, Nov. 23, 1947
3	Art Faircloth, vs. Boston, Sept. 23, 1948
3	Emlen Tunnell, vs. Green Bay, Nov. 21, 1948
3	Frank Reagan, vs. Boston, Nov. 28, 1948
3	Emlen Tunnell, vs. Washington, Oct. 9, 1949
3	Otto Schnellbacher, vs. Cleveland, Oct. 22, 1950
3	Emlen Tunnell, vs. Pittsburgh, Nov. 7, 1954
3	Tom Landry, vs. Philadelphia, Nov. 14, 1954
3	Emlen Tunnell, vs. Chi. Cardinals, Nov. 24, 1957
3	Dick Lynch, vs. St. Louis, Oct. 8, 1961
3	Dick Lynch, vs. Philadelphia, Nov. 12, 1961
3	Jim Patton, vs. Chicago, Dec. 2, 1962
3	Dick Lynch, vs. Philadelphia, Sept. 29, 1963
3	Carl Lockhart, vs. Cleveland, Dec. 4, 1966

Most Consecutive Games, Interceptions By

6	Willie Williams, 1968
5	Emlen Tunnell, 1954–55
5	Emlen Tunnell, 1954–55
5	Carl Lockhart, 1969–70

Most Yards Gained, Lifetime

1,240	Emlen Tunnell, 1948–58
712	Jim Patton, 1955–66
568	Dick Lynch, 1959–66
475	Carl Lockhart, 1965–75

Most Yards Gained, Season

251	Emlen Tunnell, 1949
251	Dick Lynch, 1963
203	Frank Reagan, 1947
195	Erich Barnes, 1961

Most Yards Gained, Game

109	Ward Cuff, vs. Philadelphia, Sept. 13, 1941
104	George Cheverko, vs. Washington, Oct. 3, 1948
102	Erich Barnes, vs. Dallas, Oct. 15, 1961

Longest Gain (in yards)

102	Erich Barnes, vs. Dallas, Oct. 15, 1961 (TD)
101	Henry Carr, vs. Los Angeles, Nov. 13, 1966 (TD)
97	Lawrence Taylor vs. Detroit, Nov. 25, 1982 (TD)
89	Bruce Maher, vs. Dallas, Nov. 10, 1968

Most Touchdowns, Lifetime

4	Emlen Tunnell, 1948–58
4	Dick Lynch, 1959–66
3	Tom Landry, 1950–55
3	Erich Barnes, 1961–64
3	Jerry Hillebrand, 1963–66
3	Carl Lockhart, 1965–72
3	George Martin, 1975–
2	Bill Petrilas, 1944–45
2	Otto Schnellbacher, 1950–51
2	Jim Patton, 1955–66
2	Tom Scott, 1959–64
2	Terry Jackson, 1978–82

Most Touchdowns, Season

3	Dick Lynch, 1963
2	Bill Petrilas, 1944
2	Emlen Tunnell, 1949
2	Tom Landry, 1951
2	Otto Schnellbacher, 1951
2	Erich Barnes, 1961
2	Carl Lockhart, 1968

Most Touchdowns, Game

1	By many players

Most Consecutive Games, Touchdowns

2	Tom Landry, vs. Cleveland, Oct. 28 vs. N.Y. Yankees, Nov. 4, 1951
2	Dick Lynch, vs. Cleveland, Oct. 13 vs. Dallas, Oct. 20, 1963
2	Carl Lockhart, vs. Philadelphia, Sept. 22 vs. Washington, Sept. 29, 1968

Most Seasons Leading League

2	Dick Lynch, 1961, 63

Punting

Most Punts, Lifetime

931	Dave Jennings, 1974–84
525	Don Chandler, 1956–64
338	Tom Landry, 1950–55

Most Punts, Season

104	Dave Jennings, 1979
100	Dave Jennings, 1977
97	Dave Jennings, 1981
95	Dave Jennings, 1978
94	Dave Jennings, 1980

Most Punts, Game

14	Carl Kinscherf, vs. Detroit, Nov. 7, 1943
11	Dave Jennings, vs. Washington, Sept. 13, 1981
11	Dave Jennings, vs. Atlanta, Oct. 25, 1981
11	Tom Landry, vs. Philadelphia, Nov. 26, 1950
11	Charlie Conerly, vs. Cleveland, Nov. 18, 1951
11	Don Chandler, vs. St. Louis, Oct. 8, 1961

Most Yards, Lifetime

38,792	Dave Jennings, 1974–84
23,019	Don Chandler, 1956–64
13,649	Tom Landry, 1950–55

Most Yards, Season

4,445	Dave Jennings, 1979
4,211	Dave Jennings, 1980
4,198	Dave Jennings, 1981
3,995	Dave Jennings, 1978
3,993	Dave Jennings, 1977

Most Yards, Game

583	Carl Kinscherf, vs. Detroit, Nov. 7, 1943 (14 punts)
511	Dave Jennings, vs. Washington, Sept. 13, 1981 (11 punts)
485	Don Chandler, vs. St. Louis, Oct. 8, 1961 (11 punts)
470	Len Barnum, vs. Green Bay, Nov. 17, 1940 (10 punts)

Longest Punt

74	Len Younce, vs. Chi. Bears, Nov. 14, 1943
74	Don Chandler, vs. Dallas, Oct. 11, 1964
73	Dave Jennings, vs. Houston, Dec. 5, 1982
72	Carl Kinscherf, vs. Phil.-Pitts., Oct. 9, 1943
72	Len Younce, vs. Brooklyn, Oct. 15, 1944
72	Dave Jennings, vs. Dallas, Nov. 4, 1979

Highest Average, Lifetime (150 punts)
- 43.8 Don Chandler, 1956–64 (525 punts)
- 43.8 Sean Lundeta, 1985– (160 punts)
- 42.0 Dave Jennings, 1974–82 (757 punts)
- 41.8 Tom Blanchard, 1971–73 (171 punts)

Highest Average, Season (35 punts)
- 46.6 Don Chandler, 1959 (55 punts)
- 45.6 Don Chandler, 1964 (73 punts)
- 44.9 Don Chandler, 1963 (59 punts)

Highest Average, Game (4 punts)
- 55.3 Dave Jennings, vs. Houston, Dec. 5, 1982 (4 punts)
- 54.1 Don Chandler, vs. Cleveland, Oct. 11, 1959 (8 punts)
- 54.0 Dave Jennings, vs. Dallas, Oct. 5, 1980 (5 punts)
- 53.1 Dave Jennings, vs. Dallas, Nov. 30, 1975 (7 punts)
- 52.1 Don Chandler, vs. Pittsburgh, Nov. 15, 1959 (7 punts)
- 52.1 Dave Jennings, vs. Kansas City, Sept. 17, 1978 (7 punts)

Most Seasons Leading League
- 1 Don Chandler, 1957
- 1 Dave Jennings, 1980

Punt Returns

Most Punt Returns, Lifetime
- 257 Emlen Tunnell, 1948–58
- 131 Phil McConkey, 1983–
- 106 Leon Bright, 1981–83
- 62 Carl Lockhart, 1965–71
- 54 Bob Hammond, 1976–78

Most Punt Returns, Season
- 52 Leon Bright, 1981
- 38 Emlen Tunnell, 1953
- 37 Leon Bright, 1982
- 35 Alvin Garrett, 1980
- 34 Emlen Tunnell, 1951

Most Punt Returns, Game
- 9 Leon Bright, vs. Philadelphia, Dec. 11, 1982
- 9 Pete Shaw, vs. Philadelphia, Nov. 20, 1983
- 8 Emlen Tunnell, vs. N.Y. Yankees, Dec. 3, 1950
- 8 Leon Bright, vs. Washington, Sept. 13, 1981
- 8 Phil McConkey, vs. Dallas, Nov. 4, 1984
- 7 Rondy Colbert, vs. New Orleans, Dec. 14, 1975
- 7 Phil McConkey, vs. Philadelphia, Sept. 8, 1985
- 6 Emlen Tunnell, vs. Philadelphia, Oct. 4, 1952
- 6 Pete Athas, vs. St. Louis, Dec. 15, 1974

Most Fair Catches, Lifetime
- 57 Carl Lockhart, 1965–71
- 45 Phil McConkey, 1983–
- 40 Bobby Duhon, 1968–72
- 21 Pete Athas, 1971–73

Most Fair Catches, Season
- 18 Phil McConkey, 1985
- 16 Bobby Duhon, 1971
- 15 Phil McConkey, 1984
- 14 Carl Lockhart, 1969
- 14 Bob Grim, 1972
- 14 Pete Athas, 1973

Most Fair Catches, Game
- 4 Eddie Dove, vs. Cleveland, Oct. 27, 1963
- 4 Carl Lockhart, vs. Minnesota, Oct. 31, 1971
- 4 Phil McConkey, vs. Washington, Sept. 16, 1984
- 4 Phil McConkey, vs. L.A. Rams, Sept. 30, 1984
- 4 Phil McConkey, vs. Philadelphia, Sept. 29, 1985

Most Yards Returned, Lifetime
- 2,206 Emlen Tunnell, 1948–58
- 1,801 Phil McConkey, 1983–
- 736 Leon Bright, 1981–82
- 491 Bob Hammond, 1976–78
- 449 Pete Athas, 1971–74

Most Yards Returned, Season
- 489 Emlen Tunnell, 1951
- 442 Phil McConkey, 1985
- 411 Emlen Tunnell, 1952
- 410 Leon Bright, 1981

Most Yards Returned, Game
- 147 Emlen Tunnell, vs. Chi. Cardinals, Oct. 14, 1951
- 143 Leon Bright, vs. Philadelphia, Dec. 11, 1982
- 106 Emlen Tunnell, vs. Washington, Dec. 7, 1952
- 103 Rondy Colbert, vs. New Orleans, Dec. 14, 1975
- 103 Phil McConkey, vs. Philadelphia, Sept. 8, 1985
- 101 Leon Bright, vs. Los Angeles, Dec. 6, 1981

Longest Return
- 83 Eddie Dove, vs. Philadelphia, Sept. 29, 1963
- 81 Emlen Tunnell, vs. Chi. Cardinals, Oct. 14, 1951
- 81 Bosh Pritchard, vs. Chi. Cardinals, Nov. 25, 1951
- 74 Emlen Tunnell, vs. N.Y. Yankees, Dec. 16, 1951

Highest Average Return, Lifetime (30 returns)
- 9.1 Bob Hammond, 1976–78 (54 returns)
- 8.8 Pete Athas, 1971–74 (51 returns)
- 8.6 Emlen Tunnell, 1948–58 (257 returns)
- 8.3 Leon Bright, 1981–82 (89 returns)
- 8.2 Alvin Garrett, 1980 (35 returns)

Highest Average Return, Season (qualifiers)
- 15.5 Merle Hapes, 1942 (11 returns)
- 14.9 George Franck, 1941 (13 returns)
- 14.4 Emlen Tunnell, 1951 (34 returns)

Highest Average Return, Game (3 returns)
- 36.8 Emlen Tunnell, vs. Chi. Cardinals, Oct. 14, 1951 (4 returns)
- 35.3 Emlen Tunnell, vs. Washington, Dec. 7, 1952 (3 returns)
- 31.0 Emlen Tunnell, vs. Washington, Oct. 7, 1951 (3 returns)

Most Touchdowns, Lifetime
- 5 Emlen Tunnell, 1948–58
- 1 By many players

Most Touchdowns, Season
- 3 Emlen Tunnell, 1951
- 1 By many players

Most Touchdowns, Game
- 1 Vic Carroll, vs. Boston, Oct. 8, 1944
- 1 Emlen Tunnell, vs. N.Y. Bulldogs, Nov. 6, 1949
- 1 Emlen Tunnell, vs. Chi. Cardinals, Oct. 14, 1951
- 1 Emlen Tunnell, vs. Philadelphia, Oct. 21, 1951
- 1 Bosh Pritchard, vs. Chi. Cardinals, Nov. 25, 1951
- 1 Emlen Tunnell, vs. N.Y. Yankees, Dec. 16, 1951
- 1 Herb Johnson, vs. Cleveland, Nov. 28, 1954
- 1 Jim Patton, vs. Washington, Oct. 30, 1955
- 1 Emlen Tunnell, vs. Philadelphia, Nov. 20, 1955
- 1 Bobby Duhon, vs. Philadelphia, Oct. 11, 1970
- 1 Rondy Colbert, vs. New Orleans, Dec. 14, 1975
- 1 Bob Hammond, vs. Dallas, Sept. 25, 1977

Most Seasons Leading League
None

Kickoff Returns

Most Kickoff Returns, Lifetime
126 Clarence Childs, 1964–67
 65 Rocky Thompson, 1971–72
 54 Joe Scott, 1948–53
 46 Emlen Tunnell, 1948–58

Most Kickoff Returns, Season
 36 Rocky Thompson, 1971
 35 Ronnie Blye, 1968
 34 Clarence Childs, 1964, 66

Most Kickoff Returns, Game
  7 Alvin Garrett, vs. San Diego, Oct. 19, 1980
  7 Gene Filipski, vs. Washington, Nov. 18, 1956
  6 Clarence Childs, vs. Cleveland, Dec. 4, 1966
  5 By many players

Most Yards Returned, Lifetime
3,163 Clarence Childs, 1964–67
1,768 Rocky Thompson, 1971–72
1,467 Joe Scott, 1948–53
1,215 Emlen Tunnell, 1948–58

Most Yards Returned, Season
987 Clarence Childs, 1964
947 Rocky Thompson, 1971
855 Clarence Childs, 1966

Most Yards Returned, Game
207 Joe Scott, vs. Los Angeles, Nov. 14, 1948
198 Rocky Thompson, vs. Detroit, Sept. 17, 1972
170 Clarence Childs, vs. Cleveland, Dec. 4, 1969
158 Clarence Childs, vs. Cleveland, Oct. 24, 1965

Longest Return
100 Emlen Tunnell, vs. N.Y. Yankees, Nov. 4, 1951
100 Clarence Childs, vs. Minnesota, Dec. 6, 1964
 99 Joe Scott, vs. Los Angeles, Nov. 14, 1948
 98 Jim Patton, vs. Washington, Oct. 30, 1955

Highest Average Return, Lifetime (40 returns)
27.2 Rocky Thompson, 1971–72 (65 returns)
27.2 Joe Scott, 1948–53 (54 returns)
26.4 Emlen Tunnell, 1948–58 (46 returns)
25.1 Clarence Childs, 1964–67 (126 returns)

Highest Average Return, Season (qualifiers)
31.6 John Salscheider, 1949 (15 returns)
30.2 John Counts, 1962 (26 returns)
29.0 Clarence Childs, 1964 (34 returns)

Highest Average Return, Game (3 returns)
51.8 Joe Scott, vs. Los Angeles, Nov. 14, 1948 (4 returns)
50.3 Ronnie Blye, vs. Pittsburgh, Sept. 15, 1968 (3 returns)
49.5 Rocky Thompson, vs. Detroit, Sept. 17, 1972 (4 returns)
44.3 Emlen Tunnell, vs. Chi. Cardinals, Nov. 1, 1953 (3 returns)

Most Touchdowns, Lifetime
  2 Rocky Thompson, 1971–72
  2 Clarence Childs, 1964–67
  1 By many players

Most Touchdowns, Season
  1 By many players, see next item.

Most Touchdowns, Game
  1 Joe Scott, vs. Los Angeles, Nov. 14, 1948
  1 Emlen Tunnell, vs. N.Y. Yankees, Nov. 4, 1951
  1 Jim Patton, vs. Washington, Oct. 30, 1955
  1 John Counts, vs. Washington, Nov. 25, 1962
  1 Clarence Childs, vs. Minnesota, Dec. 6, 1964
  1 Clarence Childs, vs. Cleveland, Dec. 4, 1966
  1 Rocky Thompson, vs. St. Louis, Oct. 3, 1971
  1 Rocky Thompson, vs. Detroit, Sept. 17, 1972

Most Seasons Leading League
  1 Joe Scott, 1948
  1 Clarence Childs, 1964

Fumbles

BY GIANTS

Most Fumbles, Lifetime
 54 Charlie Conerly, 1948–61
 48 Frank Gifford, 1952–60, 62–64
 34 Alex Webster, 1955–64

Most Fumbles, Season
 16 Phil Simms, 1985
 11 Y.A. Tittle, 1964
 11 Bobby Gaiters, 1961
 11 Charlie Conerly, 1957

Most Fumbles, Game
  5 Charlie Conerly, vs. San Francisco, Dec. 1, 1957
  4 Y. A. Tittle, vs. Philadelphia, Sept. 13, 1964

TOTAL RECOVERIES

Most Fumbles Recovered, Lifetime
 26 Charlie Conerly, 1948–61
 16 Frank Gifford, 1952–60, 62–64
 15 Joe Morrison, 1959–72

Most Fumbles Recovered, Season
  6 Emlen Tunnell, 1952

Most Fumbles Recovered, Game
  2 By many players

GIANTS' FUMBLES RECOVERED

Most Fumbles Recovered, Lifetime
 26 Charlie Conerly, 1948–61
 16 Frank Gifford, 1952–60, 62–64
 15 Joe Morrison, 1959–72

Most Fumbles Recovered, Season
  5 Phil Simms, 1985
  5 Joel Wells, 1961
  5 Frank Gifford, 1958
  5 Charlie Conerly, 1948, 57
  5 Emlen Tunnell, 1952
  5 Gene Roberts, 1950

Most Fumbles Recovered, Game
  2 By many players
  2 Last: Roy Simmons, vs. Dallas, Sept. 27, 1981

OPPONENTS' FUMBLES RECOVERED

Most Fumbles Recovered, Lifetime
19 Jim Katcavage, 1956–68
13 Cliff Livingston, 1954–61
12 Jim Patton, 1955–66
12 Brad Van Pelt, 1973–82

Most Fumbles Recovered, Season
5 Ray Poole, 1950
5 Troy Archer, 1977
5 Ernie Jones, 1978
4 Andy Stynchula, 1964
4 Erich Barnes, 1963
4 Sam Huff, 1959
4 Arnie Weinmeister, 1953
4 Frank Cope, 1946

Most Fumbles Recovered, Game
2 By many players

YARDS RETURNED

Longest Fumble Run
81 Andy Headen, vs. Dallas, Sept. 9, 1984 (TD)
72 Wendell Harris, vs. Pittsburgh, Sept. 11, 1966 (TD)
71 Roy Hilton, vs. Dallas, Oct. 27, 1974 (TD)
67 Horace Sherrod, vs. Washington, Dec. 7, 1952
65 Lindon Crow, vs. St. Louis, Oct. 30, 1960 (TD)

Most Touchdowns, Lifetime (total)
2 Sam Huff, 1959, 63 (2-opp)
2 Tom Landry, 1950, 51 (2-opp)
2 Al De Rogatis, 1949, 50 (2-opp)
2 George Martin, 1981 (2-opp)

Most Touchdowns, Season (total)
2 George Martin, vs. Washington, Sept. 13, 1981
2 George Martin, vs. St. Louis, Dec. 13, 1981

Most Touchdowns, Game (total)
1 By many players

COACHING

Year	Coach	Won	Lost	Tied	Pct.
1925	Bob Folwell	8	4	0	.667
	Regular Season				
1926	Doc Alexander	8	4	1	.667
	Regular Season				
1927–28	Earl Potteiger	15	8	3	.652
	Regular Season				
1929–30	Roy Andrews	26	5	1	.839
	Regular Season				
1931–53	Steve Owen	151	100	17	.601
	Regular Season				
	Postseason	2	8	0	.200
1954–60	Jim Lee Howell	53	27	4	.662
	Regular Season				
	Postseason	2	2	0	.500
1961–68	Allie Sherman	57	51	4	.527
	Regular Season				
	Postseason	0	3	0	.000
1969–73	Alex Webster	29	40	1	.420
	Regular Season				
1974–76	Bill Arnsparger	7	28	0	.200
	Regular Season				
1976–78	John McVay	14	23	0	.378
	Regular Season				
1979–82	Ray Perkins	23	34	0	.403
	Regular Season				
	Postseason	1	1	0	.500
1983–	Bill Parcells	38	29	1	.567
	Regular Season				
	Postseason	5	2	0	.714

MISCELLANEOUS RECORDS

Attendance

Largest Crowd, Giants Stadium
76,633 vs. Redskins, Jan. 11, 1987*
76,490 vs. Cowboys, Nov. 4, 1979

Largest Crowd, Yankee Stadium
71,163 vs. Colts, Nov. 9, 1958
68,783 vs. Eagles, Oct. 18, 1959

Largest Crowd, Away
84,213 at Browns, Nov. 27, 1963
83,193 at Browns, Dec. 1, 1968

Largest Crowd, Opening Day
76,042 vs. Cowboys, Oct. 10, 1976

Largest Attendance, Home
594,433 in 1986 (8 games)

Largest Attendance, Road
471,835 in 1986 (8 games)
446,632 in 1980 (8 games)
442,068 in 1978 (8 games)

*Playoff game.

"Best Days"

RUSHING

Yds.	Player	Date	Opponent
218	Choo Choo Roberts	11/12/50	Chi. Cardinals
202	Joe Morris	12/21/85	Pittsburgh
188	Bill Paschal	12/5/43	Washington
181	Joe Morris	10/27/86	Washington
181	Joe Morris	11/2/86	Dallas
179	Joe Morris	12/14/86	St. Louis
171	Eddie Price	12/9/51	Philadelphia
161	Rob Carpenter	12/27/81	Philadelphia
160	Ernie Koy	10/1/67	Washington
159	Tuffy Leemans	11/20/38	Philadelphia
159	Frank Gifford	11/29/59	Washington
159	Butch Woolfolk	11/20/83	Philadelphia
156	Eddie Price	12/3/50	N.Y. Yankees

PASSING

Yds.	Player	Date	Opponent
513	Phil Simms	10/13/85	Cincinnati
505	Y. A. Tittle	10/28/62	Washington
432	Phil Simms	10/6/85	Dallas
372	Randy Johnson	10/28/73	St. Louis
363	Charlie Conerly	12/5/48	Pittsburgh
357	Charlie Conerly	11/13/49	Green Bay
351	Phil Simms	11/9/80	Dallas

All-Pro Honor Roll

Eight Times:	Mel Hein
	Roosevelt Brown
Six Times:	Lawrence Taylor
Five Times:	Andy Robustelli
	Brad Van Pelt
Four Times:	Arnie Weinmeister
	Emlen Tunnell
	Frank Gifford
	Jim Patton
	Dave Jennings
	Harry Carson
Three Times:	Red Badgro
	Del Shofner
	Y. A. Tittle
	Jim Katcavage
	Mark Haynes

Retired Jersey Numbers

No.	Player
1	Ray Flaherty
7	Mel Hein
14	Y. A. Tittle
32	Al Blozis
40	Joe Morrison
42	Charlie Conerly
50	Ken Strong

First-Round Draft Choices

Year	Player	Pos.	College
1936	Art Lewis	T	Ohio U.
1937	Ed Widseth	T	Minnesota
1938	George Karamatic	HB	Gonzaga
1939	Walt Nielson	FB	Arizona
1940	Grenny Lansdell	HB	Southern California
1941	George Franck	HB	Minnesota
1942	Merle Hapes	HB	Mississippi
1943	Steve Filipowicz	FB	Fordham
1944	Billy Hillenbrand	HB	Indiana
1945	Wesley Barbour	HB	Wake Forest
1946	George Connor	T	Notre Dame
1947	Vic Schwall	HB	Northwestern
1948	Tony Minisi	HB	Pennsylvania
1949	Paul Page	HB	Southern Methodist
1950	Travis Tidwell	QB	Auburn
1951	Kyle Rote	HB	Southern Methodist
1952	Frank Gifford	HB	Southern California
1953	Bobby Marlow	HB	Alabama
1954	Ken Buck*	E	Pacific
1955	Joe Heap	HB	Notre Dame
1956	Henry Moore	FB	Arkansas
1957	Sam DeLuca*	T	South Carolina
1958	Phil King	FB	Vanderbilt
1959	Lee Grosscup	QB	Utah
1960	Lou Cordileone	G	Clemson
1961	Bruce Tarbox*	G	Syracuse
1962	Jerry Hillebrand	LB	Colorado
1963	Frank Lasky*	T	Florida
1964	Joe Don Looney	RB	Oklahoma
1965	Tucker Frederickson	RB	Auburn
1966	Francis Peay	T	Missouri
1967	Louis Thompson†	DT	Alabama
1968	Dick Buzin*	T	Penn State
1969	Fred Dryer	DE	San Diego State
1970	Jim Files	LB	Oklahoma
1971	Rocky Thompson	RB	West Texas State
1972	Eldridge Small	DB	Texas A & I
1973	Brad Van Pelt*	LB	Michigan State
1974	John Hicks	G	Ohio State
1975	Al Simpson*	T	Colorado State
1976	Troy Archer	DT	Colorado
1977	Gary Jeter	DT	Southern California
1978	Gordon King	OT	Stanford
1979	Phil Simms	QB	Morehead State
1980	Mark Haynes	DB	Colorado
1981	Lawrence Taylor	LB	North Carolina
1982	Butch Woolfolk	RB	Michigan
1983	Terry Kinard	DB	Clemson
1984	Carl Banks	LB	Michigan State
1985	George Adams	RB	Kentucky
1986	Eric Dorsey	DE	Notre Dame

*First selection came in the second round.
†First selection came in the fourth round.

273